Shojo Beat

Yona of the Dawn

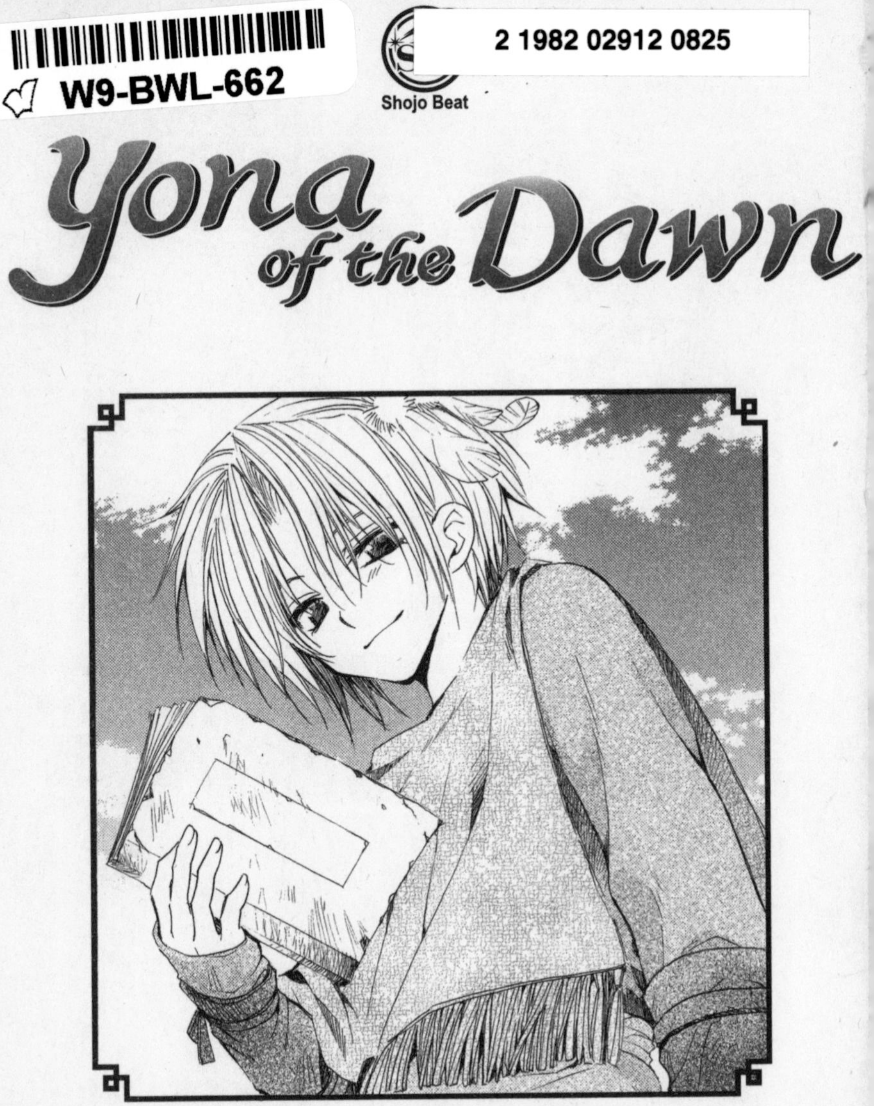

4

Story & Art by

Mizuho Kusanagi

YONA OF THE DAWN

Story Thus Far

Hak

One of the greatest heroes in the nation, known as the "Thunder Beast." He'd obeyed King Il's orders and became bodyguard to his childhood friend, Yona. He walks away from his position as general in order to protect his tribe.

Yona

While on the run, she comes to the realization that she's spent her life being protected by other people. She sets out to locate the Four Dragons in order to protect herself and the people who are most important to her.

Yun

Brilliant and intellectually curious. He may be a mouthy pretty boy, but he takes good care of people. He comes from a poor town in the Fire Tribe lands.

Gija

The White Dragon, one of the Four Dragon Warriors. Though beloved by everyone in his village, he's yearned for a master to serve. His right hand contains a dragon's might and is more powerful than ten men.

A priest. He and his predecessors were persecuted and exiled from the royal capital to a far-off land. When he met Yun, Yun had nowhere to go, so Ik-su took him in. Later, he urges Yun to travel with Yona despite how deeply he cares for him.

Ik-su

An 18-year-old scion of the royal bloodline. To keep Kohka safe from invasion by the Kai Empire to the north or the nations of Xing and Sei to the south, he is trying to create a powerful nation by uniting the Five Tribes and becoming king.

Su-won

Su-won's father and Il's older brother. Fearless and daring, he was a brilliant warrior and strategist. His death is officially recorded as an accident, but the truth is that he was stabbed to death by Il.

Yu-hon

Kohka's king, until his death. He was seen as cowardly due to his fear of weapons and avoidance of conflict. Years ago, his wife was attacked and killed by bandits. His father, the prior king, chose Il as his heir over Il's elder brother, Yu-hon.

Il

Chief of the Water Tribe
General Ahn Jung-gi

Chief of the Earth Tribe
General Yi Geun-tae

Chief of the Fire Tribe
General Kang Su-jin

Mun-deok

Chief of the Wind Tribe befor[e] Hak. Hak's adoptive grandfathe[r]

STORY

Yona, the princess of the Kingdom of Kohka*, was raised by her kind, loving father, King Il. She has dee[p] feelings for her cousin Su-won, a companion since childhood. On her 16th birthday, she goes to her father'[s] chambers to ask his blessing for a relationship between her and Su-won, but upon her arrival, she sees he[r] father just stabbed to death—by Su-won!

Driven from the palace, Yona and Hak seek counsel from a priest named Ik-su. Ik-su tells Yona that he[r] life will transform the nation and that she must locate the Four Dragon Warriors. He also informs her that th[e] White Dragon, one of the four, is protecting his bloodline in a mist-shrouded village.

When Yona and her companions locate the village and the White Dragon first sees her, his bloo[d] immediately burns, and he prostrates himself before her. He vows to serve her and tells her that he can faintl[y] sense the locations of the other Dragon Warriors.

*The Kingdom of Kohka is a coalition of five tribes: Fire, Water, Wind, Earth and Sky. The throne is held by the tribe with th[e] greatest influence, so the current royal family are of the Sky Tribe. The royal capital is Kuuto. Each tribe's chief also holds th[e] rank of general, and the Meeting of the Five Tribes is the nation's most powerful decision-making body.

Yona of the Dawn

Volume 4

CONTENTS

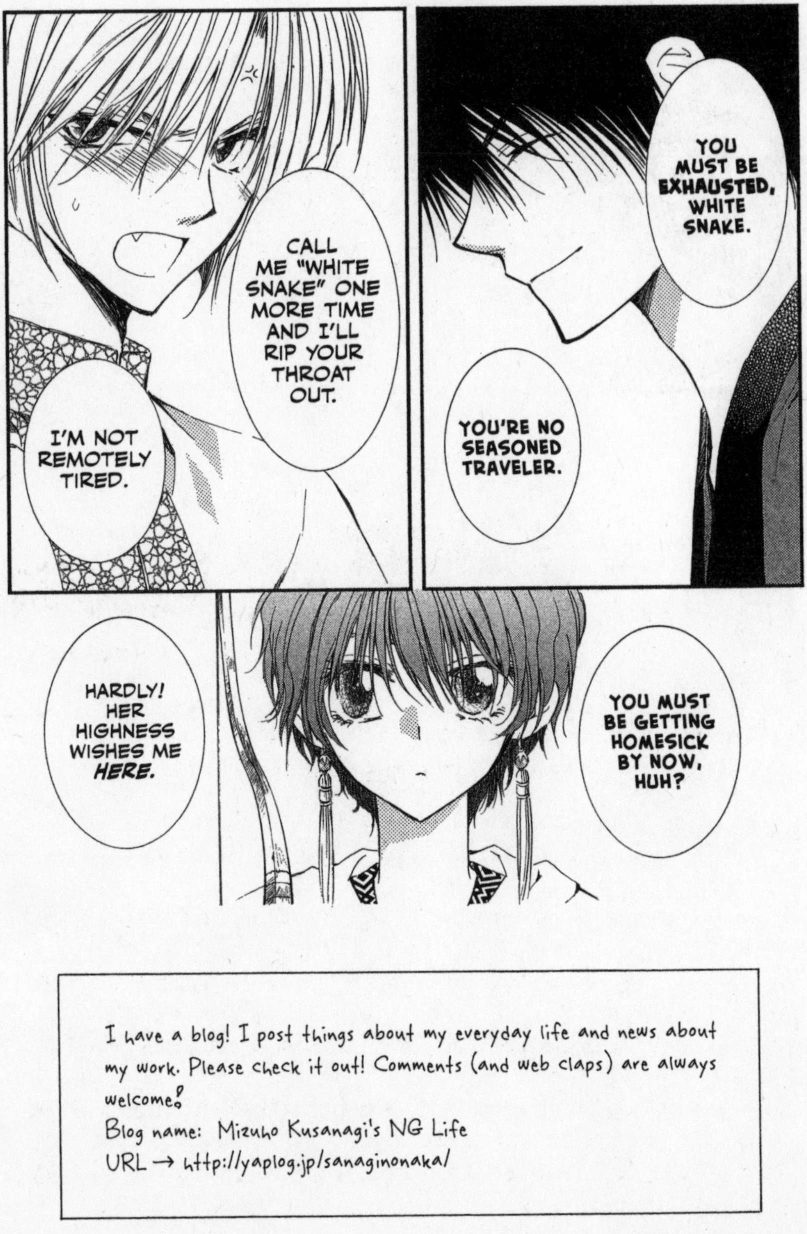
YOU MUST BE EXHAUSTED, WHITE SNAKE.
YOU'RE NO SEASONED TRAVELER.
CALL ME "WHITE SNAKE" ONE MORE TIME AND I'LL RIP YOUR THROAT OUT.
I'M NOT REMOTELY TIRED.
YOU MUST BE GETTING HOMESICK BY NOW, HUH?
HARDLY! HER HIGHNESS WISHES ME *HERE*.

I have a blog! I post things about my everyday life and news about my work. Please check it out! Comments (and web claps) are always welcome!

Blog name: Mizuho Kusanagi's NG Life

URL → http://yaplog.jp/sanaginonaka/

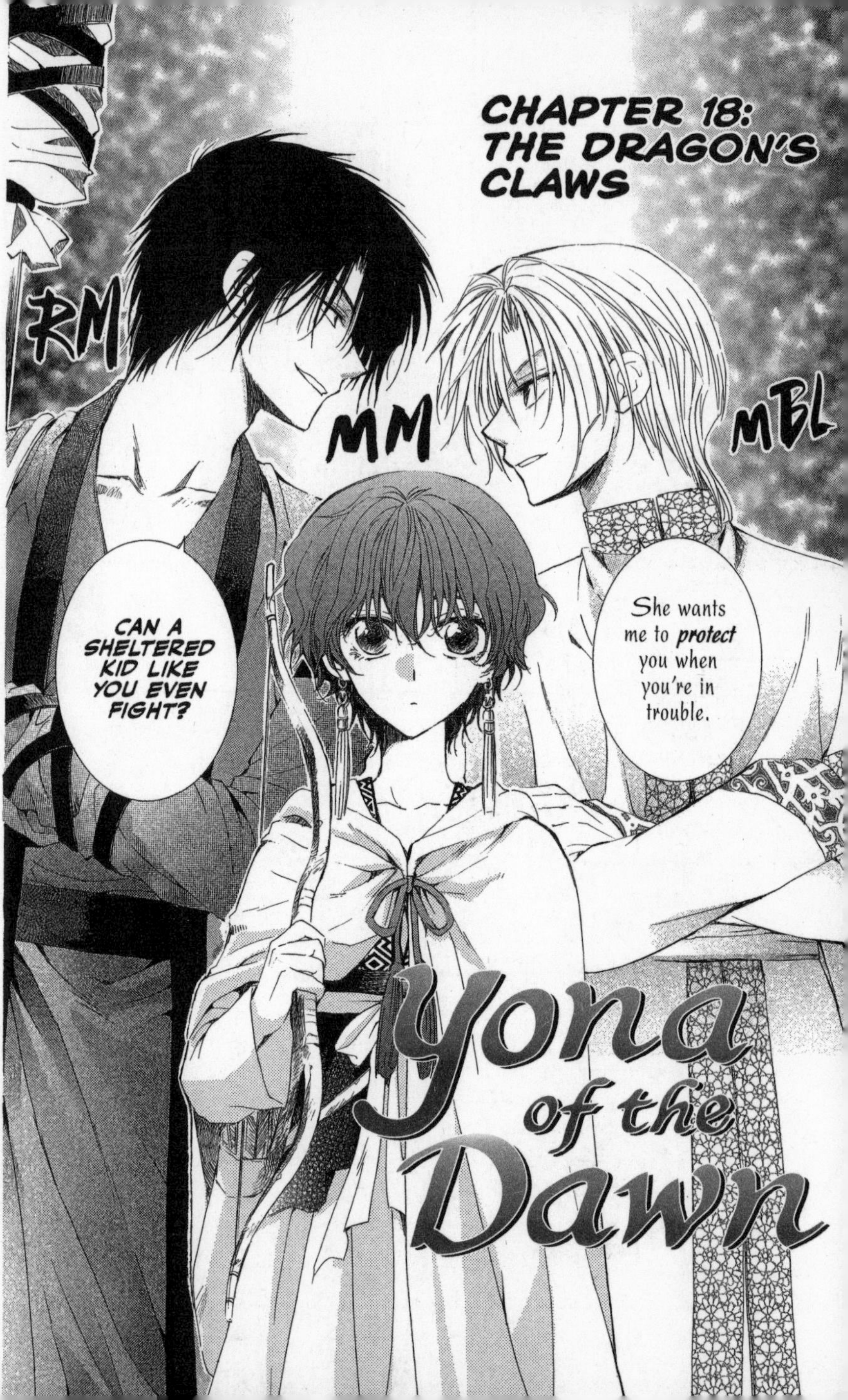
CHAPTER 18: THE DRAGON'S CLAWS
MBL
MM
RM
She wants me to ***protect*** you when you're in trouble.
CAN A SHELTERED KID LIKE YOU EVEN FIGHT?
Yona of the Dawn

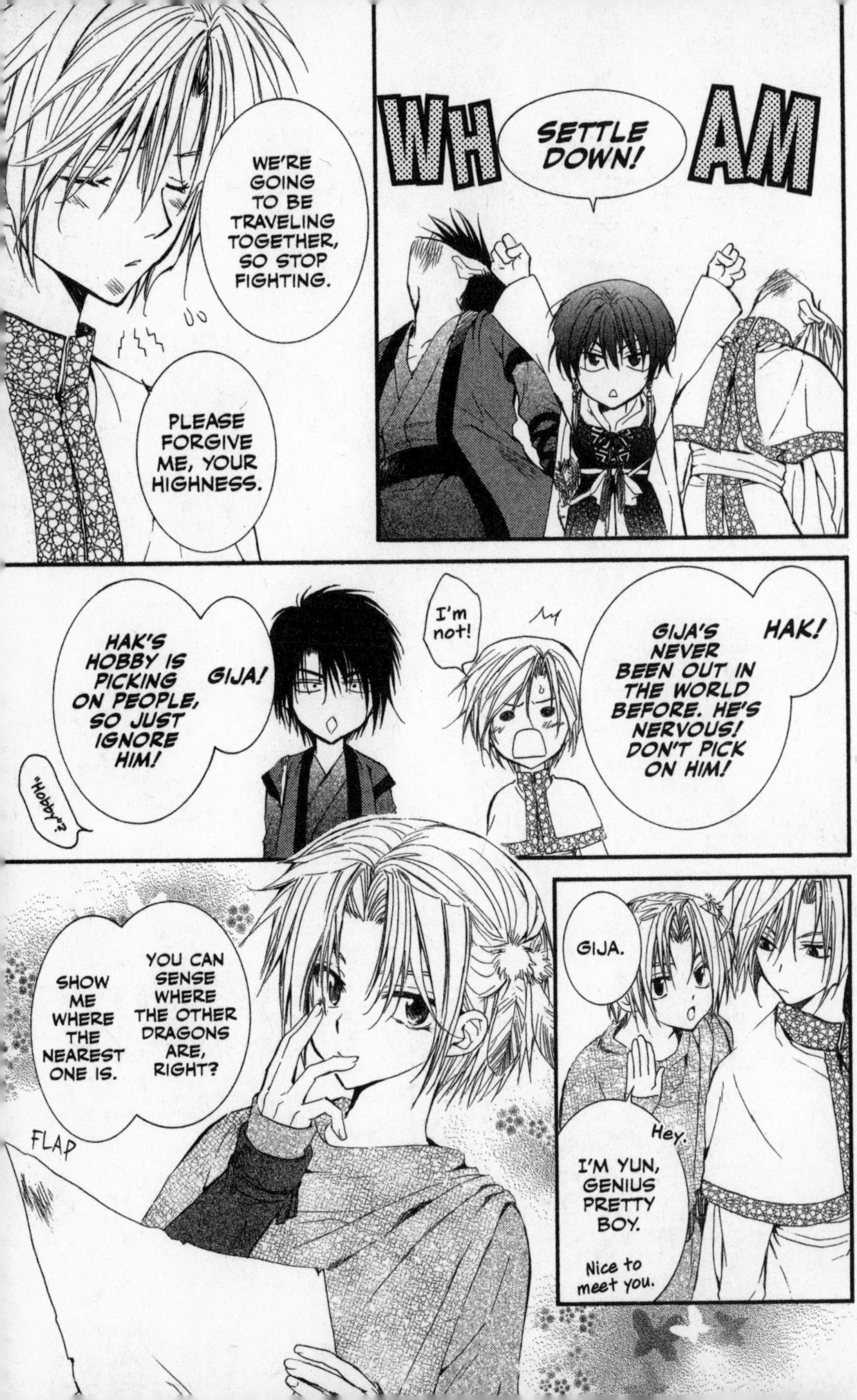
WH AM
SETTLE DOWN!
WE'RE GOING TO BE TRAVELING TOGETHER, SO STOP FIGHTING.
PLEASE FORGIVE ME, YOUR HIGHNESS.
HAK!
GIJA'S NEVER BEEN OUT IN THE WORLD BEFORE. HE'S NERVOUS! DON'T PICK ON HIM!
I'm not!
GIJA!
HAK'S HOBBY IS PICKING ON PEOPLE, SO JUST IGNORE HIM!
GIJA.
Hey.
I'M YUN, GENIUS PRETTY BOY.
Nice to meet you.
YOU CAN SENSE WHERE THE OTHER DRAGONS ARE, RIGHT?
SHOW ME WHERE THE NEAREST ONE IS.
FLAP

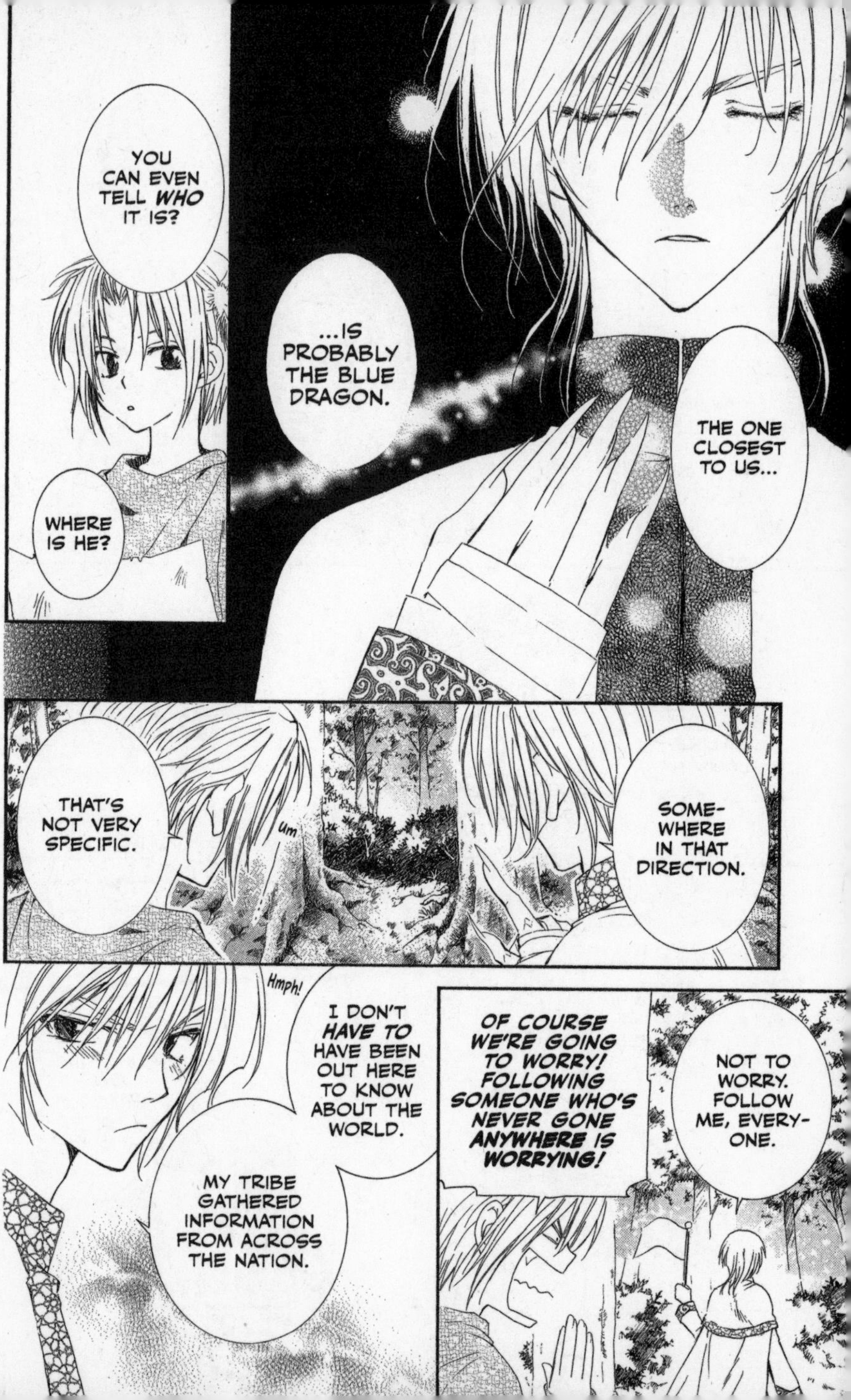
THE ONE CLOSEST TO US...
...IS PROBABLY THE BLUE DRAGON.
YOU CAN EVEN TELL *WHO* IT IS?
WHERE IS HE?
SOME-WHERE IN THAT DIRECTION.
Um
THAT'S NOT VERY SPECIFIC.
NOT TO WORRY. FOLLOW ME, EVERY-ONE.
OF COURSE WE'RE GOING TO WORRY! FOLLOWING SOMEONE WHO'S NEVER GONE ANYWHERE IS WORRYING!
Hmph!
I DON'T *HAVE TO* HAVE BEEN OUT HERE TO KNOW ABOUT THE WORLD.
MY TRIBE GATHERED INFORMATION FROM ACROSS THE NATION.

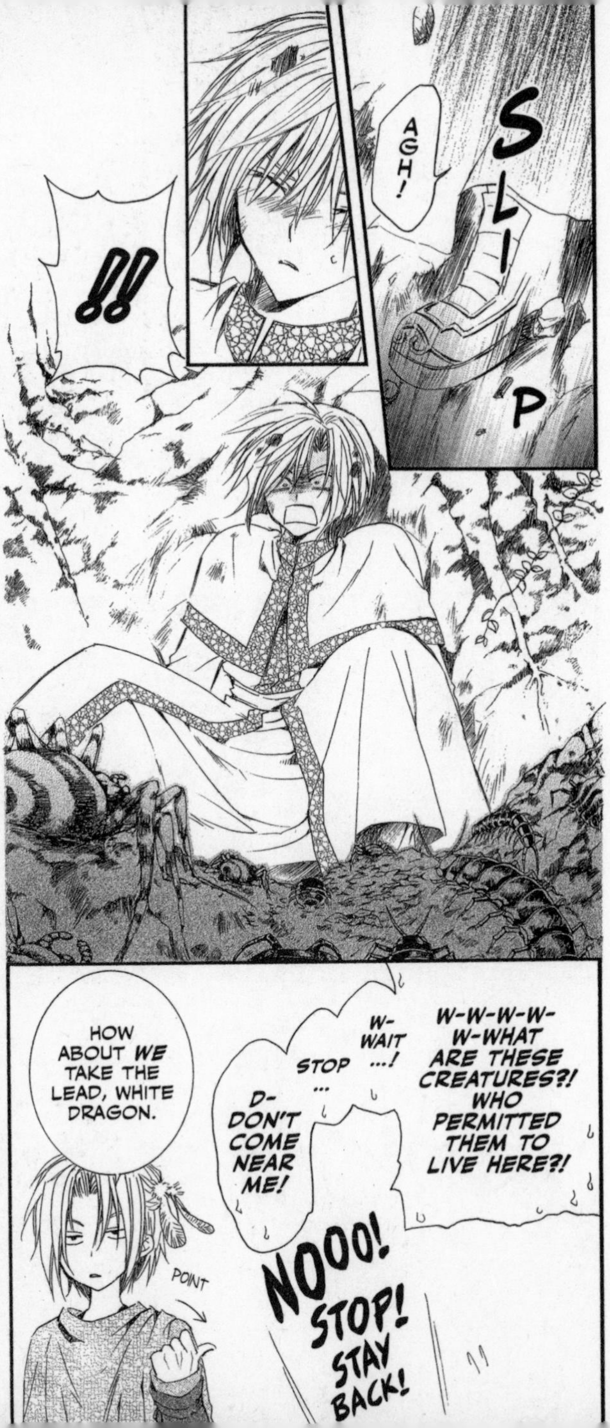
SLIP
AGH!
!!
W-W-W-W-W-WHAT ARE THESE CREATURES?! WHO PERMITTED THEM TO LIVE HERE?!
W-WAIT ...!
STOP ...
D-DON'T COME NEAR ME!
NOOO! STOP! STAY BACK!
HOW ABOUT *WE* TAKE THE LEAD, WHITE DRAGON.
POINT

Hello, this is Kusanagi!

Thank you very much for picking up Yona of the Dawn volume 4! When I started this series, writing the story felt overwhelming, but I've gotten used to it...kind of. I still struggle with my storyboards. My editor always helps me out since I'm not terribly creative.

Things are much more cheerful now that Gija's joined the group as of this volume. He's very easy to draw. As the artist, I find that helps a lot. (Smile) I hope you'll welcome him with open arms. (Smile)

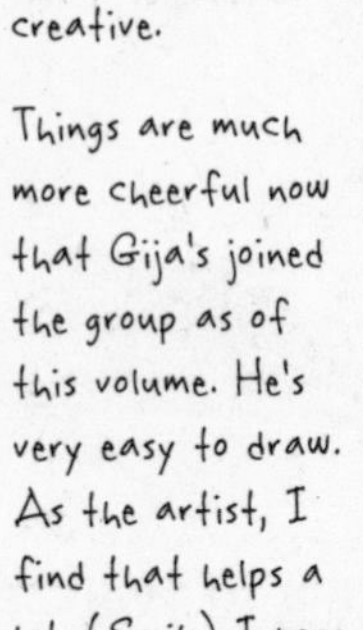
Thank you...
...for having me.

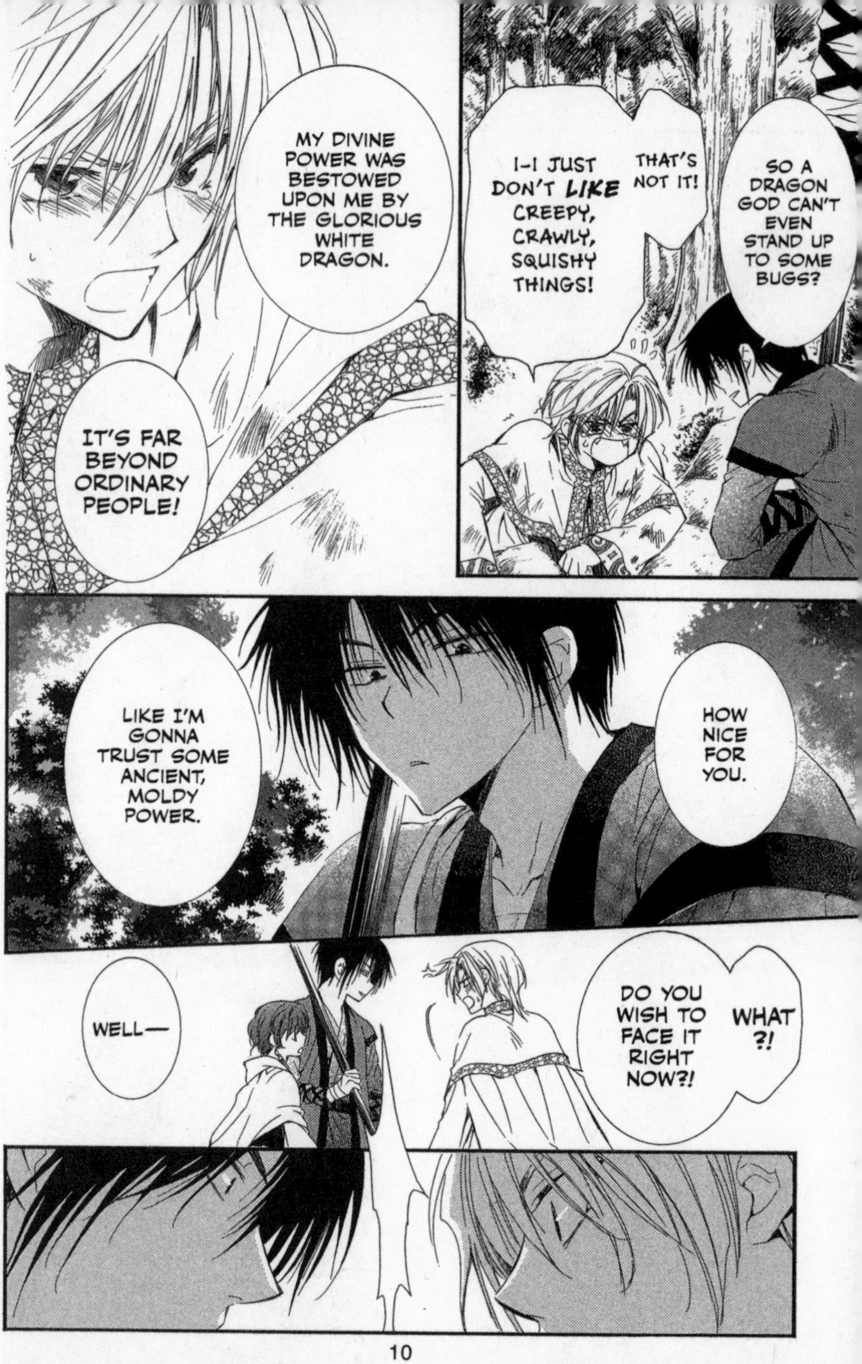
SO A DRAGON GOD CAN'T EVEN STAND UP TO SOME BUGS?
THAT'S NOT IT!
I-I JUST DON'T *LIKE* CREEPY, CRAWLY, SQUISHY THINGS!
MY DIVINE POWER WAS BESTOWED UPON ME BY THE GLORIOUS WHITE DRAGON.
IT'S FAR BEYOND ORDINARY PEOPLE!
HOW NICE FOR YOU.
LIKE I'M GONNA TRUST SOME ANCIENT, MOLDY POWER.
WHAT?!
DO YOU WISH TO FACE IT RIGHT NOW?!
WELL—

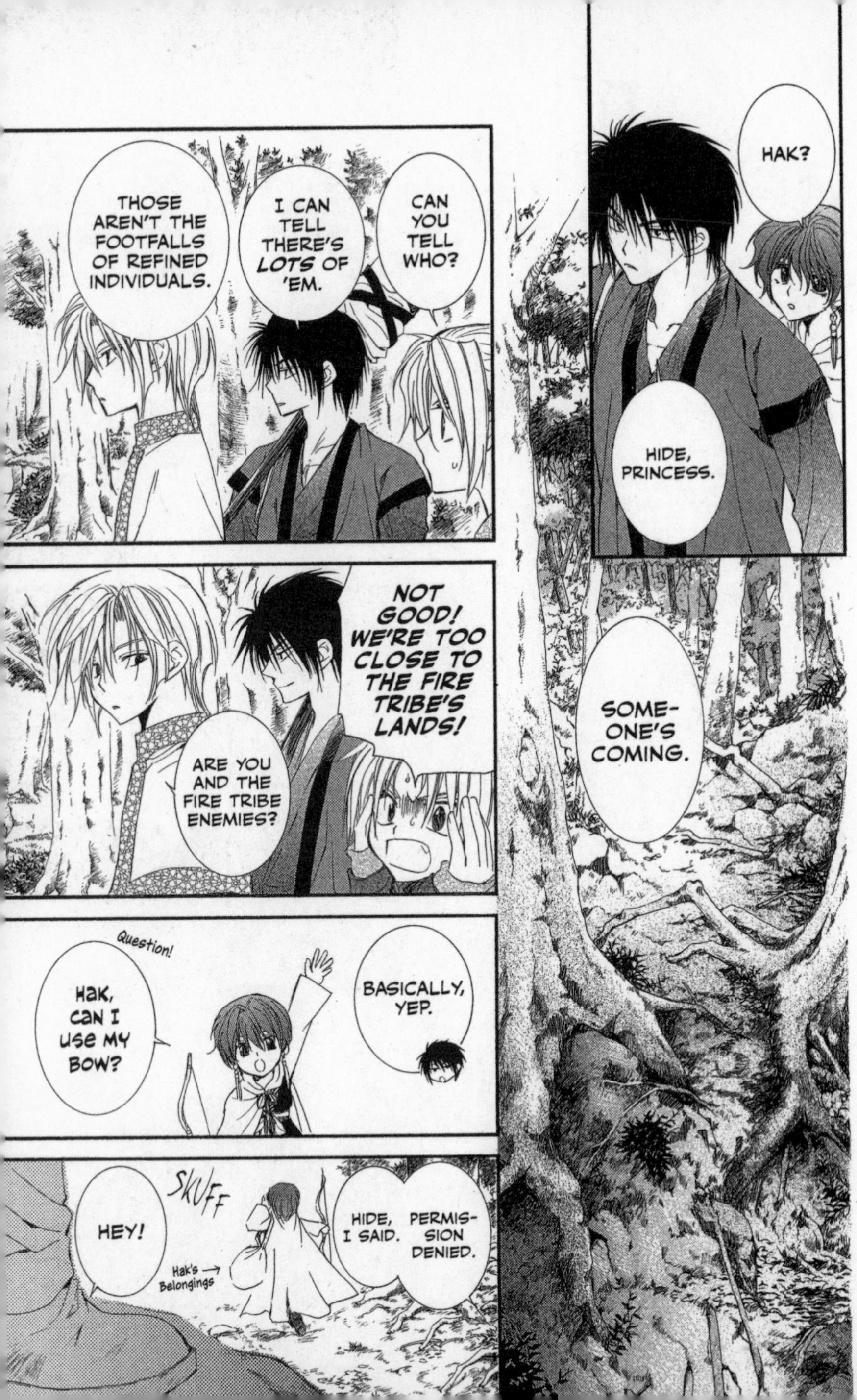
HAK?
HIDE, PRINCESS.
SOME-ONE'S COMING.
CAN YOU TELL WHO?
I CAN TELL THERE'S *LOTS* OF 'EM.
THOSE AREN'T THE FOOTFALLS OF REFINED INDIVIDUALS.
NOT GOOD! WE'RE TOO CLOSE TO THE FIRE TRIBE'S LANDS!
ARE YOU AND THE FIRE TRIBE ENEMIES?
BASICALLY, YEP.
Question!
HAK, CAN I USE MY BOW?
PERMIS-SION DENIED.
HIDE, I SAID.
SKUFF
Hak's → Belongings
HEY!

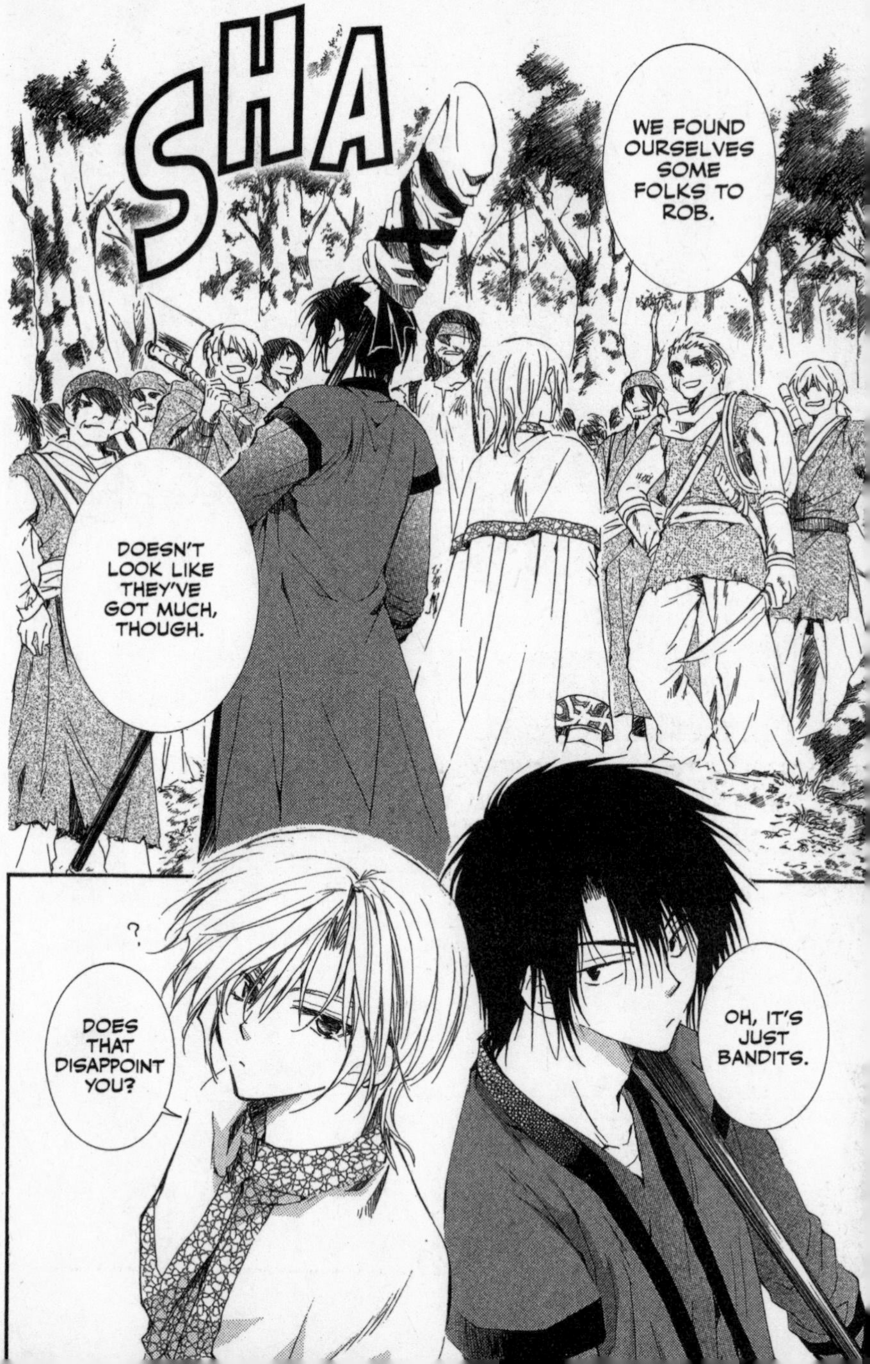
SHA
WE FOUND OURSELVES SOME FOLKS TO ROB.
DOESN'T LOOK LIKE THEY'VE GOT MUCH, THOUGH.
OH, IT'S JUST BANDITS.
?
DOES THAT DISAPPOINT YOU?

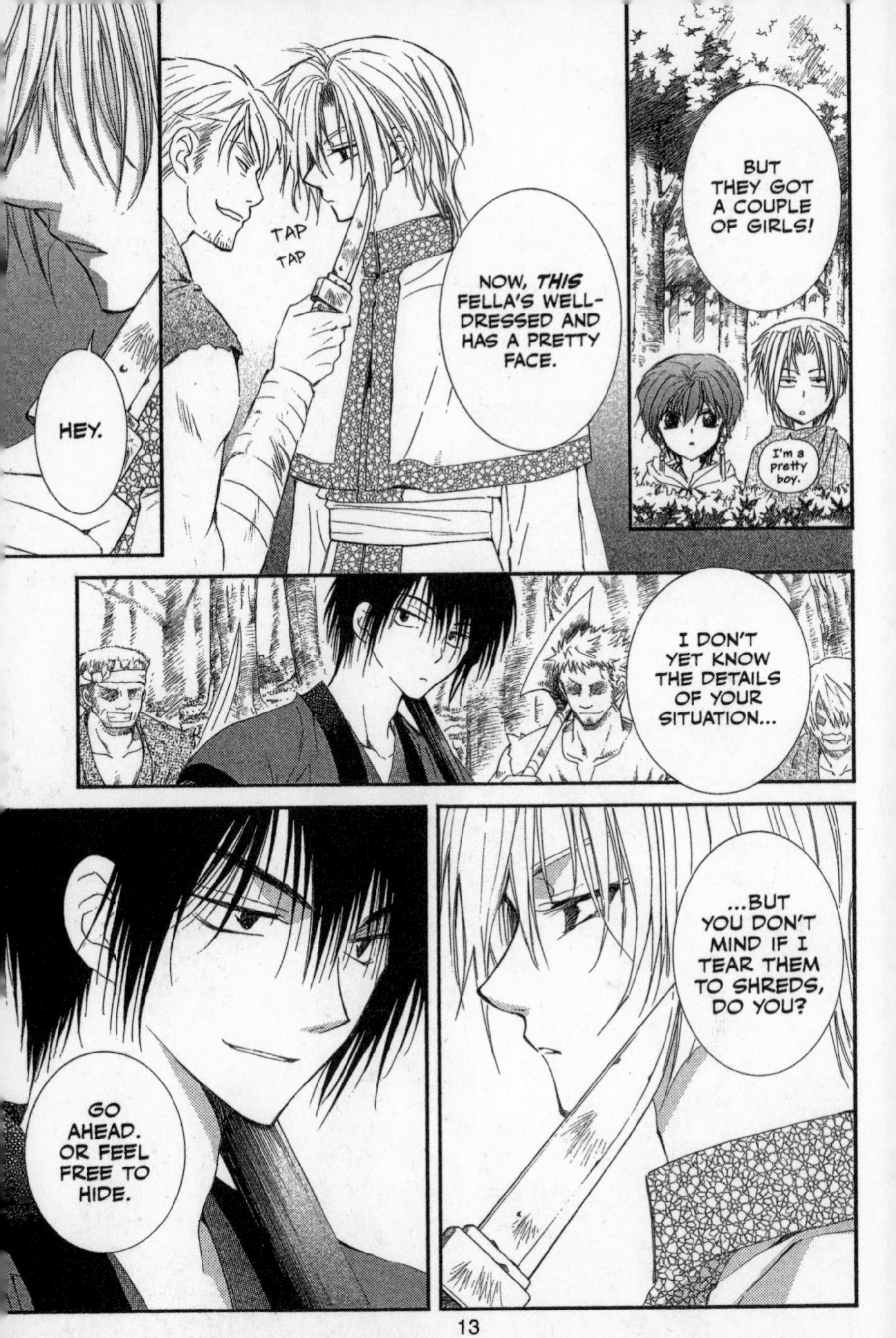
BUT THEY GOT A COUPLE OF GIRLS!
I'm a pretty boy.
NOW, *THIS* FELLA'S WELL-DRESSED AND HAS A PRETTY FACE.
TAP TAP
HEY.
I DON'T YET KNOW THE DETAILS OF YOUR SITUATION...
...BUT YOU DON'T MIND IF I TEAR THEM TO SHREDS, DO YOU?
GO AHEAD. OR FEEL FREE TO HIDE.

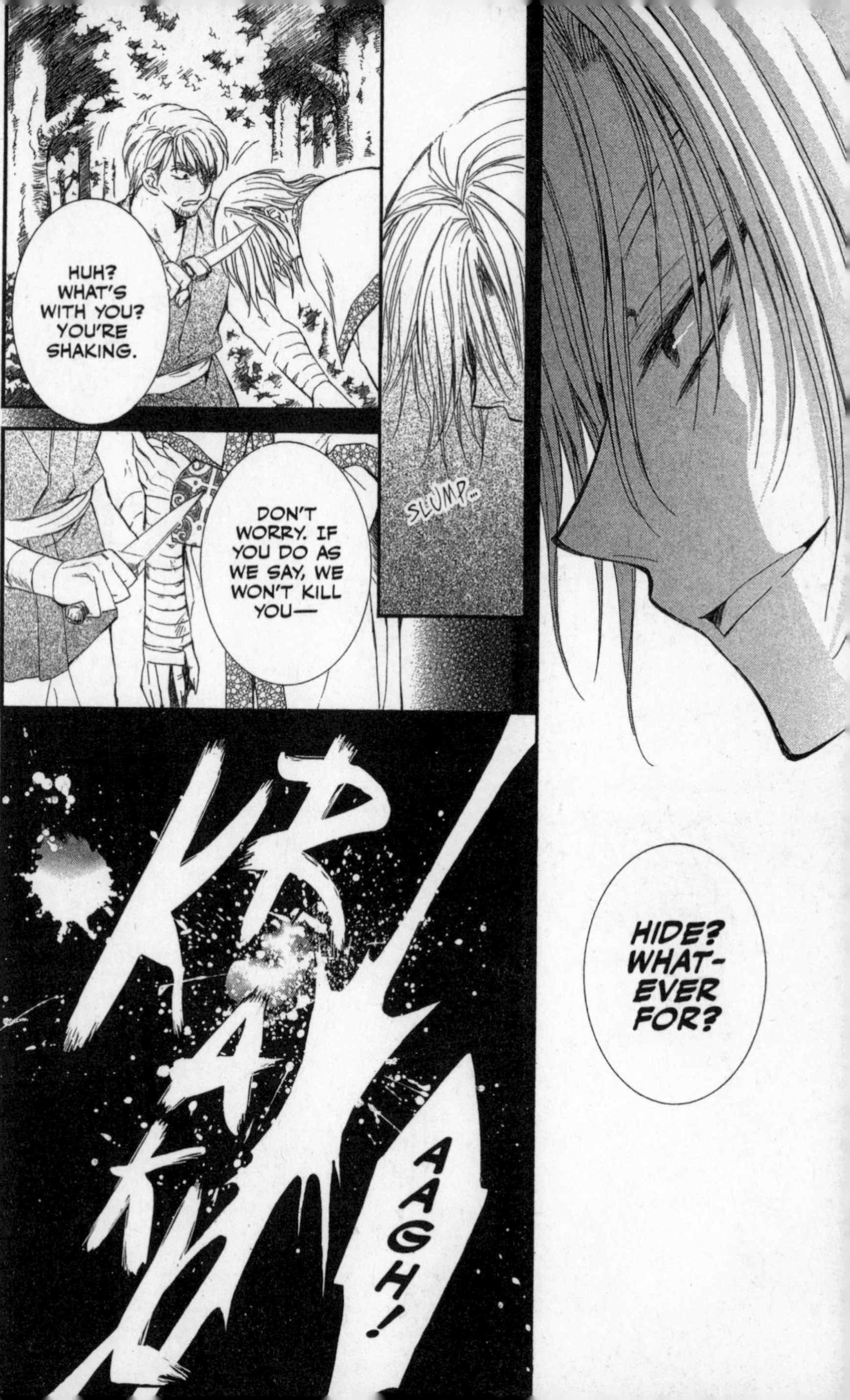
HIDE? WHAT-EVER FOR?
SLUMP...
HUH? WHAT'S WITH YOU? YOU'RE SHAKING.
DON'T WORRY. IF YOU DO AS WE SAY, WE WON'T KILL YOU—
KRAK
AAGH!

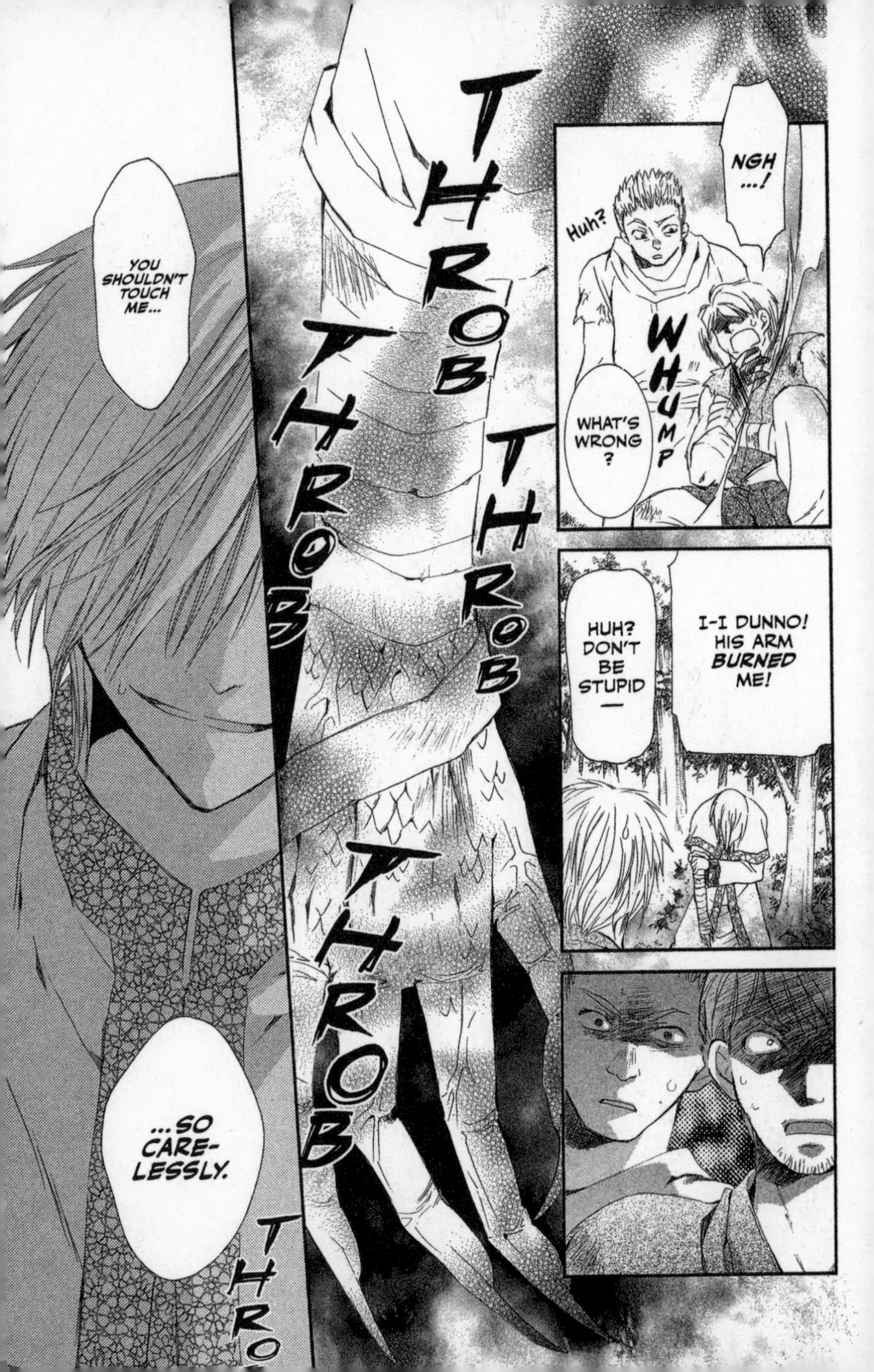
NGH ...!
Huh?
WHUMP
WHAT'S WRONG?
I-I DUNNO! HIS ARM *BURNED* ME!
HUH? DON'T BE STUPID —
THROB THROB
THROB THROB
THROB
YOU SHOULDN'T TOUCH ME...
...SO CARE-LESSLY.
THRO

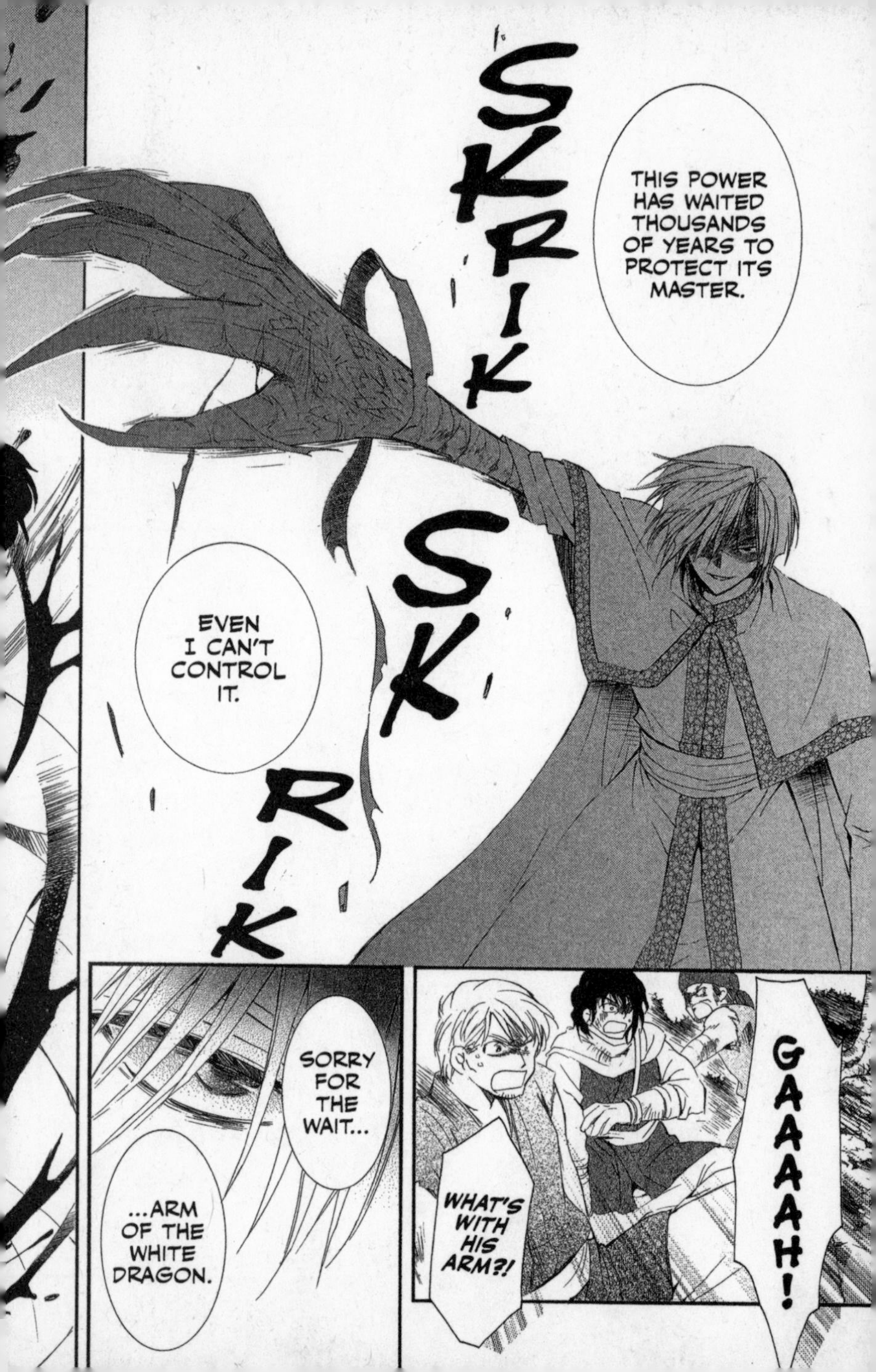
THIS POWER HAS WAITED THOUSANDS OF YEARS TO PROTECT ITS MASTER.
SKRIK
EVEN I CAN'T CONTROL IT.
SK RIK
GAAAAH!
WHAT'S WITH HIS ARM?!
SORRY FOR THE WAIT...
...ARM OF THE WHITE DRAGON.

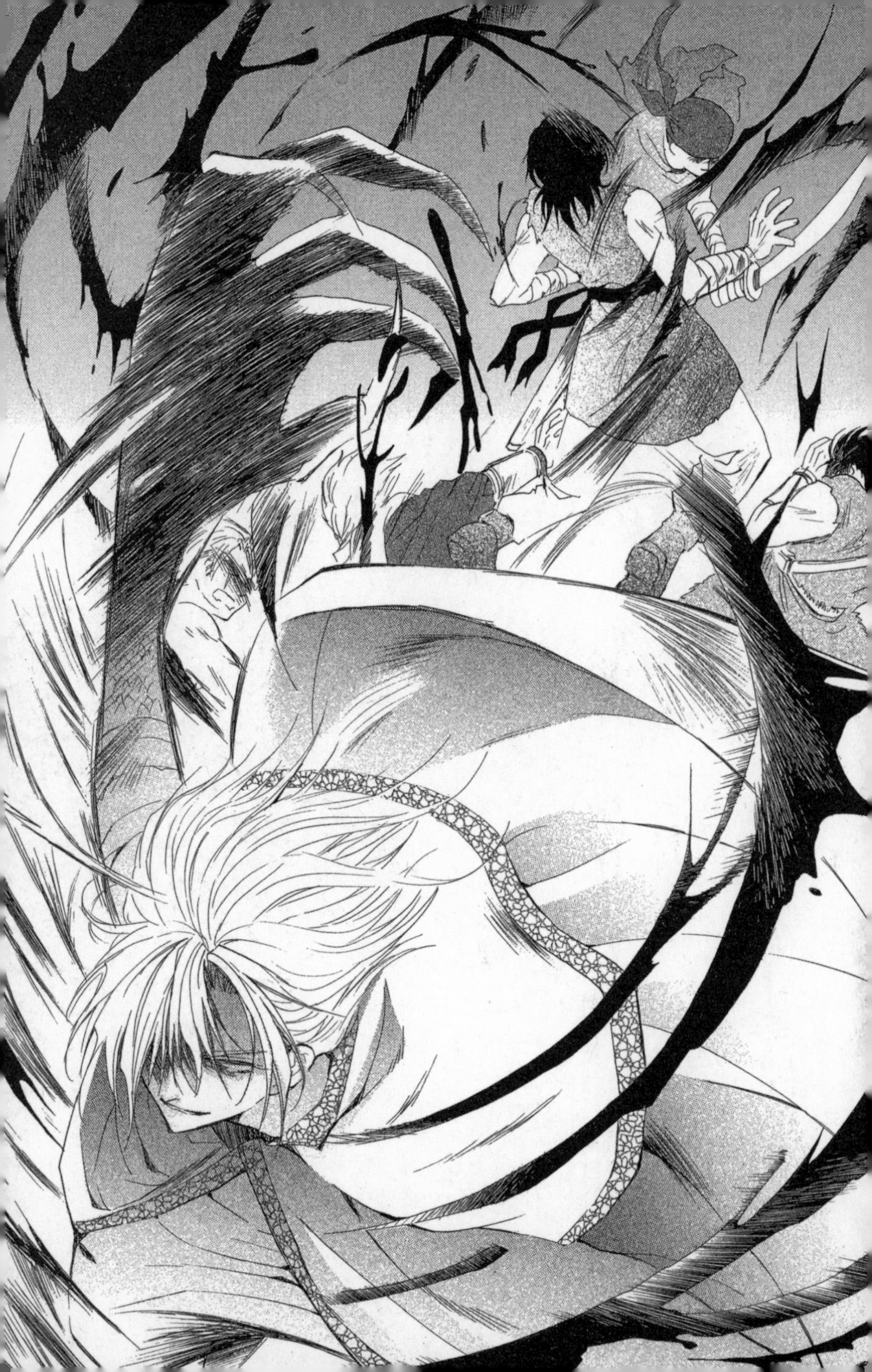

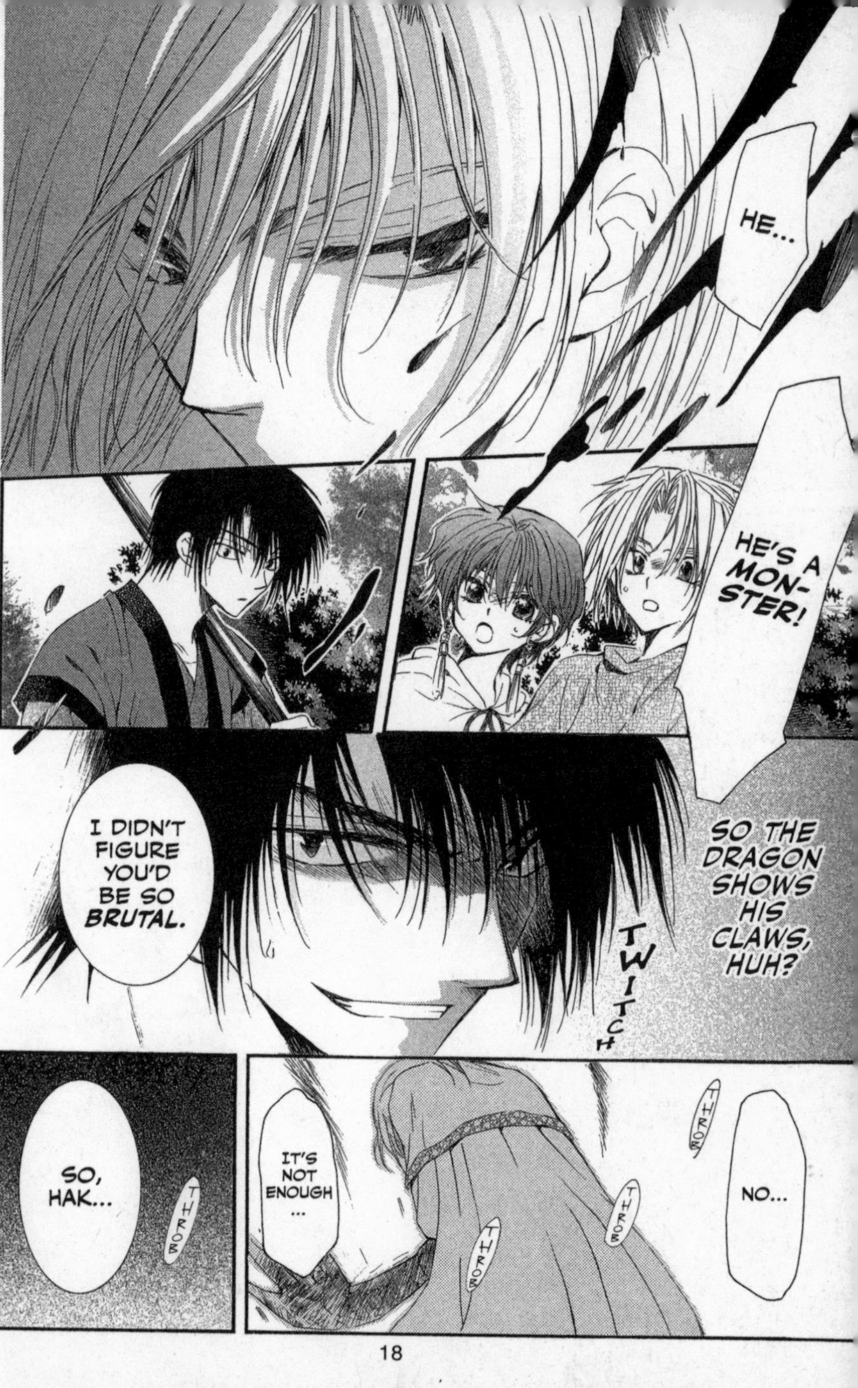
HE...
HE'S A MONSTER!
SO THE DRAGON SHOWS HIS CLAWS, HUH?
TWITCH
I DIDN'T FIGURE YOU'D BE SO BRUTAL.
NO...
THROB
THROB
THROB
IT'S NOT ENOUGH...
SO, HAK...
THROB

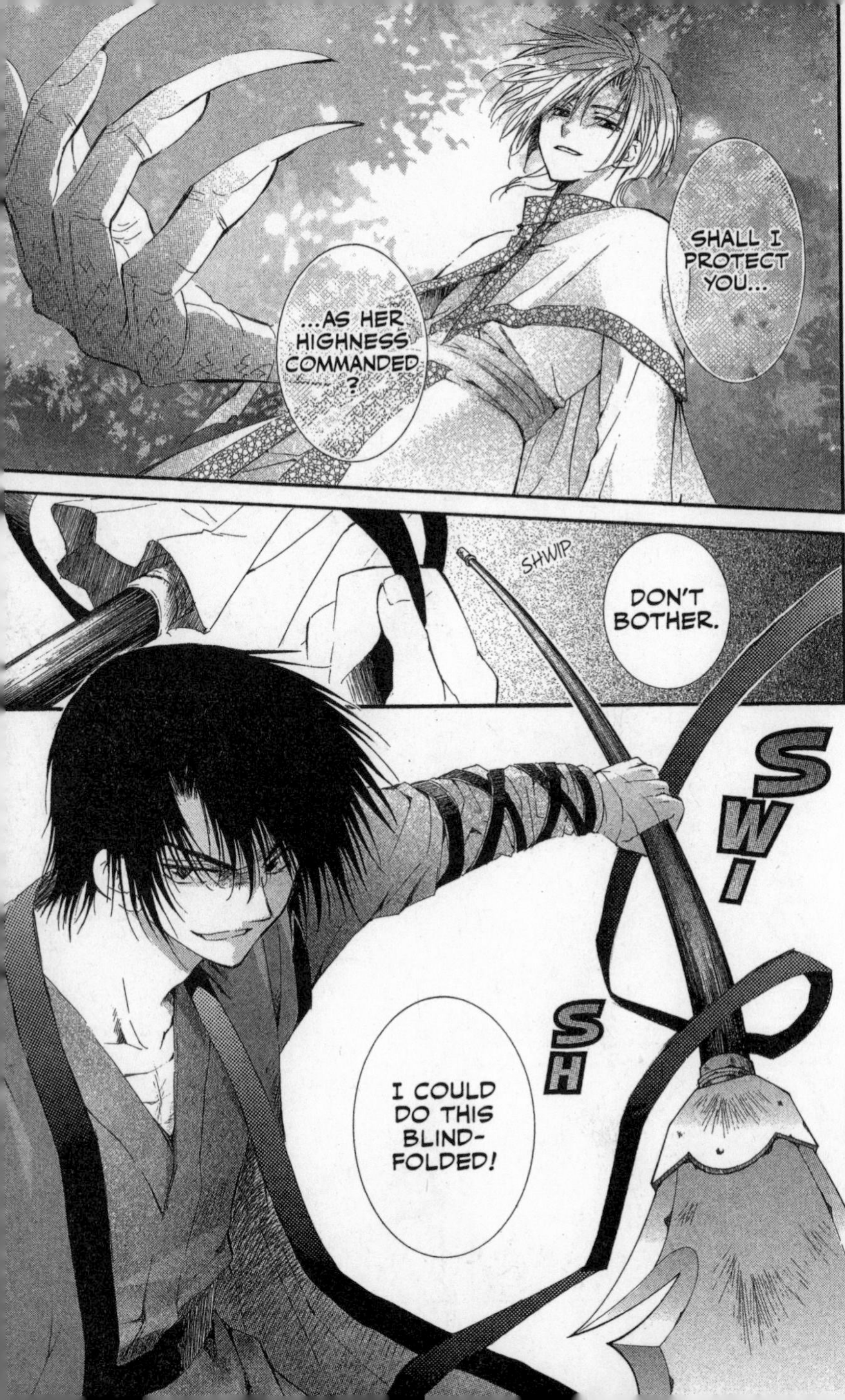
SHALL I PROTECT YOU...
...AS HER HIGHNESS COMMANDED?
SHWIP
DON'T BOTHER.
SWISH
I COULD DO THIS BLINDFOLDED!

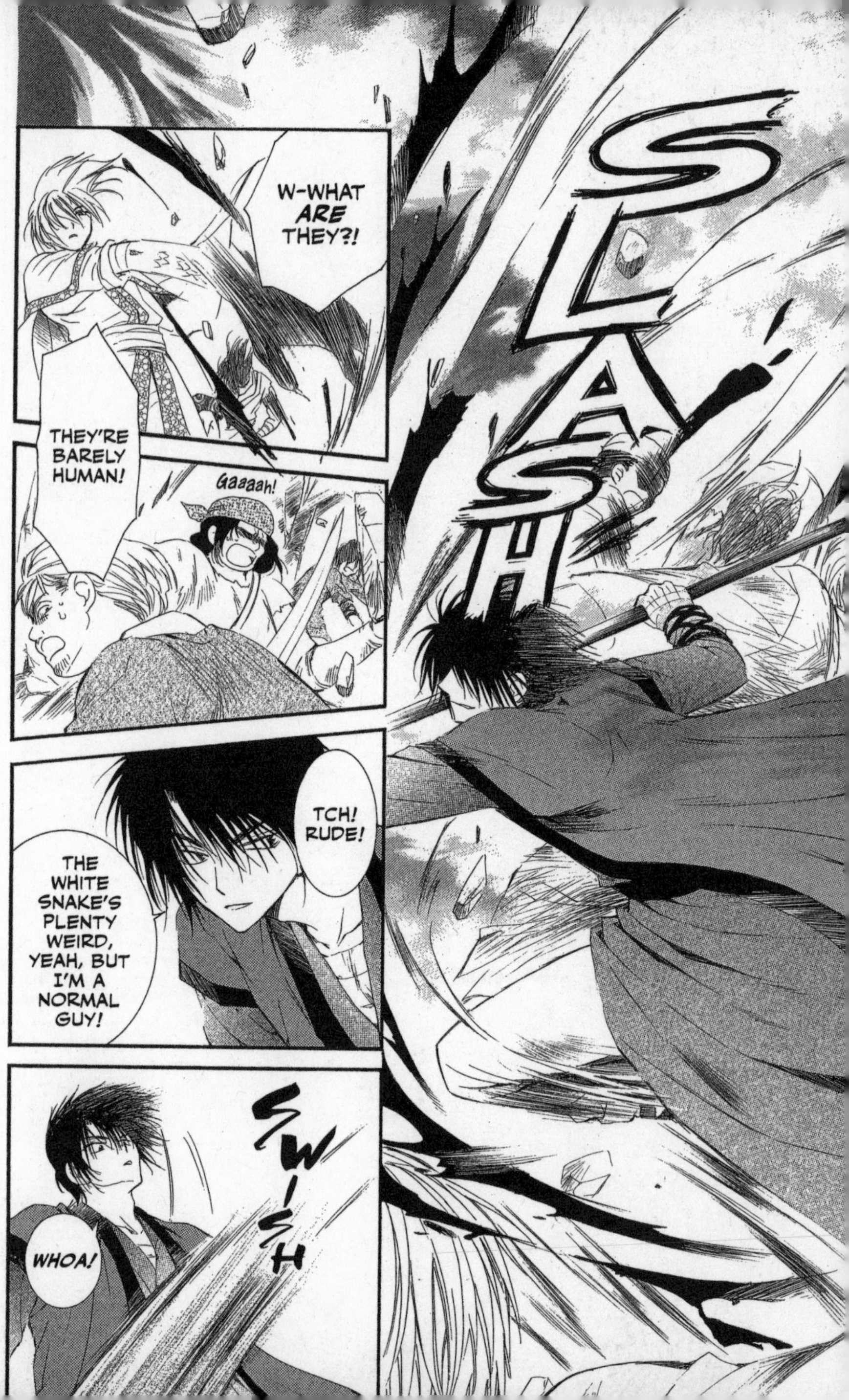
SLLASH
W-WHAT ARE THEY?!
THEY'RE BARELY HUMAN!
Gaaaah!
TCH! RUDE!
THE WHITE SNAKE'S PLENTY WEIRD, YEAH, BUT I'M A NORMAL GUY!
SWISH
WHOA!

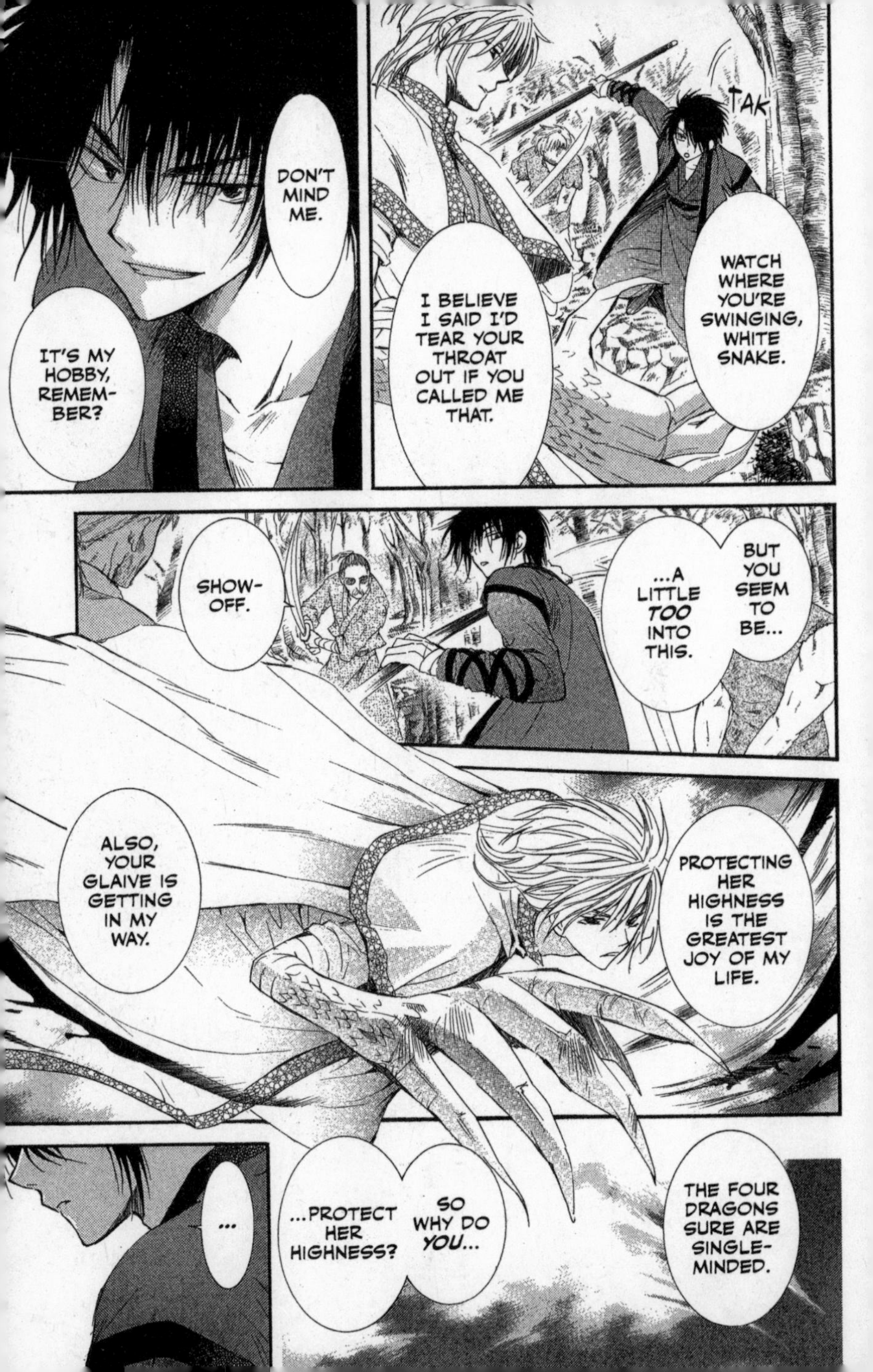
TAK
WATCH WHERE YOU'RE SWINGING, WHITE SNAKE.
I BELIEVE I SAID I'D TEAR YOUR THROAT OUT IF YOU CALLED ME THAT.
DON'T MIND ME.
IT'S MY HOBBY, REMEMBER-BER?
BUT YOU SEEM TO BE...
...A LITTLE *TOO* INTO THIS.
SHOW-OFF.
PROTECTING HER HIGHNESS IS THE GREATEST JOY OF MY LIFE.
ALSO, YOUR GLAIVE IS GETTING IN MY WAY.
THE FOUR DRAGONS SURE ARE SINGLE-MINDED.
SO WHY DO *YOU*...
...PROTECT HER HIGHNESS?
...

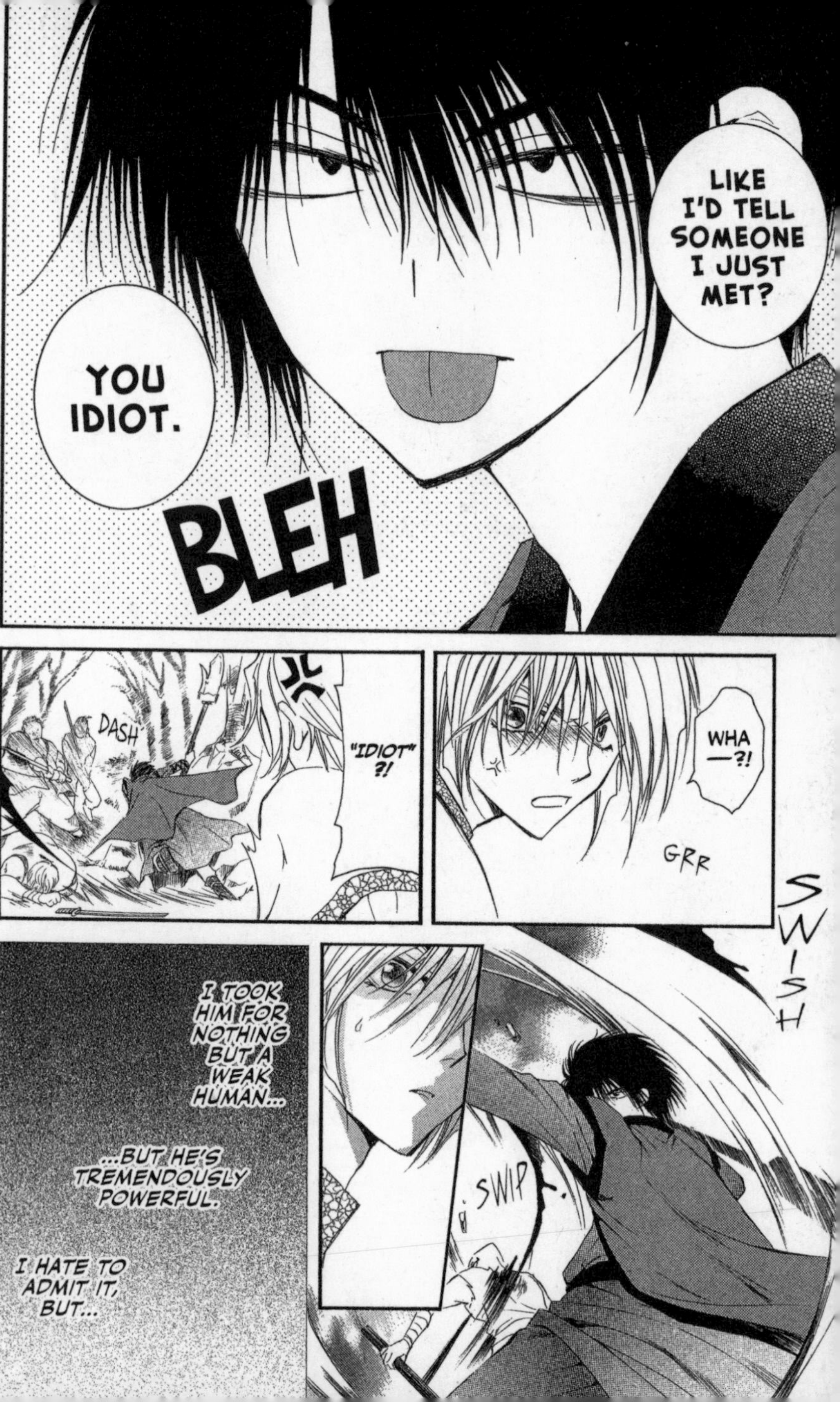
LIKE I'D TELL SOMEONE I JUST MET?
YOU IDIOT.
BLEH
WHA—?!
GRR
"IDIOT"?!
DASH
SWISH
SWIP
I TOOK HIM FOR NOTHING BUT A WEAK HUMAN...
...BUT HE'S TREMENDOUSLY POWERFUL.
I HATE TO ADMIT IT, BUT...

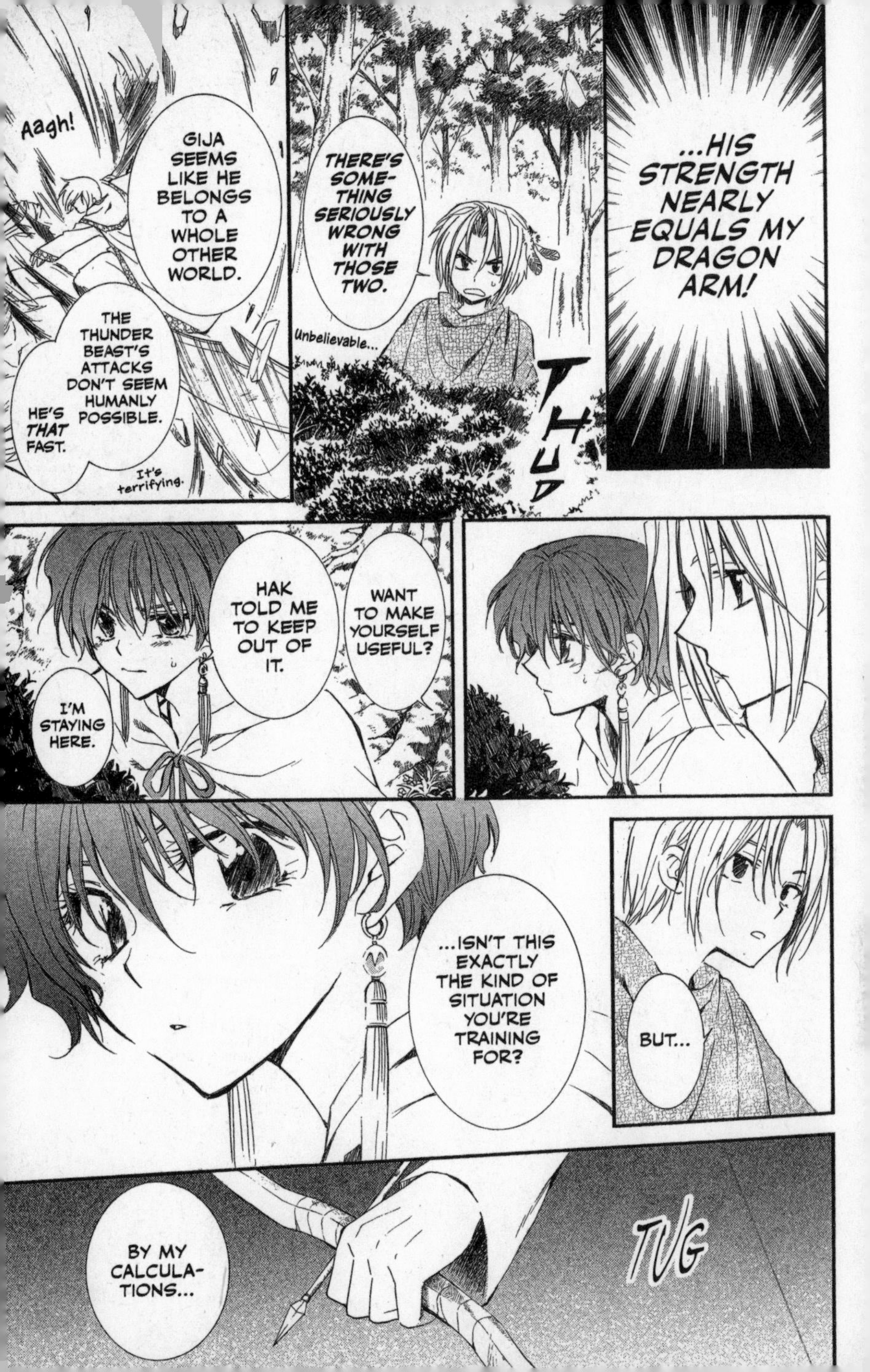
...HIS STRENGTH NEARLY EQUALS MY DRAGON ARM!
THERE'S SOME-THING SERIOUSLY WRONG WITH THOSE TWO.
Unbelievable...
THUD
GIJA SEEMS LIKE HE BELONGS TO A WHOLE OTHER WORLD.
Aagh!
THE THUNDER BEAST'S ATTACKS DON'T SEEM HUMANLY POSSIBLE.
HE'S THAT FAST.
It's terrifying.
WANT TO MAKE YOURSELF USEFUL?
HAK TOLD ME TO KEEP OUT OF IT.
I'M STAYING HERE.
BUT...
...ISN'T THIS EXACTLY THE KIND OF SITUATION YOU'RE TRAINING FOR?
TUG
BY MY CALCULA-TIONS...

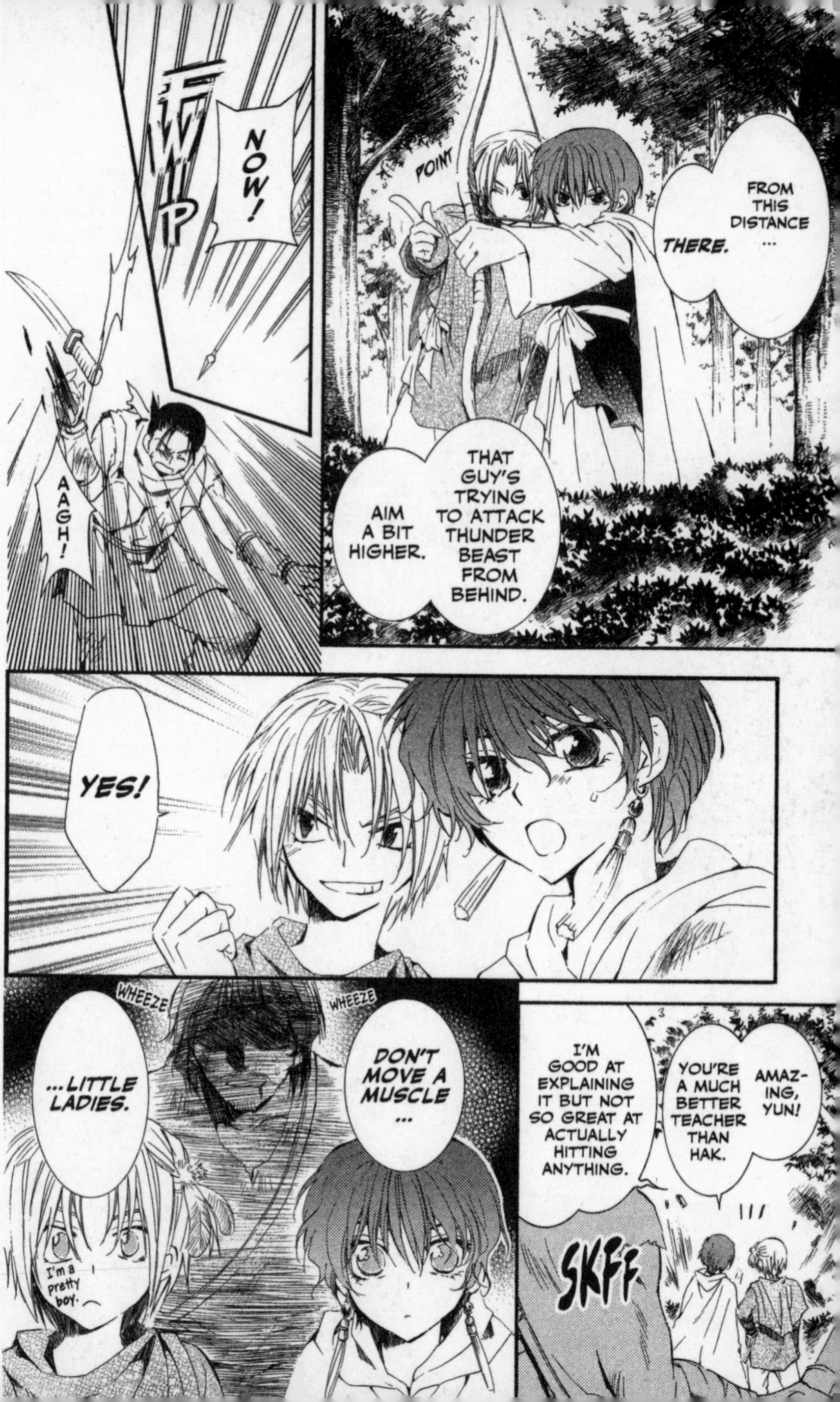
FROM THIS DISTANCE ...
THERE.
POINT
THAT GUY'S TRYING TO ATTACK THUNDER BEAST FROM BEHIND.
AIM A BIT HIGHER.
NOW!
FWIP
AAGH!
YES!
AMAZ-ING, YUN!
YOU'RE A MUCH BETTER TEACHER THAN HAK.
I'M GOOD AT EXPLAINING IT BUT NOT SO GREAT AT ACTUALLY HITTING ANYTHING.
SKFF
WHEEZE
WHEEZE
DON'T MOVE A MUSCLE ...
...LITTLE LADIES.
I'm a pretty boy.

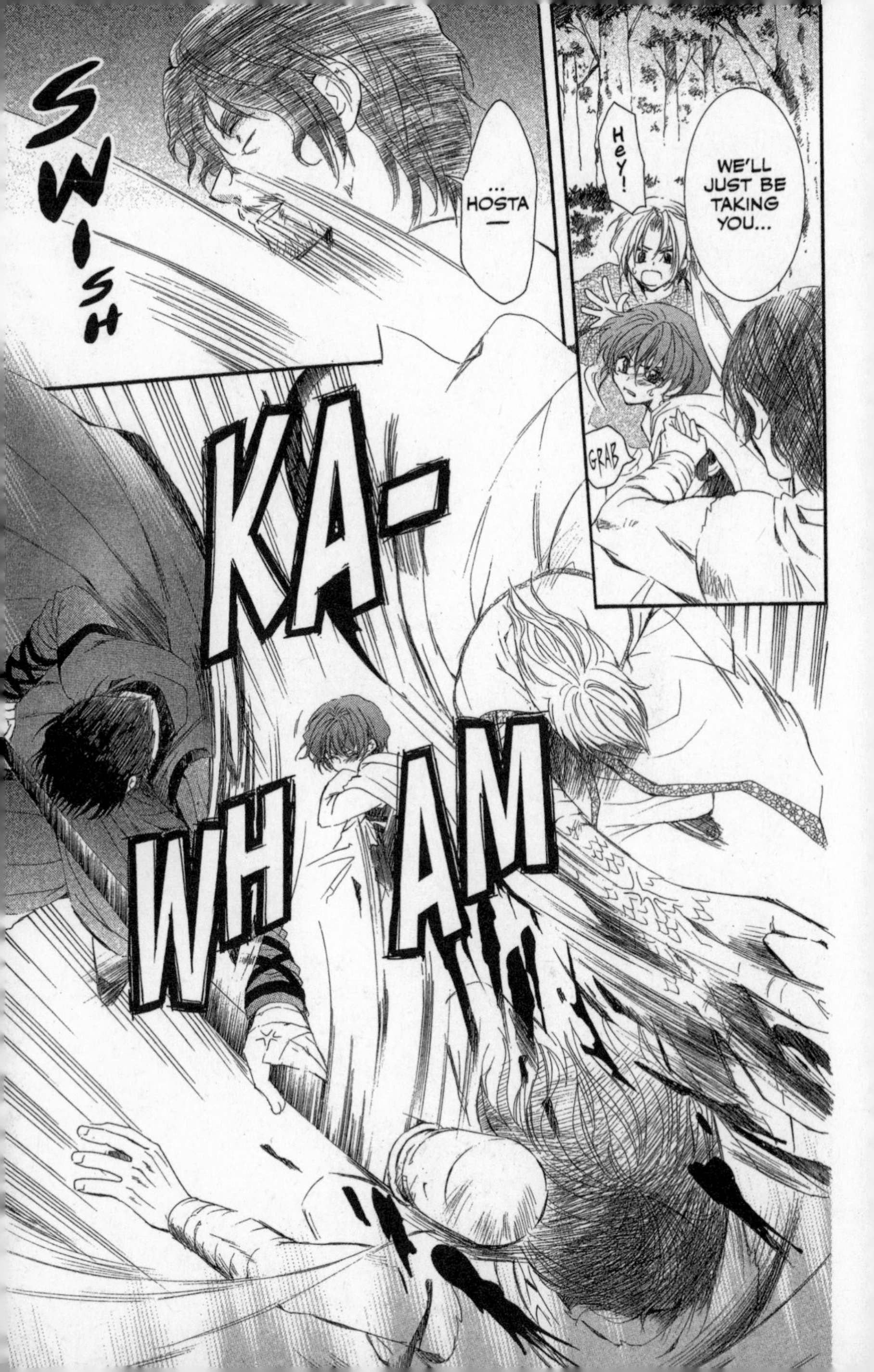
WE'LL JUST BE TAKING YOU...
HeY!
GRAB
... HOSTA —
SWISH
KA-WHAM

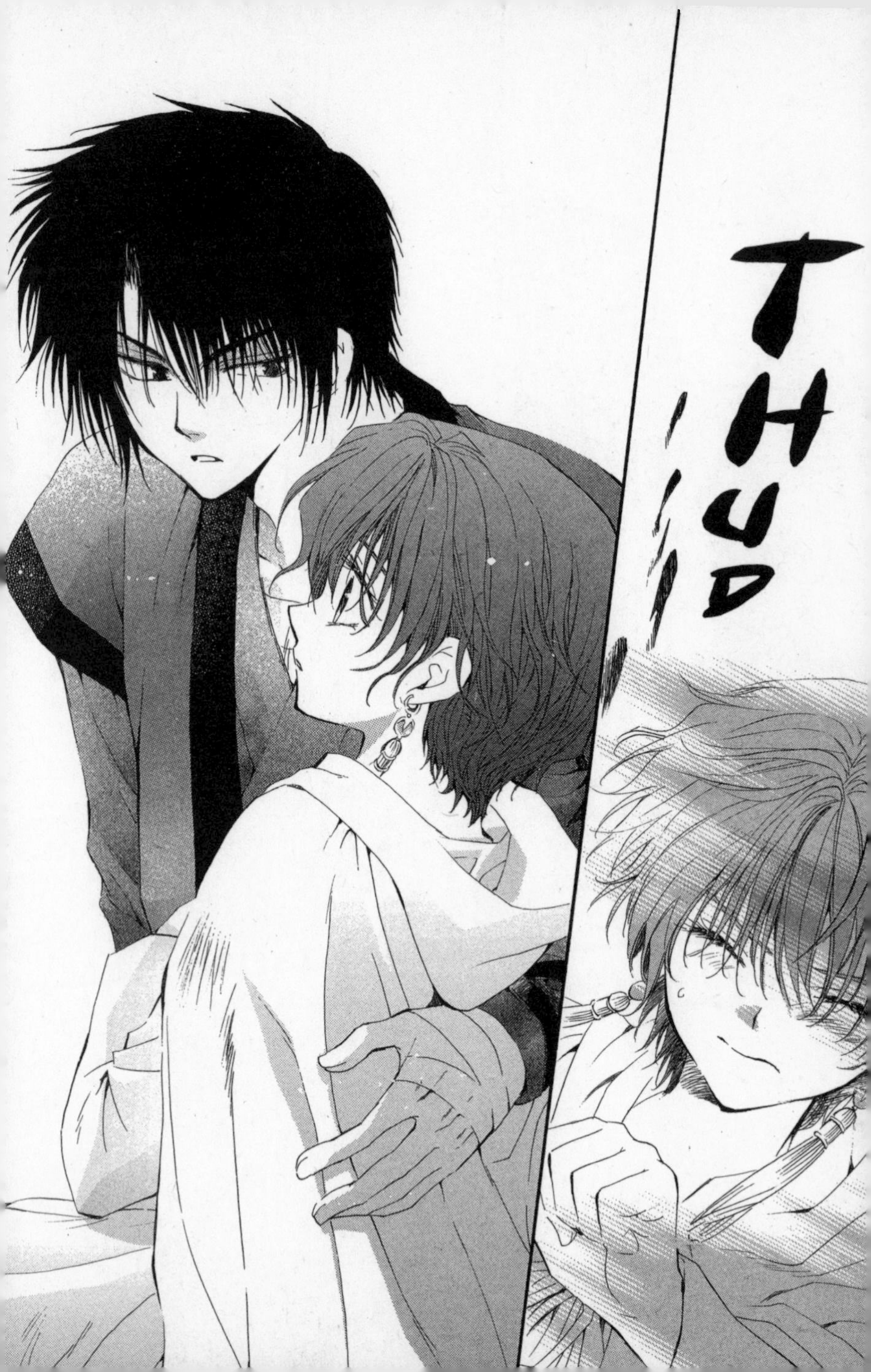
THUD

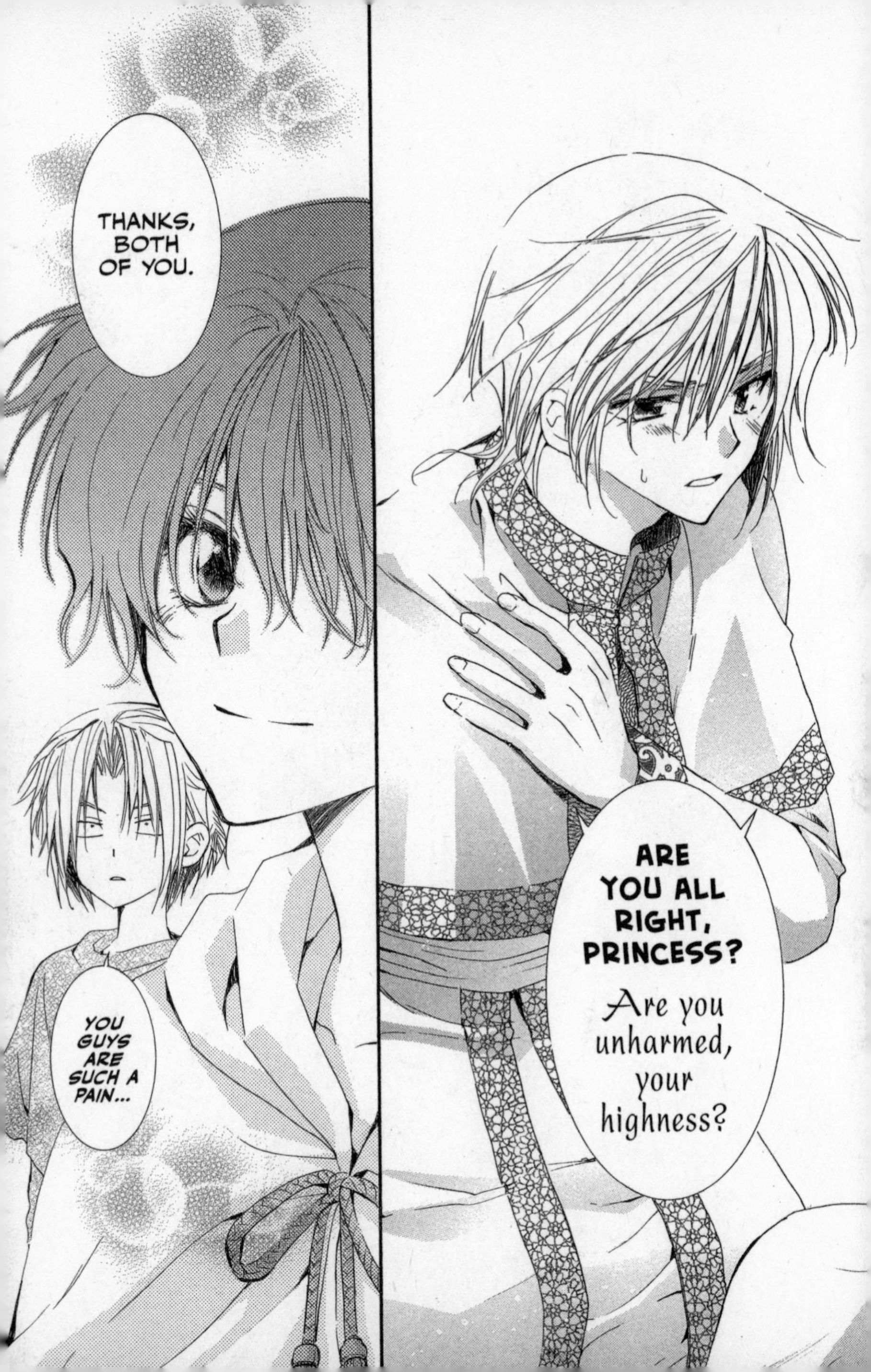
ARE YOU ALL RIGHT, PRINCESS?
Are you unharmed, your highness?
THANKS, BOTH OF YOU.
YOU GUYS ARE SUCH A PAIN...

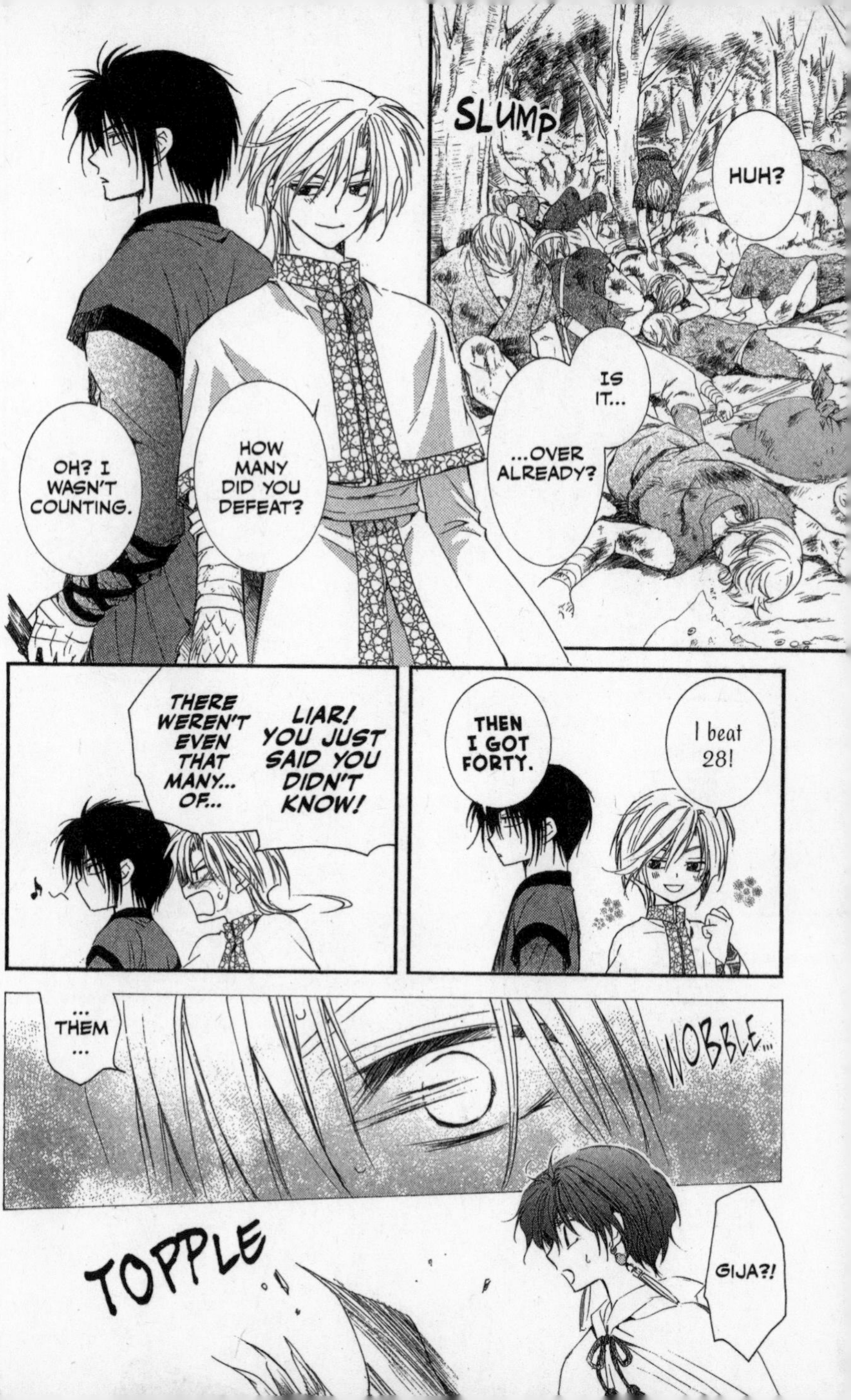
SLUMP
HUH?
IS IT...
...OVER ALREADY?
HOW MANY DID YOU DEFEAT?
OH? I WASN'T COUNTING.
I beat 28!
THEN I GOT FORTY.
LIAR! YOU JUST SAID YOU DIDN'T KNOW!
THERE WEREN'T EVEN THAT MANY... OF...
WOBBLE...
...THEM...
TOPPLE
GIJA?!

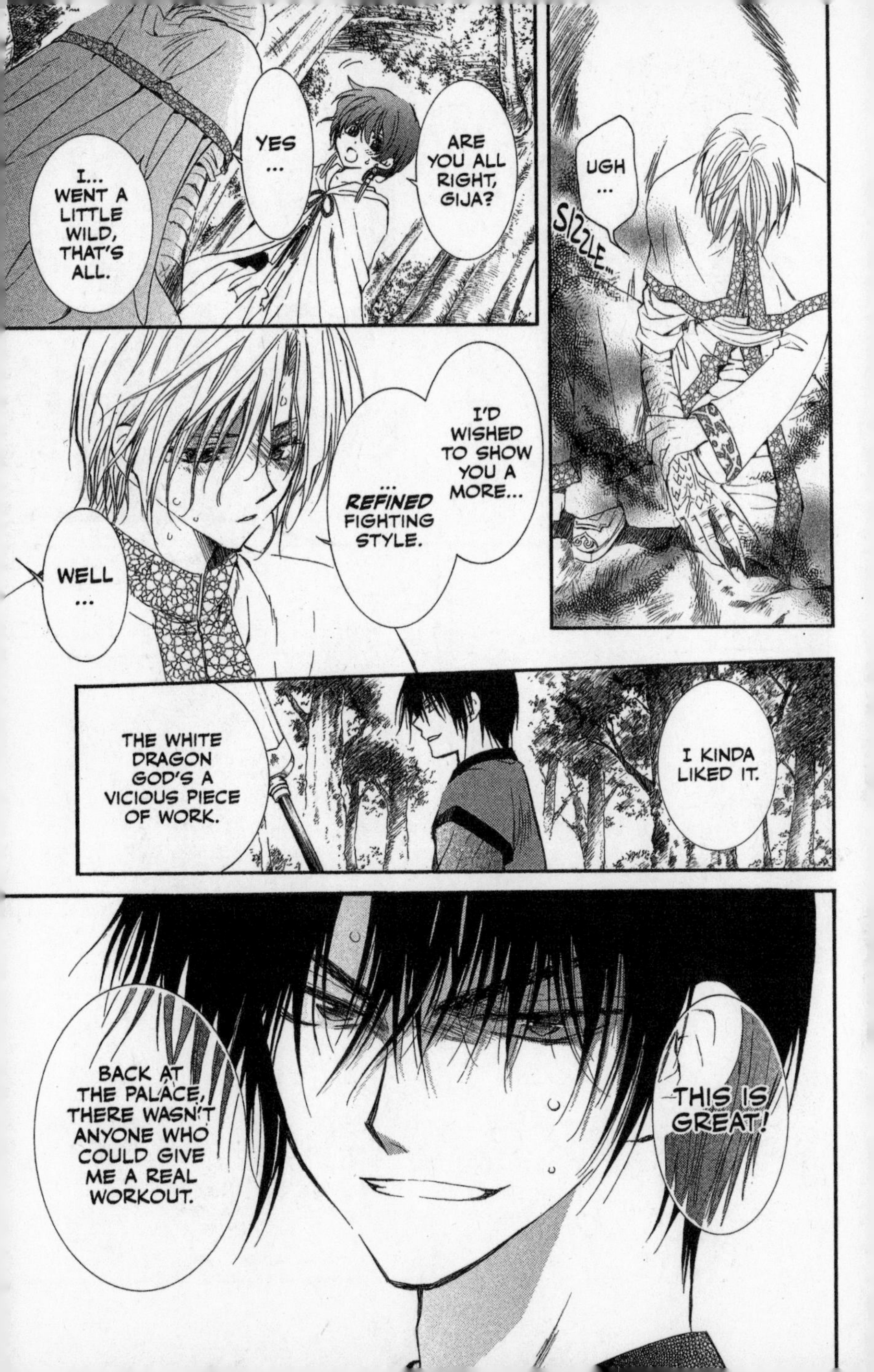
UGH ...
SIZZLE...
ARE YOU ALL RIGHT, GIJA?
YES ...
I... WENT A LITTLE WILD, THAT'S ALL.
I'D WISHED TO SHOW YOU A MORE...
... *REFINED* FIGHTING STYLE.
WELL ...
I KINDA LIKED IT.
THE WHITE DRAGON GOD'S A VICIOUS PIECE OF WORK.
THIS IS GREAT!
BACK AT THE PALACE, THERE WASN'T ANYONE WHO COULD GIVE ME A REAL WORKOUT.

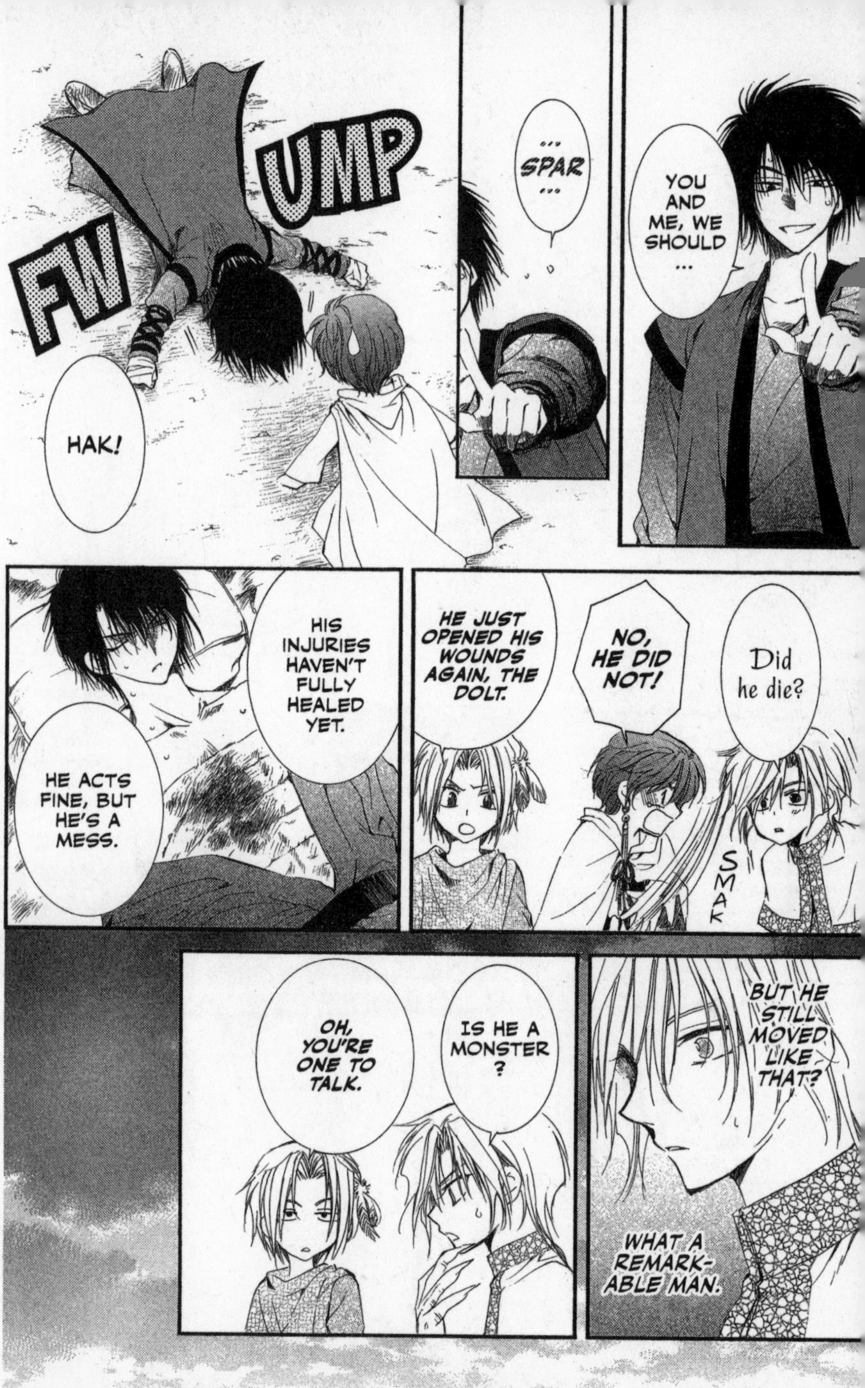
YOU AND ME, WE SHOULD ...
... SPAR ...
FWUMP
HAK!
Did he die?
NO, HE DID NOT!
SMAK
HE JUST OPENED HIS WOUNDS AGAIN, THE DOLT.
HIS INJURIES HAVEN'T FULLY HEALED YET.
HE ACTS FINE, BUT HE'S A MESS.
BUT HE STILL MOVED LIKE THAT?
WHAT A REMARK-ABLE MAN.
IS HE A MONSTER ?
OH, YOU'RE ONE TO TALK.

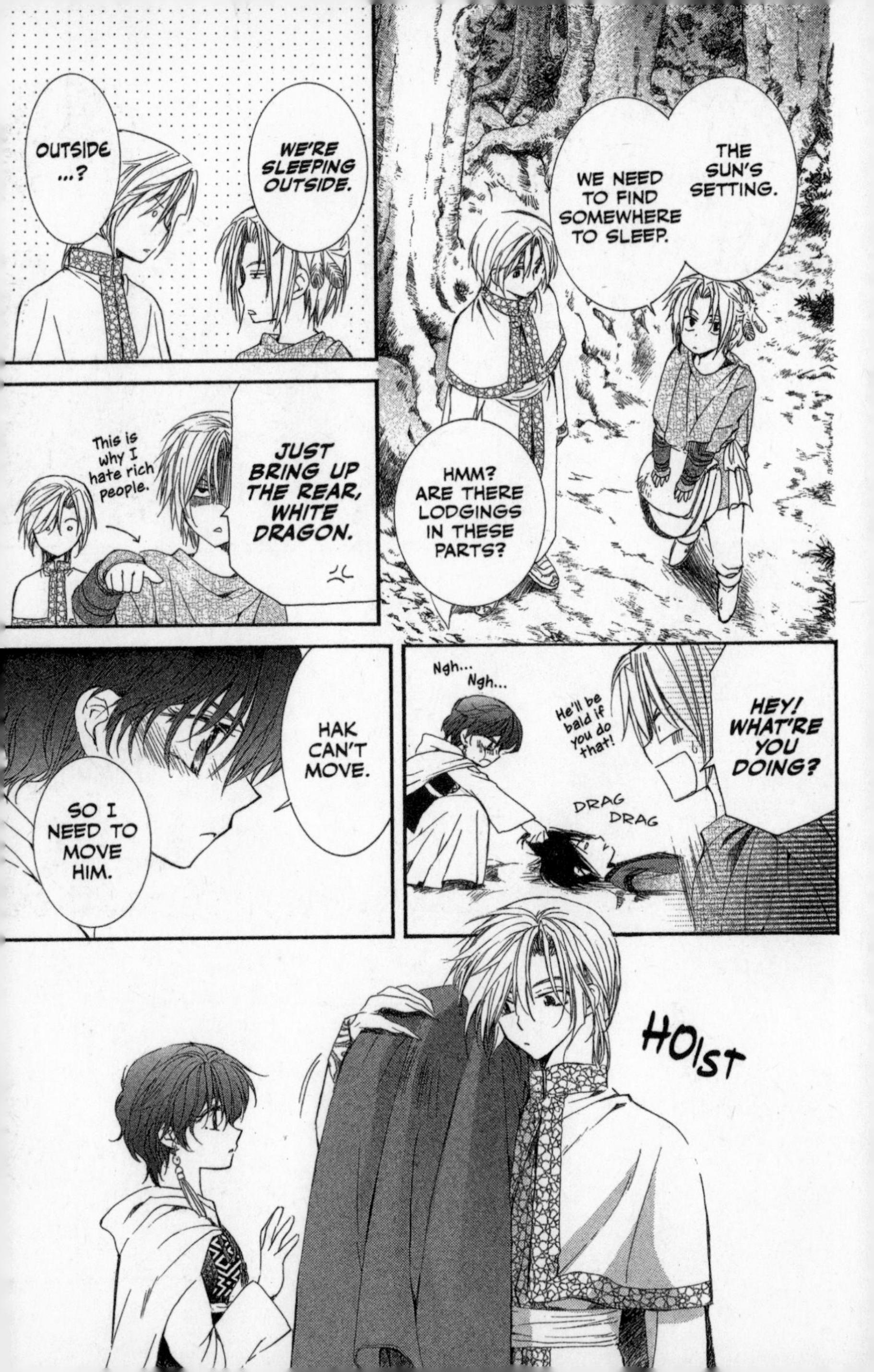
THE SUN'S SETTING.
WE NEED TO FIND SOMEWHERE TO SLEEP.
HMM? ARE THERE LODGINGS IN THESE PARTS?
WE'RE SLEEPING OUTSIDE.
OUTSIDE ...?
JUST BRING UP THE REAR, WHITE DRAGON.
This is why I hate rich people.
HEY! WHAT'RE YOU DOING?
He'll be bald if you do that!
Ngh... Ngh...
DRAG DRAG
HAK CAN'T MOVE.
SO I NEED TO MOVE HIM.
HOIST

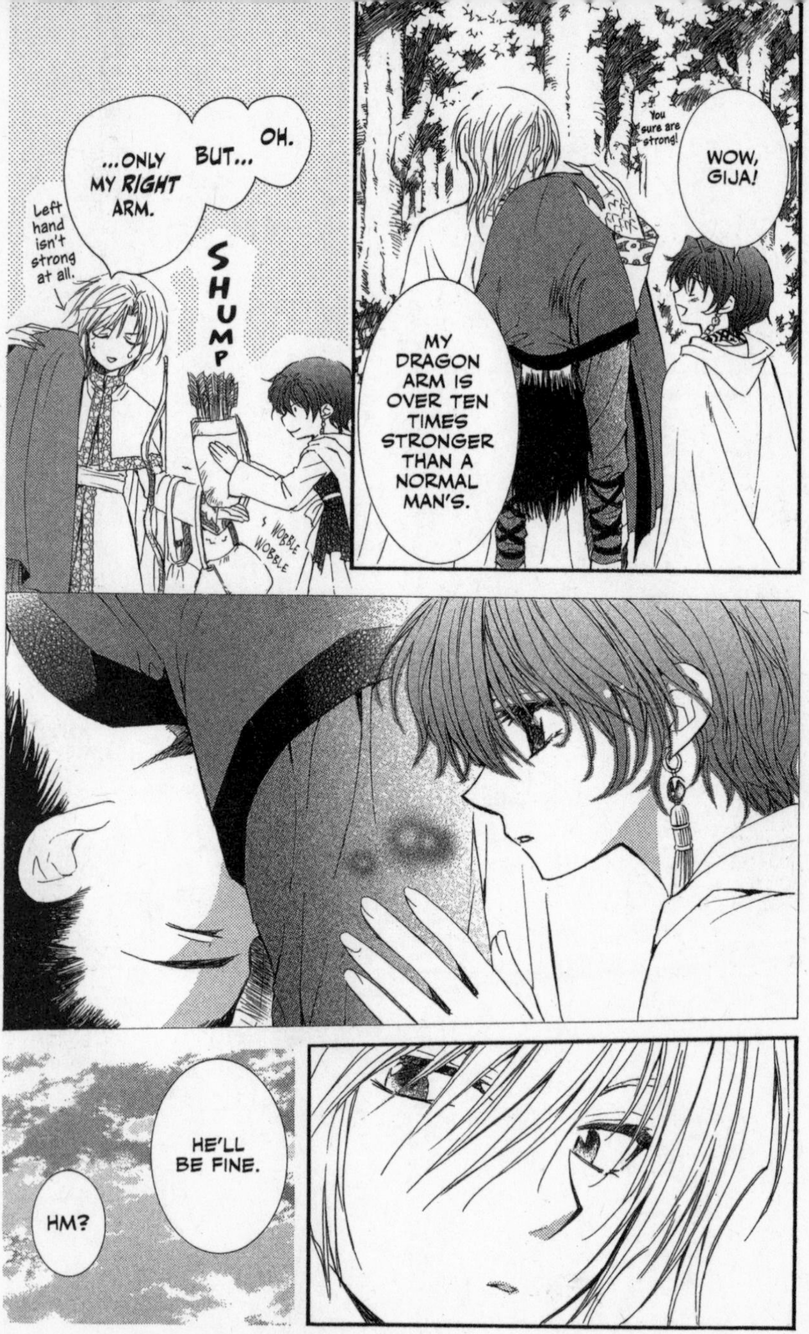
WOW, GIJA!
You sure are strong!
MY DRAGON ARM IS OVER TEN TIMES STRONGER THAN A NORMAL MAN'S.
OH.
BUT...
...ONLY MY RIGHT ARM.
Left hand isn't strong at all.
SHUMP
WOBBLE WOBBLE
HE'LL BE FINE.
HM?

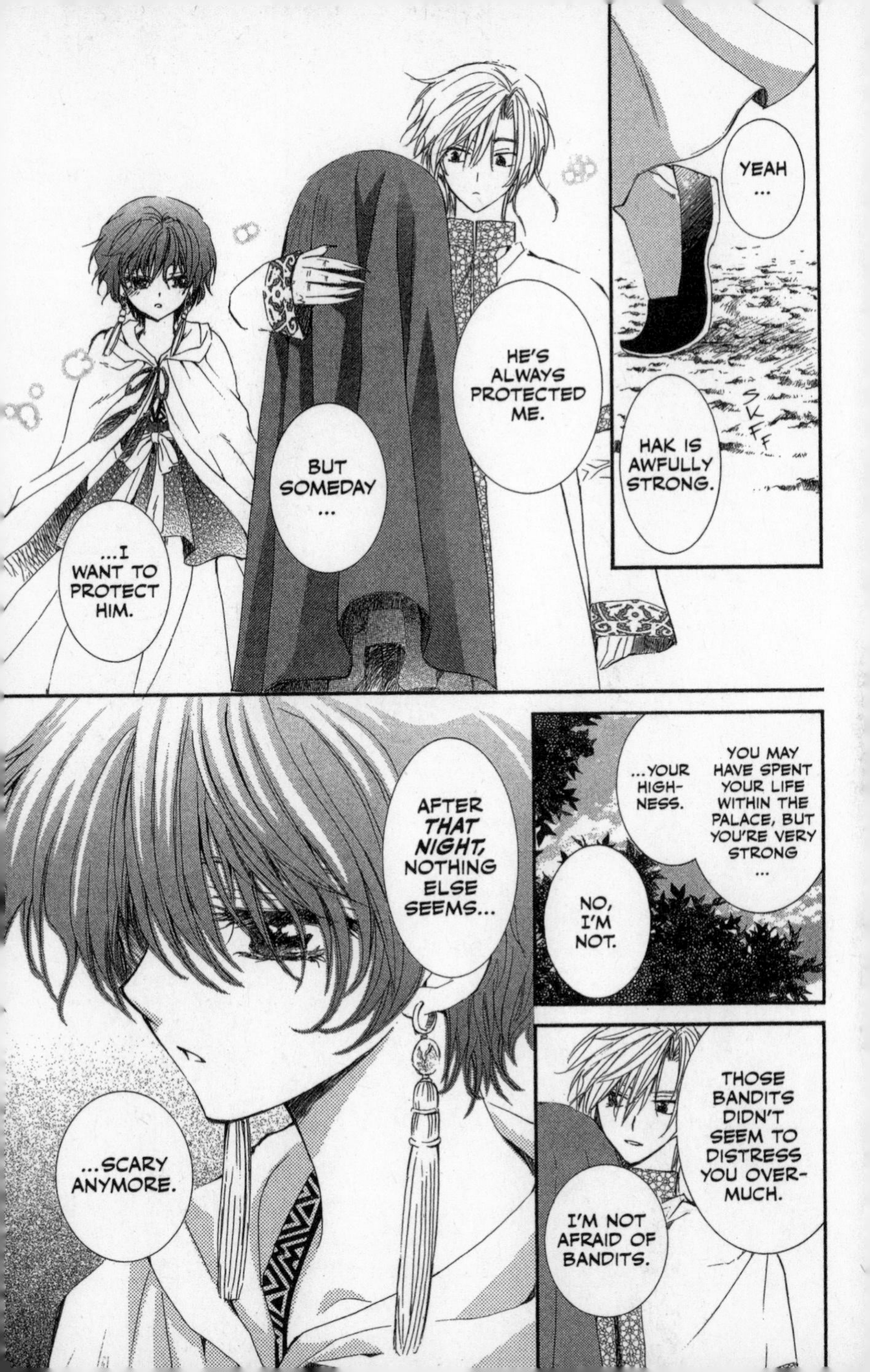
YEAH ...
HAK IS AWFULLY STRONG.
SKFF
HE'S ALWAYS PROTECTED ME.
BUT SOMEDAY ...
...I WANT TO PROTECT HIM.
YOU MAY HAVE SPENT YOUR LIFE WITHIN THE PALACE, BUT YOU'RE VERY STRONG ...
...YOUR HIGHNESS.
NO, I'M NOT.
THOSE BANDITS DIDN'T SEEM TO DISTRESS YOU OVERMUCH.
I'M NOT AFRAID OF BANDITS.
AFTER *THAT NIGHT,* NOTHING ELSE SEEMS...
...SCARY ANYMORE.

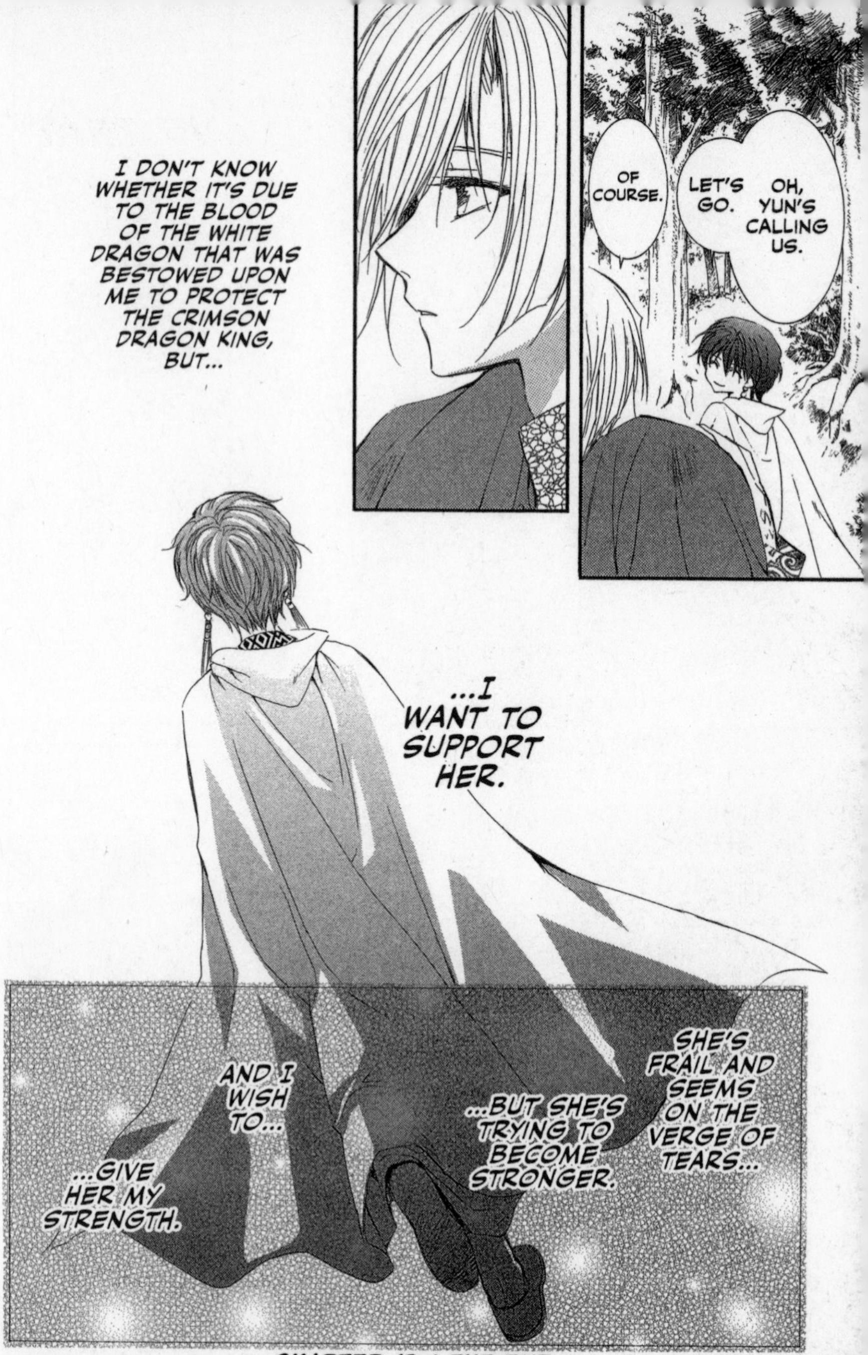
OH, YUN'S CALLING US.
LET'S GO.
OF COURSE.
I DON'T KNOW WHETHER IT'S DUE TO THE BLOOD OF THE WHITE DRAGON THAT WAS BESTOWED UPON ME TO PROTECT THE CRIMSON DRAGON KING, BUT...
...I WANT TO SUPPORT HER.
SHE'S FRAIL AND SEEMS ON THE VERGE OF TEARS...
...BUT SHE'S TRYING TO BECOME STRONGER.
AND I WISH TO...
...GIVE HER MY STRENGTH.

CHAPTER 18 / THE END

CHAPTER 19: THIS WAY AND THAT

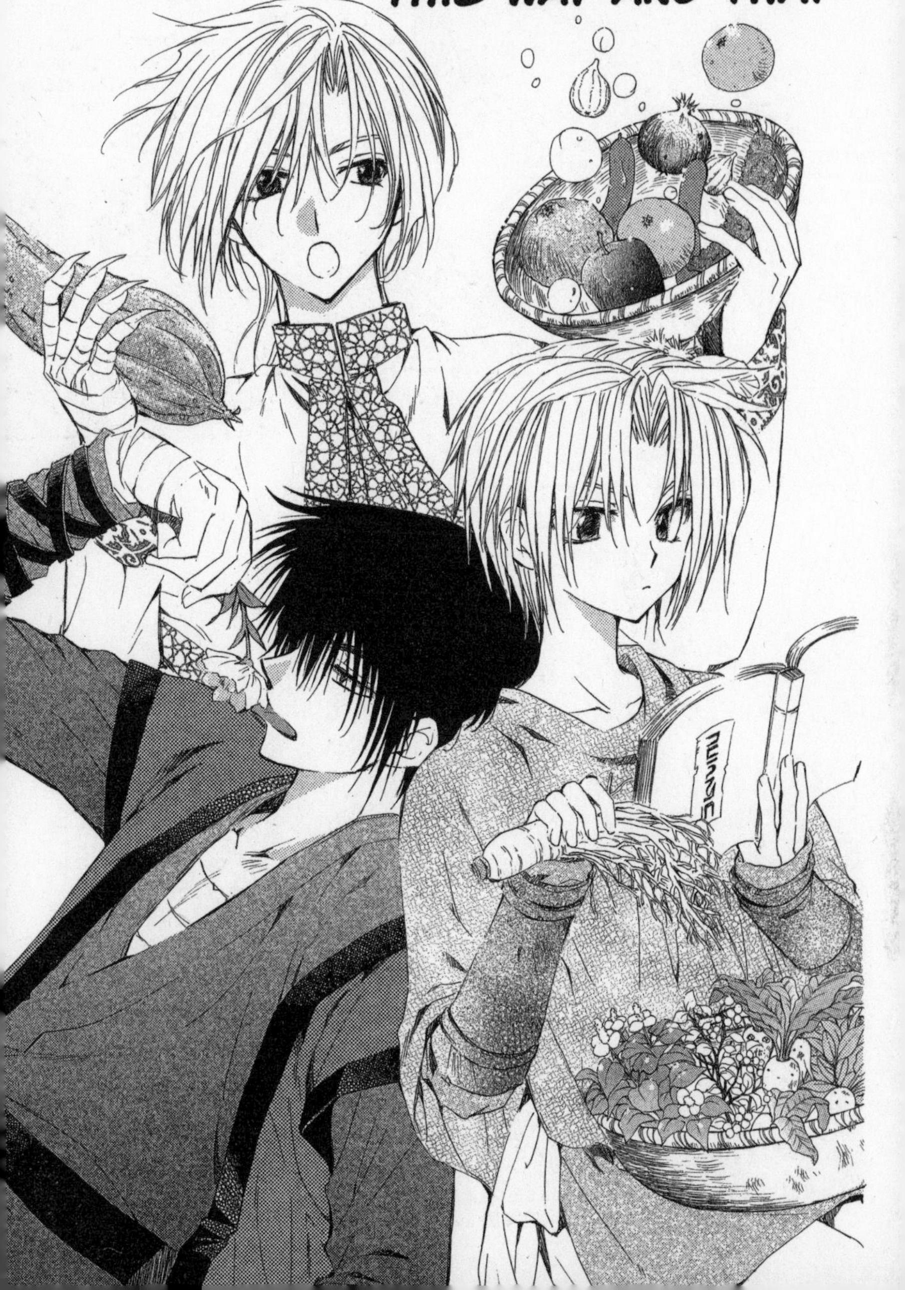

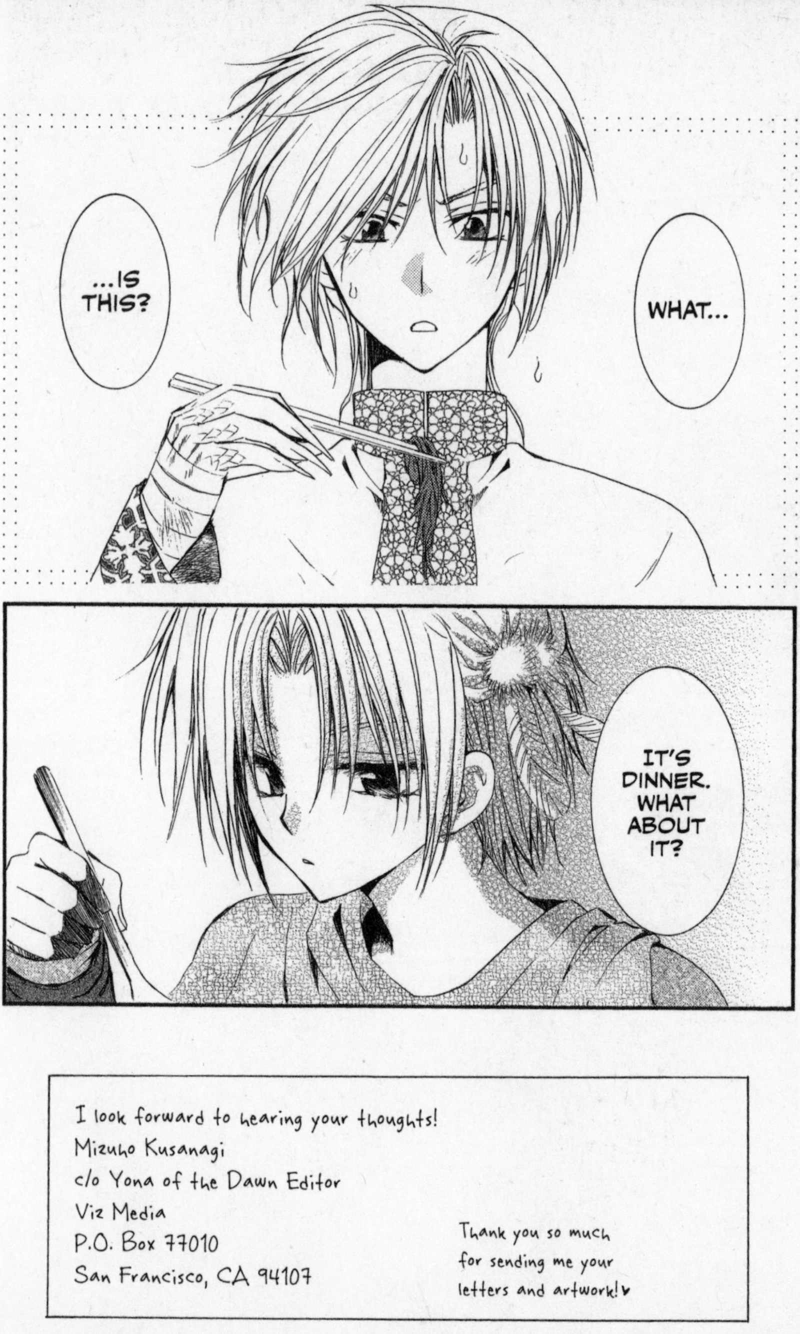
WHAT...
...IS THIS?
IT'S DINNER. WHAT ABOUT IT?

I look forward to hearing your thoughts!
Mizuho Kusanagi
c/o Yona of the Dawn Editor
Viz Media
P.O. Box 77010
San Francisco, CA 94107

Thank you so much for sending me your letters and artwork!♥

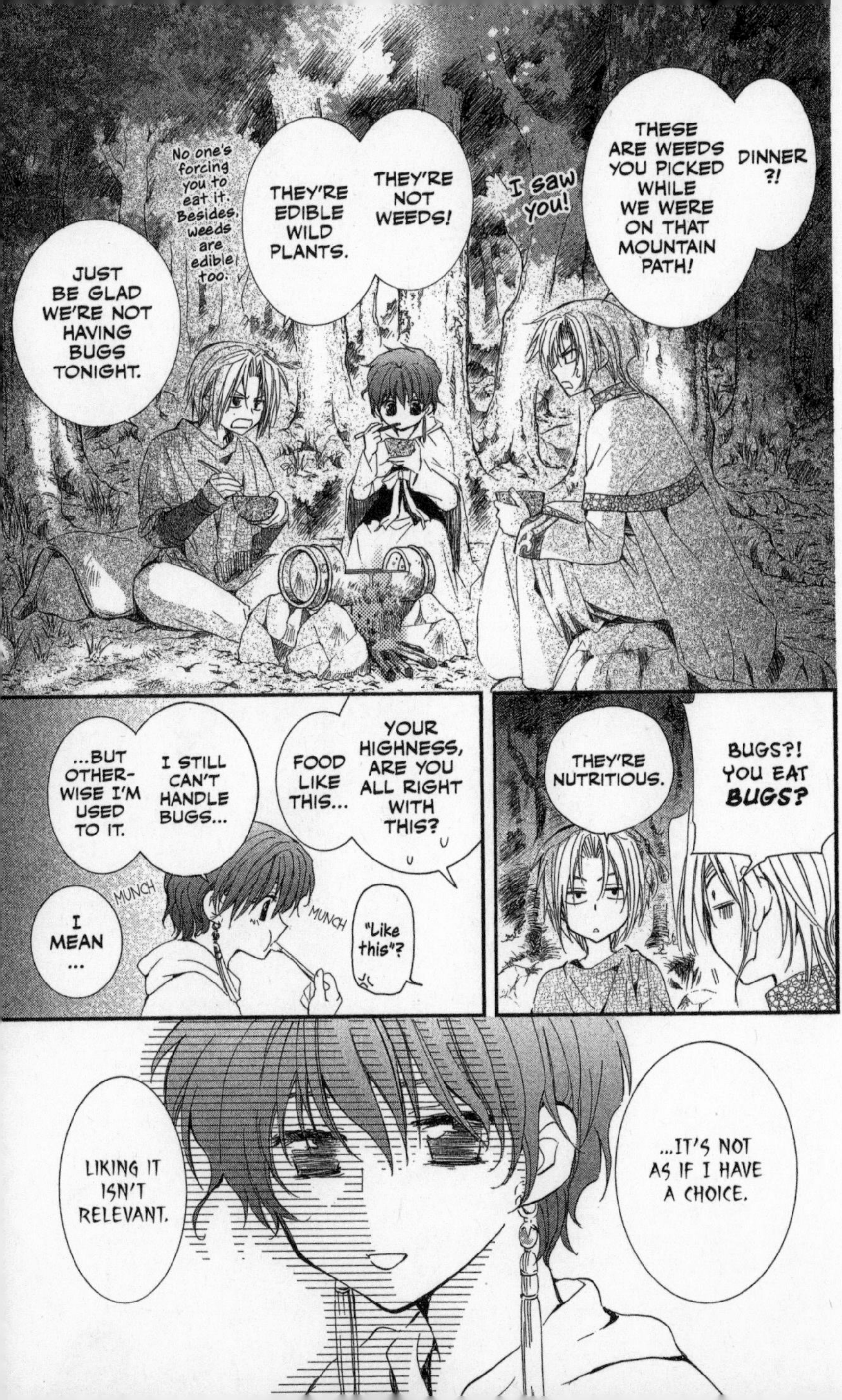
DINNER ?!
THESE ARE WEEDS YOU PICKED WHILE WE WERE ON THAT MOUNTAIN PATH!
I saw you!
THEY'RE NOT WEEDS!
THEY'RE EDIBLE WILD PLANTS.
No one's forcing you to eat it. Besides, weeds are edible too.
JUST BE GLAD WE'RE NOT HAVING BUGS TONIGHT.
BUGS?! YOU EAT **BUGS?**
THEY'RE NUTRITIOUS.
YOUR HIGHNESS, ARE YOU ALL RIGHT WITH THIS?
FOOD LIKE THIS...
"Like this"?
MUNCH
I STILL CAN'T HANDLE BUGS...
...BUT OTHER-WISE I'M USED TO IT.
MUNCH
I MEAN ...
...IT'S NOT AS IF I HAVE A CHOICE.
LIKING IT ISN'T RELEVANT.

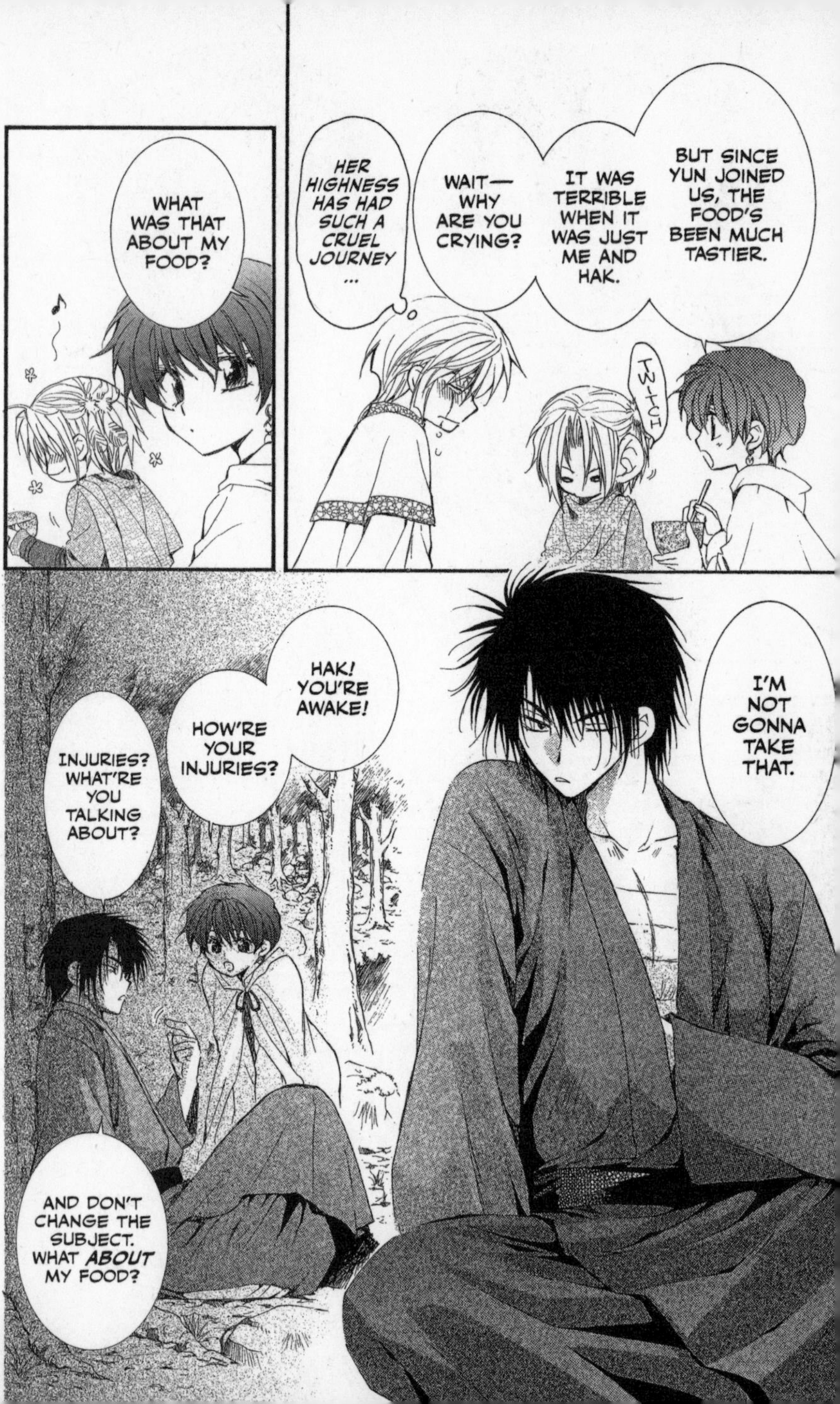
BUT SINCE YUN JOINED US, THE FOOD'S BEEN MUCH TASTIER.
IT WAS TERRIBLE WHEN IT WAS JUST ME AND HAK.
WAIT— WHY ARE YOU CRYING?
TWITCH
HER HIGHNESS HAS HAD SUCH A CRUEL JOURNEY ...
WHAT WAS THAT ABOUT MY FOOD?
I'M NOT GONNA TAKE THAT.
HAK! YOU'RE AWAKE!
HOW'RE YOUR INJURIES?
INJURIES? WHAT'RE YOU TALKING ABOUT?
AND DON'T CHANGE THE SUBJECT. WHAT *ABOUT* MY FOOD?

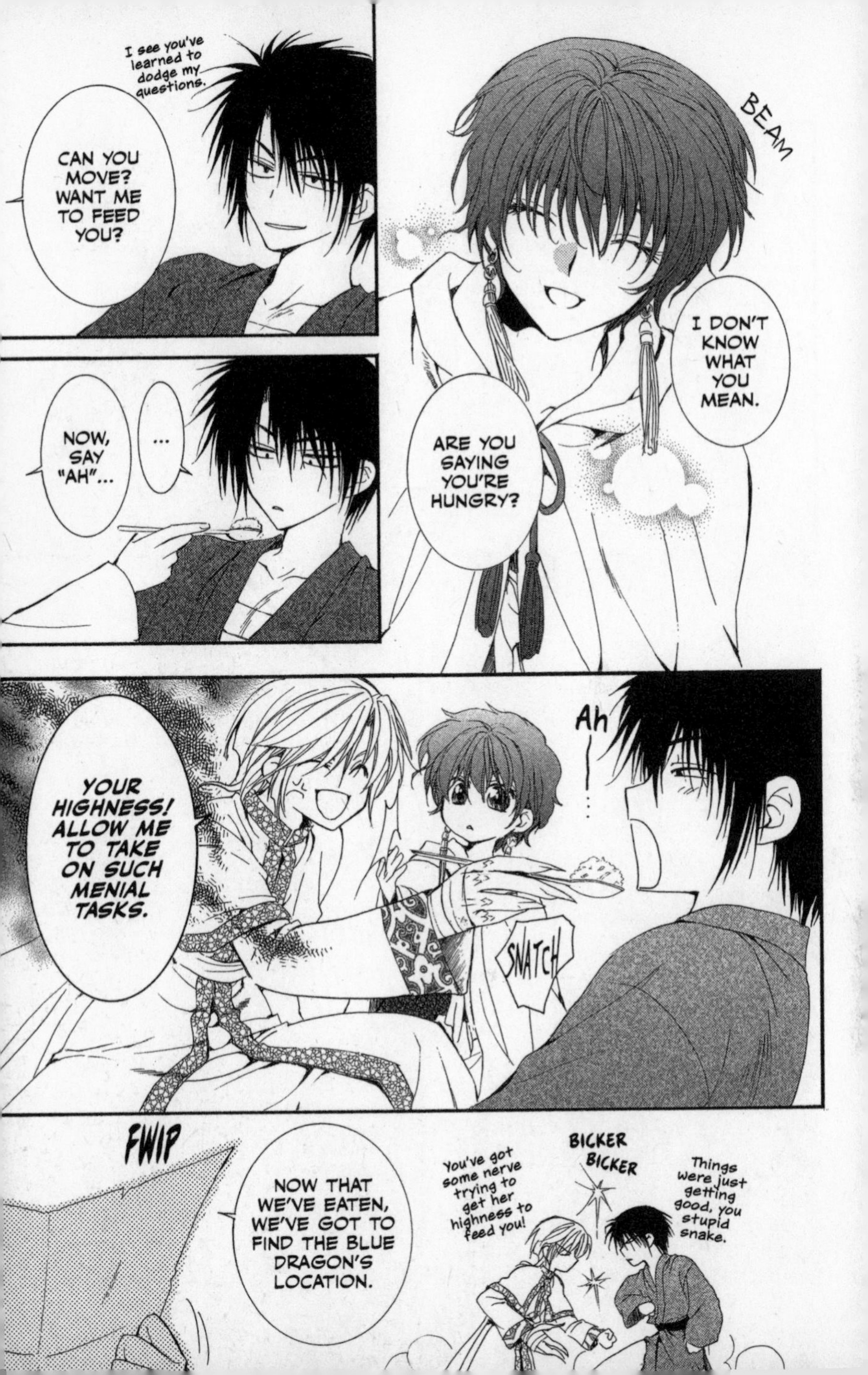
BEAM
I DON'T KNOW WHAT YOU MEAN.
ARE YOU SAYING YOU'RE HUNGRY?
I see you've learned to dodge my questions.
CAN YOU MOVE? WANT ME TO FEED YOU?
...
NOW, SAY "AH"...
Ah...
YOUR HIGHNESS! ALLOW ME TO TAKE ON SUCH MENIAL TASKS.
SNATCH
BICKER BICKER
Things were just getting good, you stupid snake.
You've got some nerve trying to get her highness to feed you!
FWIP
NOW THAT WE'VE EATEN, WE'VE GOT TO FIND THE BLUE DRAGON'S LOCATION.

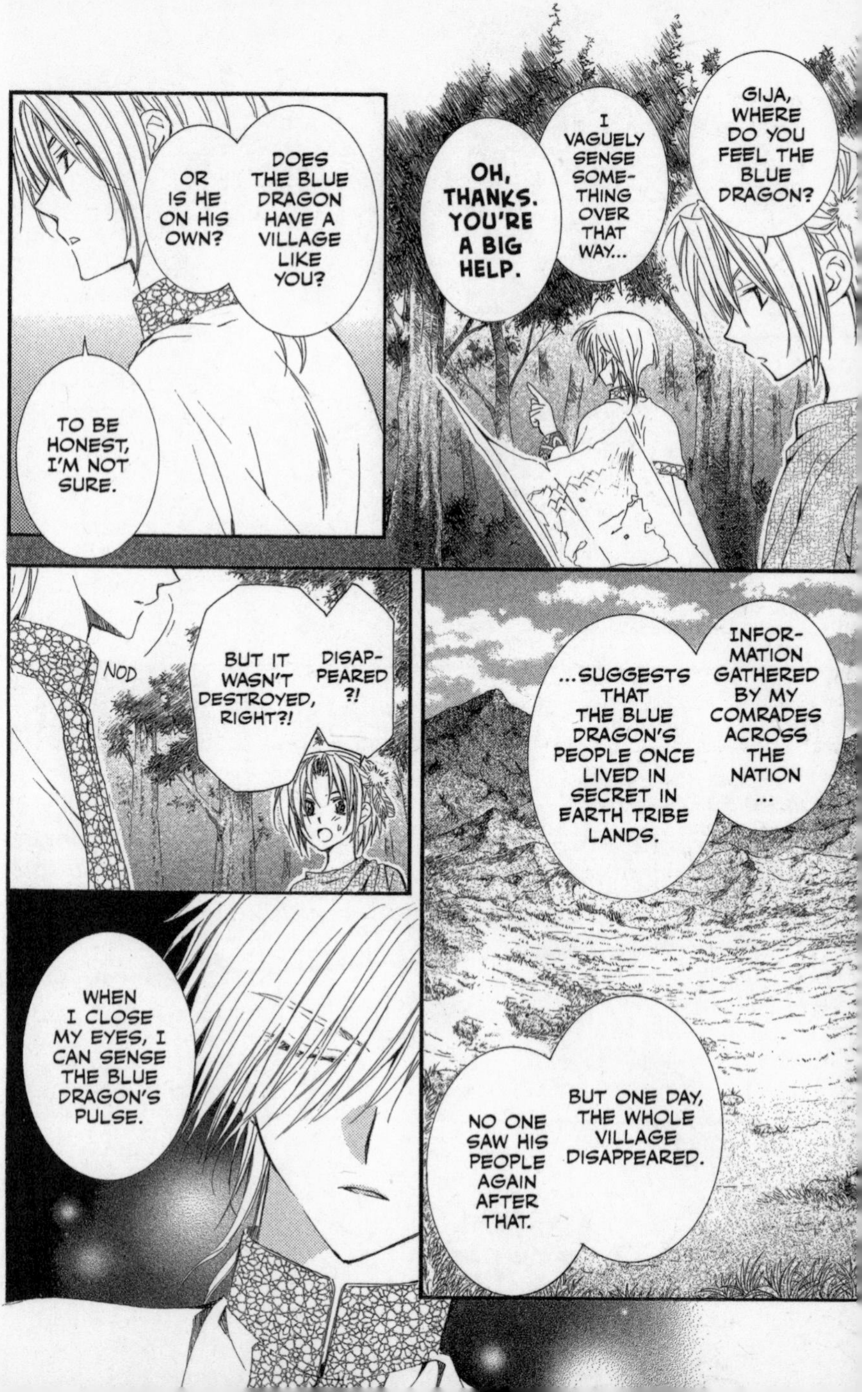
GIJA, WHERE DO YOU FEEL THE BLUE DRAGON?
I VAGUELY SENSE SOMETHING OVER THAT WAY...
OH, THANKS. YOU'RE A BIG HELP.
DOES THE BLUE DRAGON HAVE A VILLAGE LIKE YOU?
OR IS HE ON HIS OWN?
TO BE HONEST, I'M NOT SURE.
INFORMATION GATHERED BY MY COMRADES ACROSS THE NATION...
...SUGGESTS THAT THE BLUE DRAGON'S PEOPLE ONCE LIVED IN SECRET IN EARTH TRIBE LANDS.
BUT ONE DAY, THE WHOLE VILLAGE DISAPPEARED.
NO ONE SAW HIS PEOPLE AGAIN AFTER THAT.
DISAPPEARED?!
BUT IT WASN'T DESTROYED, RIGHT?!
NOD
WHEN I CLOSE MY EYES, I CAN SENSE THE BLUE DRAGON'S PULSE.

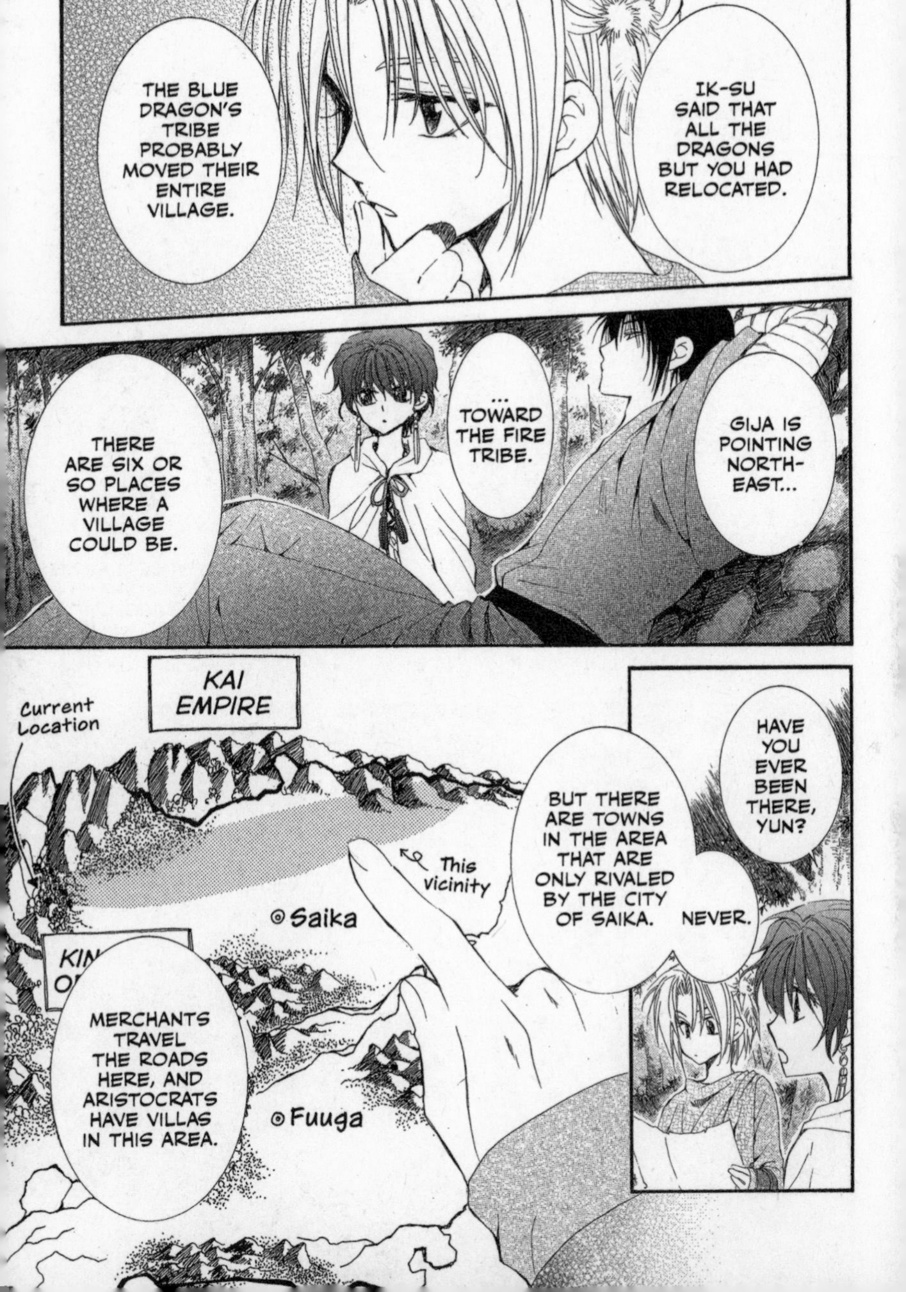
IK-SU SAID THAT ALL THE DRAGONS BUT YOU HAD RELOCATED.
THE BLUE DRAGON'S TRIBE PROBABLY MOVED THEIR ENTIRE VILLAGE.
GIJA IS POINTING NORTH-EAST...
... TOWARD THE FIRE TRIBE.
THERE ARE SIX OR SO PLACES WHERE A VILLAGE COULD BE.
HAVE YOU EVER BEEN THERE, YUN?
NEVER.
BUT THERE ARE TOWNS IN THE AREA THAT ARE ONLY RIVALED BY THE CITY OF SAIKA.
KAI EMPIRE
Current Location
This Vicinity
Saika
Fuuga
MERCHANTS TRAVEL THE ROADS HERE, AND ARISTOCRATS HAVE VILLAS IN THIS AREA.

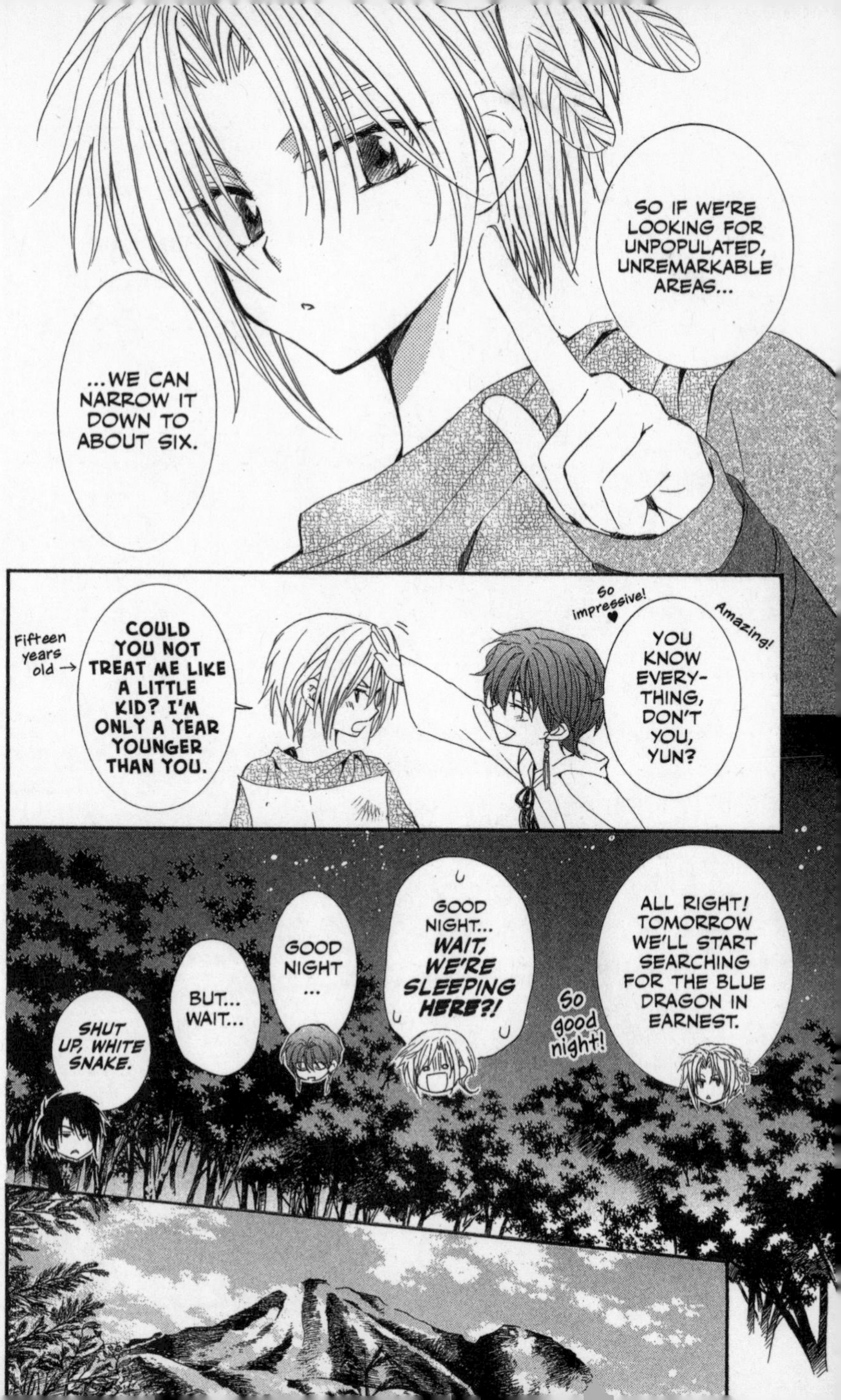
SO IF WE'RE LOOKING FOR UNPOPULATED, UNREMARKABLE AREAS...
...WE CAN NARROW IT DOWN TO ABOUT SIX.
Amazing!
So impressive! ♥
YOU KNOW EVERYTHING, DON'T YOU, YUN?
COULD YOU NOT TREAT ME LIKE A LITTLE KID? I'M ONLY A YEAR YOUNGER THAN YOU.
Fifteen years old →
ALL RIGHT! TOMORROW WE'LL START SEARCHING FOR THE BLUE DRAGON IN EARNEST.
So good night!
GOOD NIGHT... WAIT, WE'RE SLEEPING HERE?!
GOOD NIGHT ...
BUT... WAIT...
SHUT UP, WHITE SNAKE.

The editor-in-chief came up with the title *Yona of the Dawn*. Coming up with titles is very difficult! (For me, anyway.) I have a harder time thinking up titles than creating storyboards. I struggle with the titles for all of my works and come up with a ton of ideas. At first, *Yona* was called "Yona of the Flower Crown," but I thought it didn't have enough punch, so it was back to the drawing board.

I wanted red to be the heroine's color, so I thought of about thirty titles incorporating it, but none of them quite worked.

To be continued in the next column...

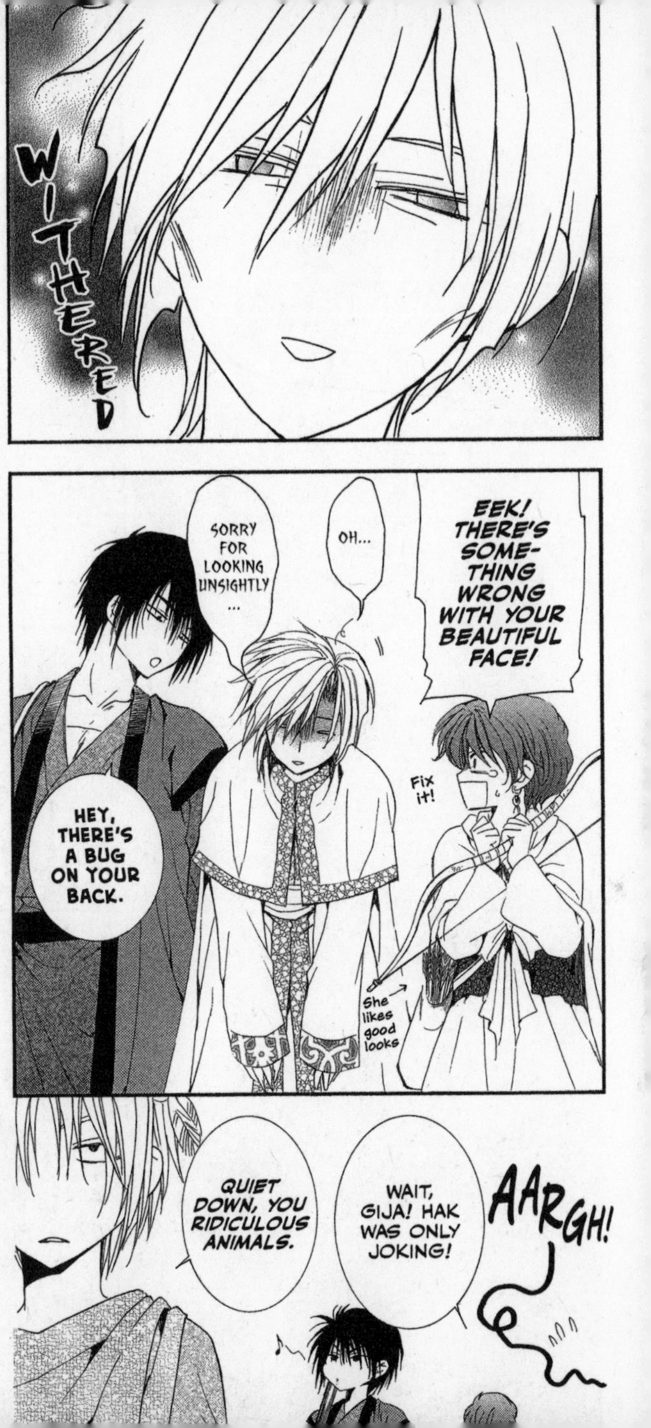
WITHERED
EEK! THERE'S SOMETHING WRONG WITH YOUR BEAUTIFUL FACE!
Fix it!
OH...
SORRY FOR LOOKING UNSIGHTLY ...
HEY, THERE'S A BUG ON YOUR BACK.
She likes good looks
AARGH!
WAIT, GIJA! HAK WAS ONLY JOKING!
QUIET DOWN, YOU RIDICULOUS ANIMALS.

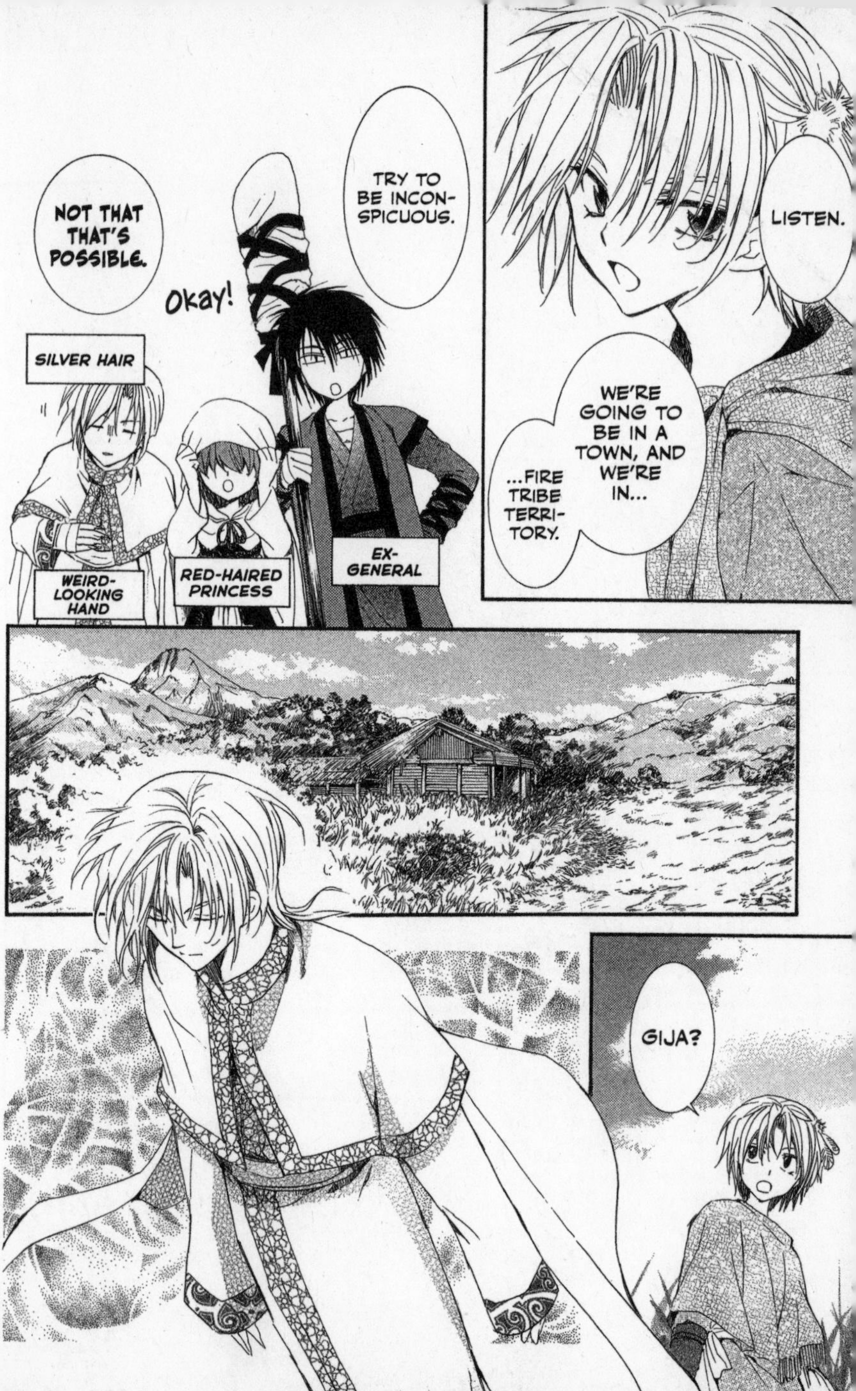
LISTEN.
WE'RE GOING TO BE IN A TOWN, AND WE'RE IN...
...FIRE TRIBE TERRITORY.
TRY TO BE INCON-SPICUOUS.
Okay!
NOT THAT THAT'S POSSIBLE.
EX-GENERAL
RED-HAIRED PRINCESS
SILVER HAIR
WEIRD-LOOKING HAND
GIJA?

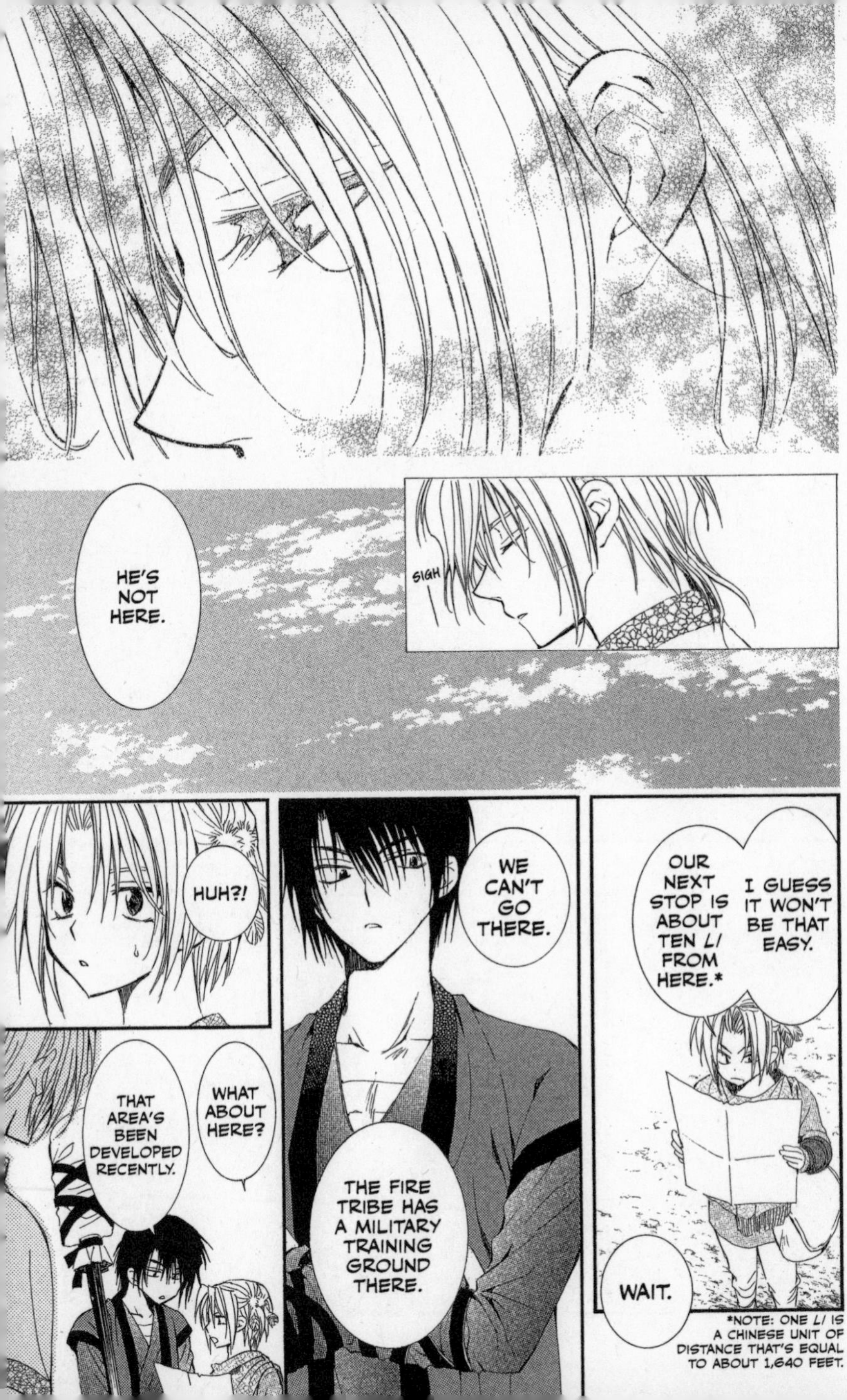
SIGH
HE'S NOT HERE.
I GUESS IT WON'T BE THAT EASY.
OUR NEXT STOP IS ABOUT TEN *LI* FROM HERE.*
WAIT.
WE CAN'T GO THERE.
THE FIRE TRIBE HAS A MILITARY TRAINING GROUND THERE.
HUH?!
WHAT ABOUT HERE?
THAT AREA'S BEEN DEVELOPED RECENTLY.

*NOTE: ONE *LI* IS A CHINESE UNIT OF DISTANCE THAT'S EQUAL TO ABOUT 1,640 FEET.

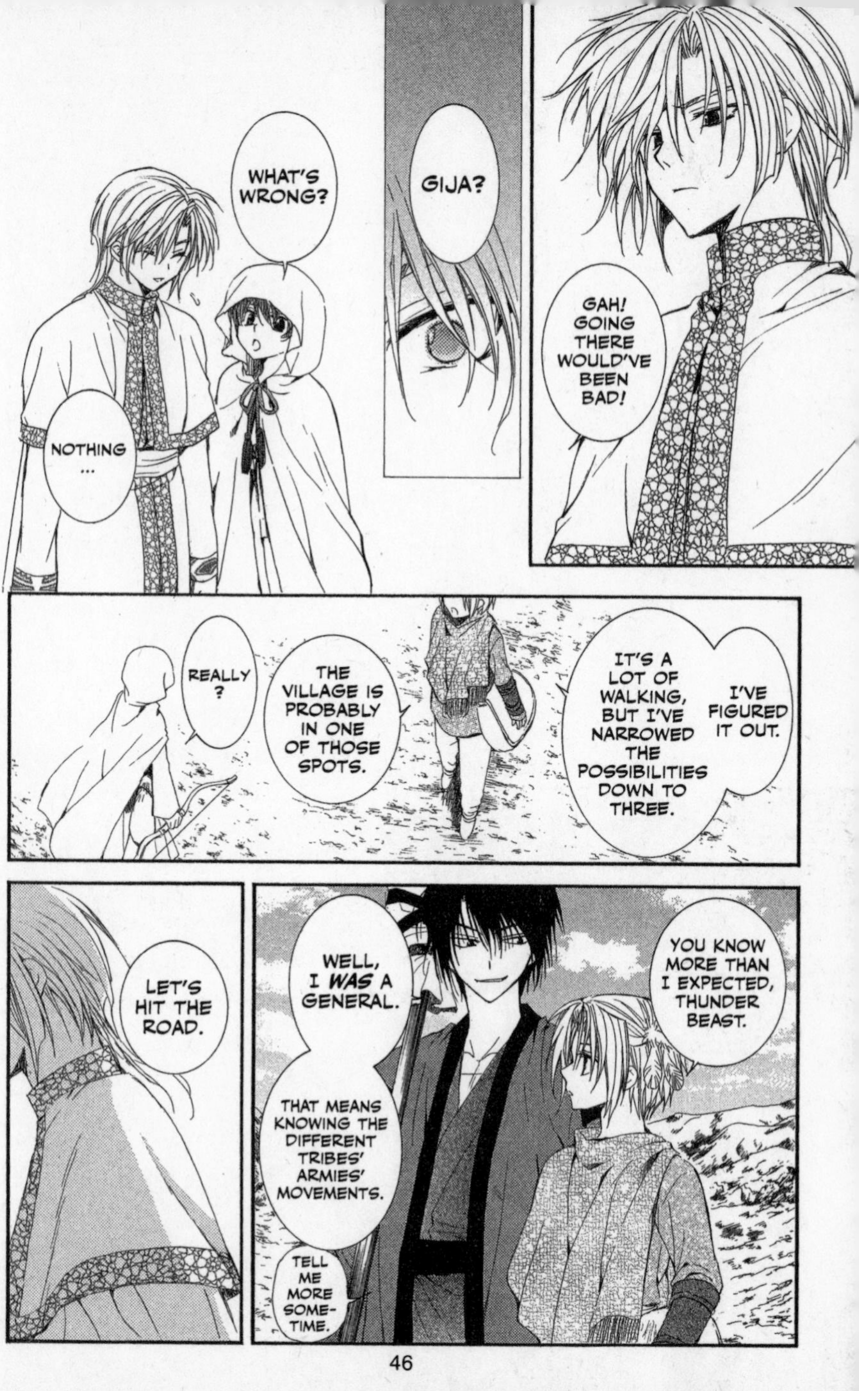
GAH! GOING THERE WOULD'VE BEEN BAD!
GIJA?
WHAT'S WRONG?
NOTHING ...
I'VE FIGURED IT OUT.
IT'S A LOT OF WALKING, BUT I'VE NARROWED THE POSSIBILITIES DOWN TO THREE.
THE VILLAGE IS PROBABLY IN ONE OF THOSE SPOTS.
REALLY?
YOU KNOW MORE THAN I EXPECTED, THUNDER BEAST.
WELL, I *WAS* A GENERAL.
THAT MEANS KNOWING THE DIFFERENT TRIBES' ARMIES' MOVEMENTS.
TELL ME MORE SOME-TIME.
LET'S HIT THE ROAD.

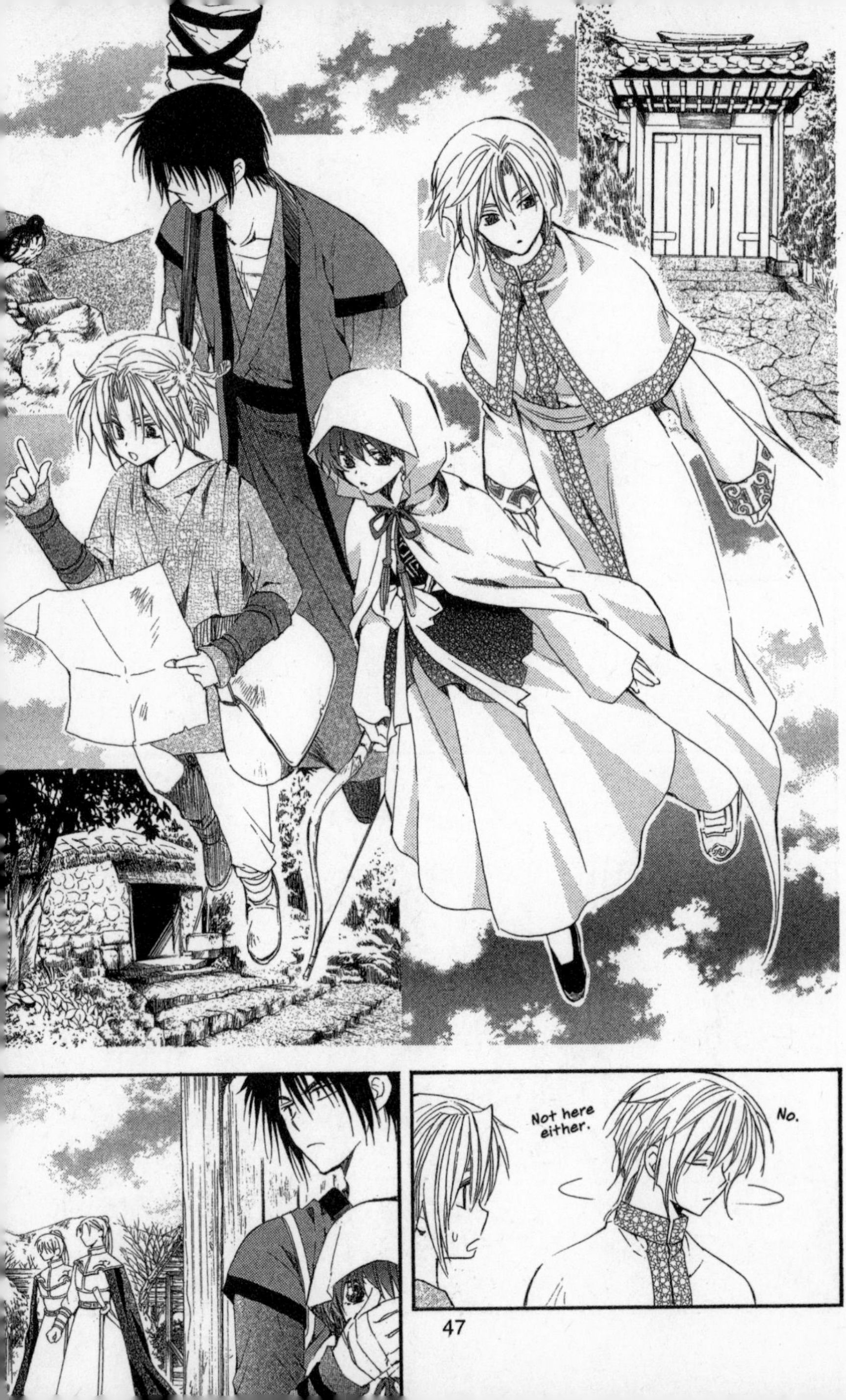
No.
Not here either.

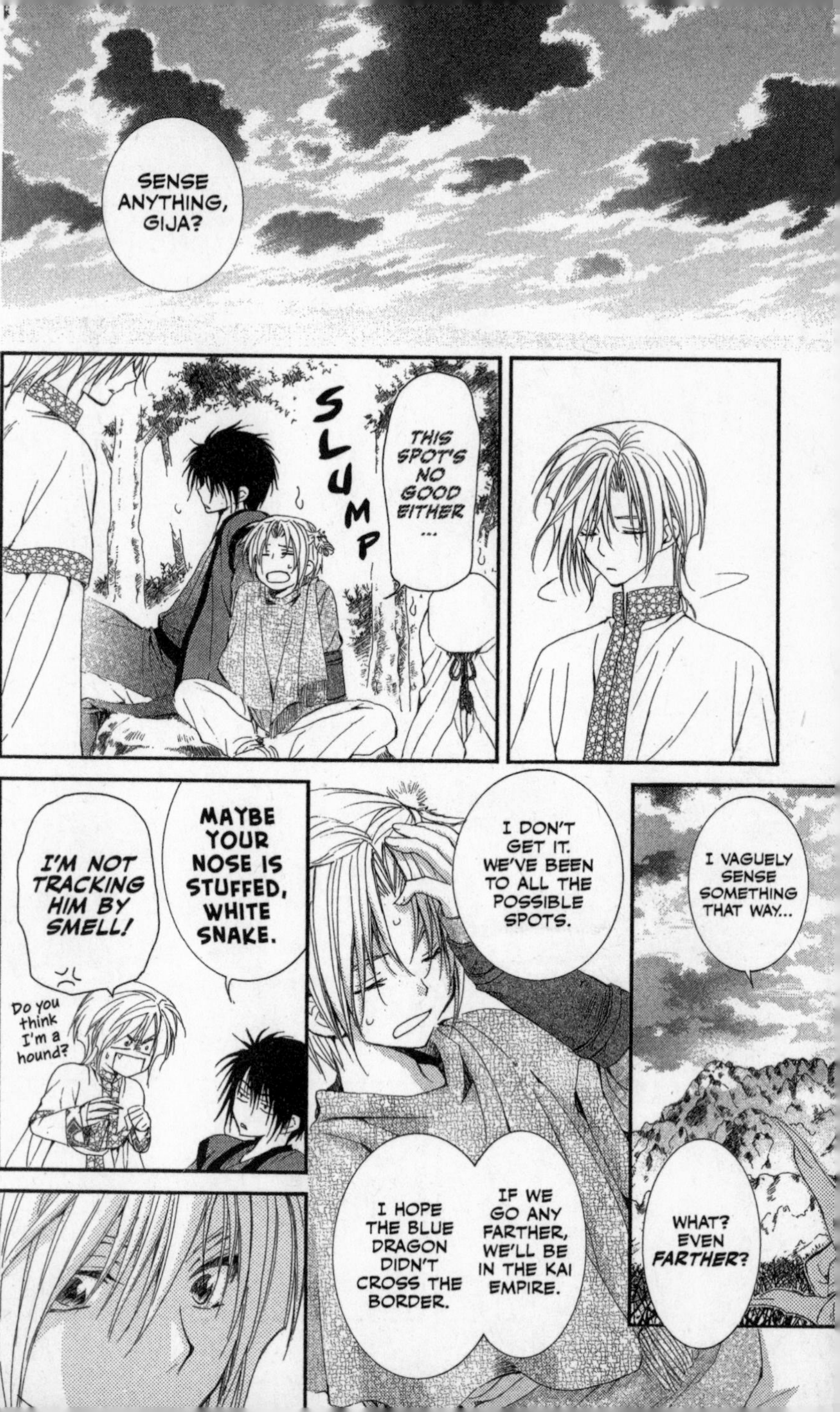
SENSE ANYTHING, GIJA?
THIS SPOT'S NO GOOD EITHER ...
SLUMP
I VAGUELY SENSE SOMETHING THAT WAY...
WHAT? EVEN *FARTHER*?
I DON'T GET IT. WE'VE BEEN TO ALL THE POSSIBLE SPOTS.
IF WE GO ANY FARTHER, WE'LL BE IN THE KAI EMPIRE.
I HOPE THE BLUE DRAGON DIDN'T CROSS THE BORDER.
MAYBE YOUR NOSE IS STUFFED, WHITE SNAKE.
I'M NOT TRACKING HIM BY SMELL!
Do you think I'm a hound?

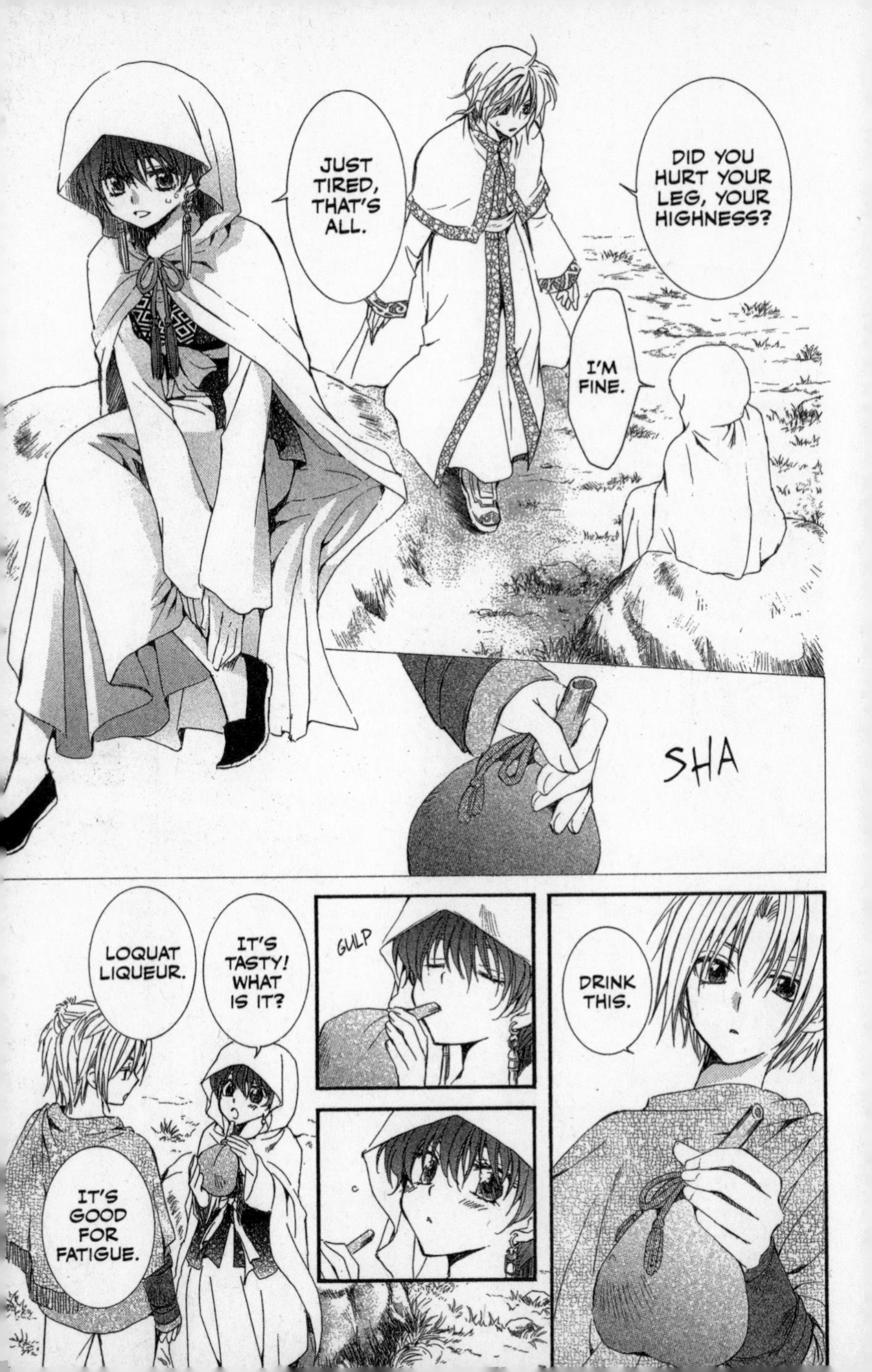
DID YOU HURT YOUR LEG, YOUR HIGHNESS?
I'M FINE.
JUST TIRED, THAT'S ALL.
SHA
DRINK THIS.
GULP
IT'S TASTY! WHAT IS IT?
LOQUAT LIQUEUR.
IT'S GOOD FOR FATIGUE.

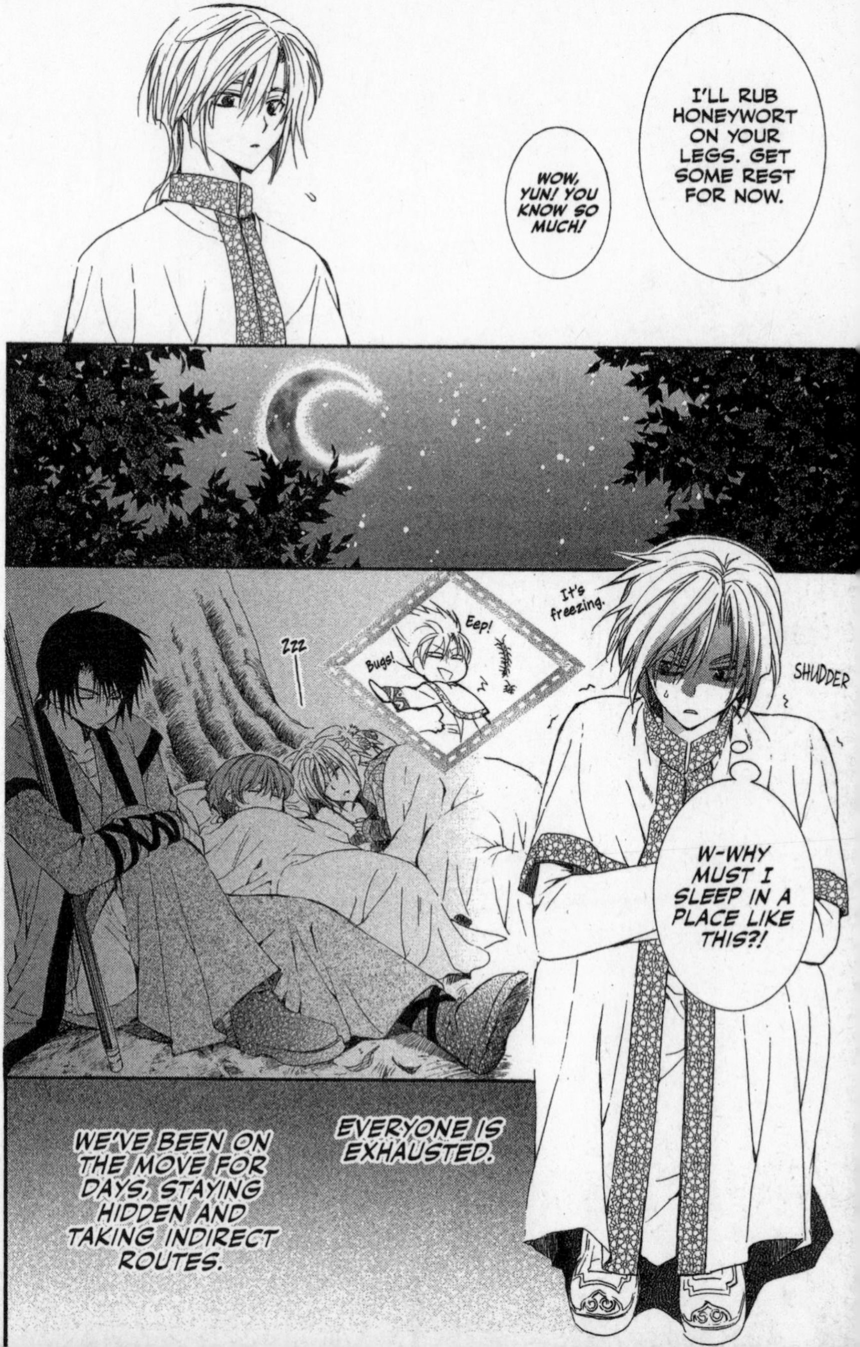
I'LL RUB HONEYWORT ON YOUR LEGS. GET SOME REST FOR NOW.
WOW, YUN! YOU KNOW SO MUCH!
SHUDDER
It's freezing.
W-WHY MUST I SLEEP IN A PLACE LIKE THIS?!
Eep!
Bugs!
Zzz
EVERYONE IS EXHAUSTED.
WE'VE BEEN ON THE MOVE FOR DAYS, STAYING HIDDEN AND TAKING INDIRECT ROUTES.

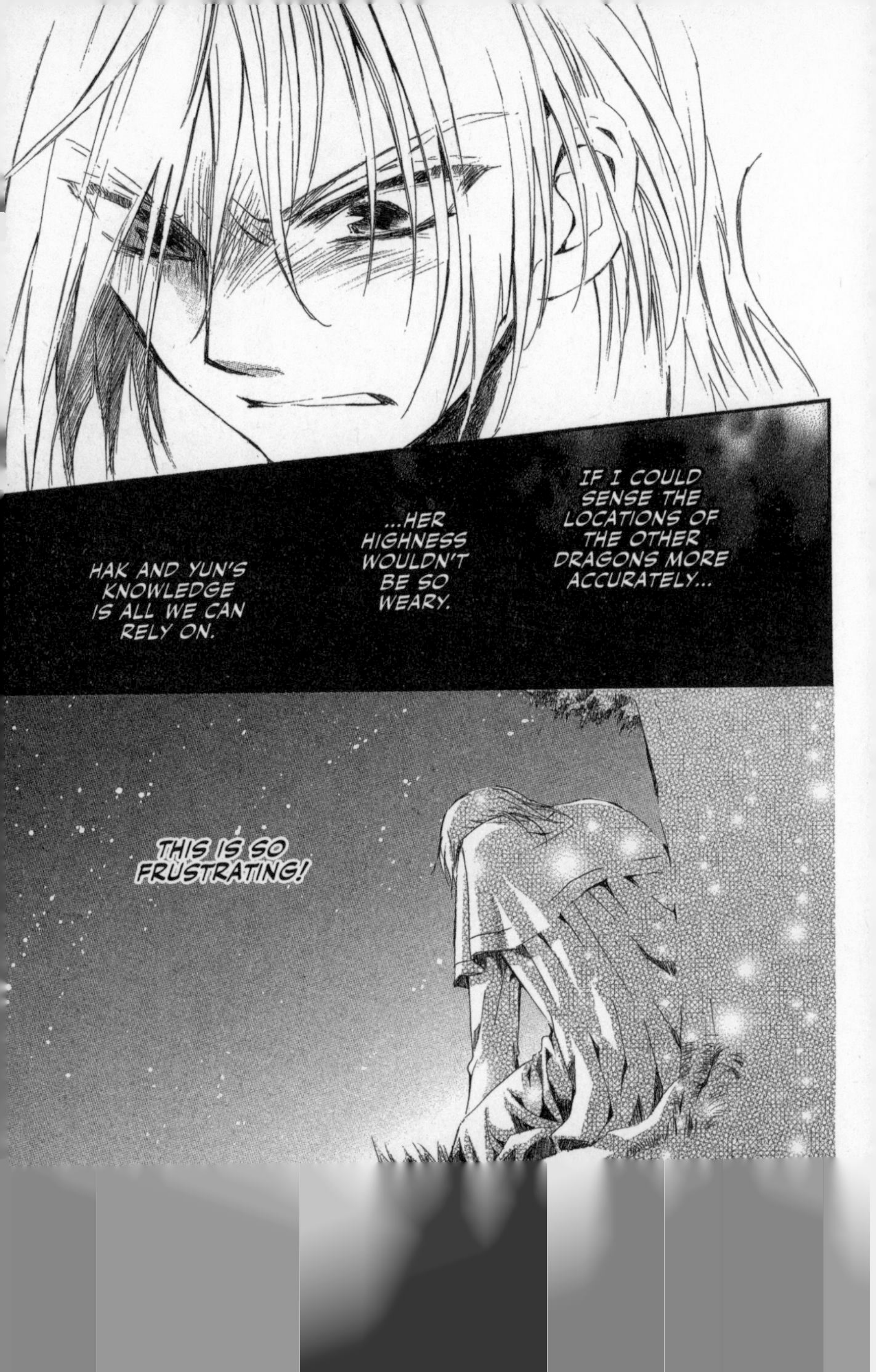
IF I COULD SENSE THE LOCATIONS OF THE OTHER DRAGONS MORE ACCURATELY...
...HER HIGHNESS WOULDN'T BE SO WEARY.
HAK AND YUN'S KNOWLEDGE IS ALL WE CAN RELY ON.
THIS IS SO FRUSTRATING!

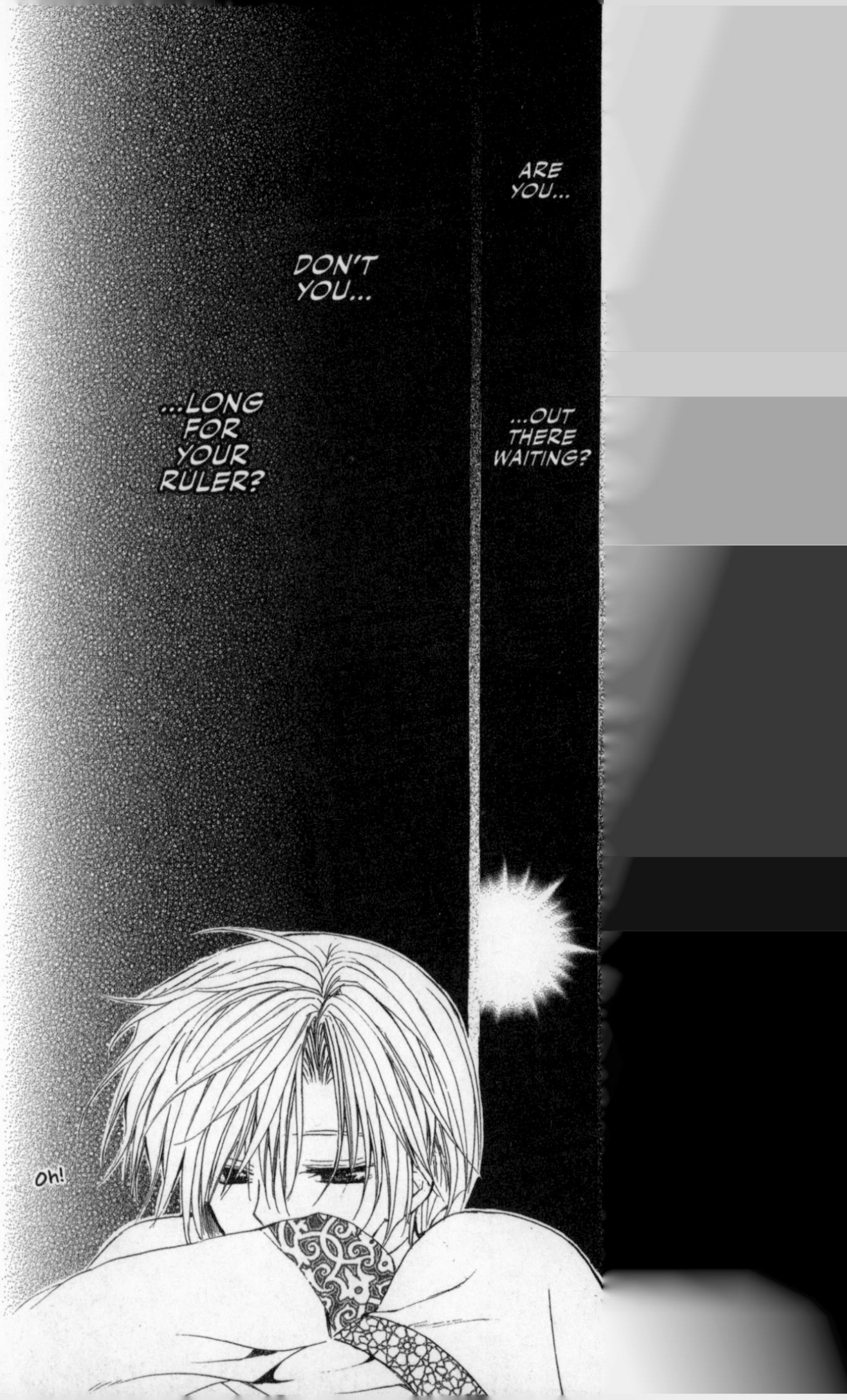
ARE YOU...
...OUT THERE WAITING?
DON'T YOU...
...LONG FOR YOUR RULER?
Oh!

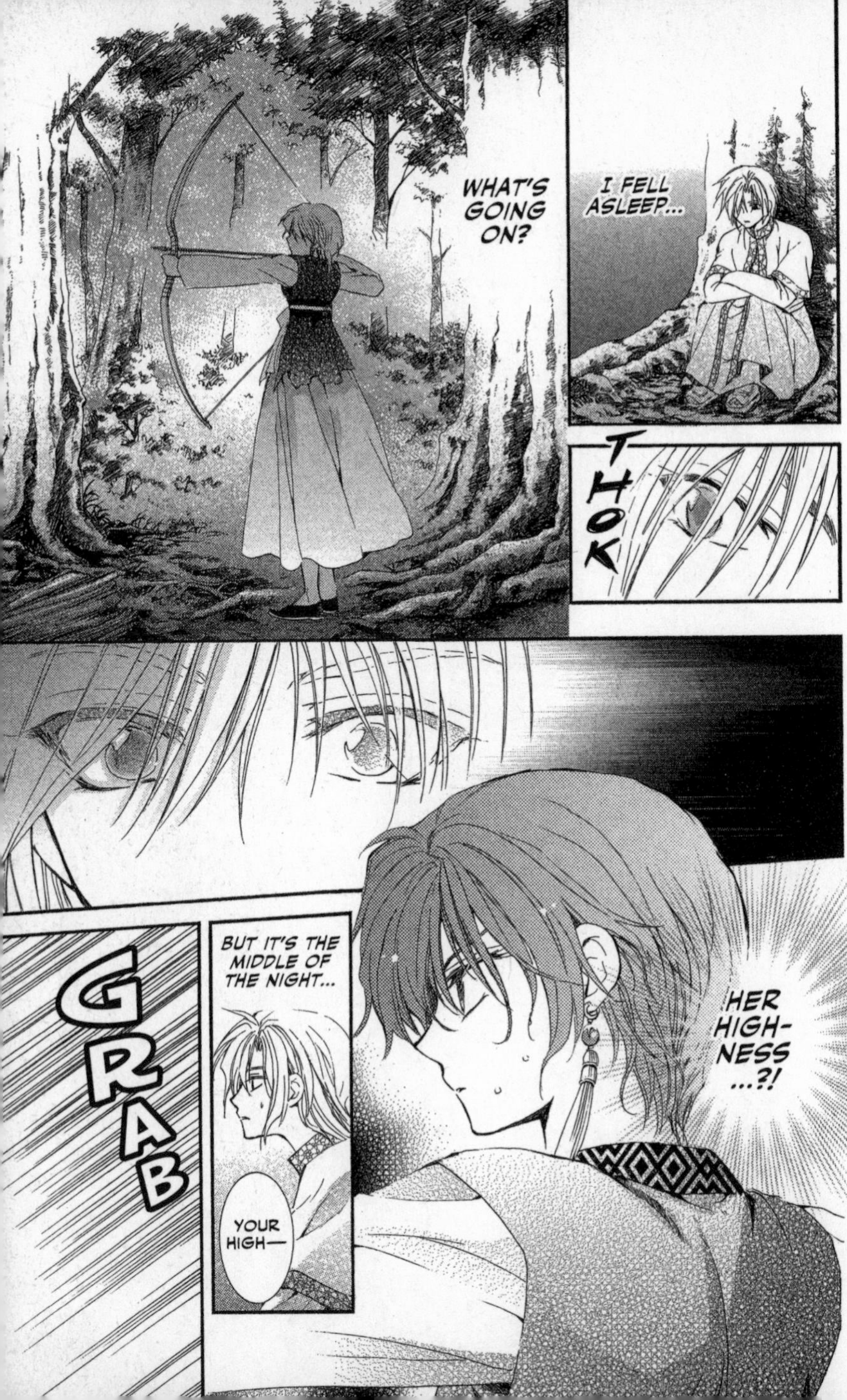
I FELL ASLEEP...
THOK
WHAT'S GOING ON?
HER HIGH-NESS ...?!
BUT IT'S THE MIDDLE OF THE NIGHT...
YOUR HIGH—
GRAB

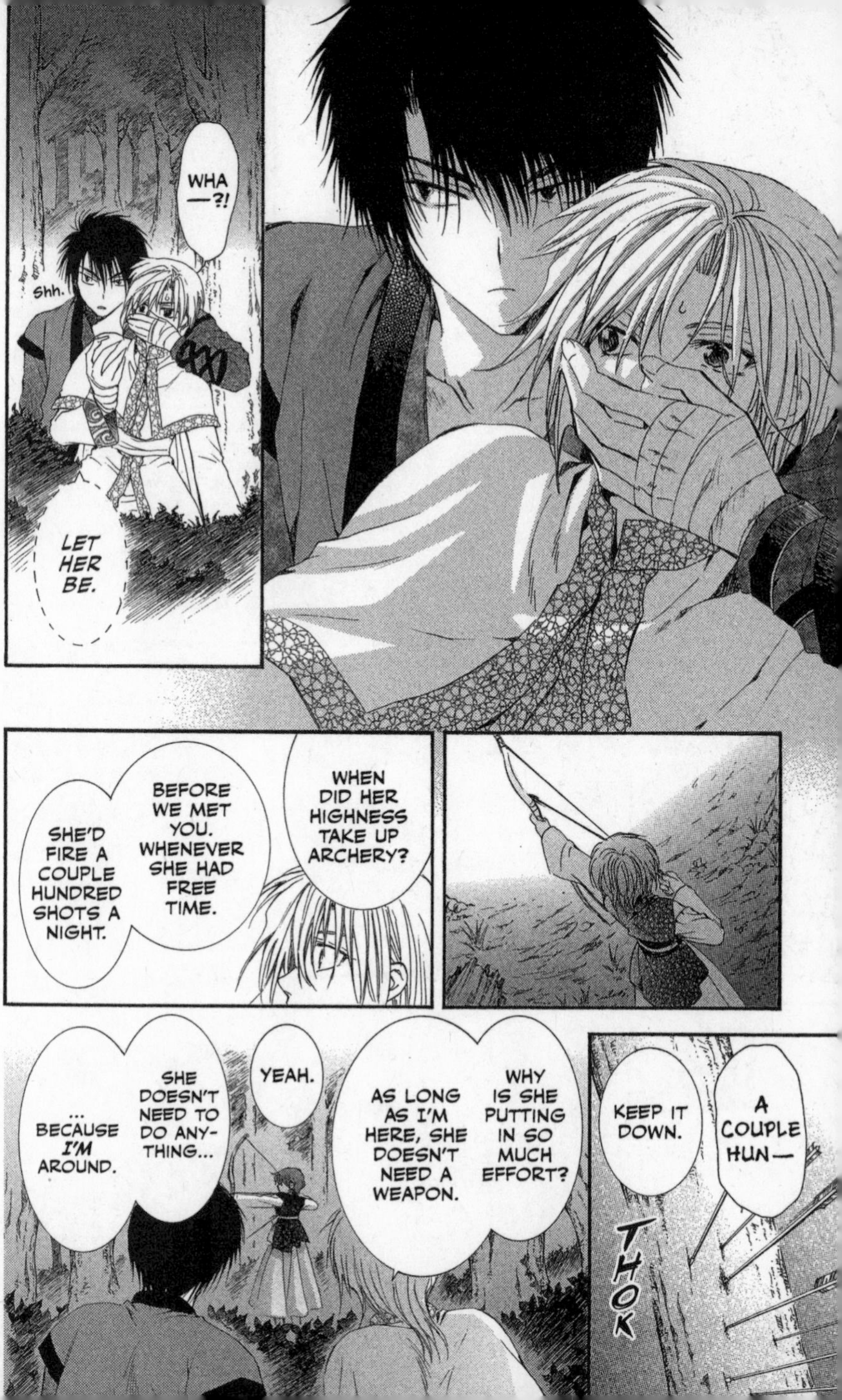
WHA—?!
Shh.
LET HER BE.
WHEN DID HER HIGHNESS TAKE UP ARCHERY?
BEFORE WE MET YOU. WHENEVER SHE HAD FREE TIME.
SHE'D FIRE A COUPLE HUNDRED SHOTS A NIGHT.
A COUPLE HUN—
KEEP IT DOWN.
THOK
WHY IS SHE PUTTING IN SO MUCH EFFORT?
AS LONG AS I'M HERE, SHE DOESN'T NEED A WEAPON.
YEAH.
SHE DOESN'T NEED TO DO ANY-THING...
...BECAUSE *I'M* AROUND.

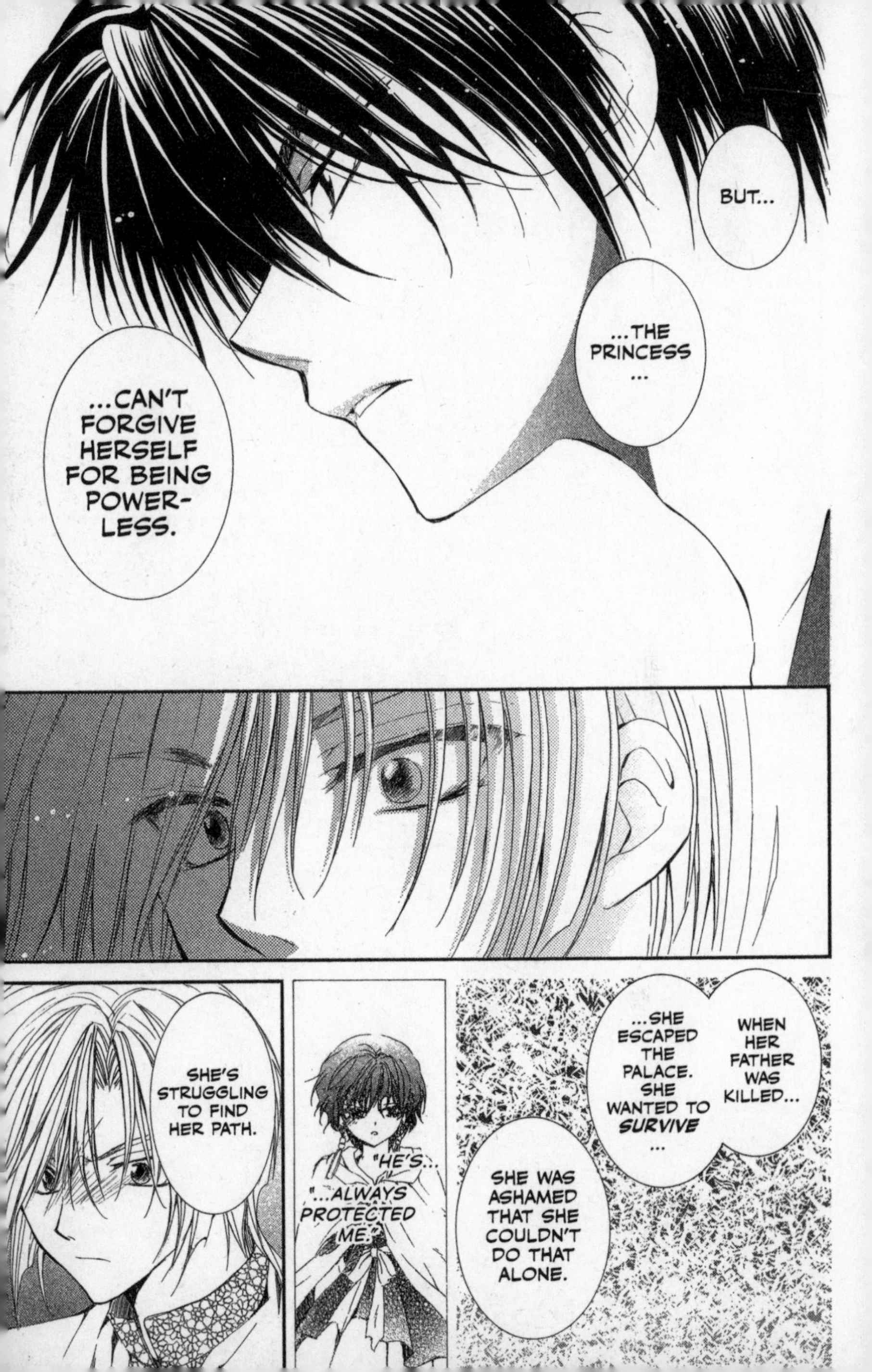
BUT...
...THE PRINCESS ...
...CAN'T FORGIVE HERSELF FOR BEING POWER-LESS.
WHEN HER FATHER WAS KILLED...
...SHE ESCAPED THE PALACE. SHE WANTED TO *SURVIVE* ...
SHE WAS ASHAMED THAT SHE COULDN'T DO THAT ALONE.
"HE'S...
"...ALWAYS PROTECTED ME."
SHE'S STRUGGLING TO FIND HER PATH.

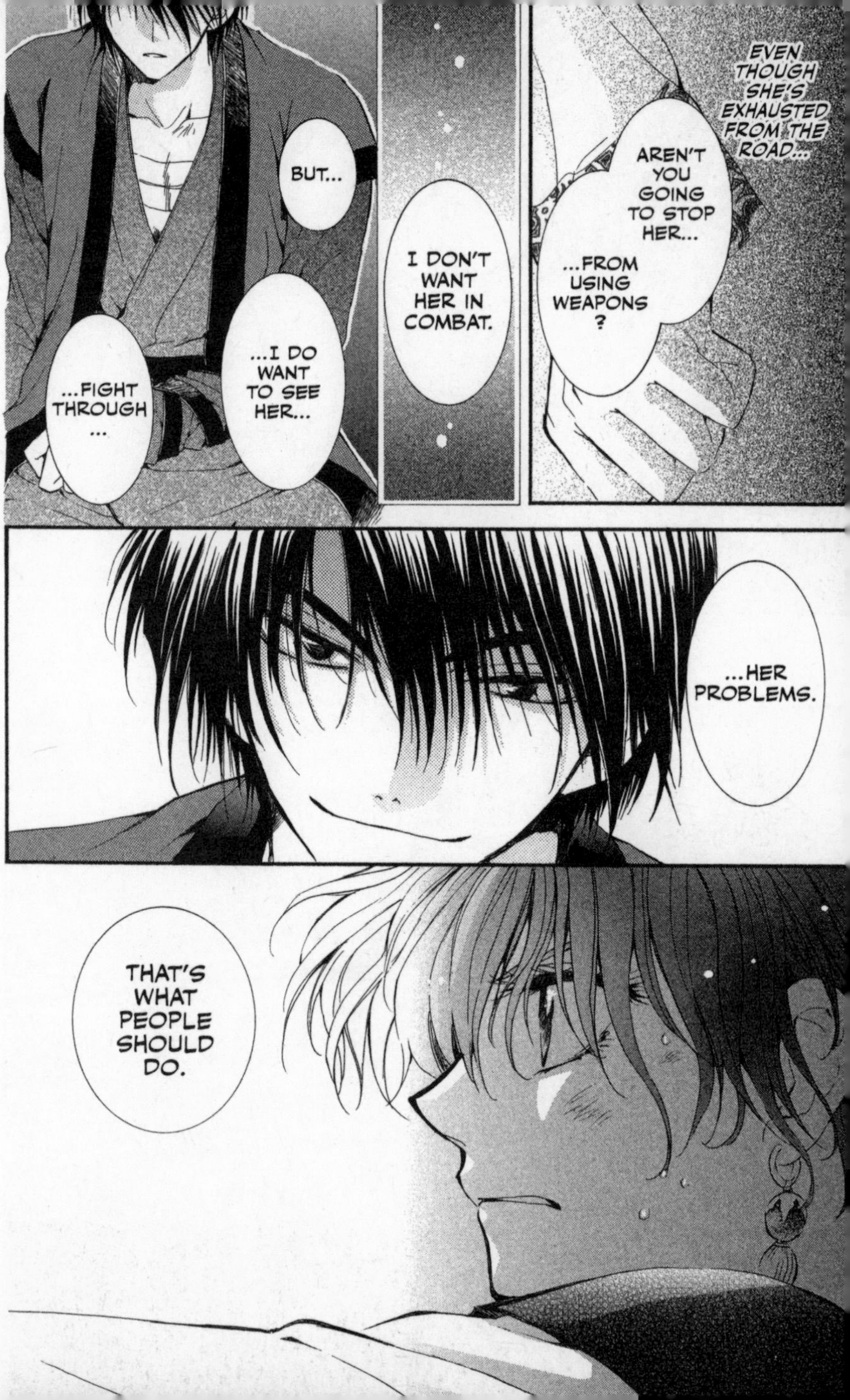
EVEN THOUGH SHE'S EXHAUSTED FROM THE ROAD...
AREN'T YOU GOING TO STOP HER...
...FROM USING WEAPONS?
I DON'T WANT HER IN COMBAT.
BUT...
...I DO WANT TO SEE HER...
...FIGHT THROUGH...
...HER PROBLEMS.
THAT'S WHAT PEOPLE SHOULD DO.

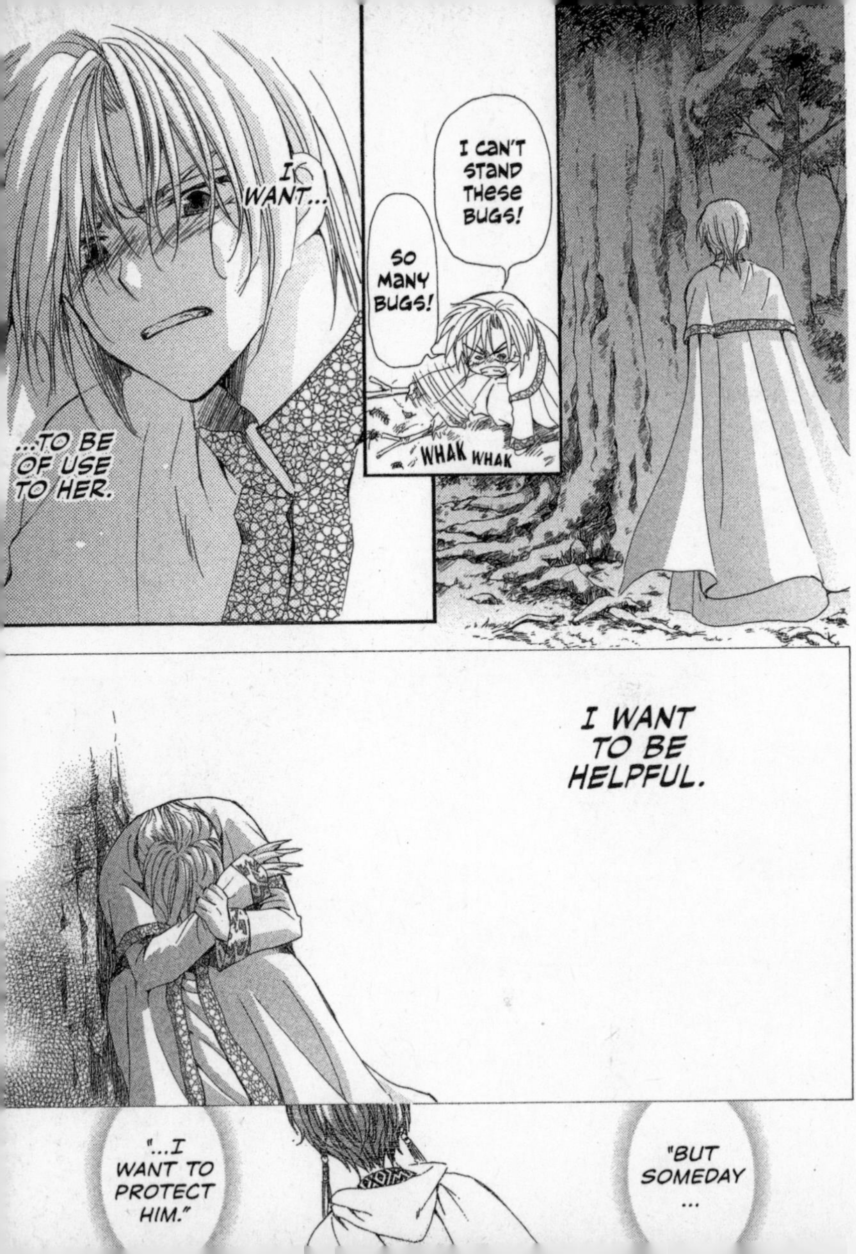
I CAN'T STAND THESE BUGS!
SO MANY BUGS!
WHAK WHAK
I WANT...
...TO BE OF USE TO HER.
I WANT TO BE HELPFUL.
"BUT SOMEDAY...
"...I WANT TO PROTECT HIM."

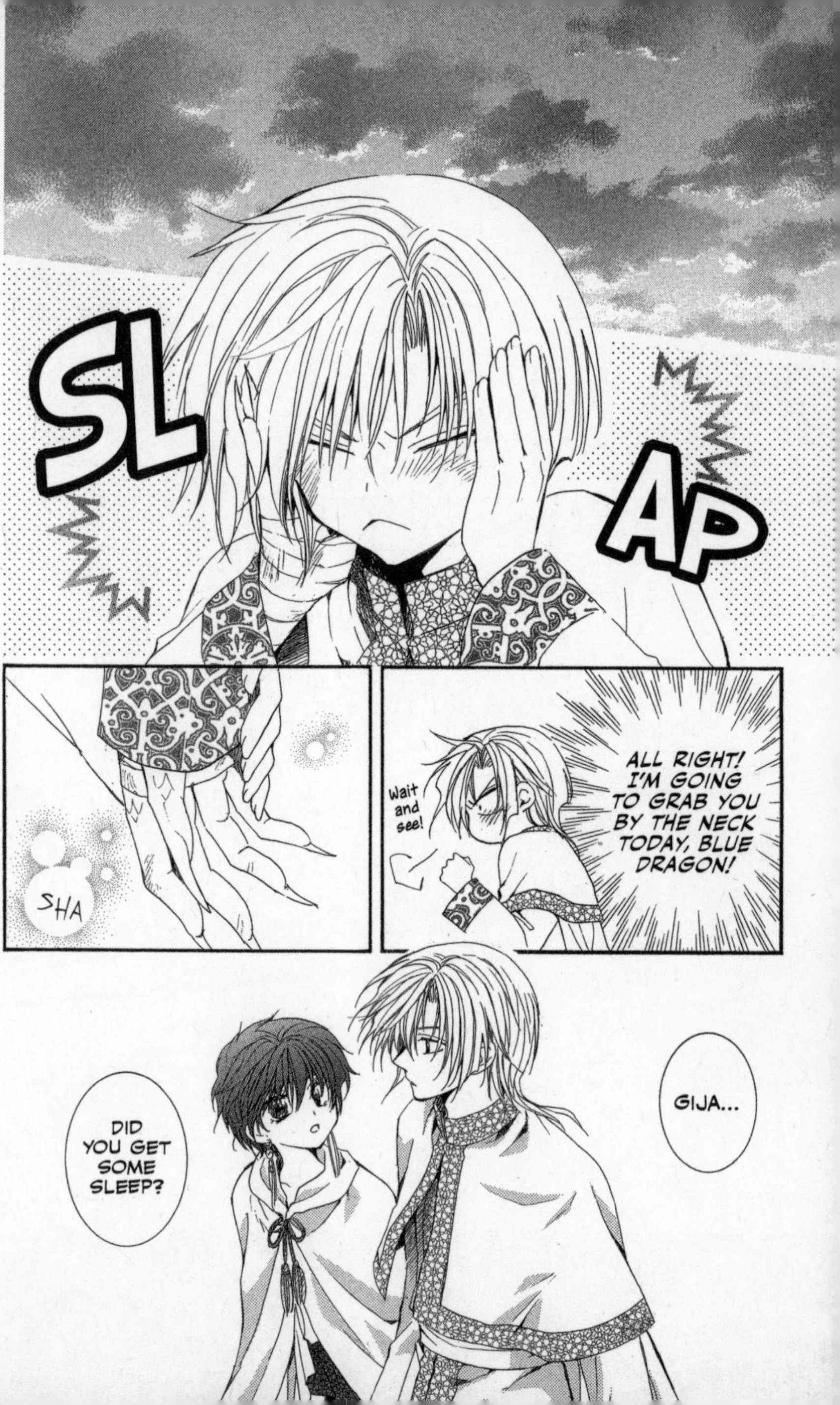
SL
AP
ALL RIGHT! I'M GOING TO GRAB YOU BY THE NECK TODAY, BLUE DRAGON!
Wait and see!
SHA
GIJA...
DID YOU GET SOME SLEEP?

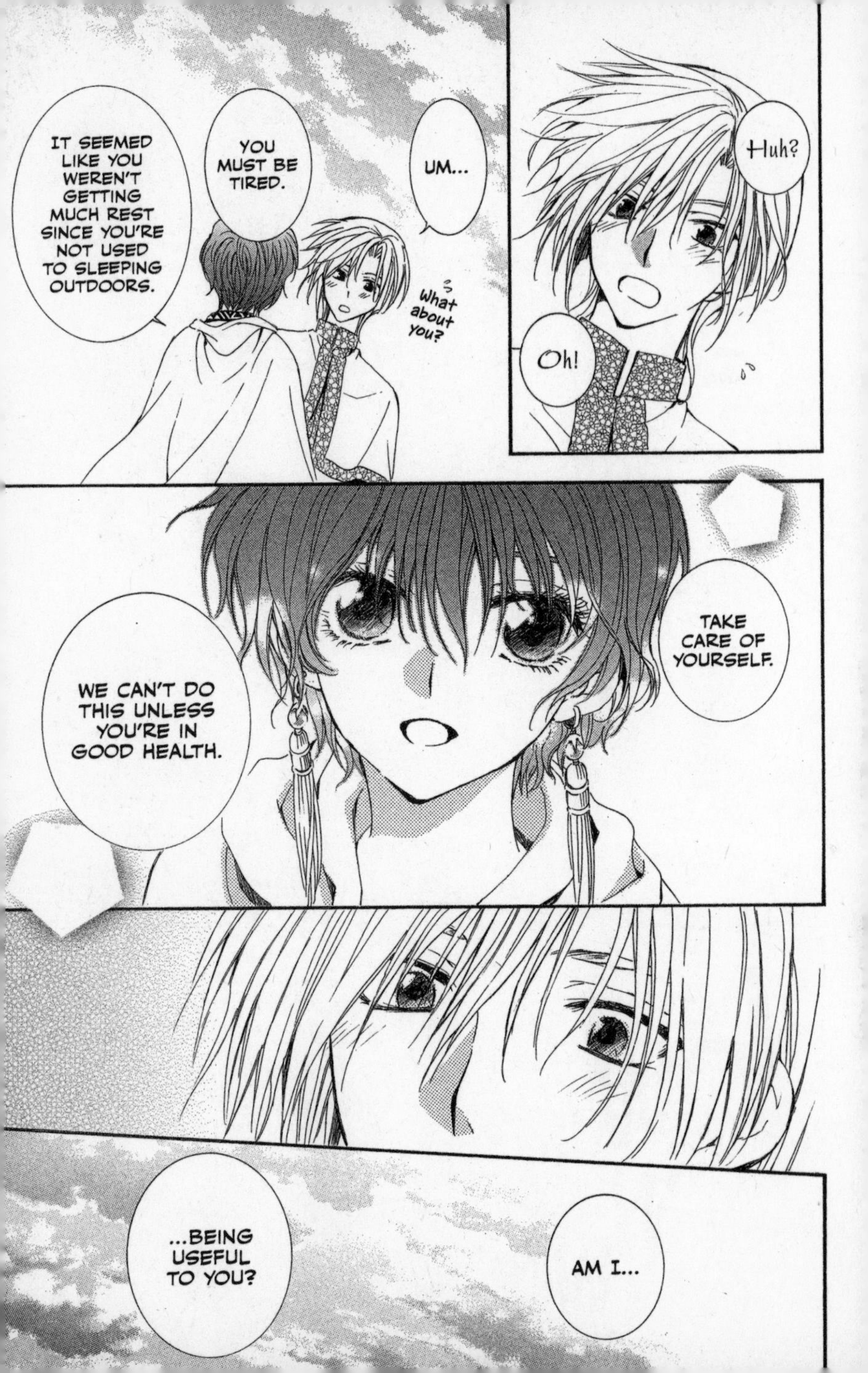
Huh?
Oh!
UM...
What about you?
YOU MUST BE TIRED.
IT SEEMED LIKE YOU WEREN'T GETTING MUCH REST SINCE YOU'RE NOT USED TO SLEEPING OUTDOORS.
TAKE CARE OF YOURSELF.
WE CAN'T DO THIS UNLESS YOU'RE IN GOOD HEALTH.
AM I...
...BEING USEFUL TO YOU?

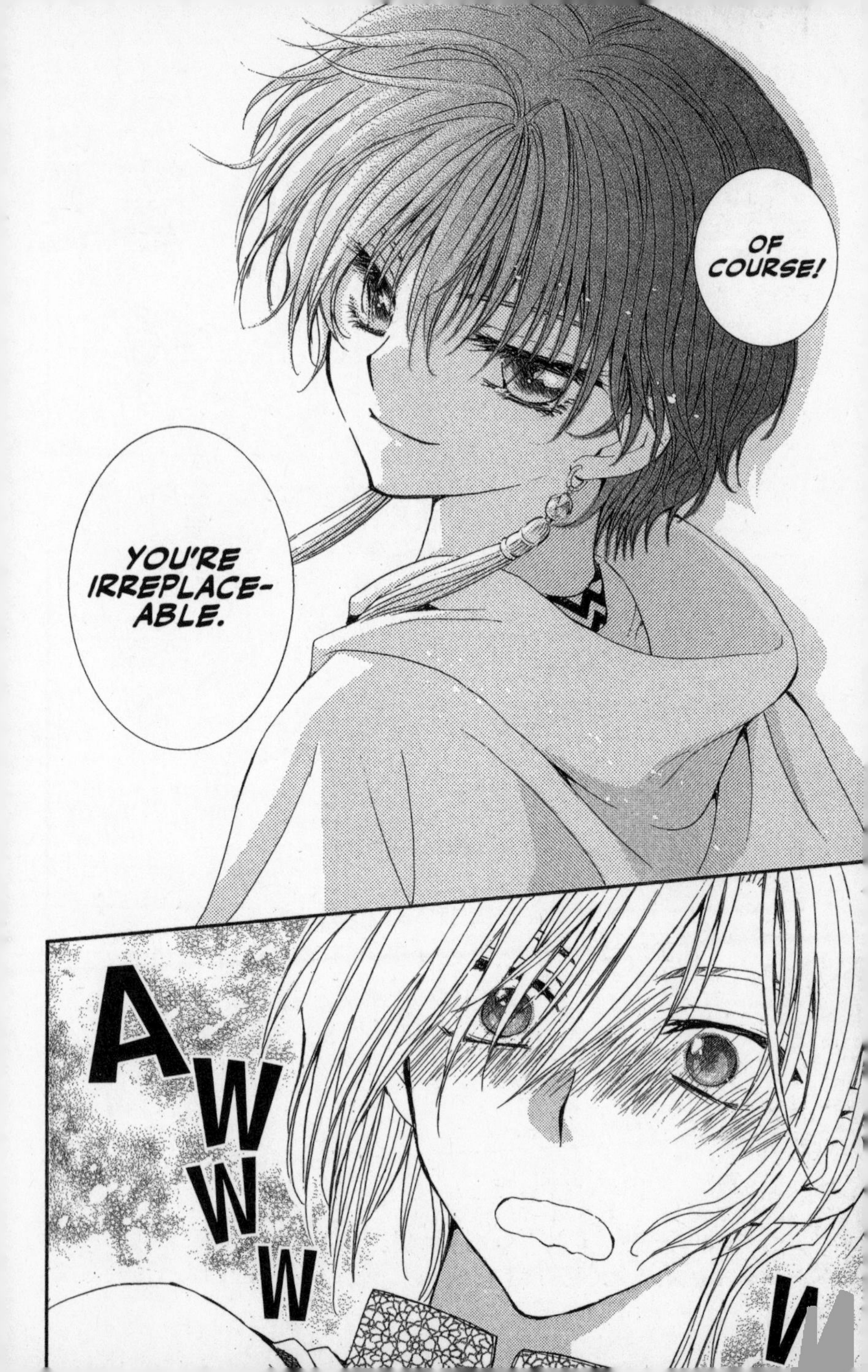
OF COURSE!
YOU'RE IRREPLACE-ABLE.
AWWWW

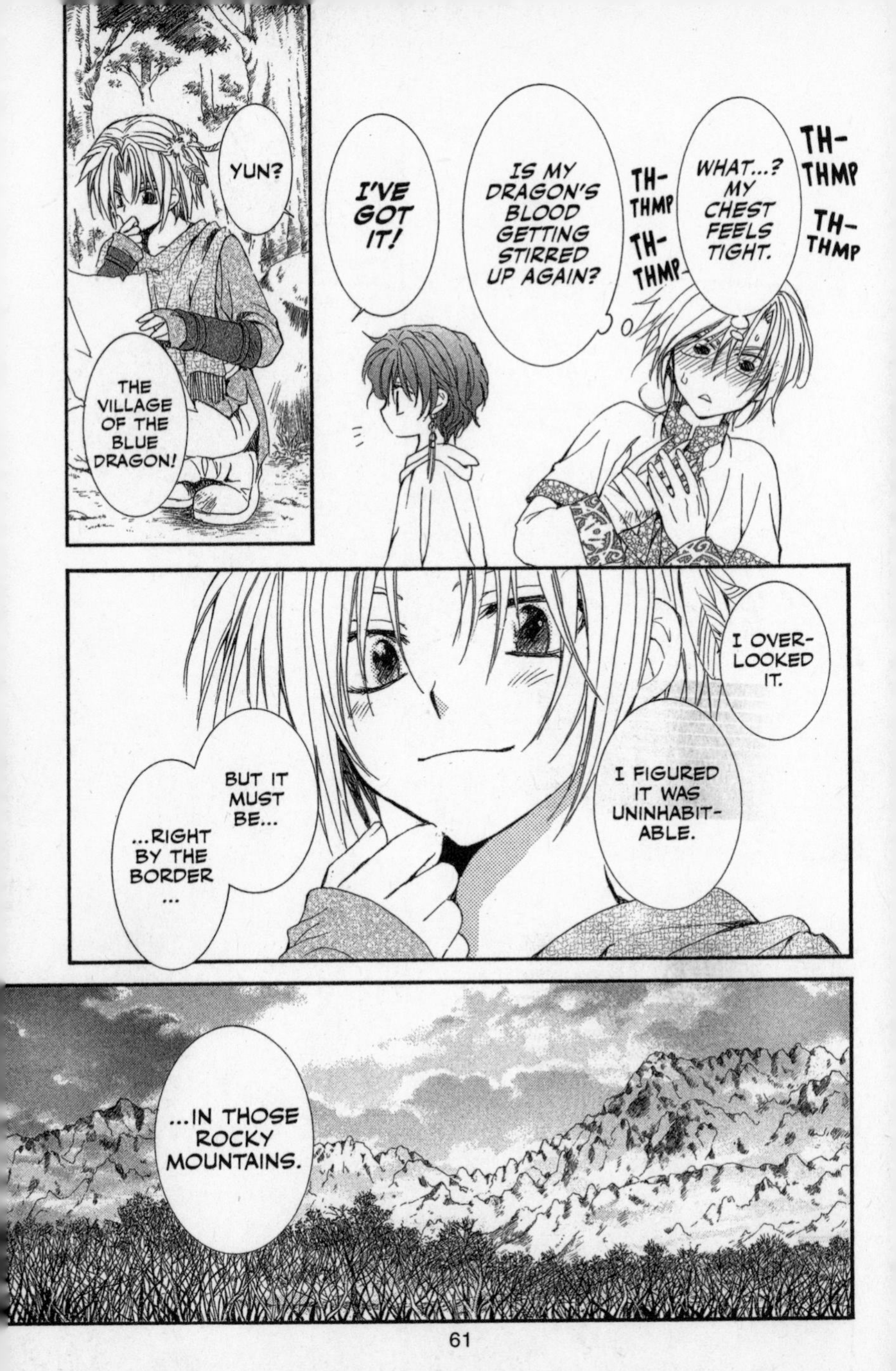
TH-THMP
TH-THMP
WHAT...? MY CHEST FEELS TIGHT.
TH-THMP
TH-THMP
IS MY DRAGON'S BLOOD GETTING STIRRED UP AGAIN?
I'VE GOT IT!
YUN?
THE VILLAGE OF THE BLUE DRAGON!
I OVER-LOOKED IT.
I FIGURED IT WAS UNINHABIT-ABLE.
BUT IT MUST BE...
...RIGHT BY THE BORDER...
...IN THOSE ROCKY MOUNTAINS.

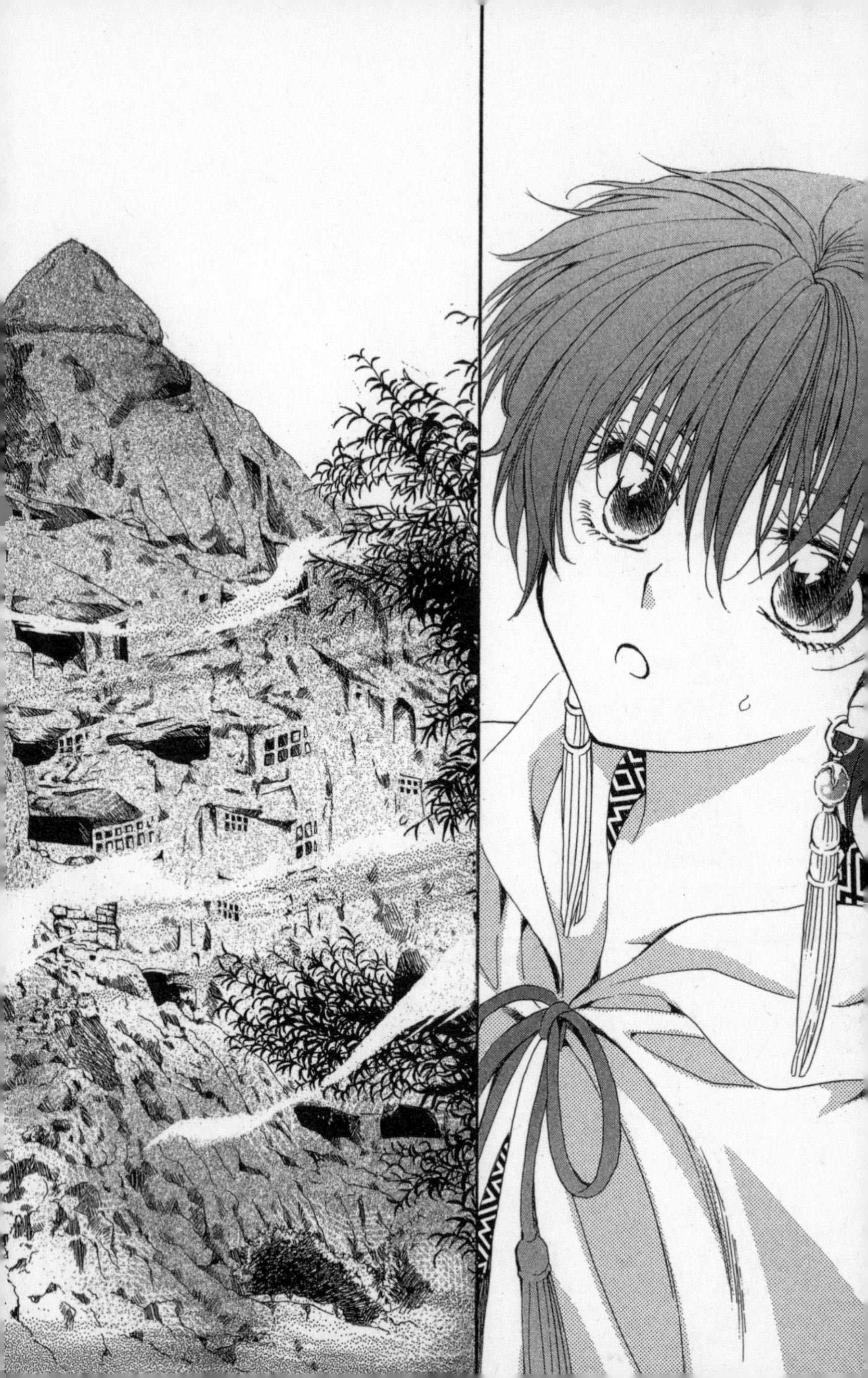

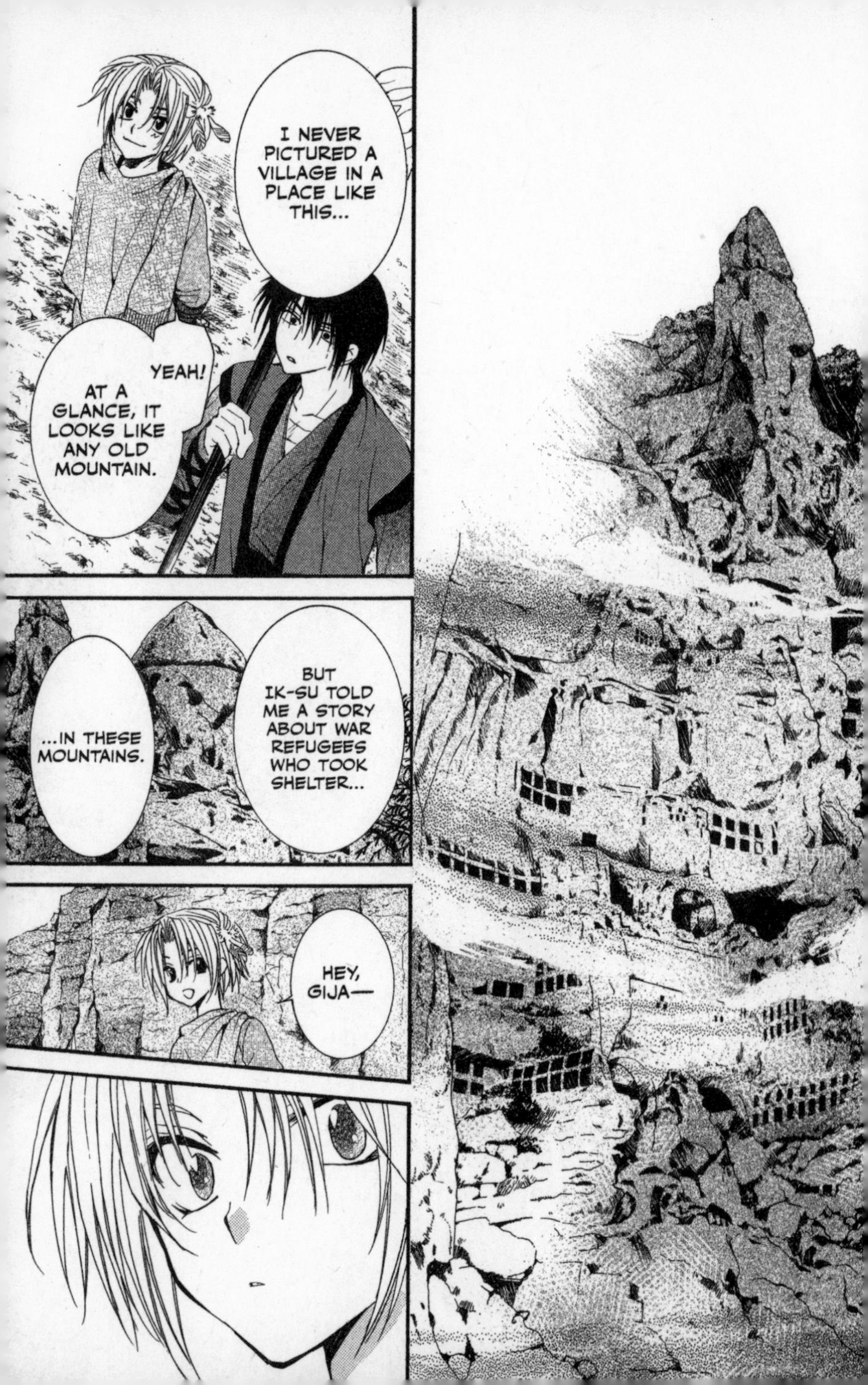
I NEVER PICTURED A VILLAGE IN A PLACE LIKE THIS...
YEAH! AT A GLANCE, IT LOOKS LIKE ANY OLD MOUNTAIN.
BUT IK-SU TOLD ME A STORY ABOUT WAR REFUGEES WHO TOOK SHELTER...
...IN THESE MOUNTAINS.
HEY, GIJA—

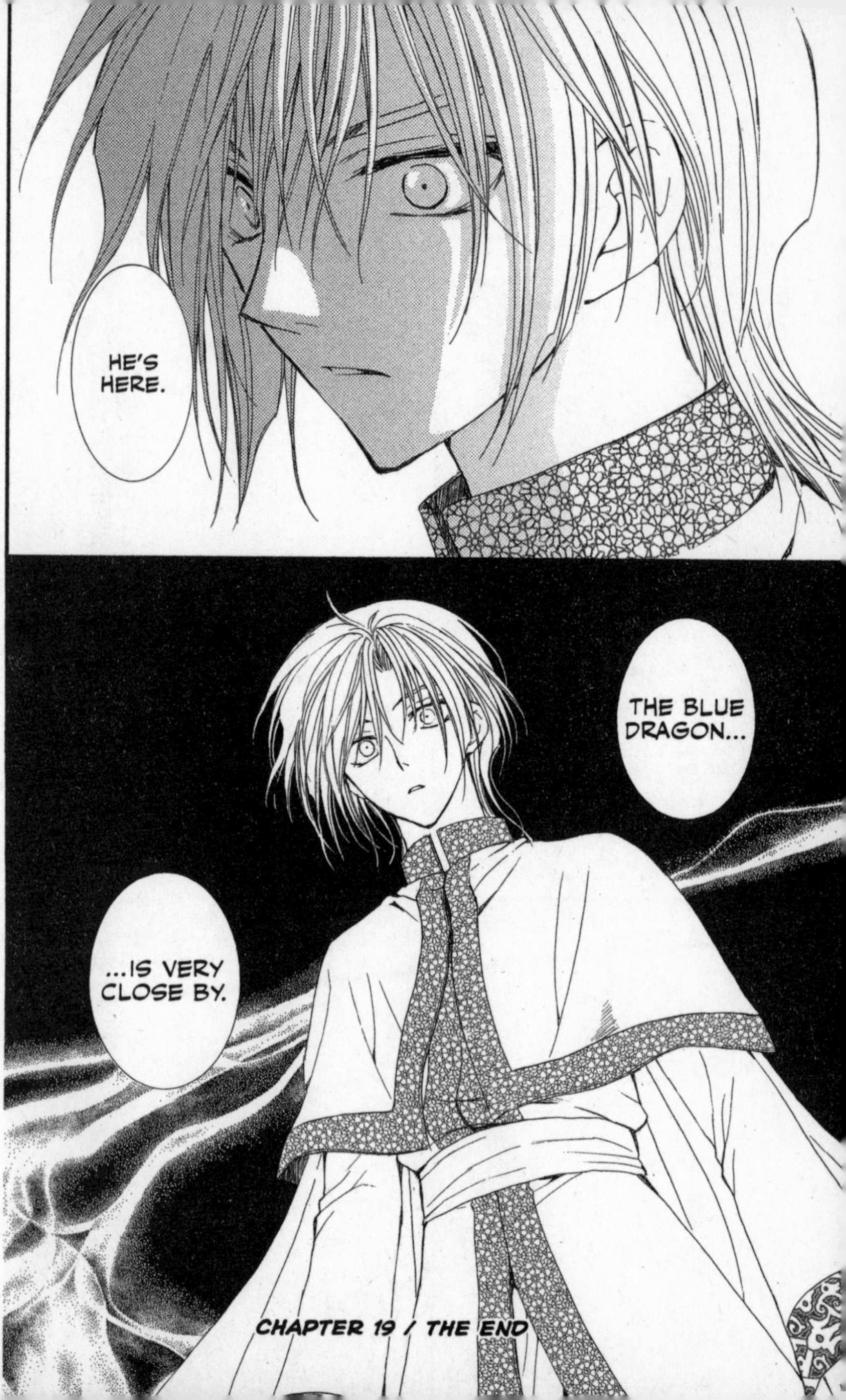
HE'S HERE.
THE BLUE DRAGON...
...IS VERY CLOSE BY.
CHAPTER 19 / THE END

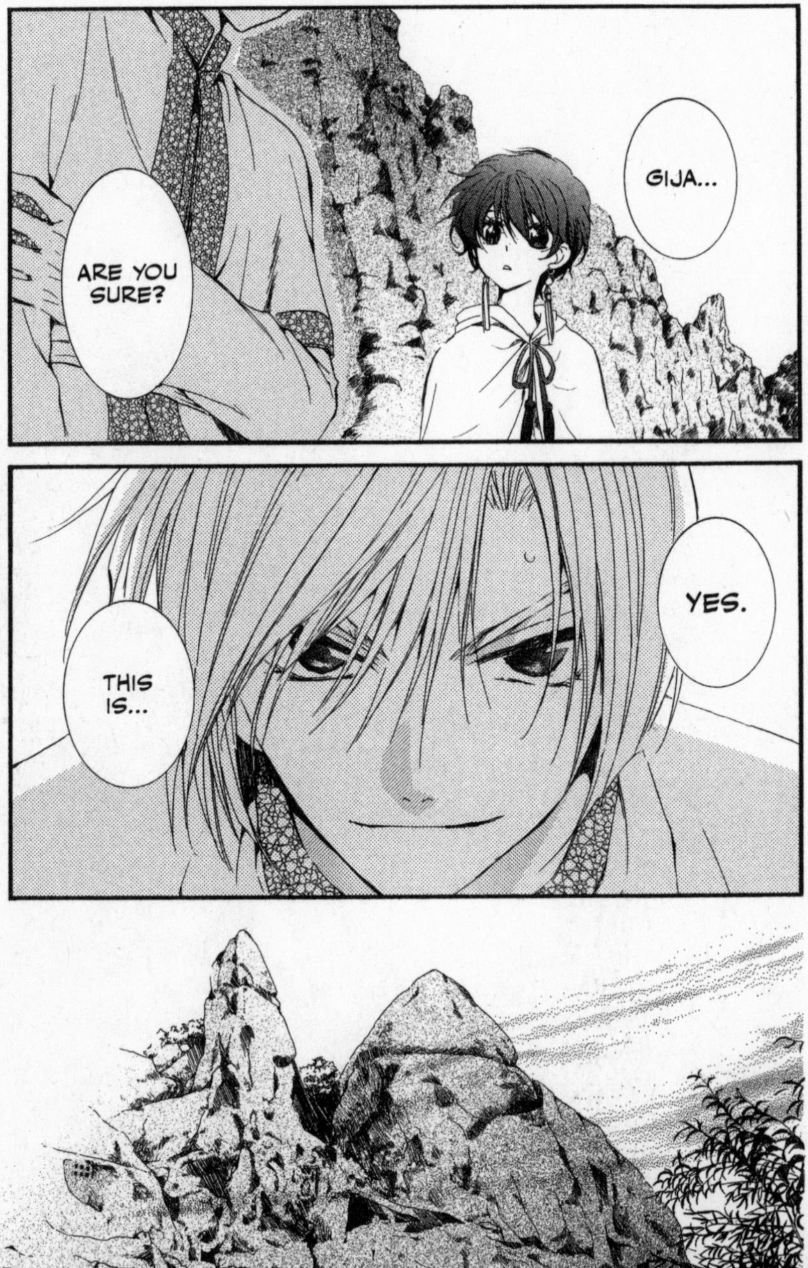
GIJA...
ARE YOU SURE?
YES.
THIS IS...

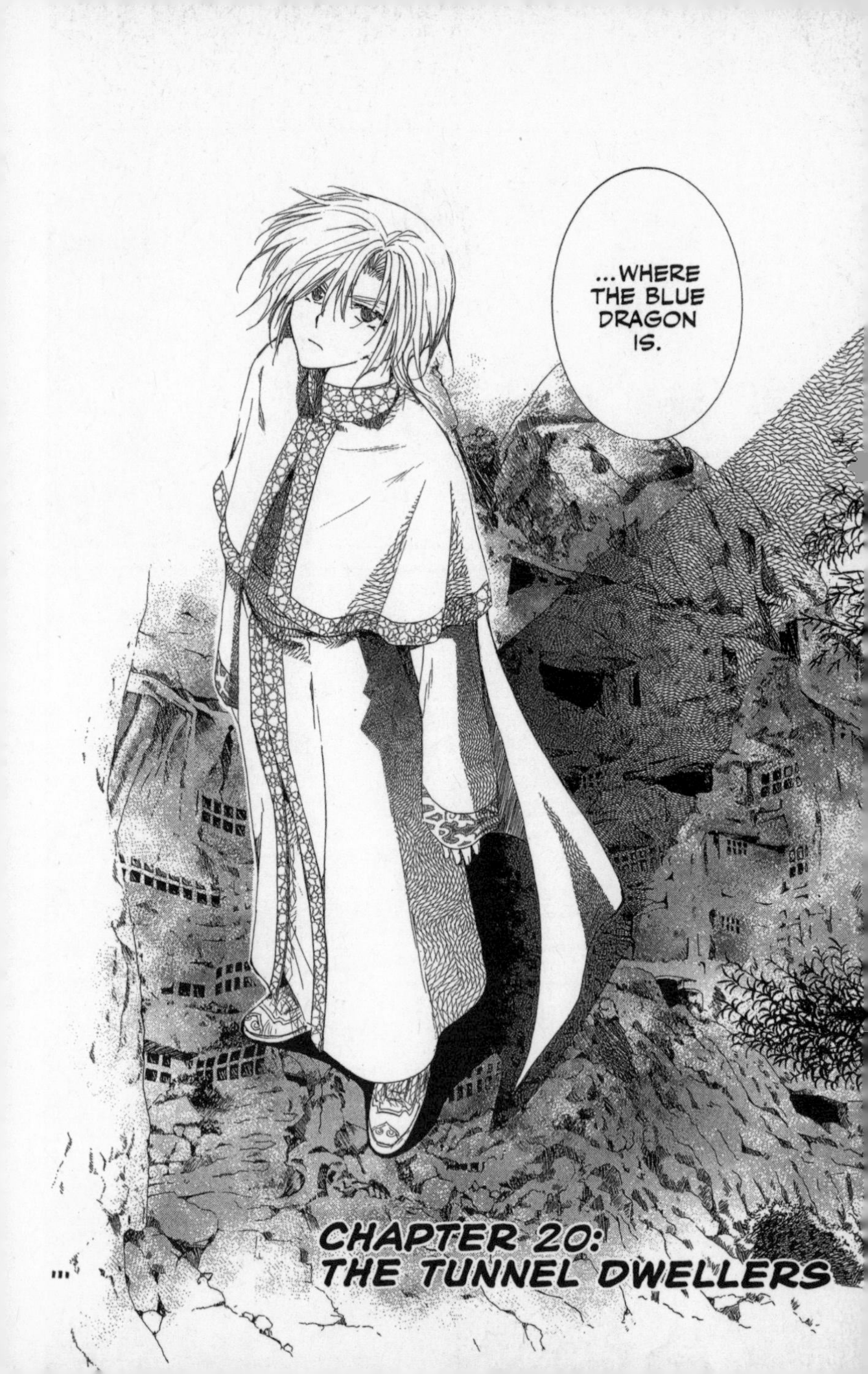
...WHERE THE BLUE DRAGON IS.
...
CHAPTER 20: THE TUNNEL DWELLERS

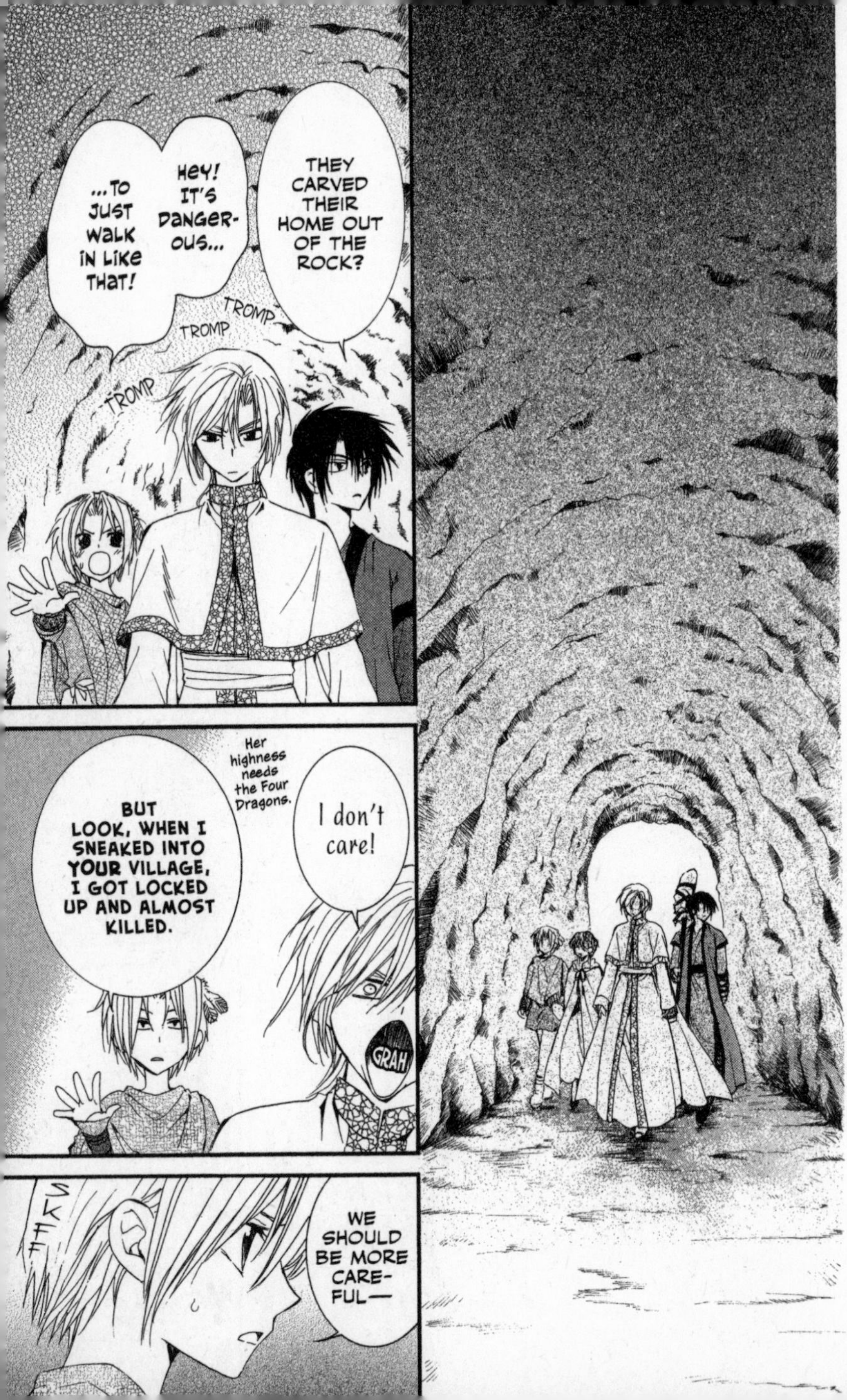
THEY CARVED THEIR HOME OUT OF THE ROCK?
HEY! IT'S DANGER-OUS...
...TO JUST WALK IN LIKE THAT!
TROMP
TROMP
TROMP
Her highness needs the Four Dragons.
I don't care!
BUT LOOK, WHEN I SNEAKED INTO YOUR VILLAGE, I GOT LOCKED UP AND ALMOST KILLED.
GRAH
WE SHOULD BE MORE CARE-FUL—
SKFF

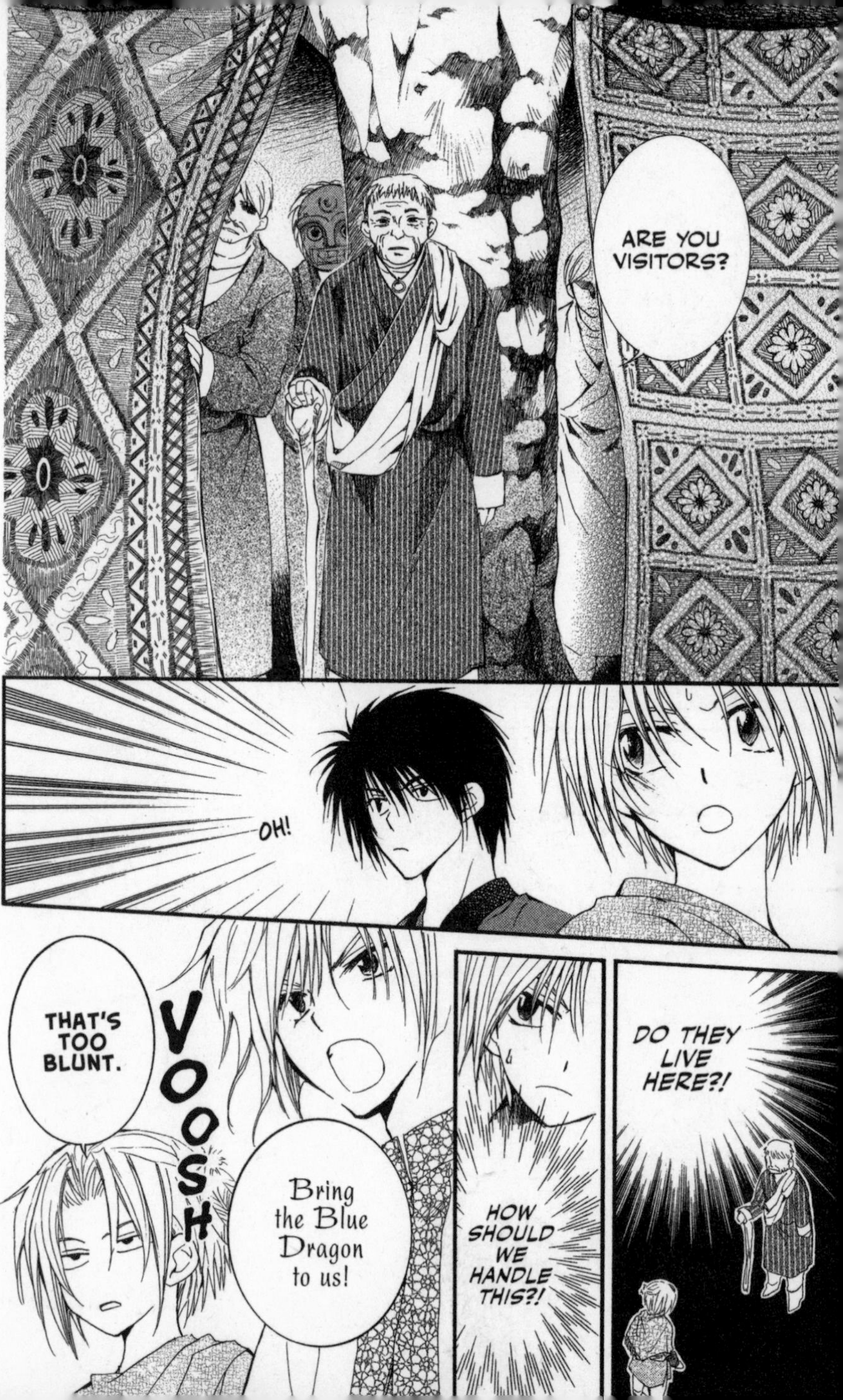
ARE YOU VISITORS?
OH!
DO THEY LIVE HERE?!
HOW SHOULD WE HANDLE THIS?!
Bring the Blue Dragon to us!
VOOSH
THAT'S TOO BLUNT.

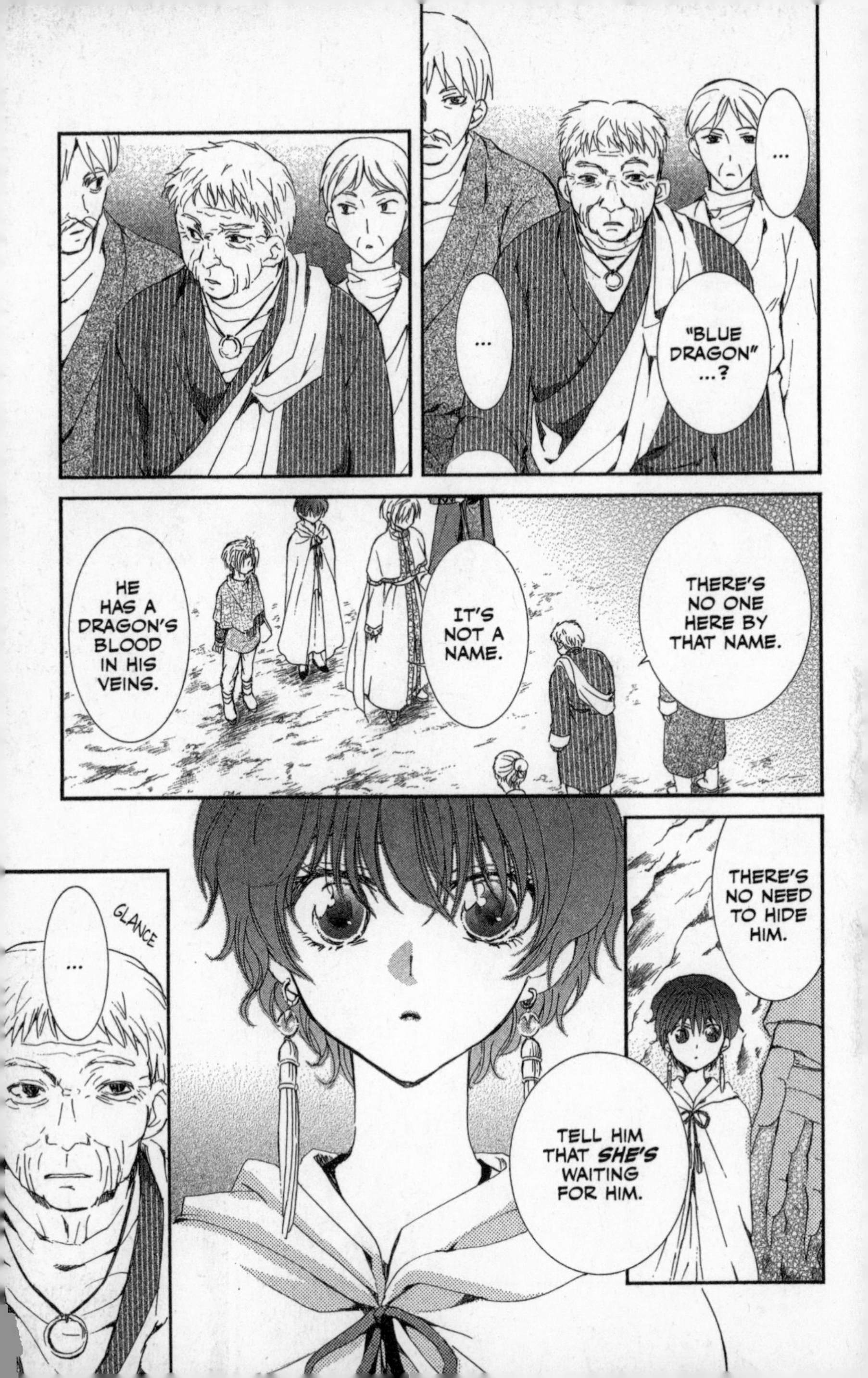
...
"BLUE DRAGON" ...?
...
THERE'S NO ONE HERE BY THAT NAME.
IT'S NOT A NAME.
HE HAS A DRAGON'S BLOOD IN HIS VEINS.
THERE'S NO NEED TO HIDE HIM.
TELL HIM THAT *SHE'S* WAITING FOR HIM.
GLANCE
...

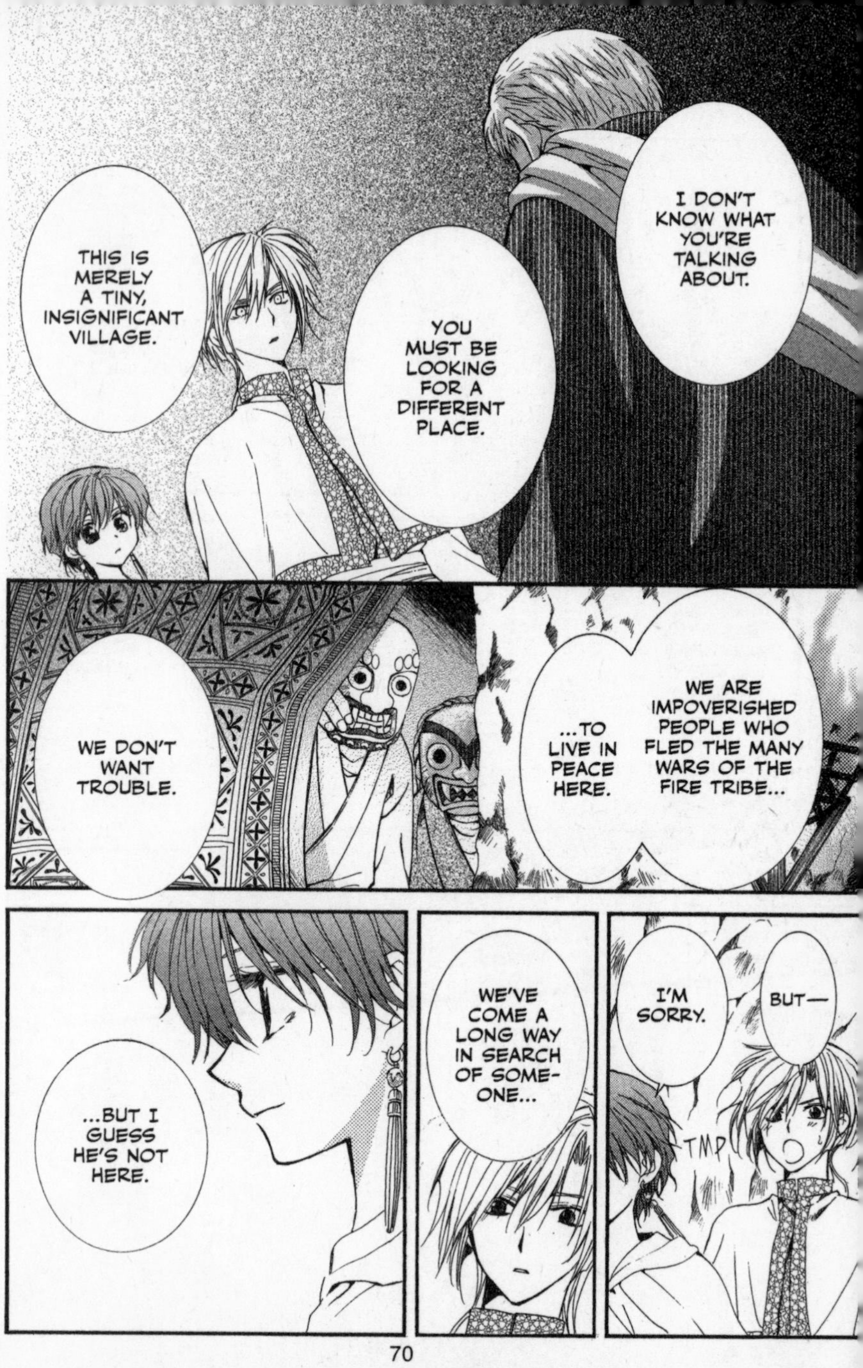
I DON'T KNOW WHAT YOU'RE TALKING ABOUT.
YOU MUST BE LOOKING FOR A DIFFERENT PLACE.
THIS IS MERELY A TINY, INSIGNIFICANT VILLAGE.
WE ARE IMPOVERISHED PEOPLE WHO FLED THE MANY WARS OF THE FIRE TRIBE...
...TO LIVE IN PEACE HERE.
WE DON'T WANT TROUBLE.
BUT—
I'M SORRY.
TMP
WE'VE COME A LONG WAY IN SEARCH OF SOME-ONE...
...BUT I GUESS HE'S NOT HERE.

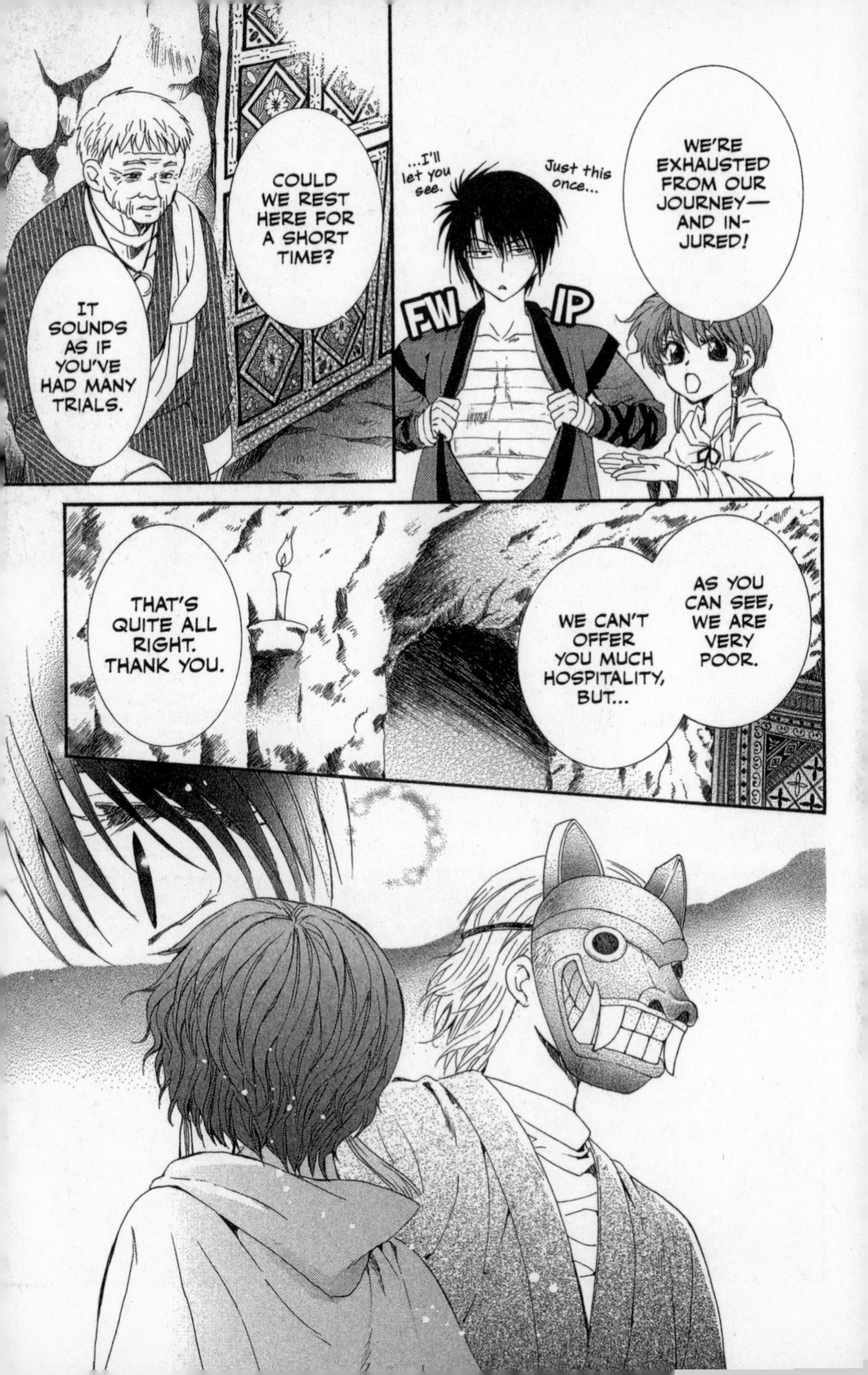
WE'RE EXHAUSTED FROM OUR JOURNEY— AND IN- JURED!
Just this once...
...I'll let you see.
FW IP
COULD WE REST HERE FOR A SHORT TIME?
IT SOUNDS AS IF YOU'VE HAD MANY TRIALS.
AS YOU CAN SEE, WE ARE VERY POOR.
WE CAN'T OFFER YOU MUCH HOSPITALITY, BUT...
THAT'S QUITE ALL RIGHT. THANK YOU.

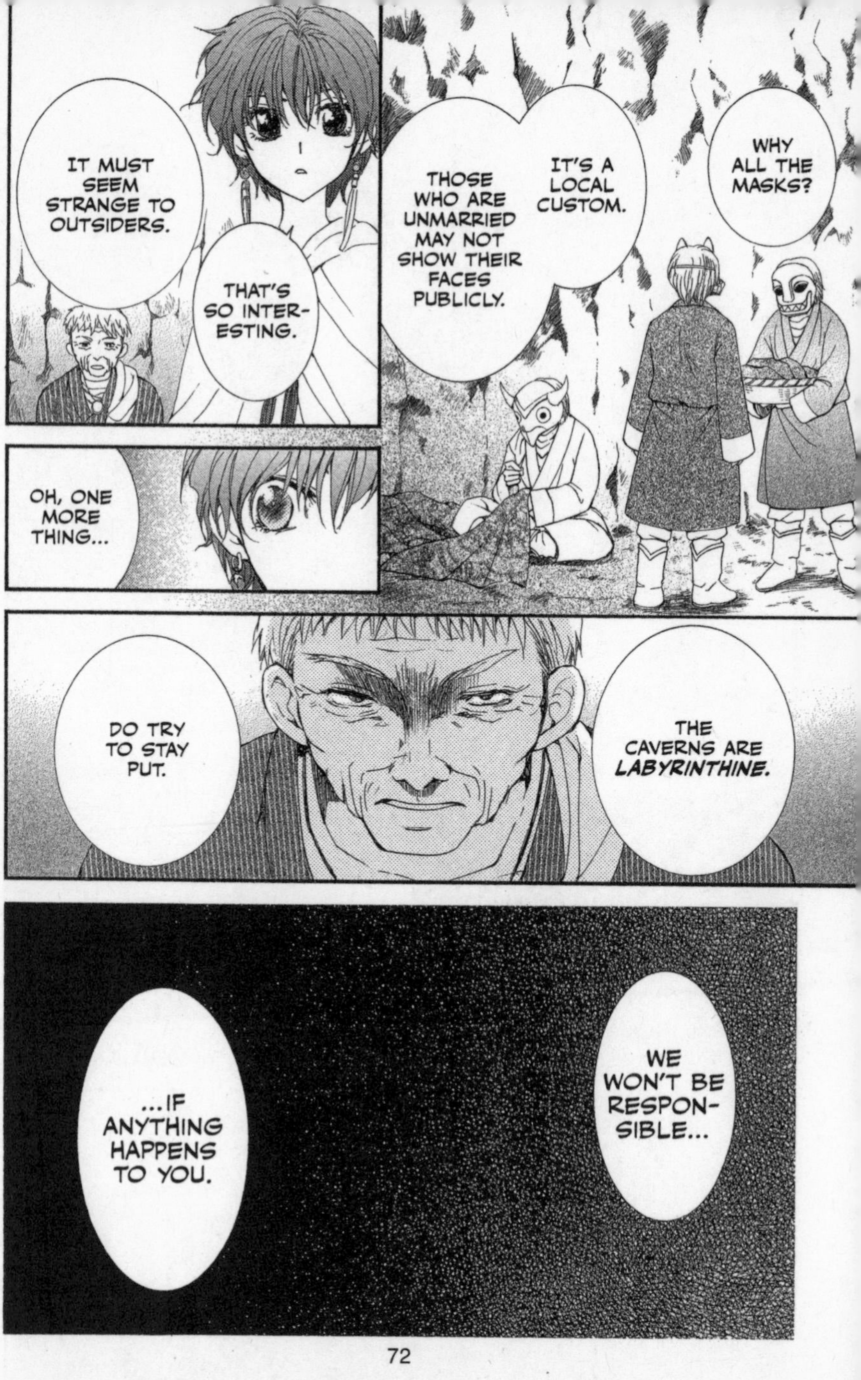
WHY ALL THE MASKS?
IT'S A LOCAL CUSTOM.
THOSE WHO ARE UNMARRIED MAY NOT SHOW THEIR FACES PUBLICLY.
IT MUST SEEM STRANGE TO OUTSIDERS.
THAT'S SO INTER-ESTING.
OH, ONE MORE THING...
THE CAVERNS ARE *LABYRINTHINE.*
DO TRY TO STAY PUT.
WE WON'T BE RESPON-SIBLE...
...IF ANYTHING HAPPENS TO YOU.

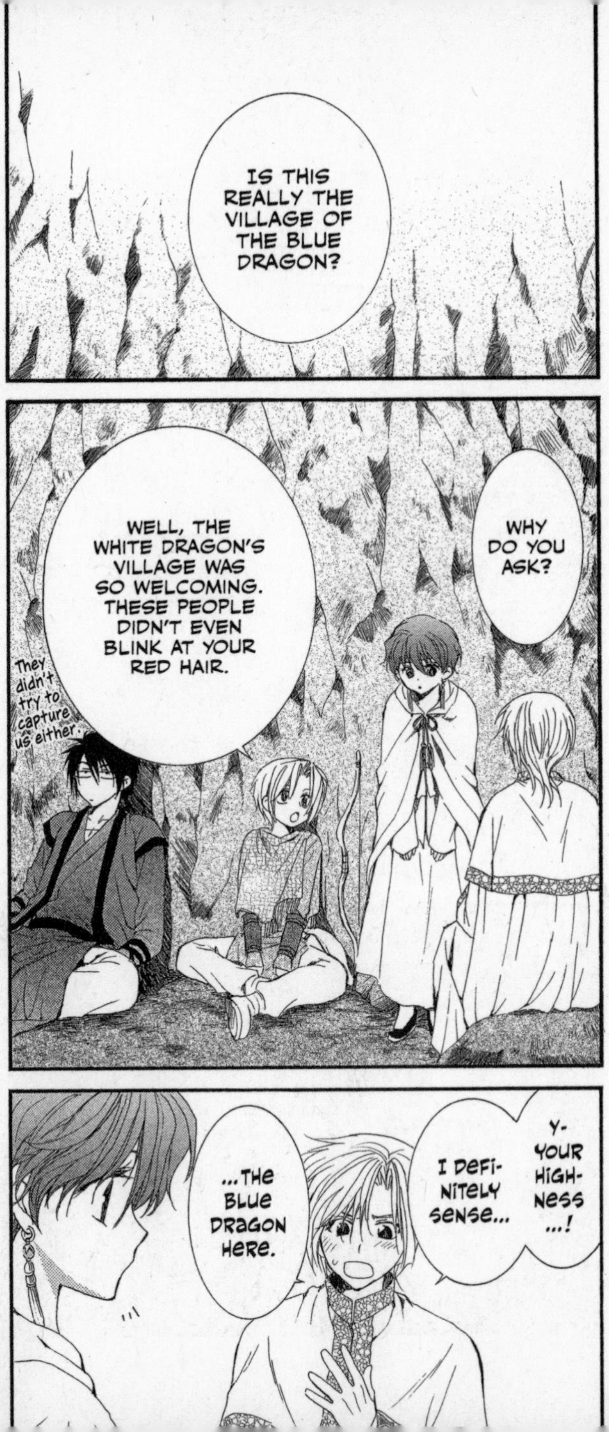
IS THIS REALLY THE VILLAGE OF THE BLUE DRAGON?
WHY DO YOU ASK?
WELL, THE WHITE DRAGON'S VILLAGE WAS SO WELCOMING. THESE PEOPLE DIDN'T EVEN BLINK AT YOUR RED HAIR.
They didn't try to capture us either.
Y-YOUR HIGHNESS...!
I DEFINITELY SENSE...
...THE BLUE DRAGON HERE.

※ Continued from the previous column.

I didn't know what to do, but then the editor-in-chief suggested "Yona of the Dawn." My editor and I agreed that it sounded good. (I was in Tokyo for a meeting when it happened.) Morning and daybreak... I thought of several titles that carried the image of dawn, so it stuck with me. Thank you, editor-in-chief! The title logo is very pretty. I love it! ♥ I used to be so nervous whenever I was at the editorial office, but I've gotten used to it. (*Smile*) The editors are always helping me out.

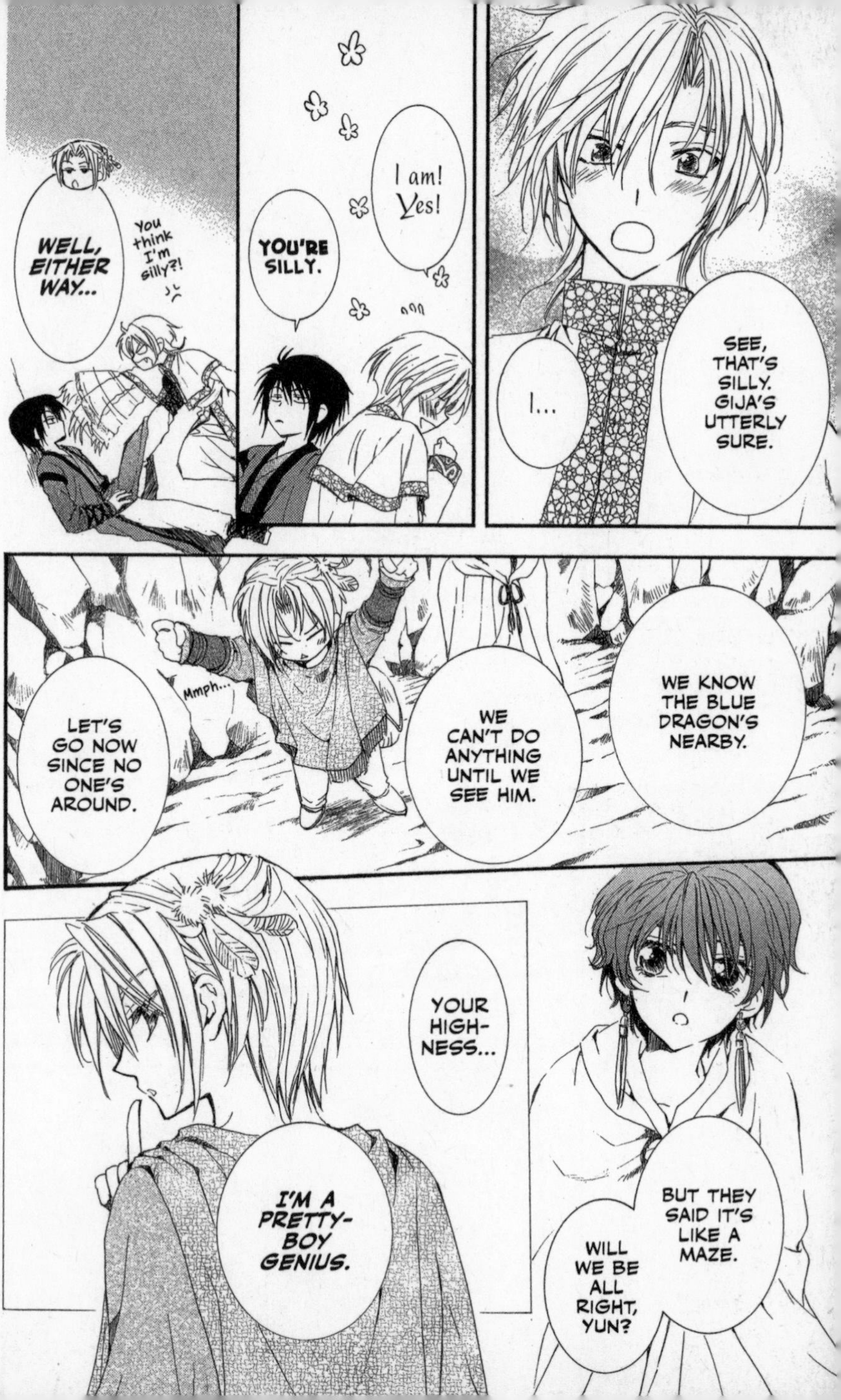
SEE, THAT'S SILLY. GIJA'S UTTERLY SURE.
I...
I am! Yes!
YOU'RE SILLY.
You think I'm silly?!
WELL, EITHER WAY...
WE KNOW THE BLUE DRAGON'S NEARBY.
WE CAN'T DO ANYTHING UNTIL WE SEE HIM.
Mmph...
LET'S GO NOW SINCE NO ONE'S AROUND.
BUT THEY SAID IT'S LIKE A MAZE.
WILL WE BE ALL RIGHT, YUN?
YOUR HIGHNESS...
I'M A PRETTY-BOY GENIUS.

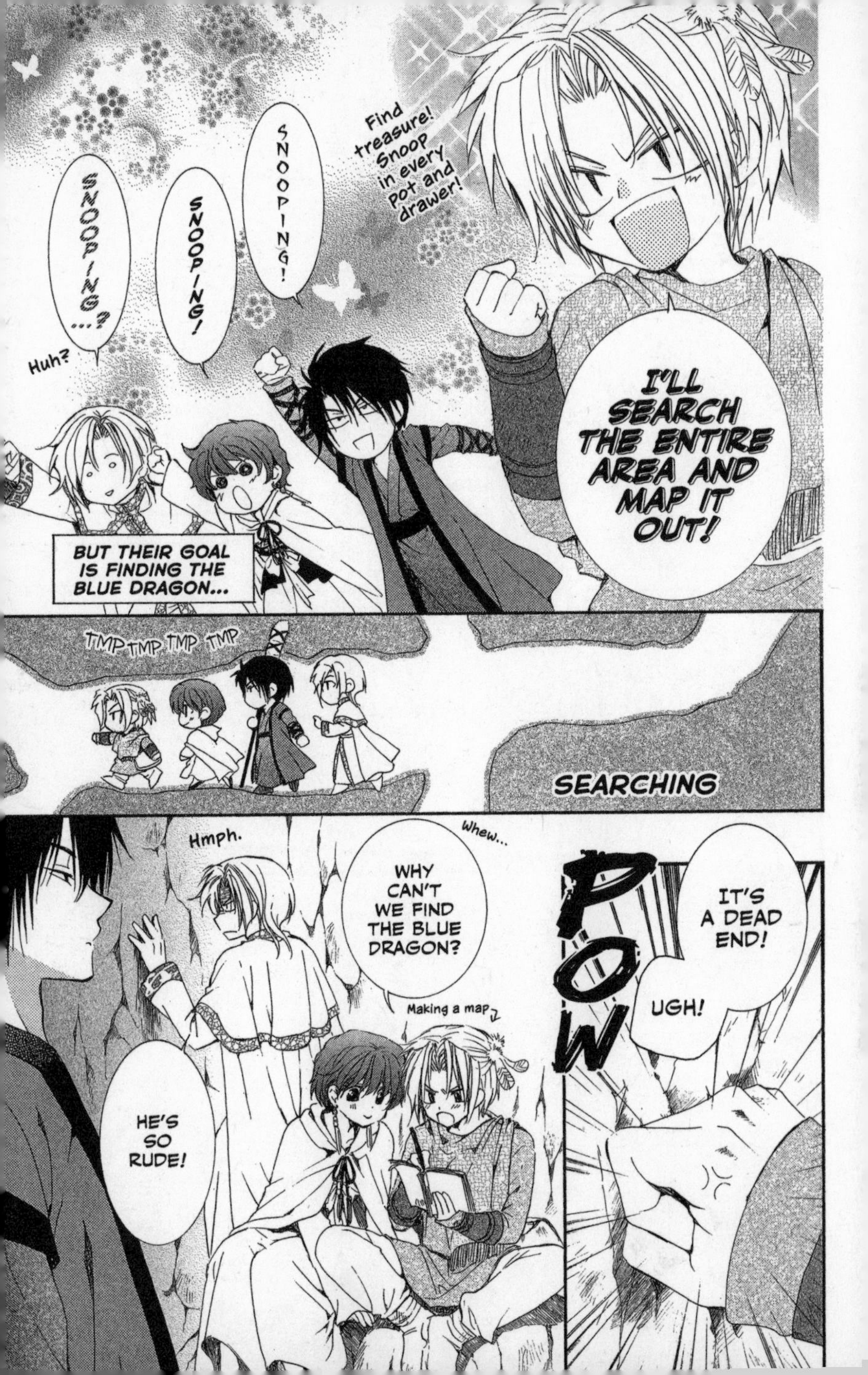
I'LL SEARCH THE ENTIRE AREA AND MAP IT OUT!
Find treasure! Snoop in every pot and drawer!
SNOOPING!
SNOOPING!
SNOOPING...?
Huh?
BUT THEIR GOAL IS FINDING THE BLUE DRAGON...
TMP TMP TMP TMP
SEARCHING
IT'S A DEAD END!
POW
UGH!
Whew...
WHY CAN'T WE FIND THE BLUE DRAGON?
Hmph.
Making a map
HE'S SO RUDE!

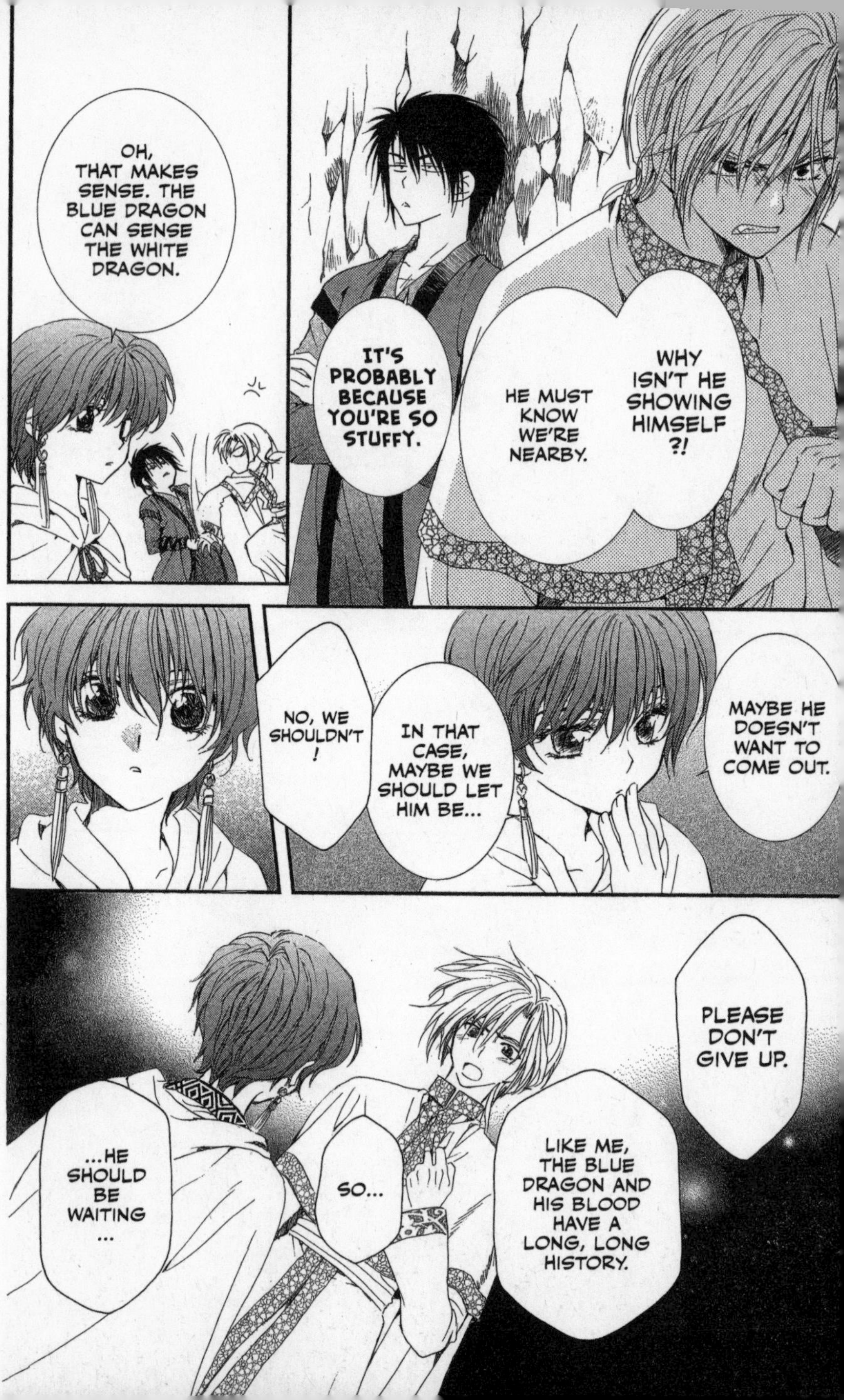
WHY ISN'T HE SHOWING HIMSELF?!
HE MUST KNOW WE'RE NEARBY.
IT'S PROBABLY BECAUSE YOU'RE SO STUFFY.
OH, THAT MAKES SENSE. THE BLUE DRAGON CAN SENSE THE WHITE DRAGON.
MAYBE HE DOESN'T WANT TO COME OUT.
IN THAT CASE, MAYBE WE SHOULD LET HIM BE...
NO, WE SHOULDN'T!
PLEASE DON'T GIVE UP.
LIKE ME, THE BLUE DRAGON AND HIS BLOOD HAVE A LONG, LONG HISTORY.
SO...
...HE SHOULD BE WAITING...

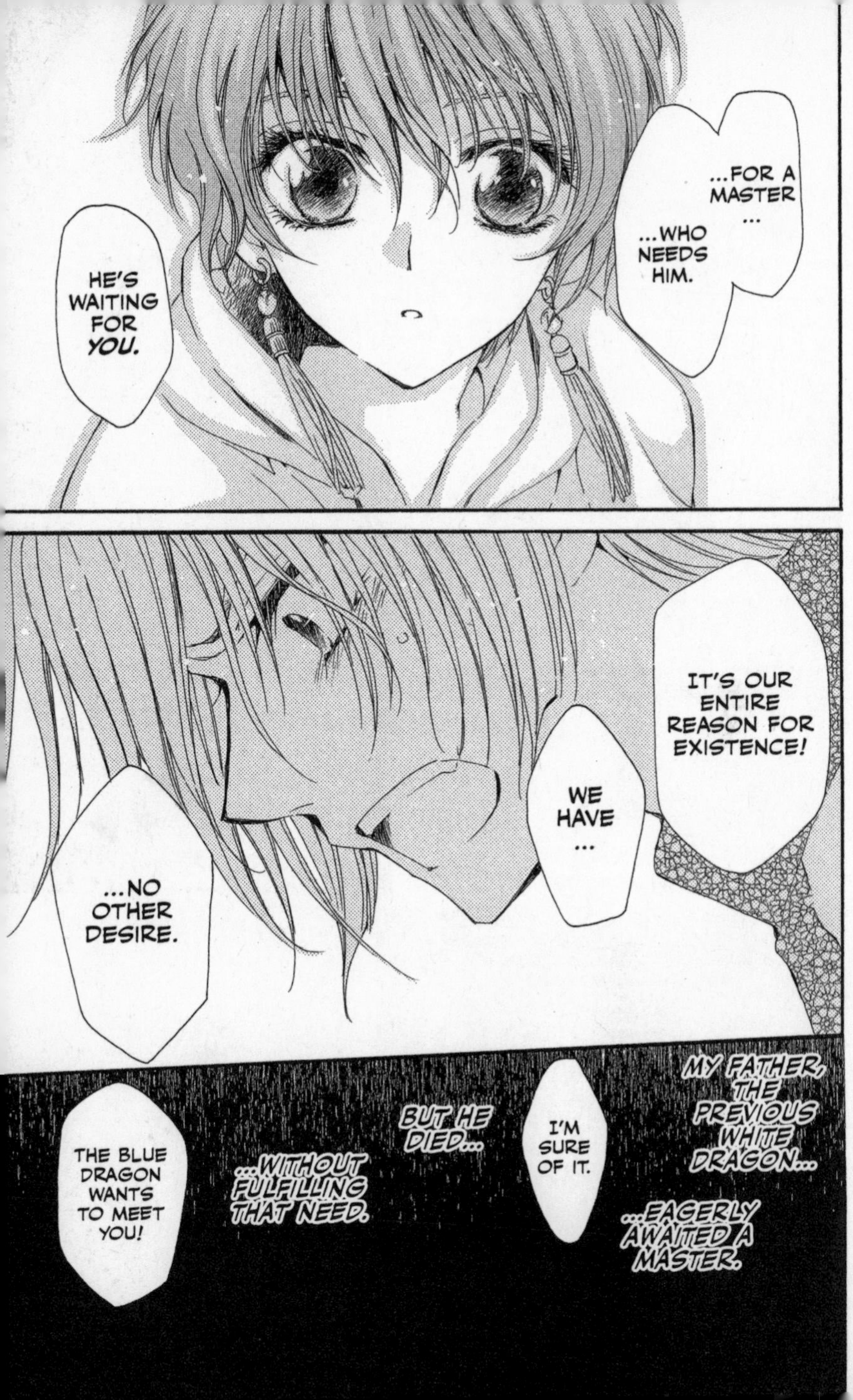
...FOR A MASTER ...
...WHO NEEDS HIM.
HE'S WAITING FOR *YOU.*
IT'S OUR ENTIRE REASON FOR EXISTENCE!
WE HAVE ...
...NO OTHER DESIRE.
MY FATHER, THE PREVIOUS WHITE DRAGON...
...EAGERLY AWAITED A MASTER.
I'M SURE OF IT.
BUT HE DIED...
...WITHOUT FULFILLING THAT NEED.
THE BLUE DRAGON WANTS TO MEET YOU!

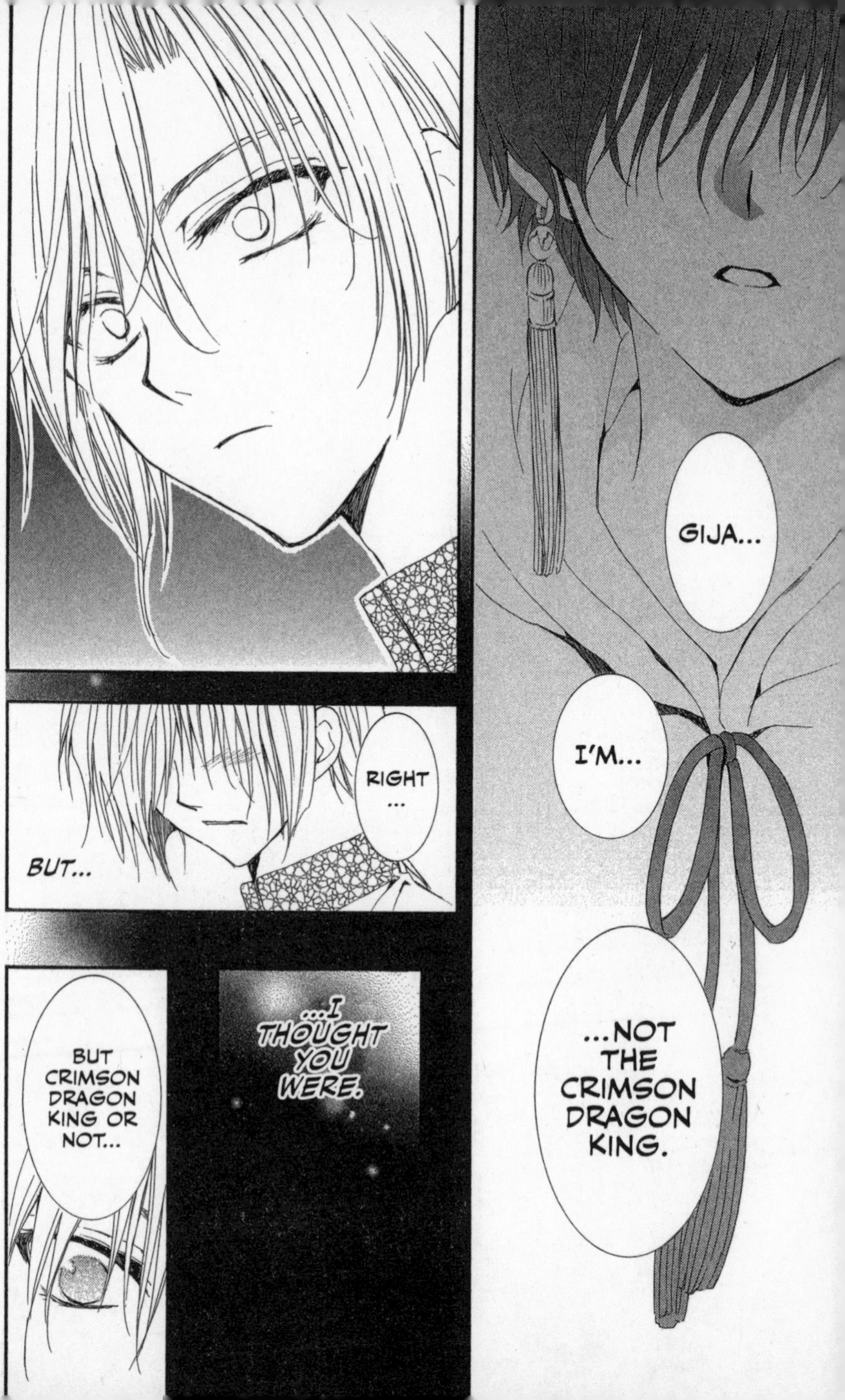
GIJA...
I'M...
...NOT THE CRIMSON DRAGON KING.
RIGHT ...
BUT...
...I THOUGHT YOU WERE.
BUT CRIMSON DRAGON KING OR NOT...

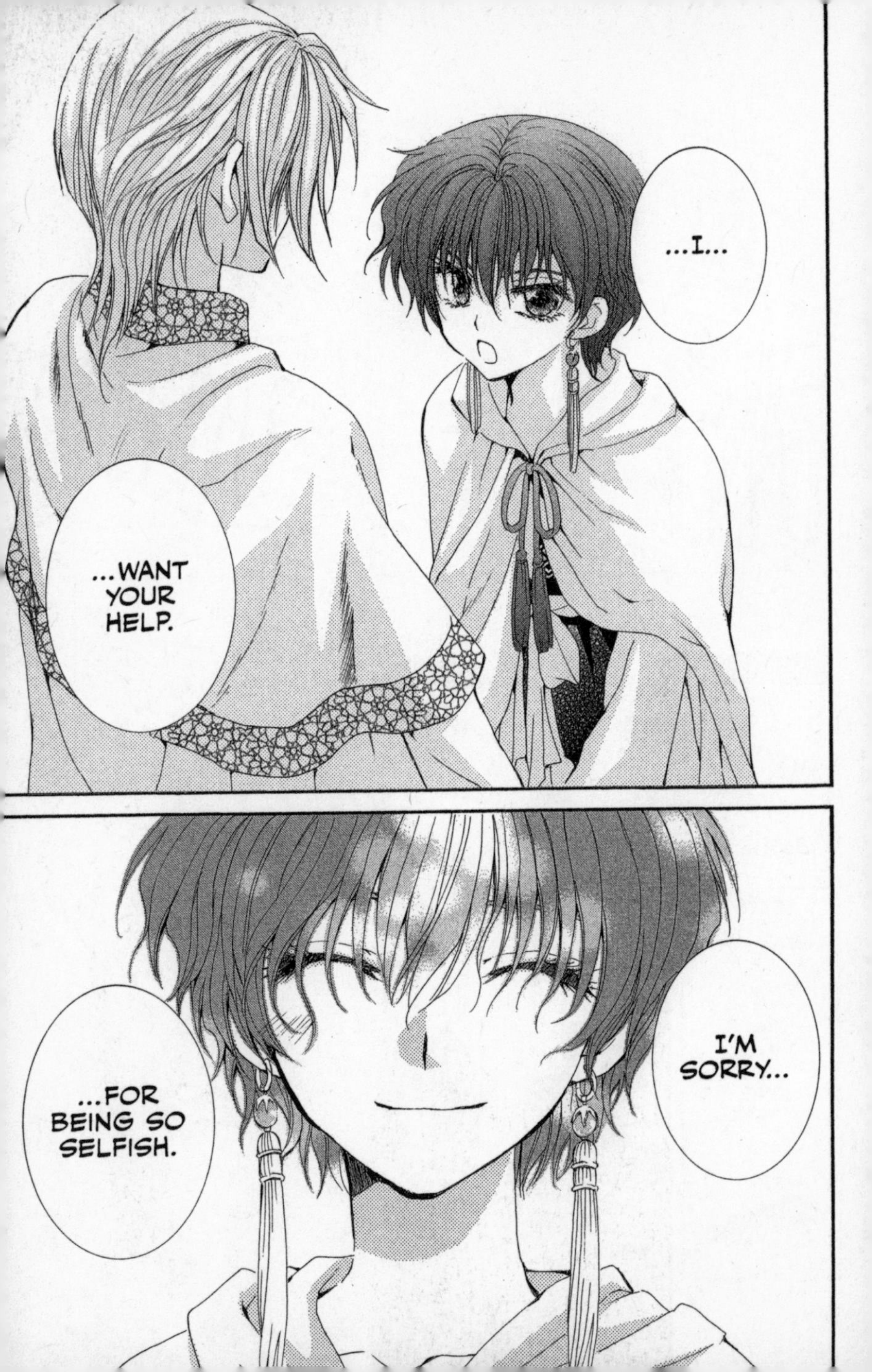
...I...
...WANT YOUR HELP.
I'M SORRY...
...FOR BEING SO SELFISH.

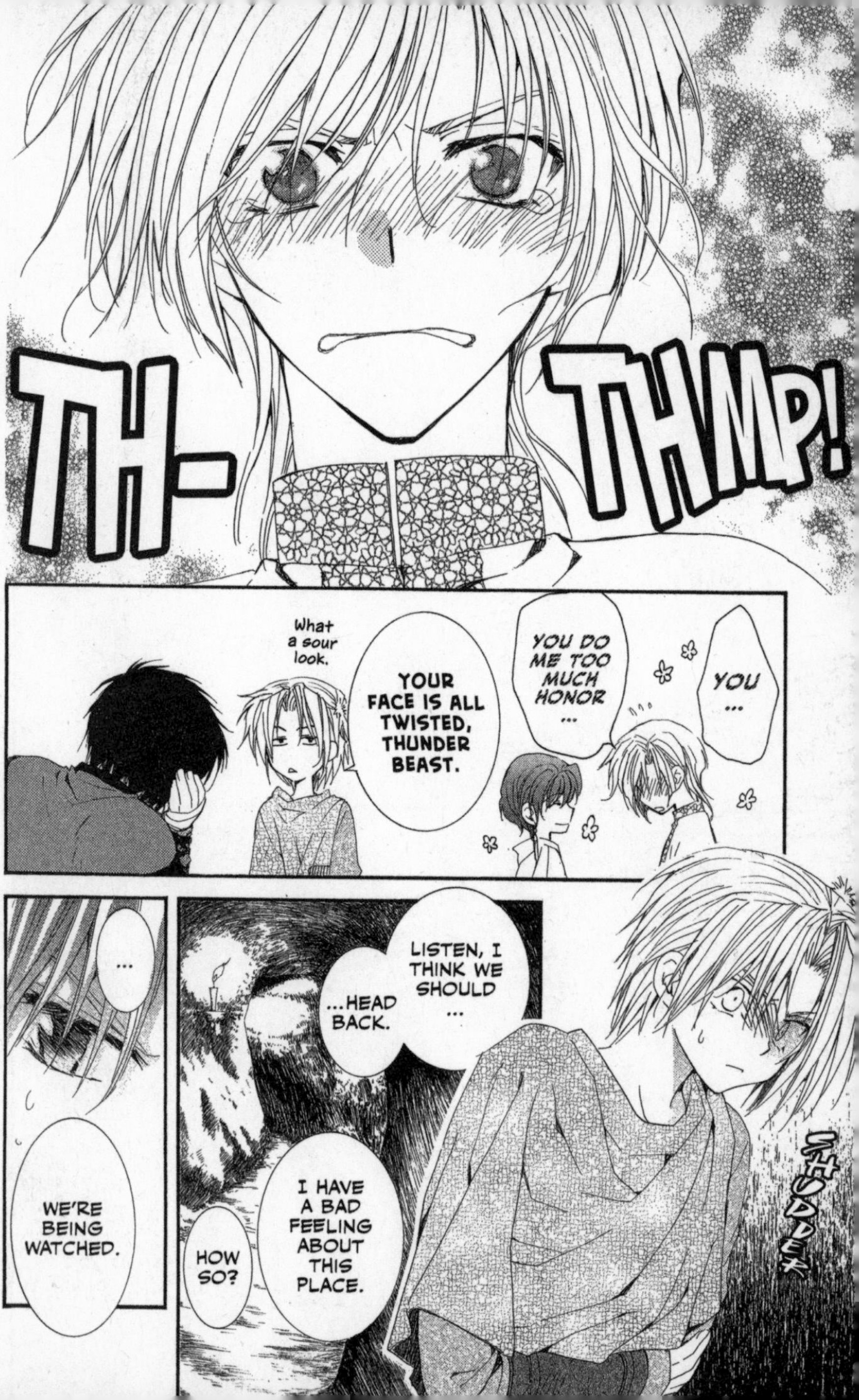
TH-
THMP!
YOU ...
YOU DO ME TOO MUCH HONOR ...
YOUR FACE IS ALL TWISTED, THUNDER BEAST.
What a sour look.
SHUDDER
LISTEN, I THINK WE SHOULD ...
...HEAD BACK.
I HAVE A BAD FEELING ABOUT THIS PLACE.
HOW SO?
...
WE'RE BEING WATCHED.

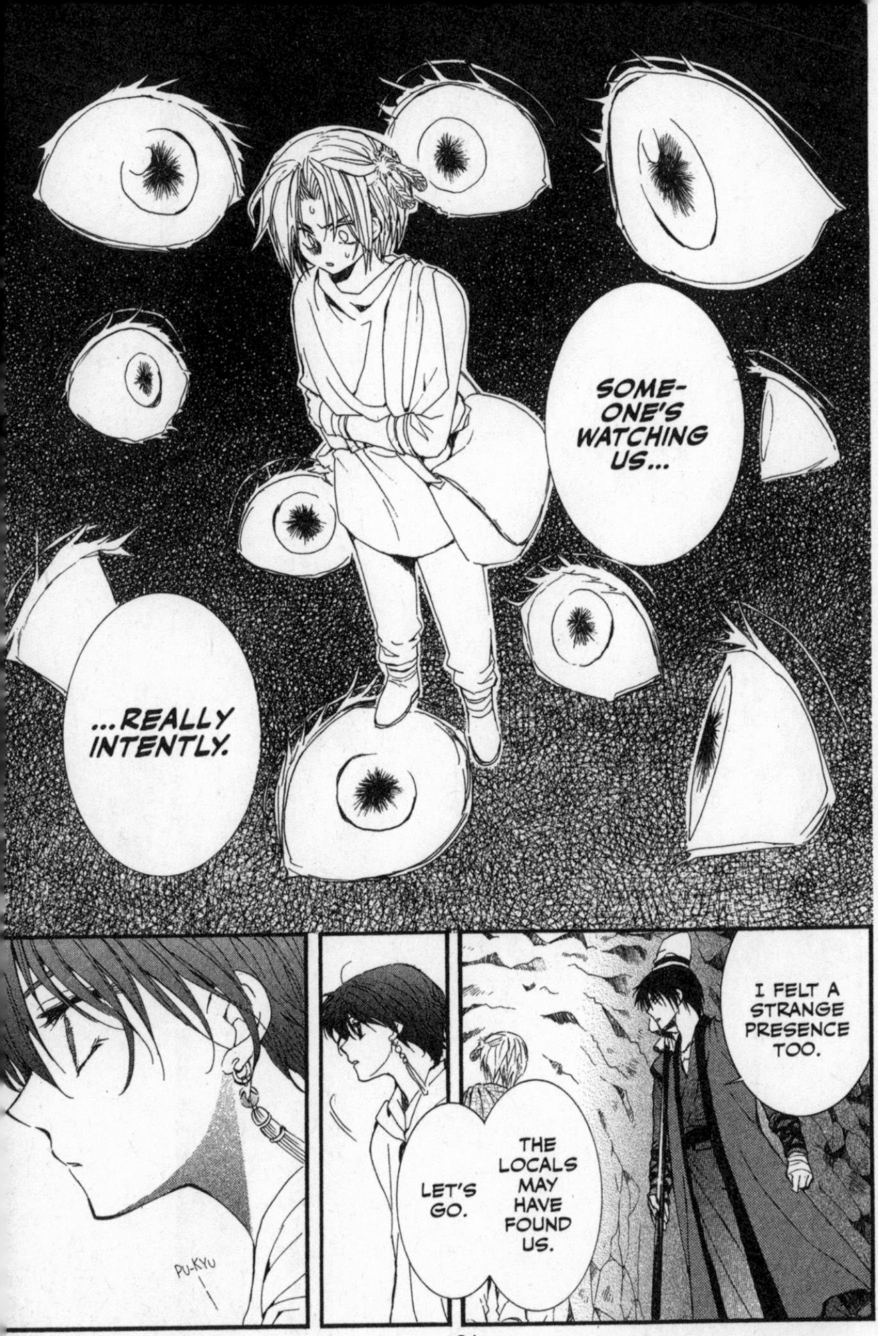
SOME-ONE'S WATCHING US...
...REALLY INTENTLY.
I FELT A STRANGE PRESENCE TOO.
THE LOCALS MAY HAVE FOUND US.
LET'S GO.
PU-KYU

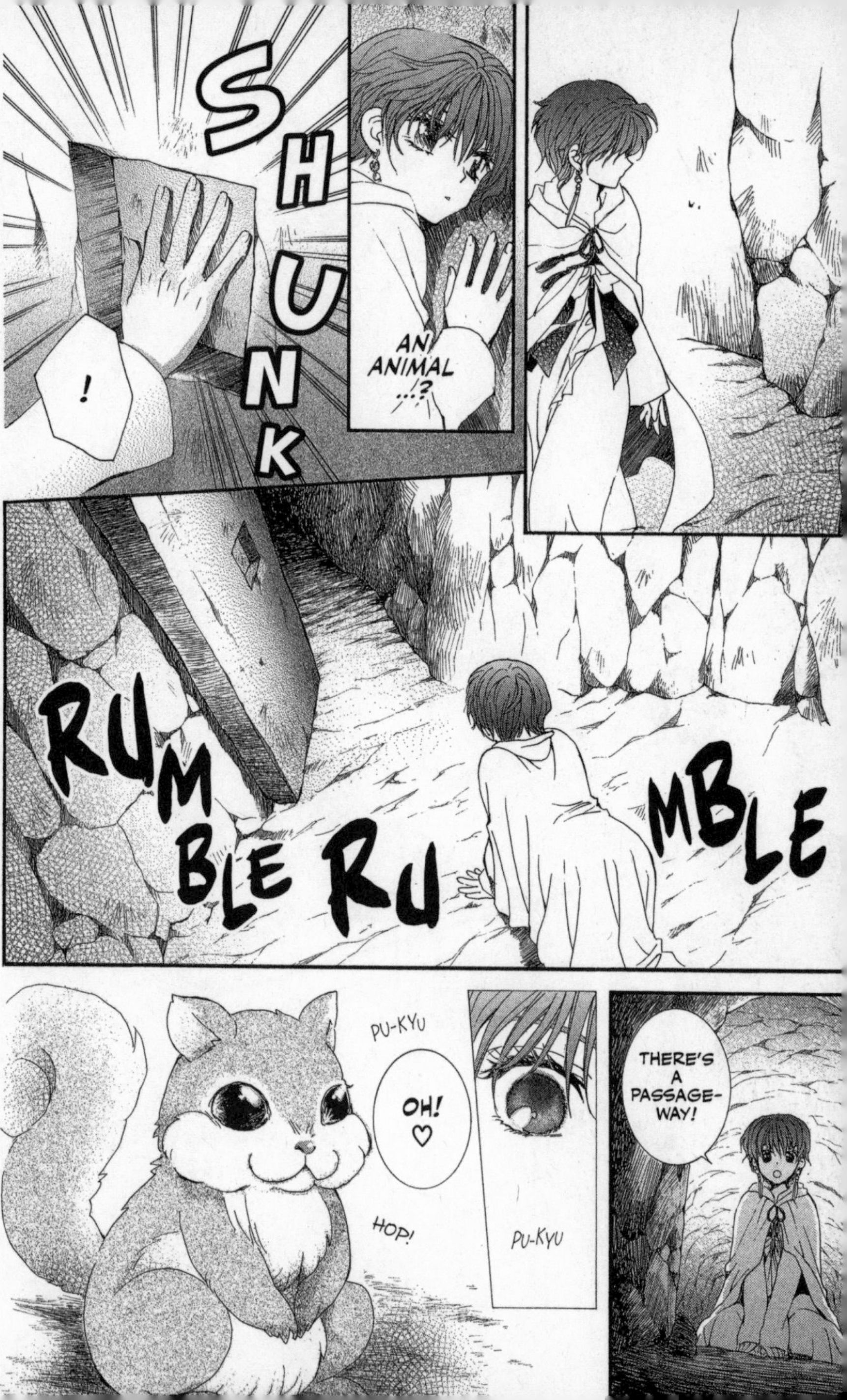
AN ANIMAL ...!?
SHUNK
!
RUMBLE RUMBLE
THERE'S A PASSAGE-WAY!
PU-KYU
PU-KYU
OH! ♡
HOP!

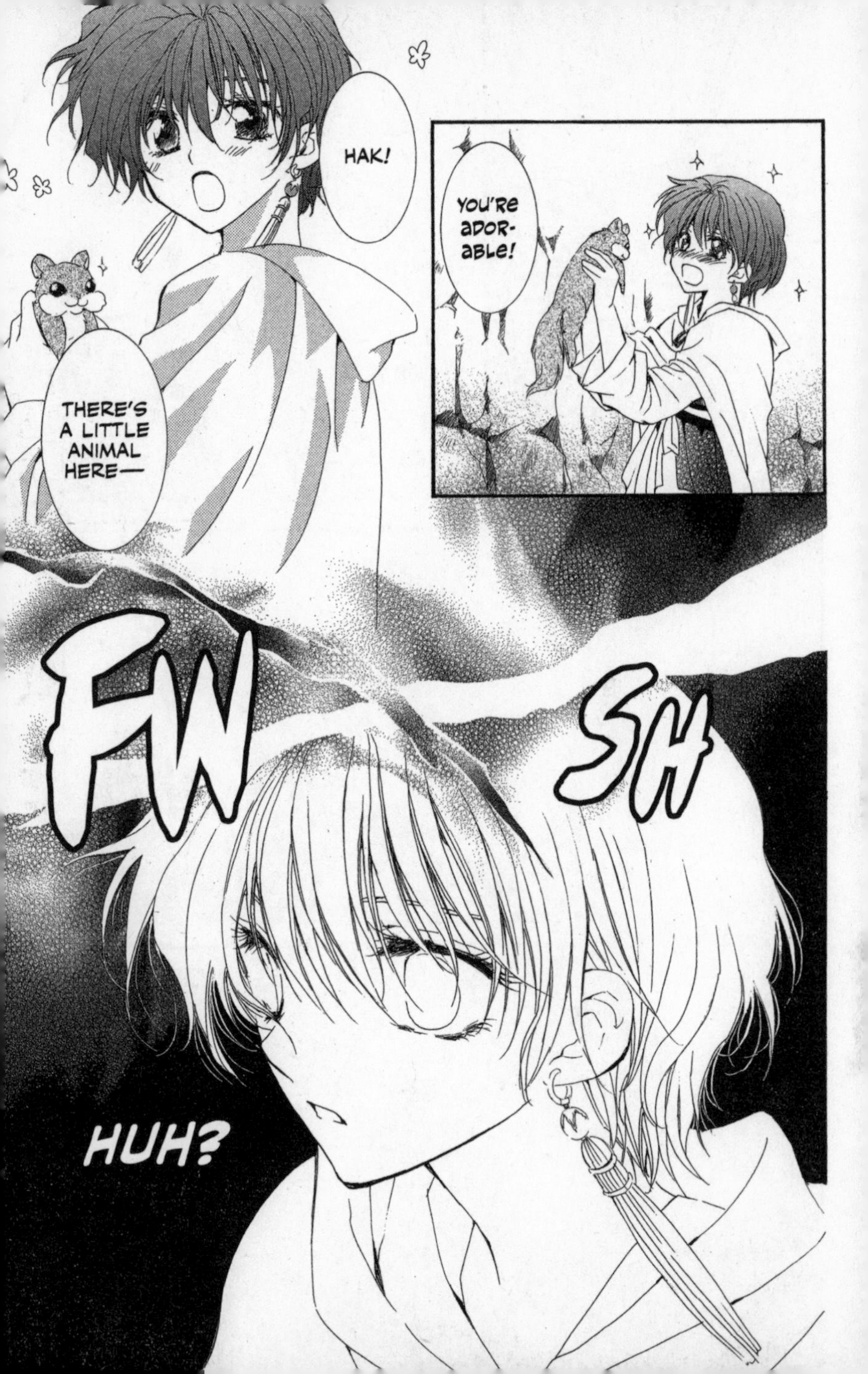
YOU'RE ADORABLE!
HAK!
THERE'S A LITTLE ANIMAL HERE—
FWSH
HUH?

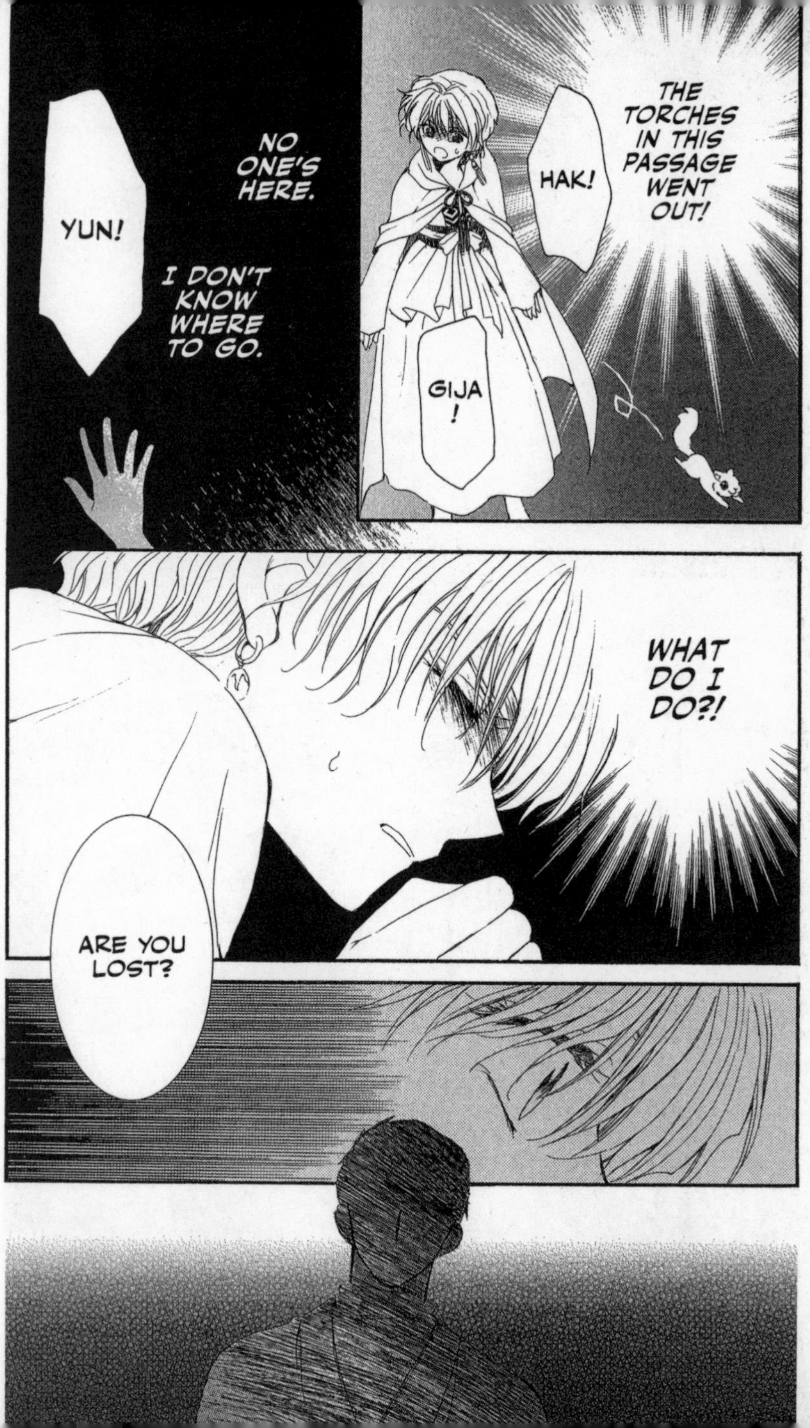
THE TORCHES IN THIS PASSAGE WENT OUT!
HAK!
GIJA!
NO ONE'S HERE.
YUN!
I DON'T KNOW WHERE TO GO.
WHAT DO I DO?!
ARE YOU LOST?

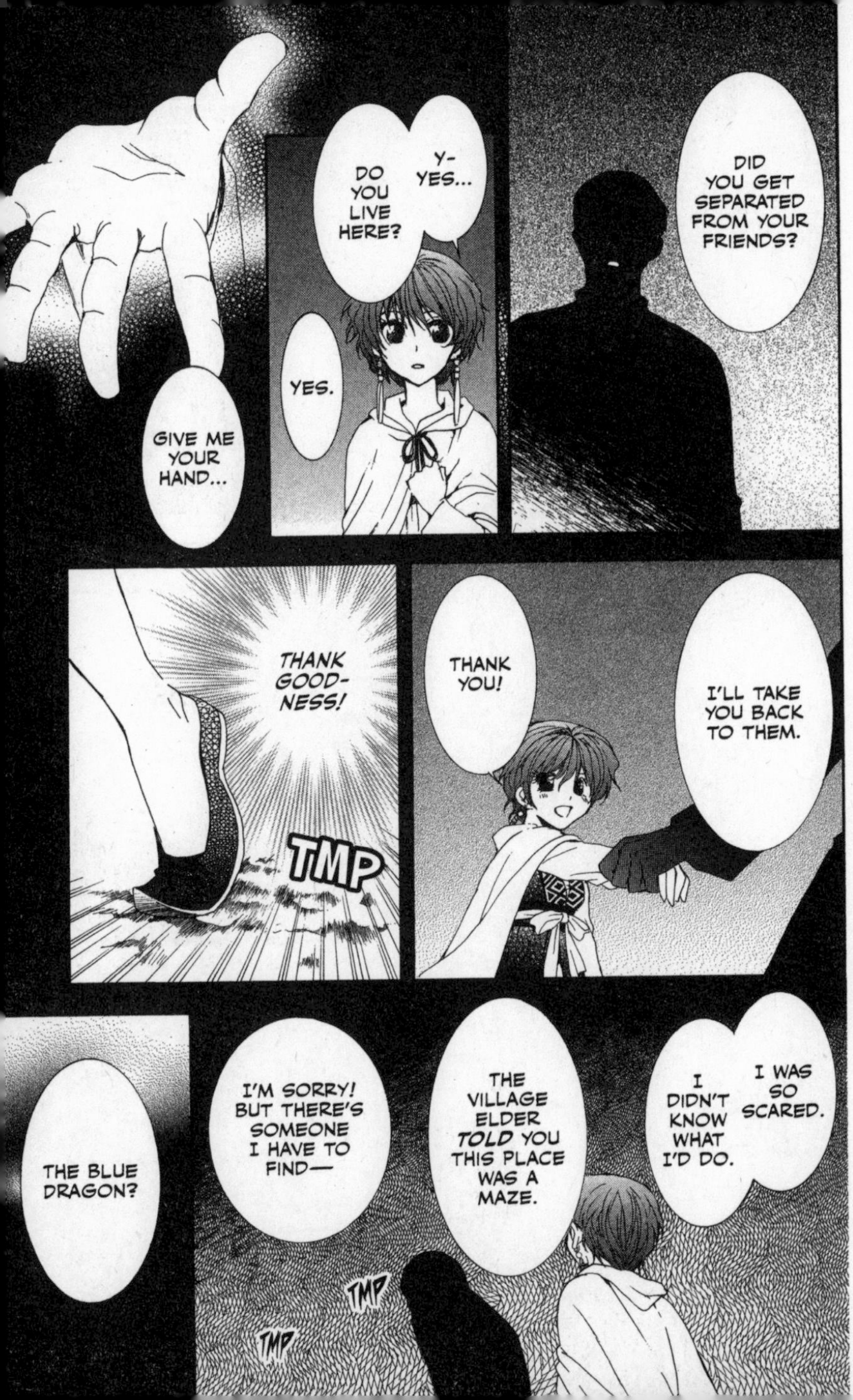
DID YOU GET SEPARATED FROM YOUR FRIENDS?
Y-YES...
DO YOU LIVE HERE?
YES.
GIVE ME YOUR HAND...
I'LL TAKE YOU BACK TO THEM.
THANK YOU!
THANK GOODNESS!
TMP
I WAS SO SCARED.
I DIDN'T KNOW WHAT I'D DO.
THE VILLAGE ELDER TOLD YOU THIS PLACE WAS A MAZE.
I'M SORRY! BUT THERE'S SOMEONE I HAVE TO FIND—
TMP
TMP
THE BLUE DRAGON?

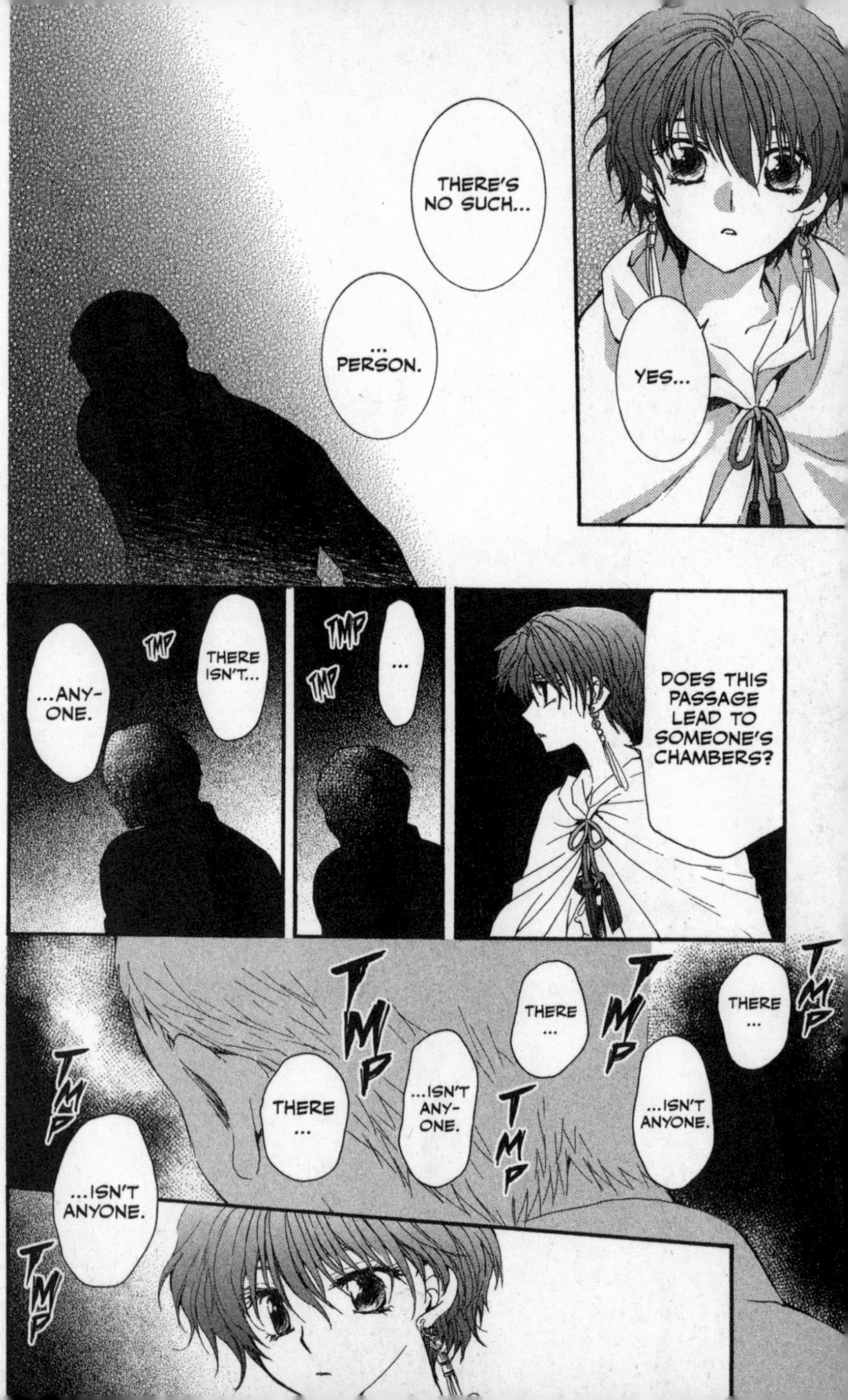
YES...
THERE'S NO SUCH...
... PERSON.
DOES THIS PASSAGE LEAD TO SOMEONE'S CHAMBERS?
TMP
TMP
...
THERE ISN'T...
TMP
...ANY-ONE.
TMP
THERE ...
...ISN'T ANYONE.
TMP
THERE ...
TMP
...ISN'T ANY-ONE.
THERE ...
TMP
TMP
...ISN'T ANYONE.
TMP

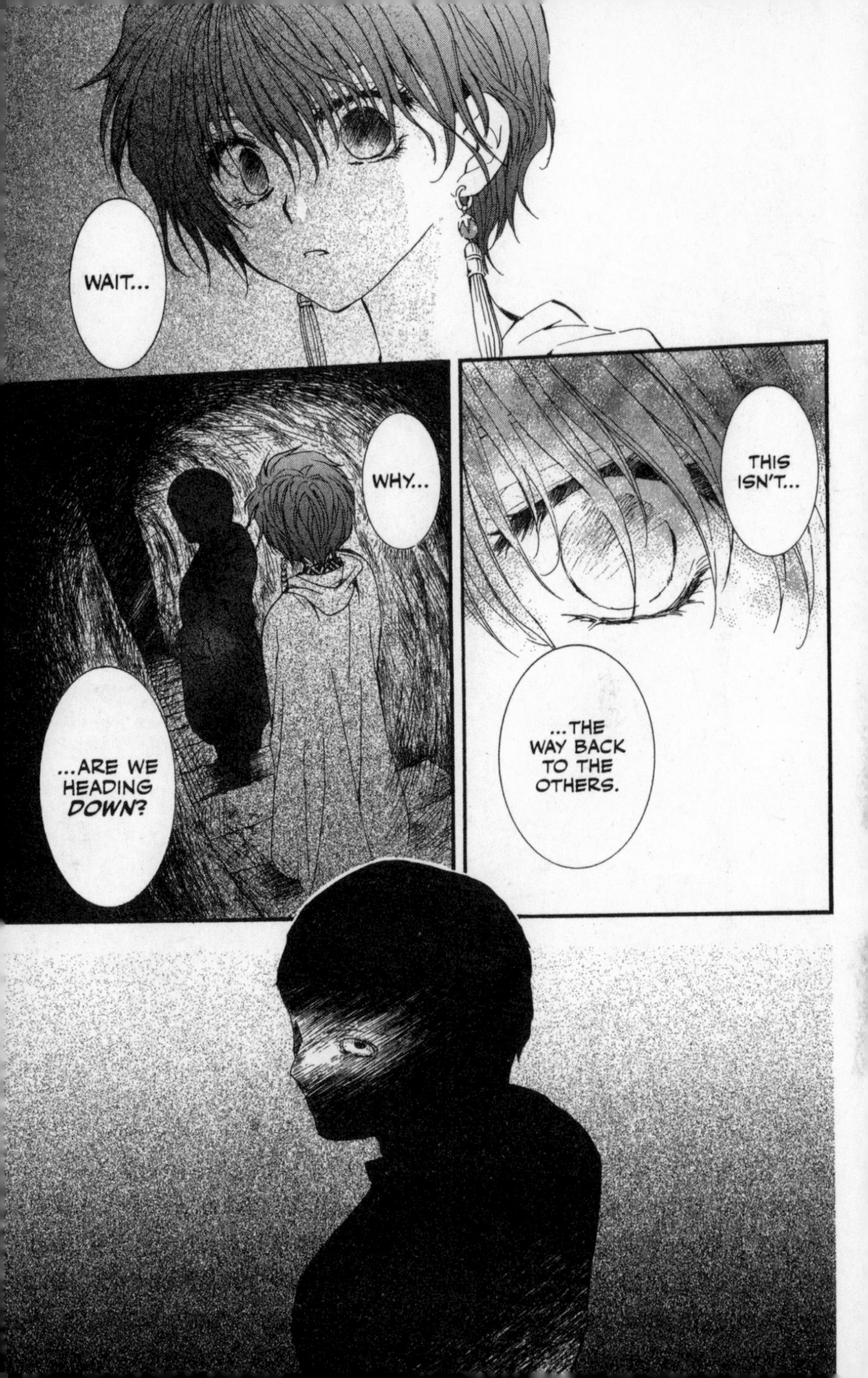
WAIT...
THIS ISN'T...
...THE WAY BACK TO THE OTHERS.
WHY...
...ARE WE HEADING *DOWN*?

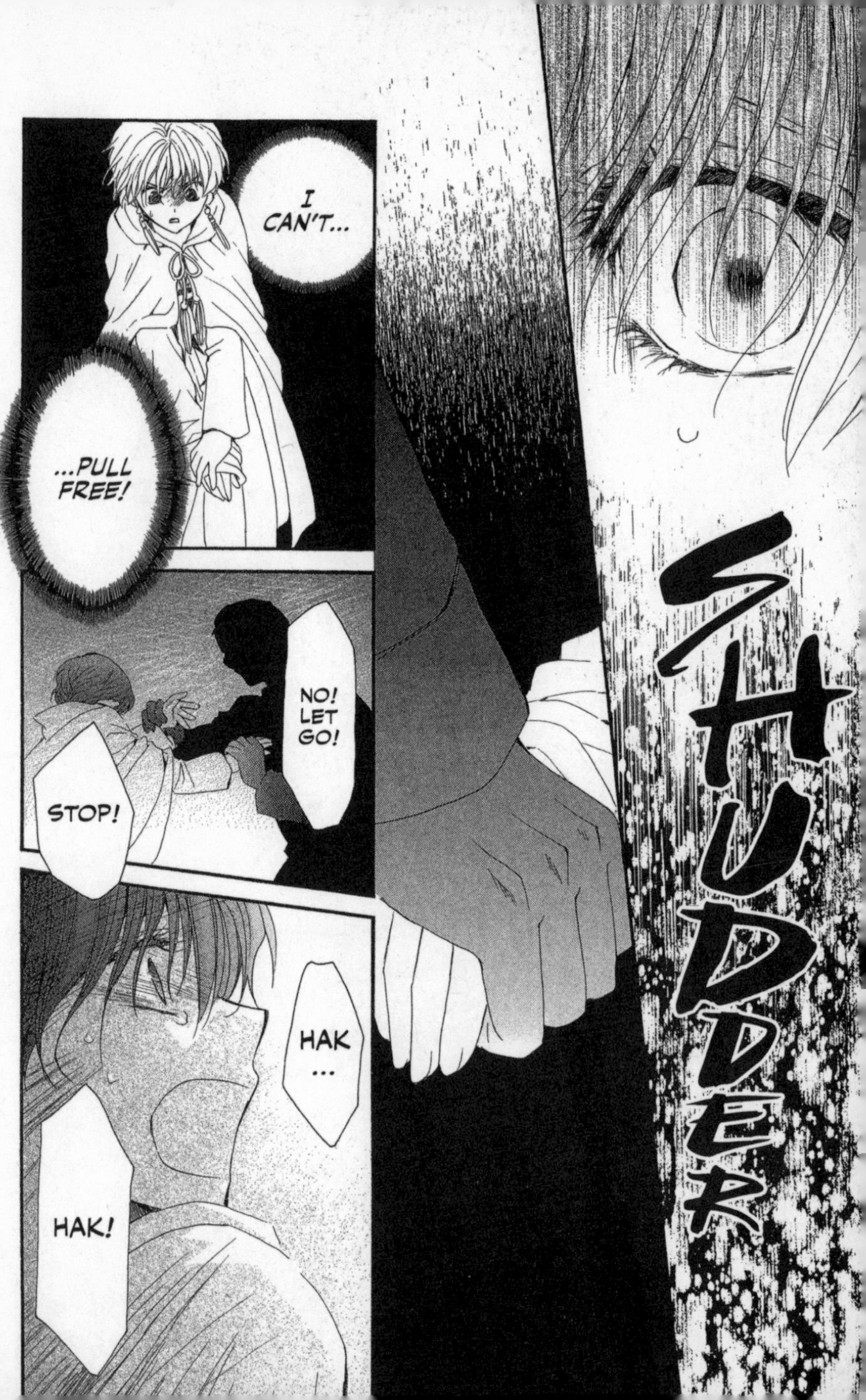
SHUDDER
I CAN'T...
...PULL FREE!
NO! LET GO!
STOP!
HAK...
HAK!

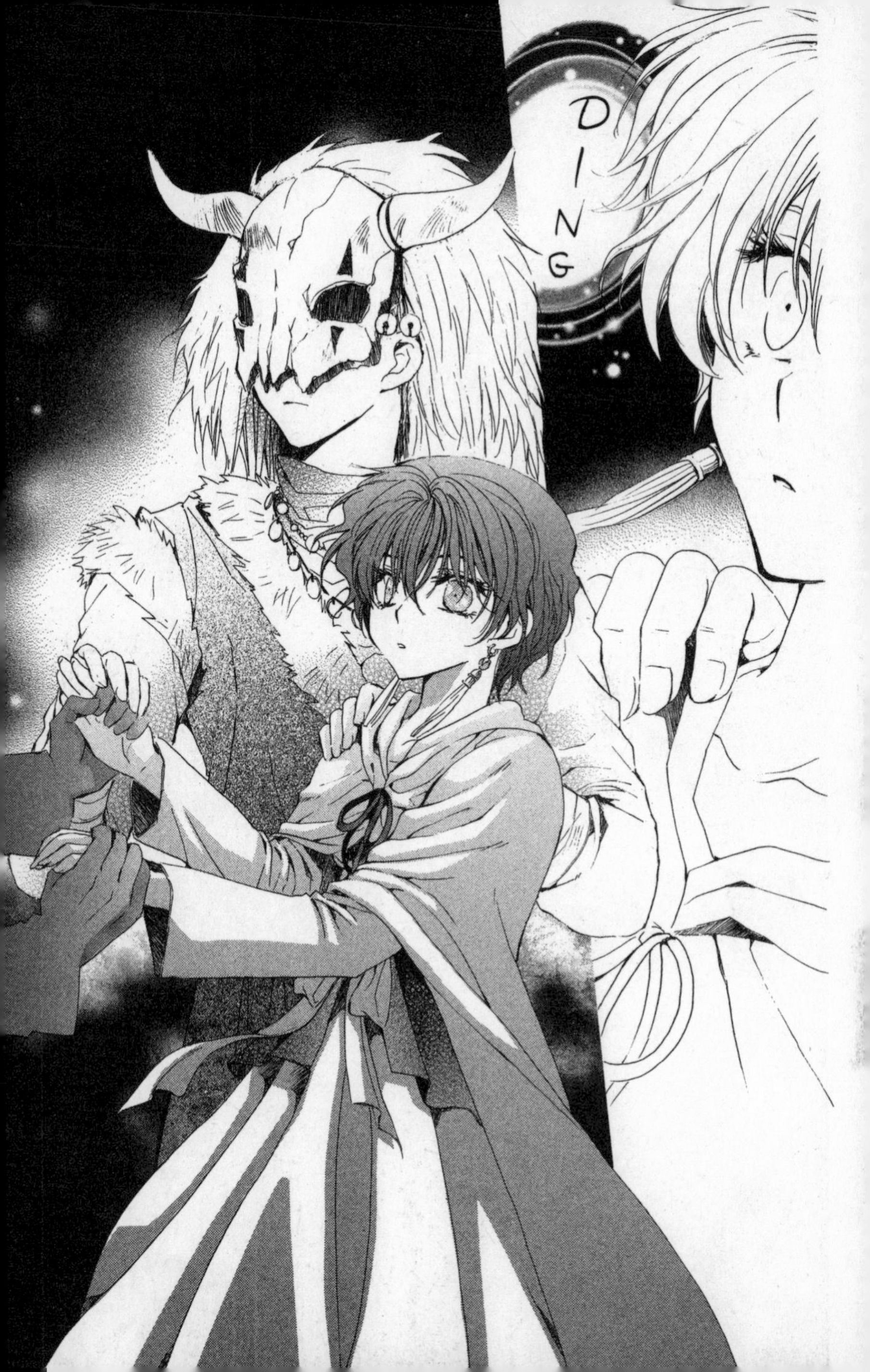
DING

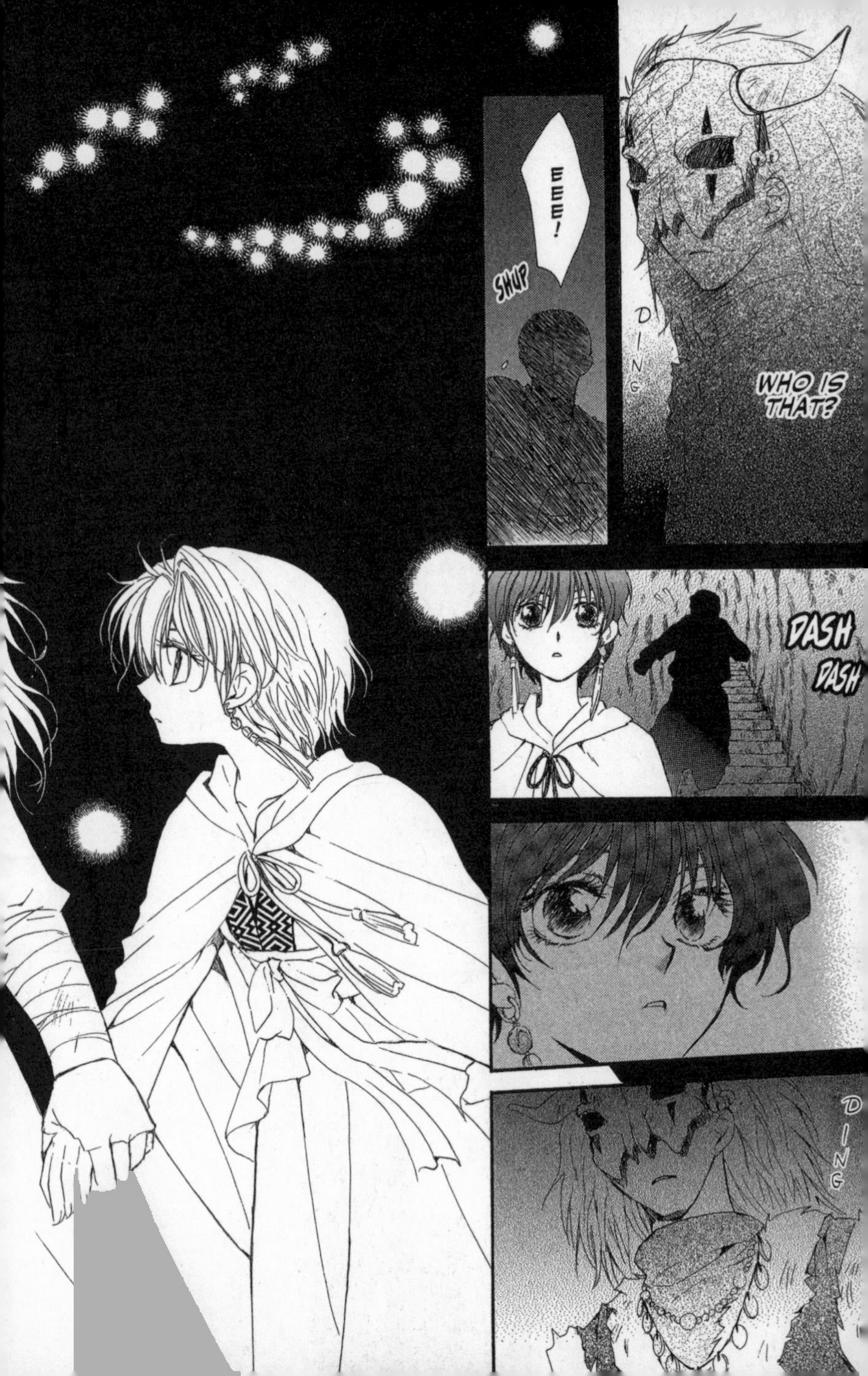
DING
WHO IS THAT?
EEEE!
SHUP
DASH
DASH
DING

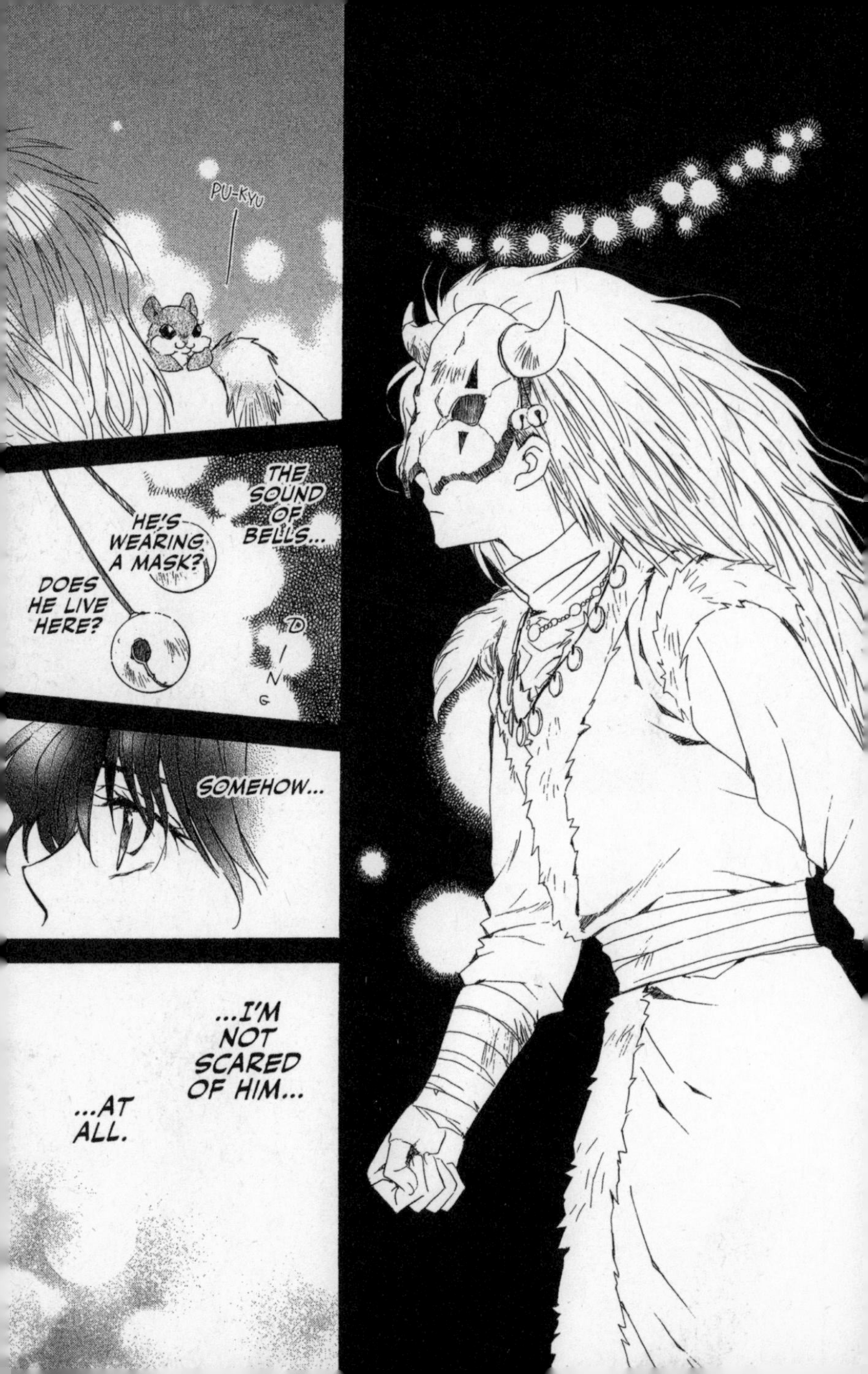
PU-KYU
THE SOUND OF BELLS...
HE'S WEARING A MASK?
DOES HE LIVE HERE?
DING
SOMEHOW...
...I'M NOT SCARED OF HIM...
...AT ALL.

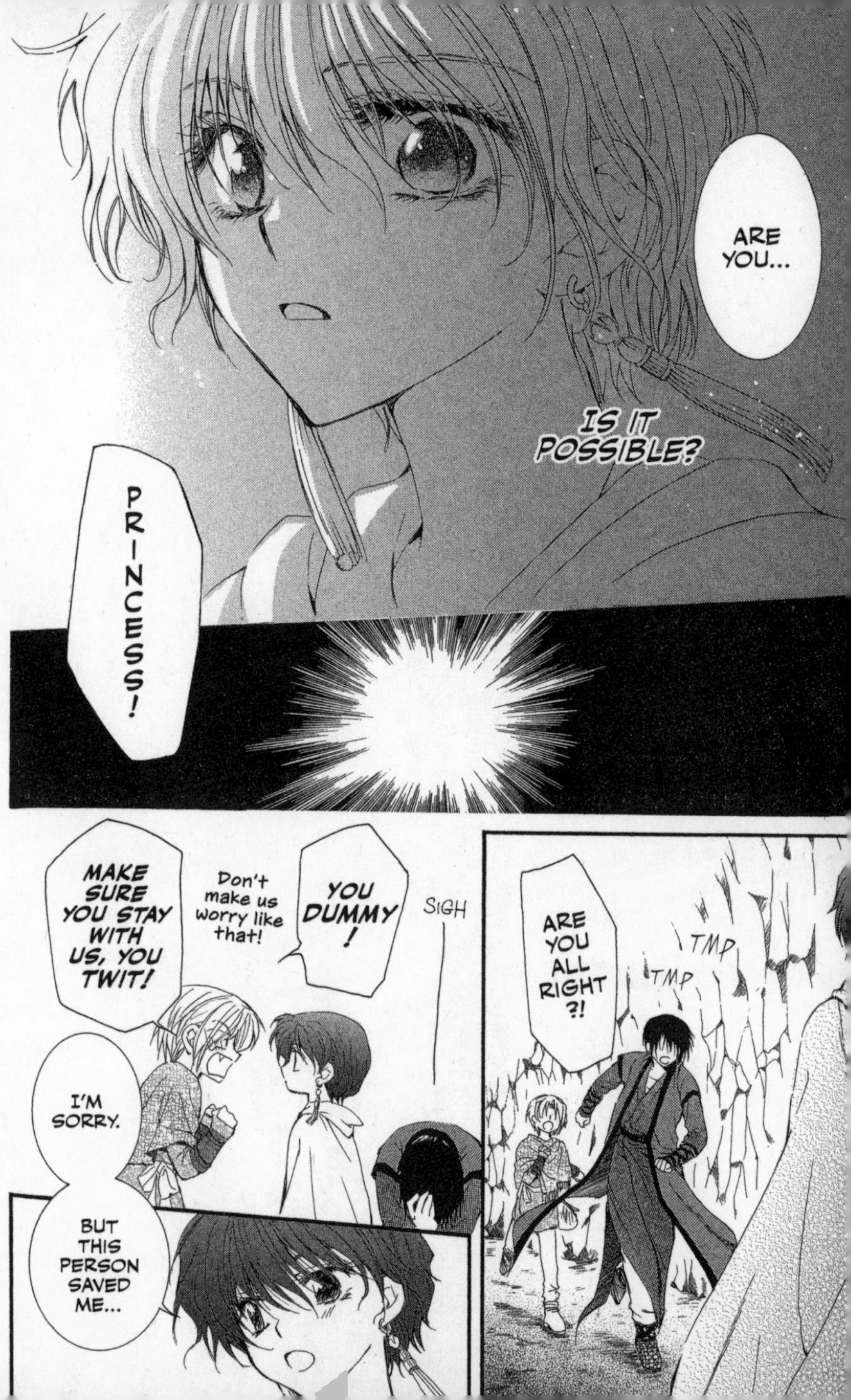
ARE YOU...
IS IT POSSIBLE?
PRINCESS!
ARE YOU ALL RIGHT?!
TMP
TMP
SIGH
YOU DUMMY!
Don't make us worry like that!
MAKE SURE YOU STAY WITH US, YOU TWIT!
I'M SORRY.
BUT THIS PERSON SAVED ME...

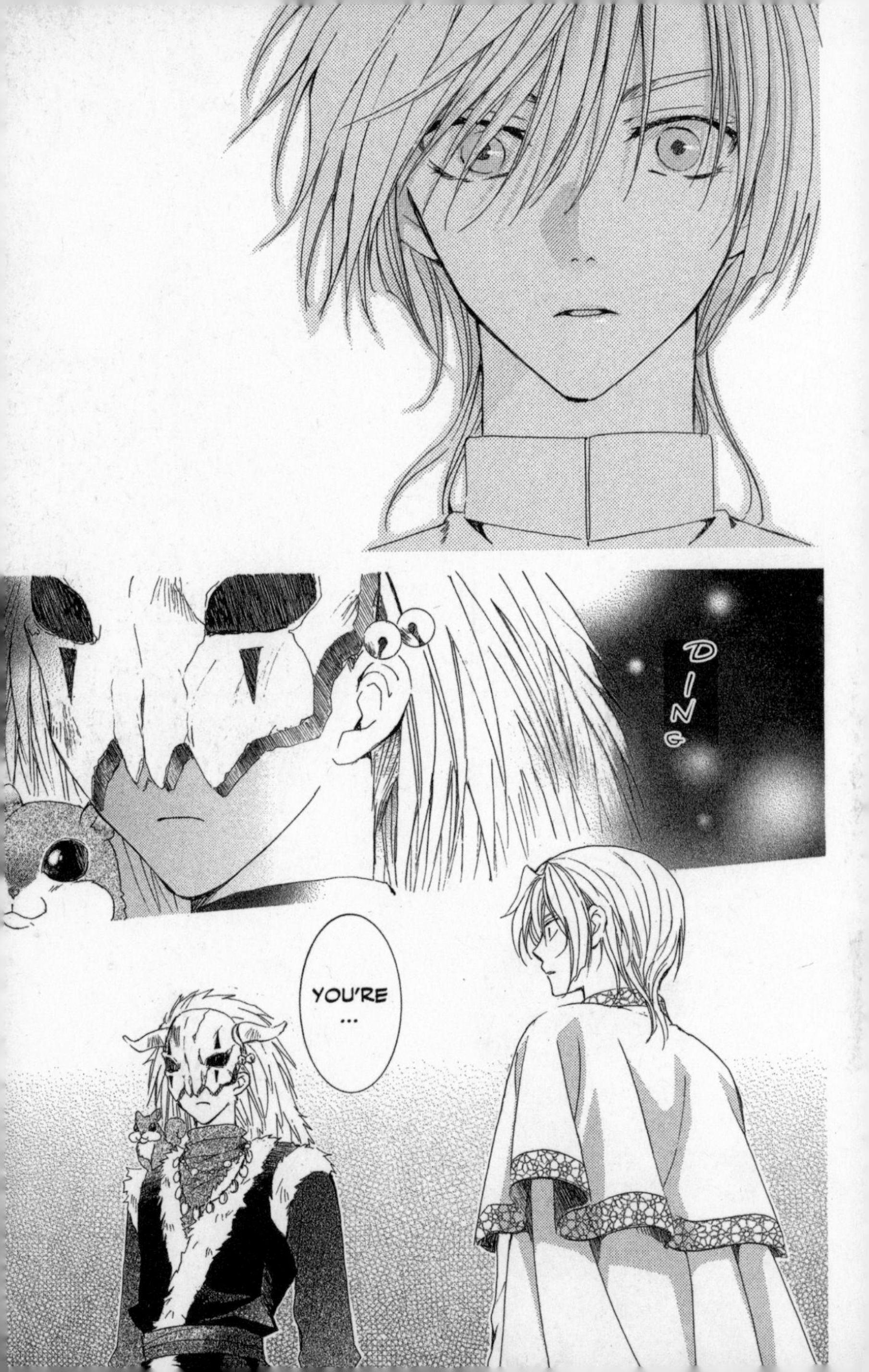
DING
YOU'RE ...

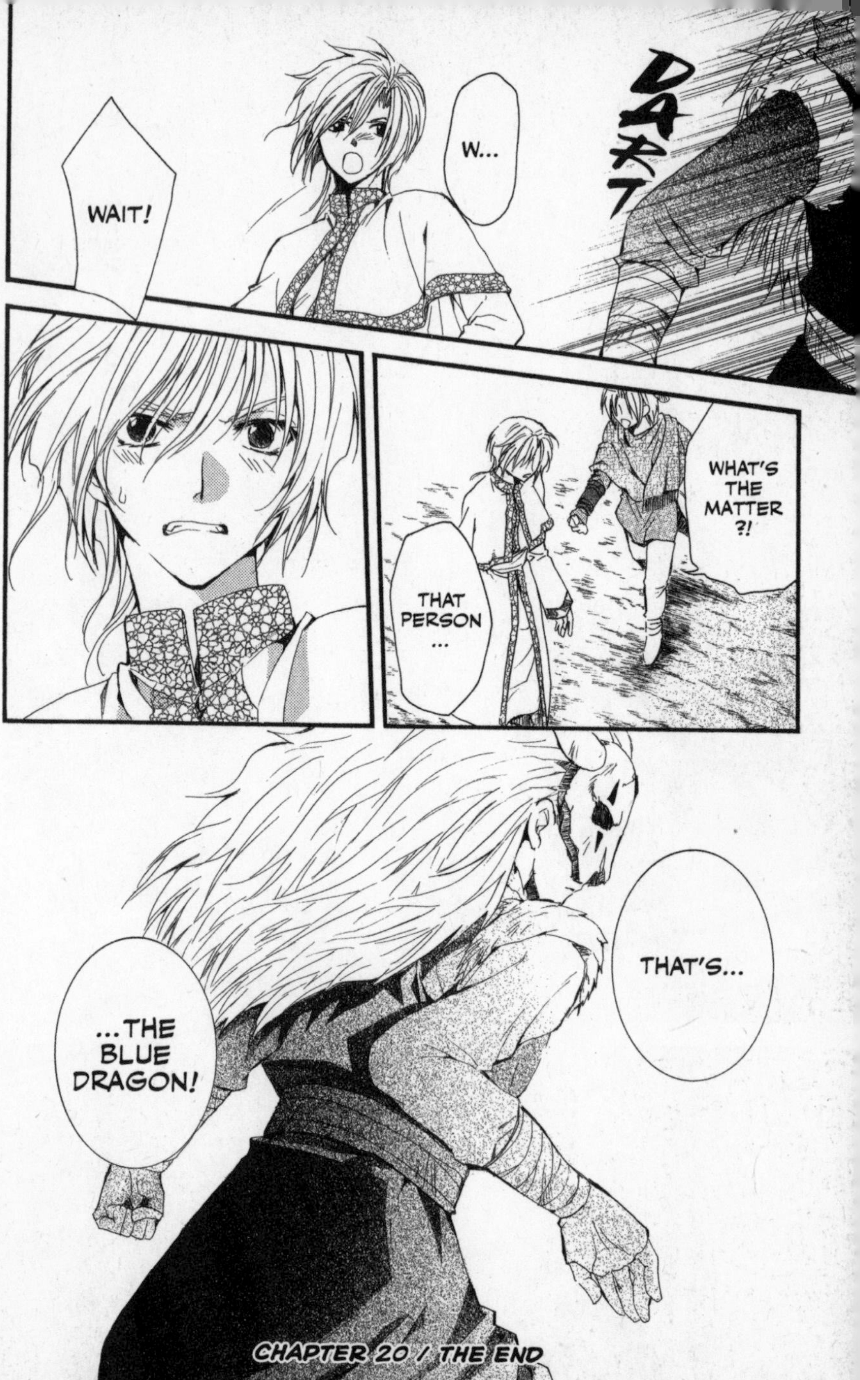
DART
W...
WAIT!
WHAT'S THE MATTER ?!
THAT PERSON ...
THAT'S...
...THE BLUE DRAGON!
CHAPTER 20 / THE END

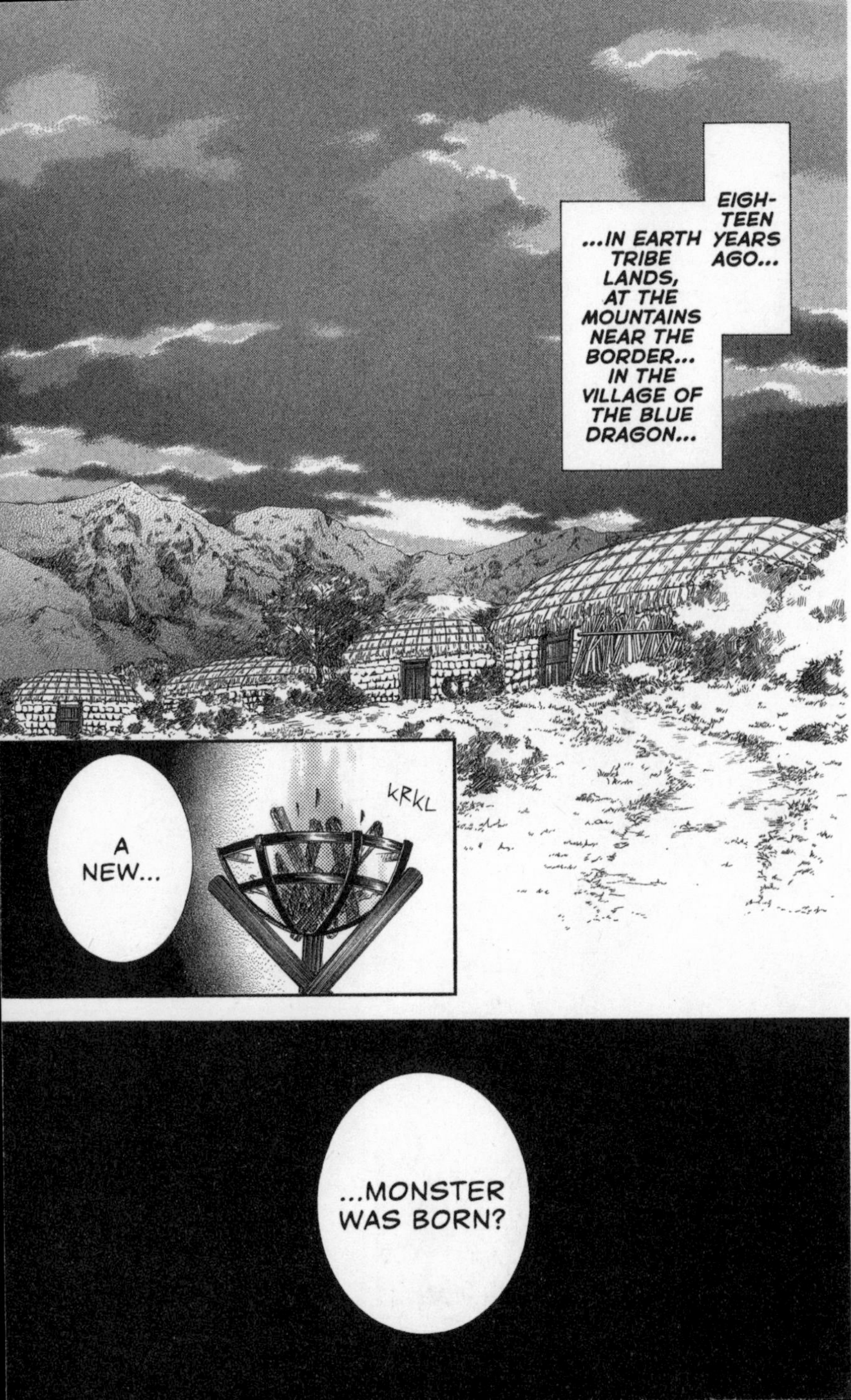
EIGHTEEN YEARS AGO...
...IN EARTH TRIBE LANDS, AT THE MOUNTAINS NEAR THE BORDER... IN THE VILLAGE OF THE BLUE DRAGON...
KRKL
A NEW...
...MONSTER WAS BORN?

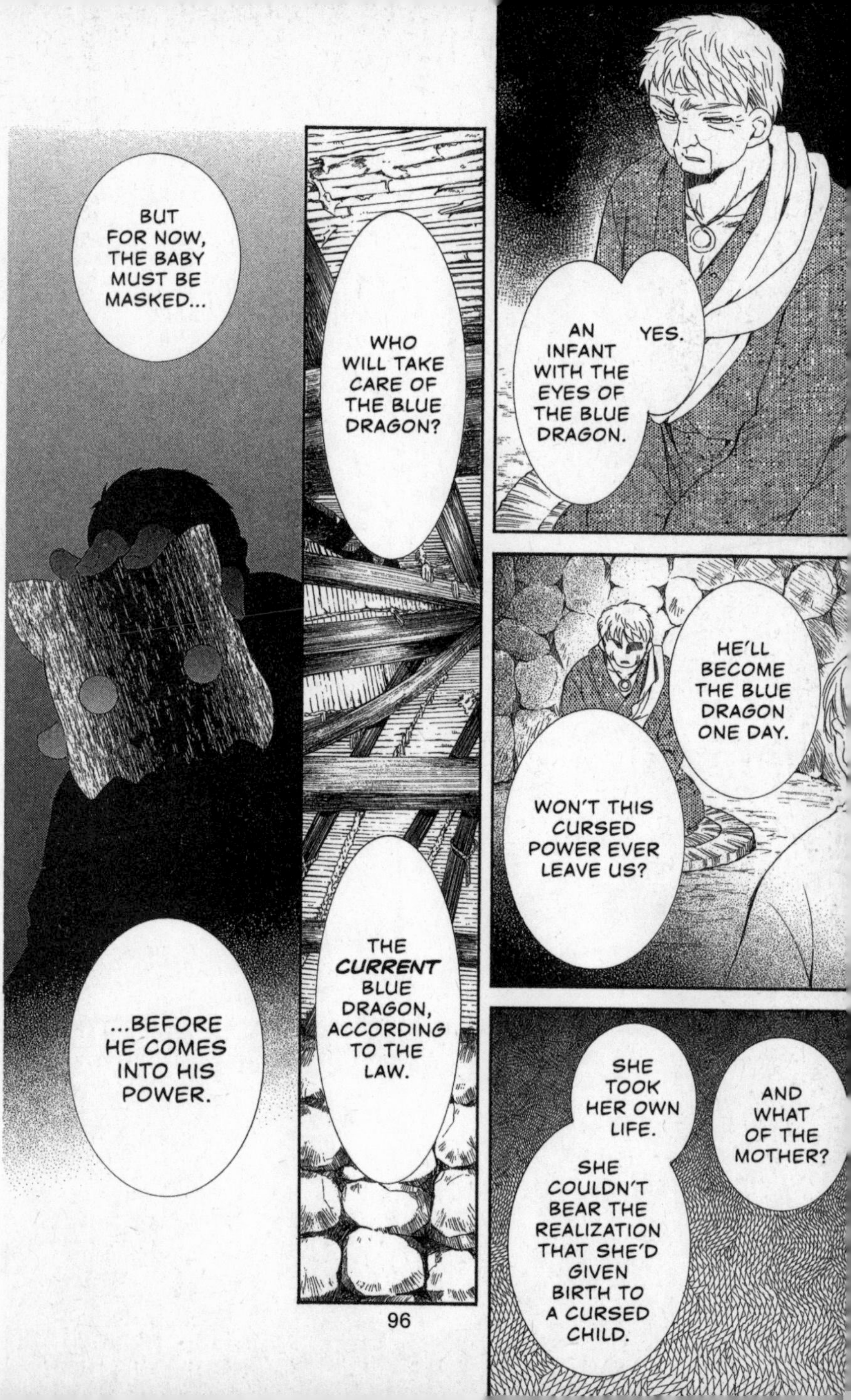
YES.
AN INFANT WITH THE EYES OF THE BLUE DRAGON.
HE'LL BECOME THE BLUE DRAGON ONE DAY.
WON'T THIS CURSED POWER EVER LEAVE US?
AND WHAT OF THE MOTHER?
SHE TOOK HER OWN LIFE.
SHE COULDN'T BEAR THE REALIZATION THAT SHE'D GIVEN BIRTH TO A CURSED CHILD.
WHO WILL TAKE CARE OF THE BLUE DRAGON?
THE *CURRENT* BLUE DRAGON, ACCORDING TO THE LAW.
BUT FOR NOW, THE BABY MUST BE MASKED...
...BEFORE HE COMES INTO HIS POWER.

CHAPTER 21: THE BLINDFOLDED DRAGON

MY FIRST
MEMORY...

...WAS OF
DARKNESS.

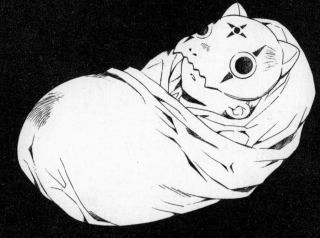

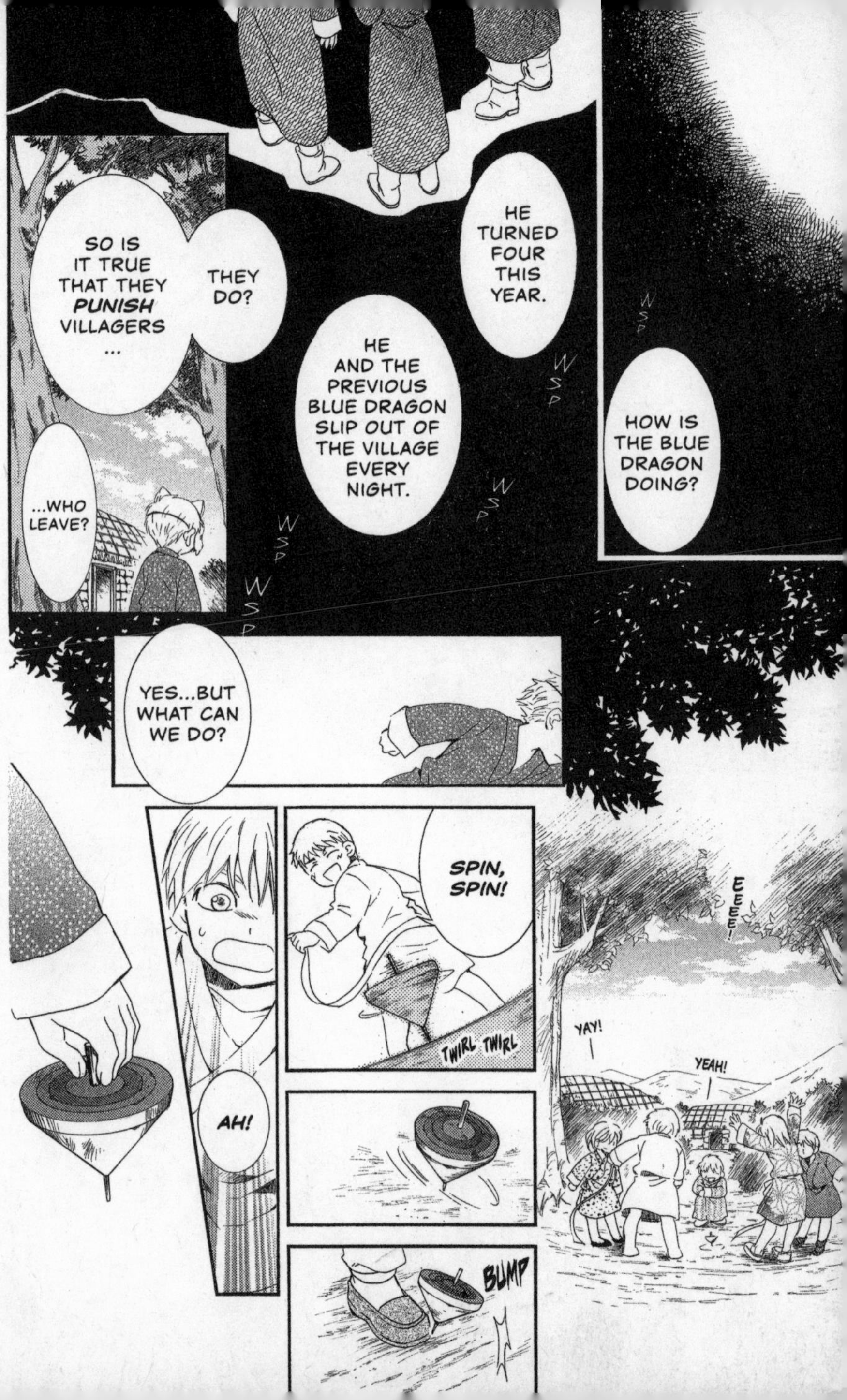
HOW IS THE BLUE DRAGON DOING?
HE TURNED FOUR THIS YEAR.
HE AND THE PREVIOUS BLUE DRAGON SLIP OUT OF THE VILLAGE EVERY NIGHT.
WSP
WSP
WSP
WSP
THEY DO?
SO IS IT TRUE THAT THEY *PUNISH* VILLAGERS ...
...WHO LEAVE?
YES...BUT WHAT CAN WE DO?
EEEE!
YAY!
YEAH!
SPIN, SPIN!
TWIRL TWIRL
BUMP
AH!

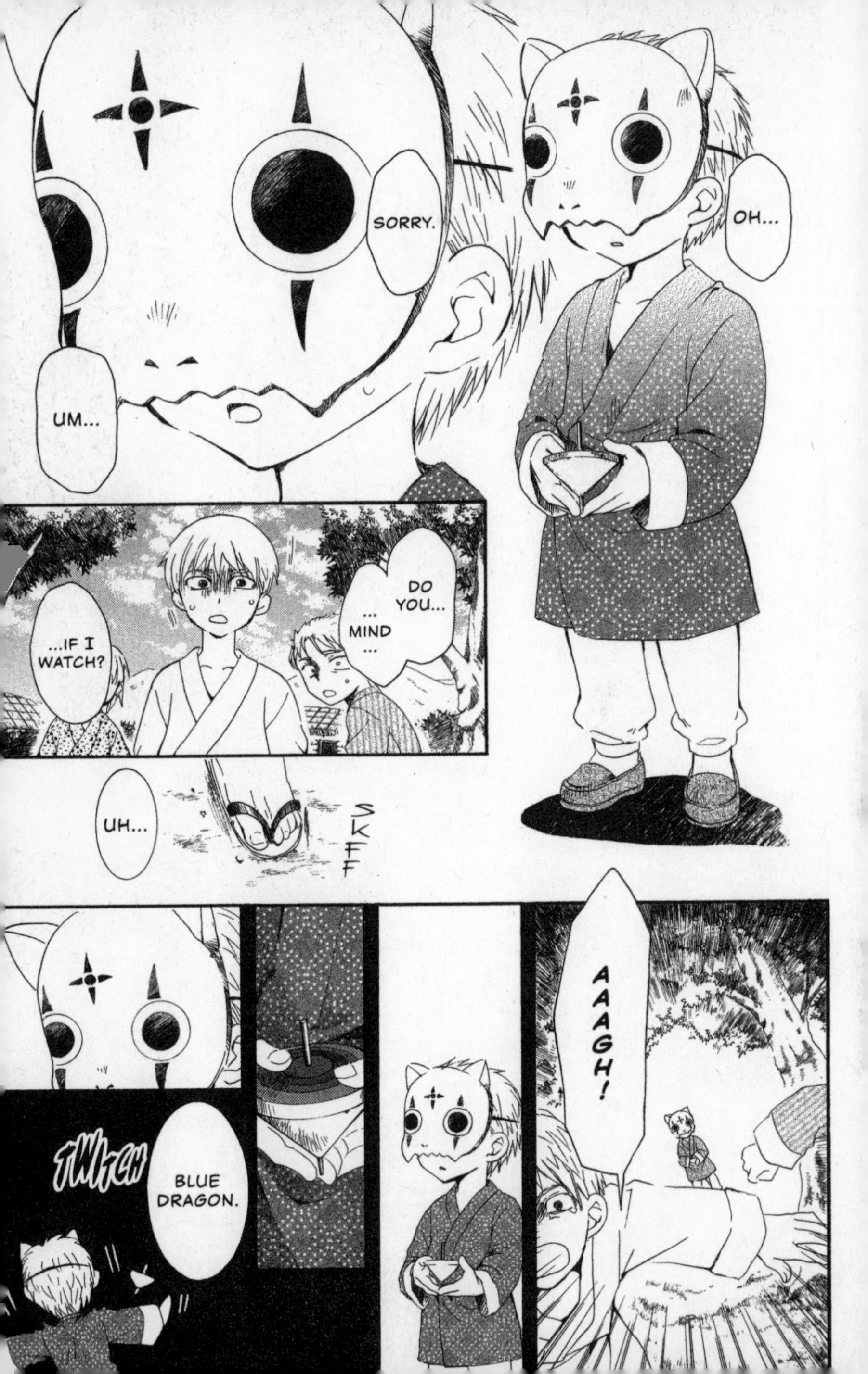
OH...
SORRY.
UM...
DO YOU...
...MIND...
...IF I WATCH?
UH...
SKFF
AAAGH!
TWITCH
BLUE DRAGON.

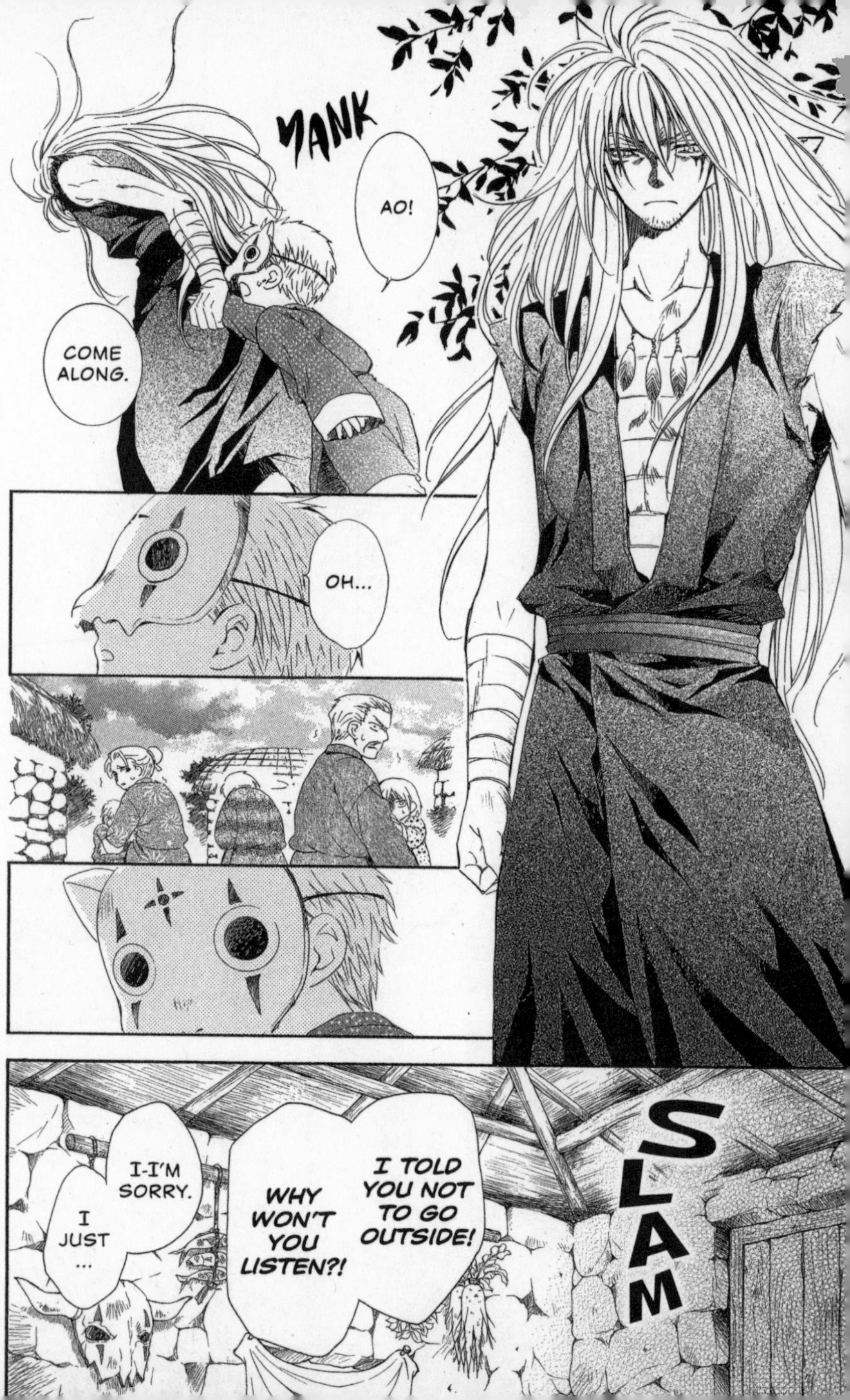
YANK
AO!
COME ALONG.
OH...
SLAM
I TOLD YOU NOT TO GO OUTSIDE!
WHY WON'T YOU LISTEN?!
I-I'M SORRY.
I JUST ...

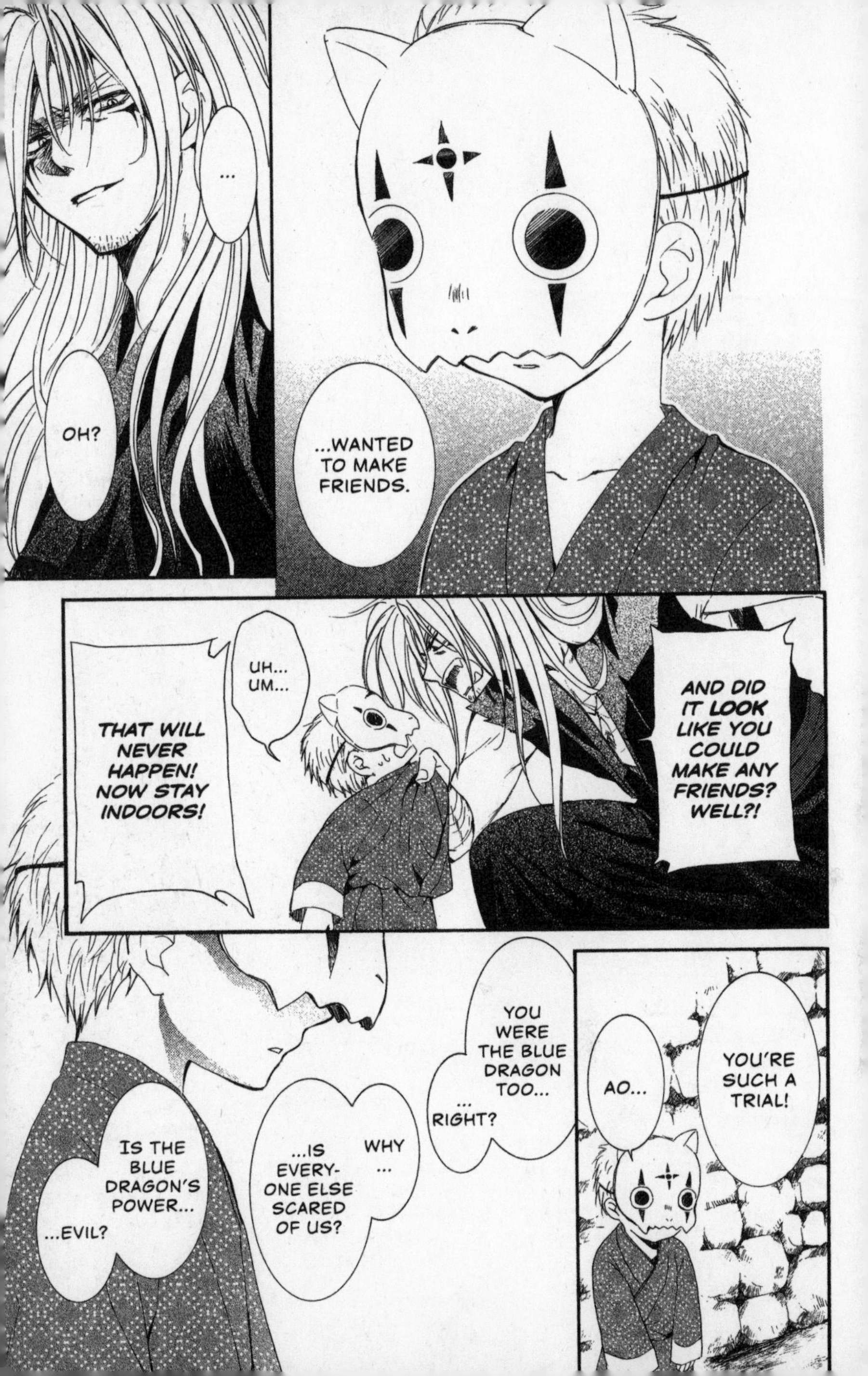
...WANTED TO MAKE FRIENDS.
...
OH?
AND DID IT LOOK LIKE YOU COULD MAKE ANY FRIENDS? WELL?!
UH... UM...
THAT WILL NEVER HAPPEN! NOW STAY INDOORS!
YOU'RE SUCH A TRIAL!
AO...
YOU WERE THE BLUE DRAGON TOO... ...RIGHT?
WHY ...
...IS EVERY-ONE ELSE SCARED OF US?
IS THE BLUE DRAGON'S POWER...
...EVIL?

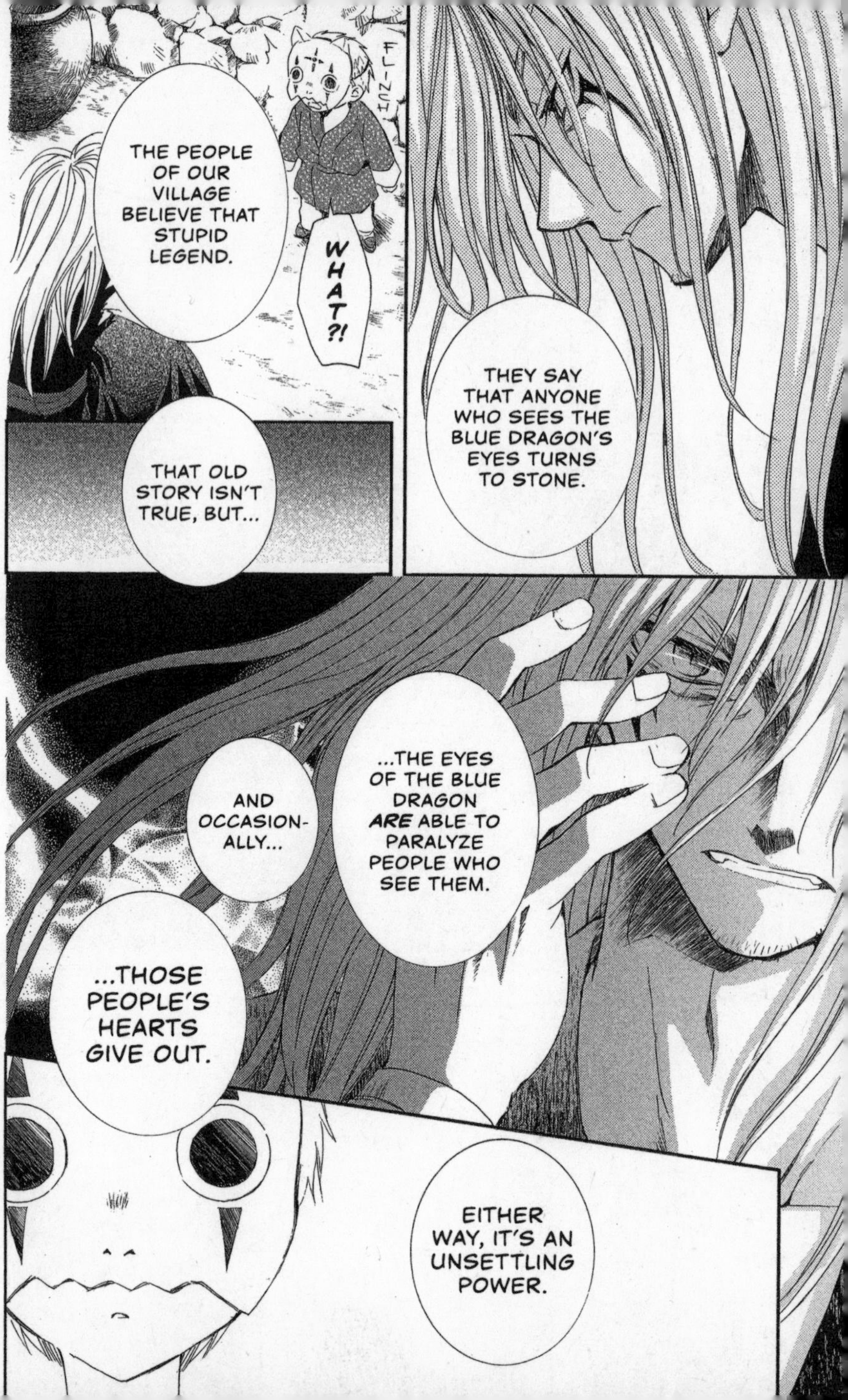
THEY SAY THAT ANYONE WHO SEES THE BLUE DRAGON'S EYES TURNS TO STONE.
FLINCH
THE PEOPLE OF OUR VILLAGE BELIEVE THAT STUPID LEGEND.
WHAT?!
THAT OLD STORY ISN'T TRUE, BUT...
...THE EYES OF THE BLUE DRAGON *ARE* ABLE TO PARALYZE PEOPLE WHO SEE THEM.
AND OCCASIONALLY...
...THOSE PEOPLE'S HEARTS GIVE OUT.
EITHER WAY, IT'S AN UNSETTLING POWER.

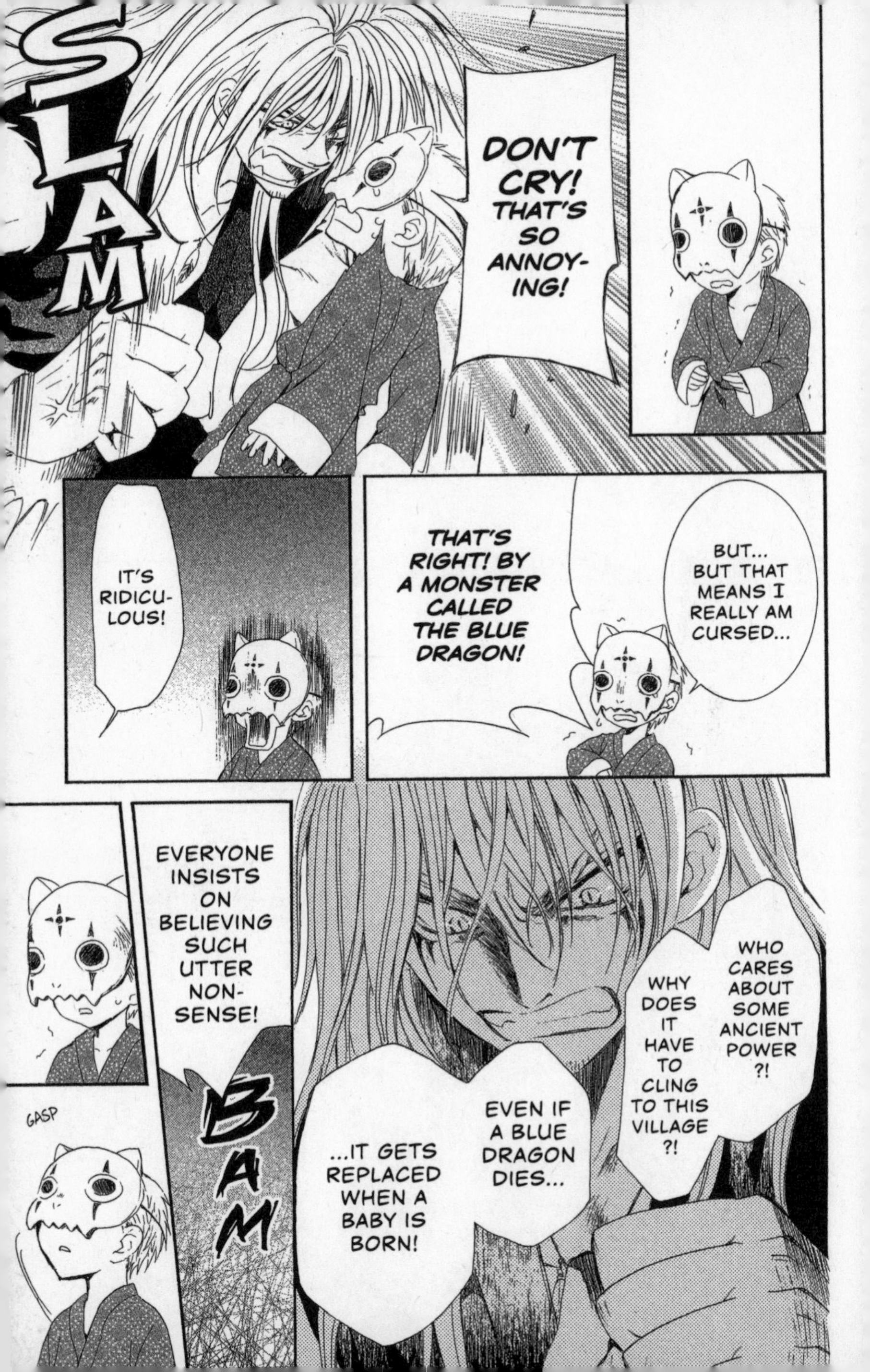
DON'T CRY! THAT'S SO ANNOYING!
SLAM
BUT... BUT THAT MEANS I REALLY AM CURSED...
THAT'S RIGHT! BY A MONSTER CALLED THE BLUE DRAGON!
IT'S RIDICULOUS!
WHO CARES ABOUT SOME ANCIENT POWER?!
WHY DOES IT HAVE TO CLING TO THIS VILLAGE?!
EVEN IF A BLUE DRAGON DIES...
...IT GETS REPLACED WHEN A BABY IS BORN!
EVERYONE INSISTS ON BELIEVING SUCH UTTER NONSENSE!
BAM
GASP

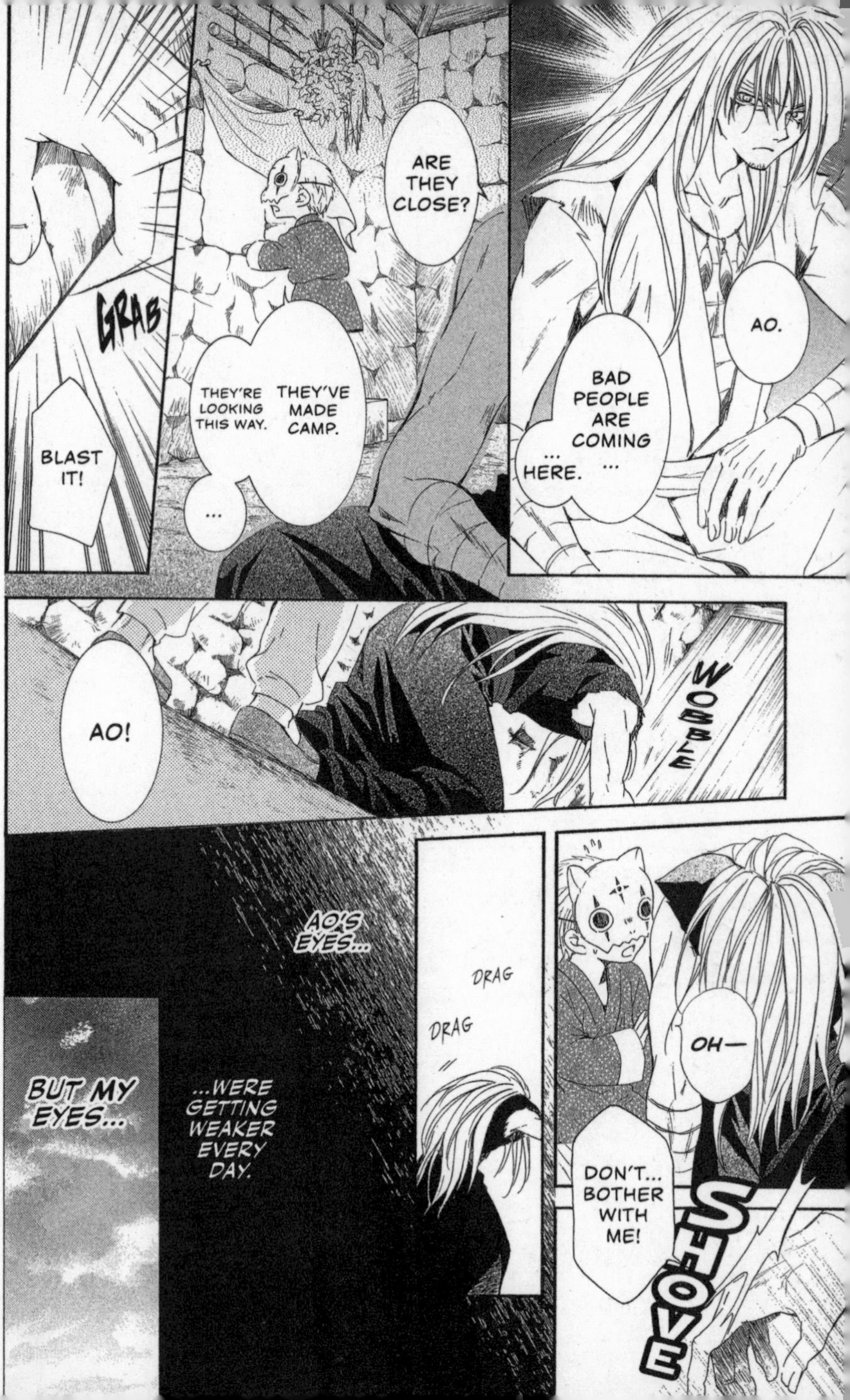

AO.
BAD PEOPLE ARE COMING ... ... HERE.
ARE THEY CLOSE?
THEY'VE MADE CAMP.
THEY'RE LOOKING THIS WAY.
...
GRAB
BLAST IT!
WOBBLE
AO!
OH—
DON'T... BOTHER WITH ME!
SHOVE
DRAG
DRAG
AO'S EYES...
...WERE GETTING WEAKER EVERY DAY.
BUT MY EYES...

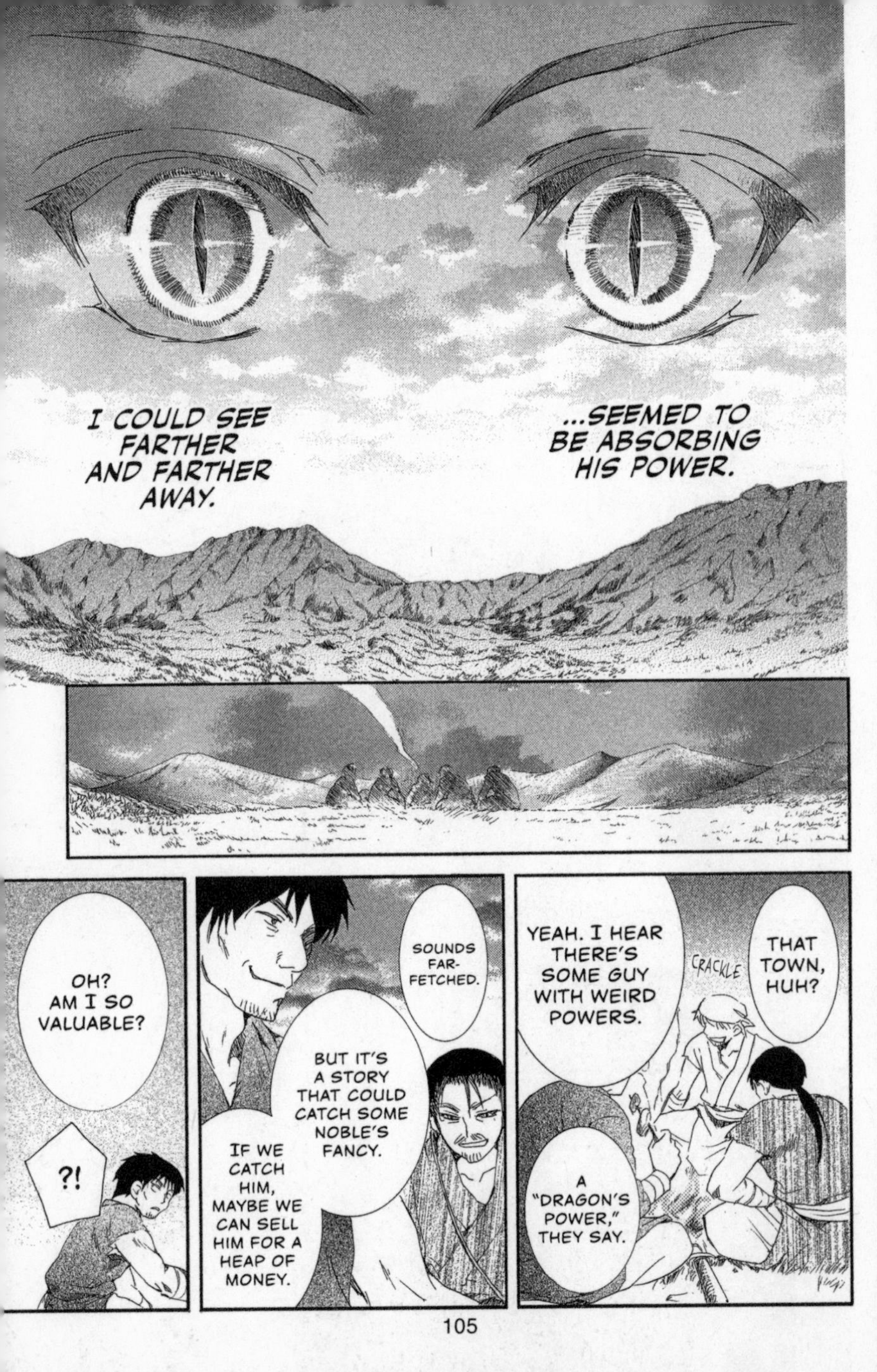
...SEEMED TO BE ABSORBING HIS POWER.
I COULD SEE FARTHER AND FARTHER AWAY.
THAT TOWN, HUH?
CRACKLE
YEAH. I HEAR THERE'S SOME GUY WITH WEIRD POWERS.
A "DRAGON'S POWER," THEY SAY.
SOUNDS FAR-FETCHED.
BUT IT'S A STORY THAT COULD CATCH SOME NOBLE'S FANCY.
IF WE CATCH HIM, MAYBE WE CAN SELL HIM FOR A HEAP OF MONEY.
OH? AM I SO VALUABLE?
?!

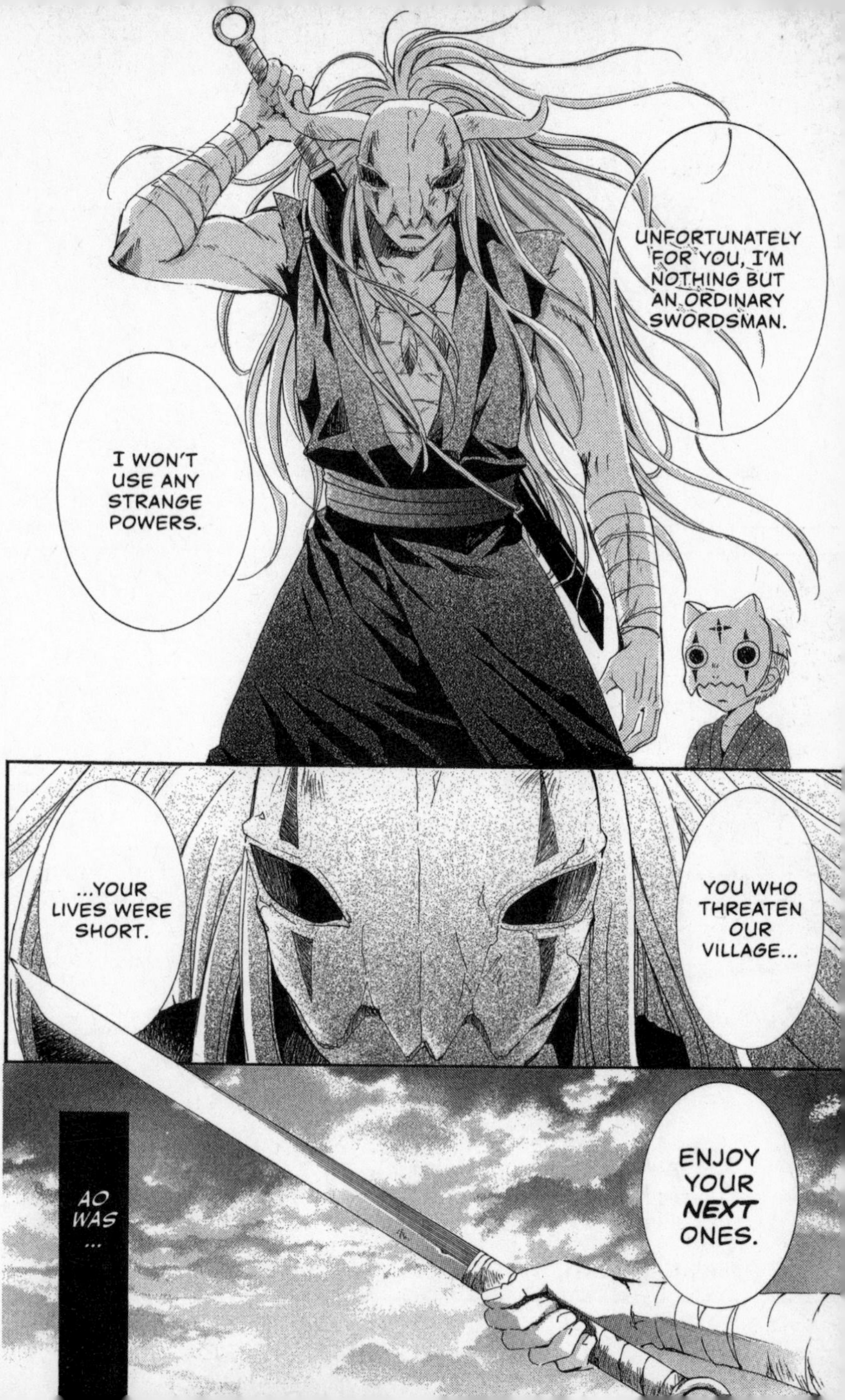
UNFORTUNATELY FOR YOU, I'M NOTHING BUT AN ORDINARY SWORDSMAN.
I WON'T USE ANY STRANGE POWERS.
YOU WHO THREATEN OUR VILLAGE...
...YOUR LIVES WERE SHORT.
ENJOY YOUR **NEXT** ONES.
AO WAS ...

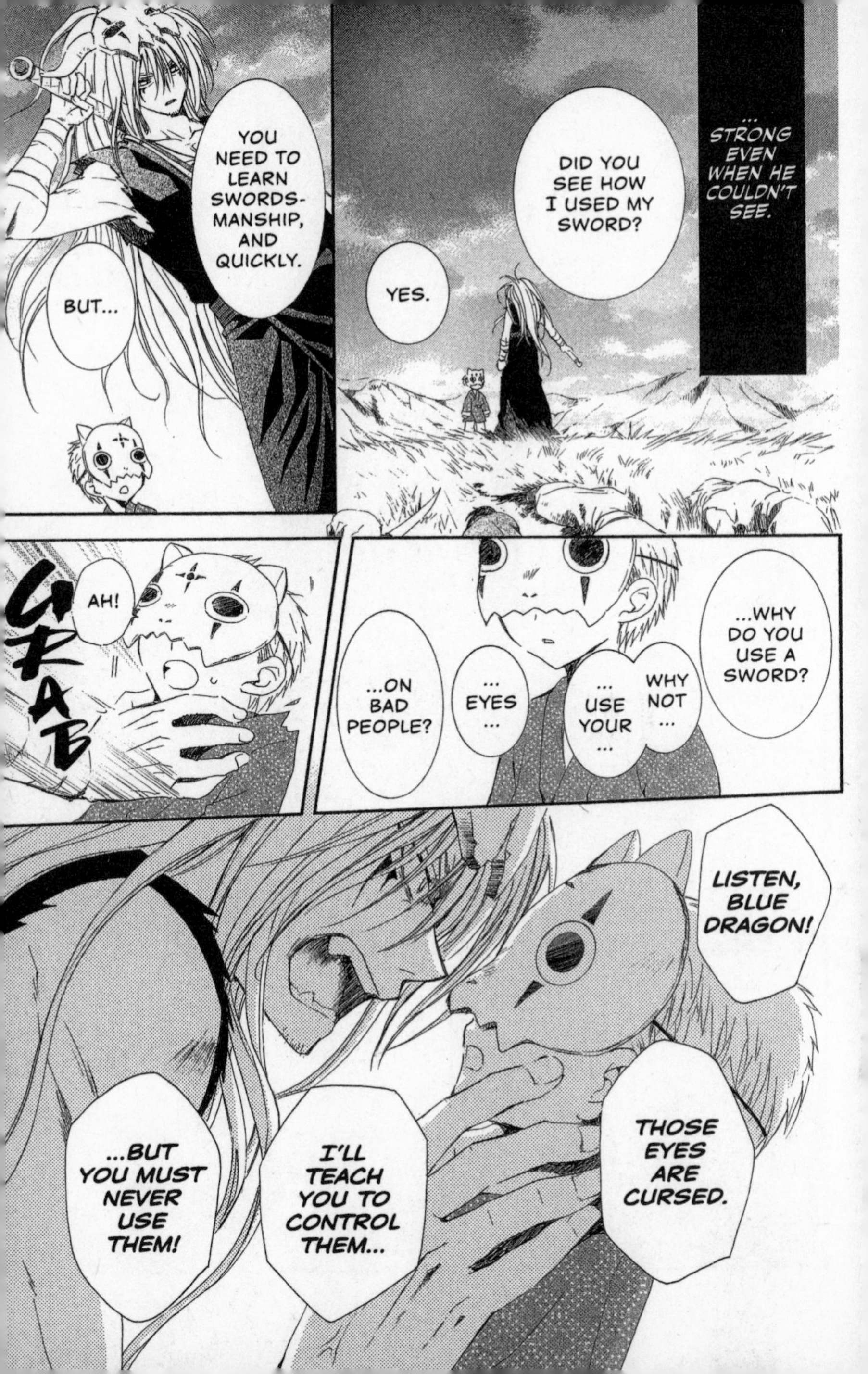
... STRONG EVEN WHEN HE COULDN'T SEE.
DID YOU SEE HOW I USED MY SWORD?
YES.
YOU NEED TO LEARN SWORDS-MANSHIP, AND QUICKLY.
BUT...
...WHY DO YOU USE A SWORD?
WHY NOT ...
... USE YOUR ...
... EYES ...
...ON BAD PEOPLE?
AH!
GRAB
LISTEN, BLUE DRAGON!
THOSE EYES ARE CURSED.
I'LL TEACH YOU TO CONTROL THEM...
...BUT YOU MUST NEVER USE THEM!

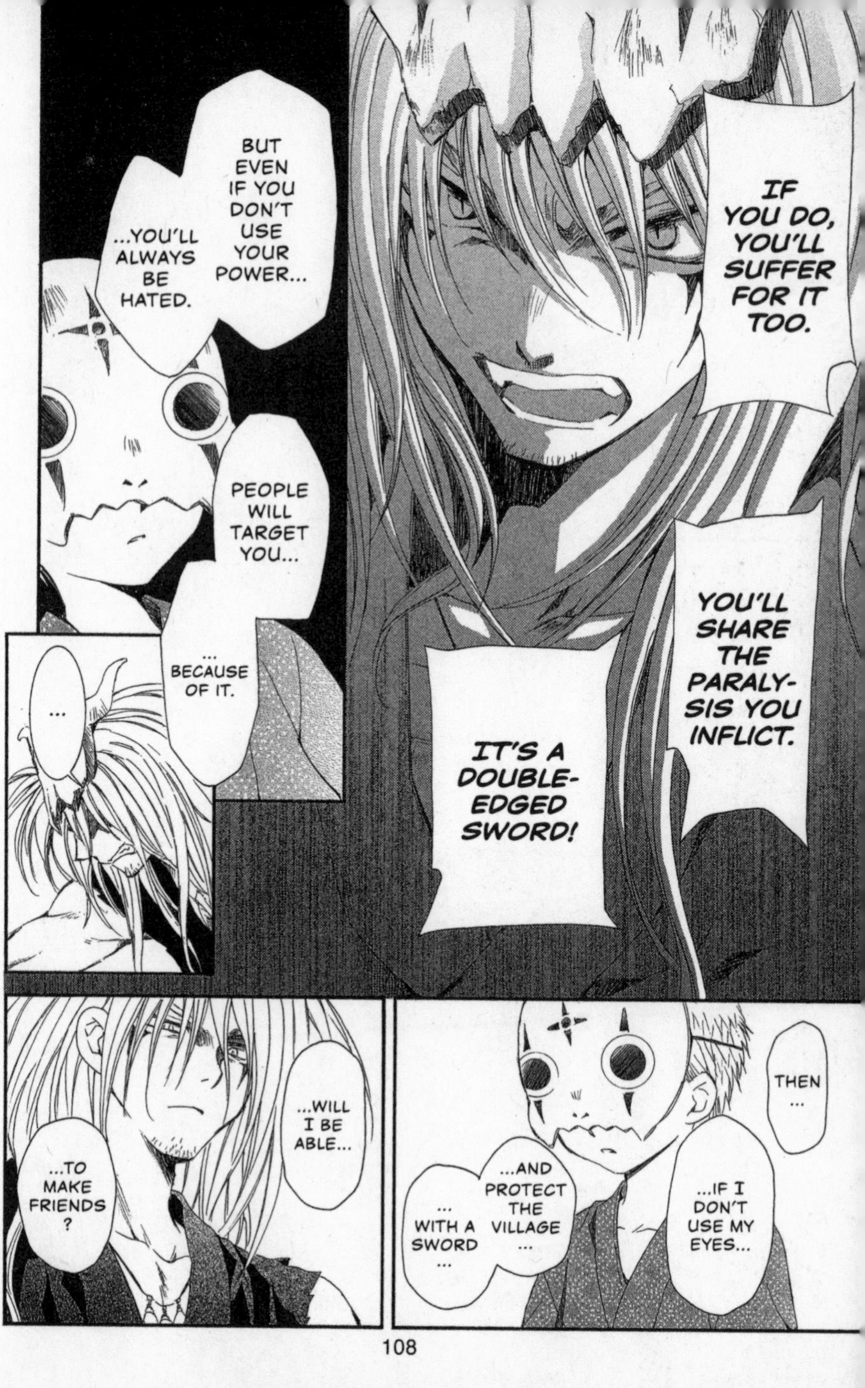
IF YOU DO, YOU'LL SUFFER FOR IT TOO.
YOU'LL SHARE THE PARALYSIS YOU INFLICT.
IT'S A DOUBLE-EDGED SWORD!
BUT EVEN IF YOU DON'T USE YOUR POWER...
...YOU'LL ALWAYS BE HATED.
PEOPLE WILL TARGET YOU...
...BECAUSE OF IT.
...
THEN...
...IF I DON'T USE MY EYES...
...AND PROTECT THE VILLAGE...
...WITH A SWORD...
...WILL I BE ABLE...
...TO MAKE FRIENDS?

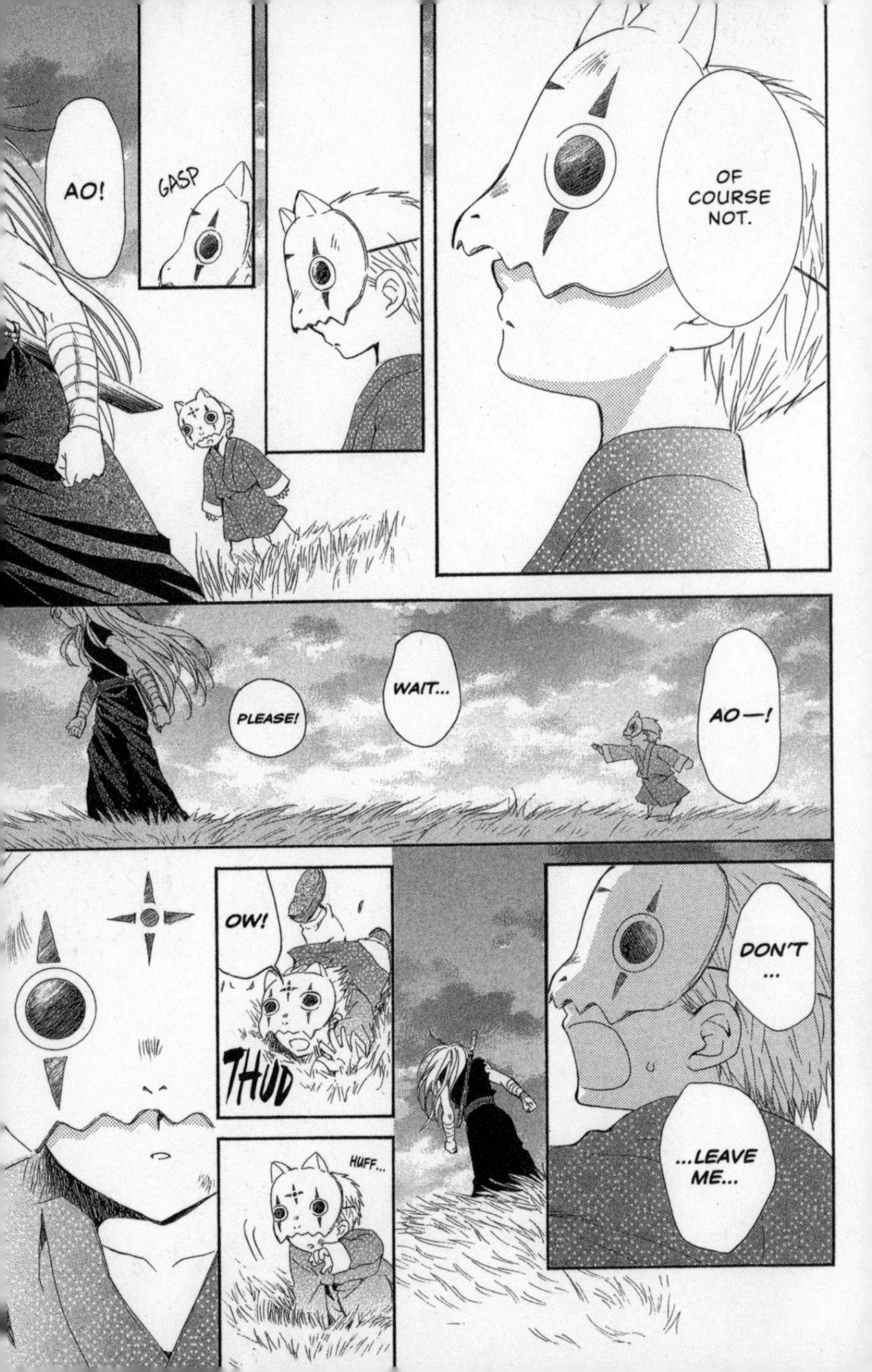
OF COURSE NOT.
GASP
AO!
AO—!
WAIT...
PLEASE!
DON'T ...
...LEAVE ME...
OW!
THUD
HUFF...

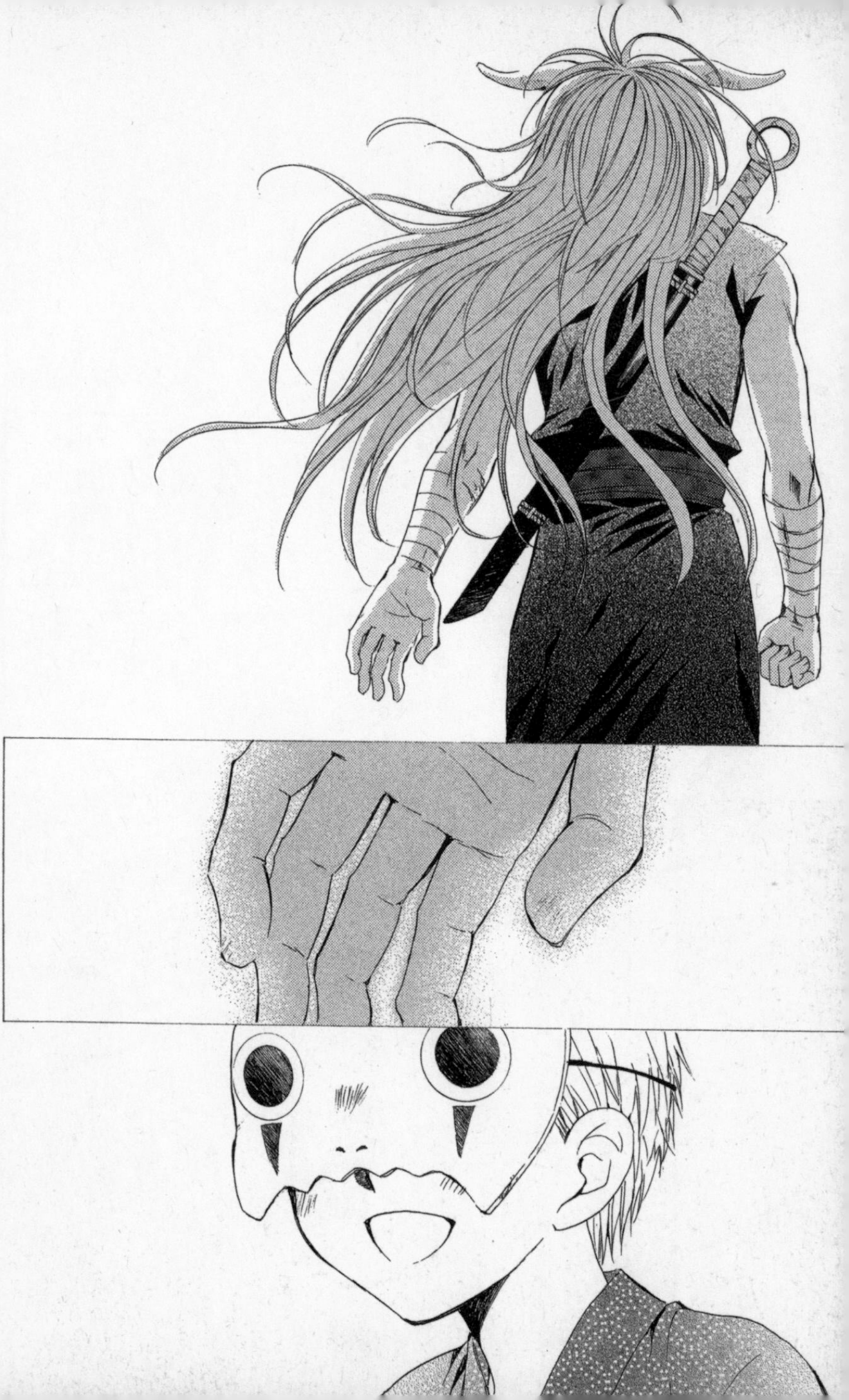

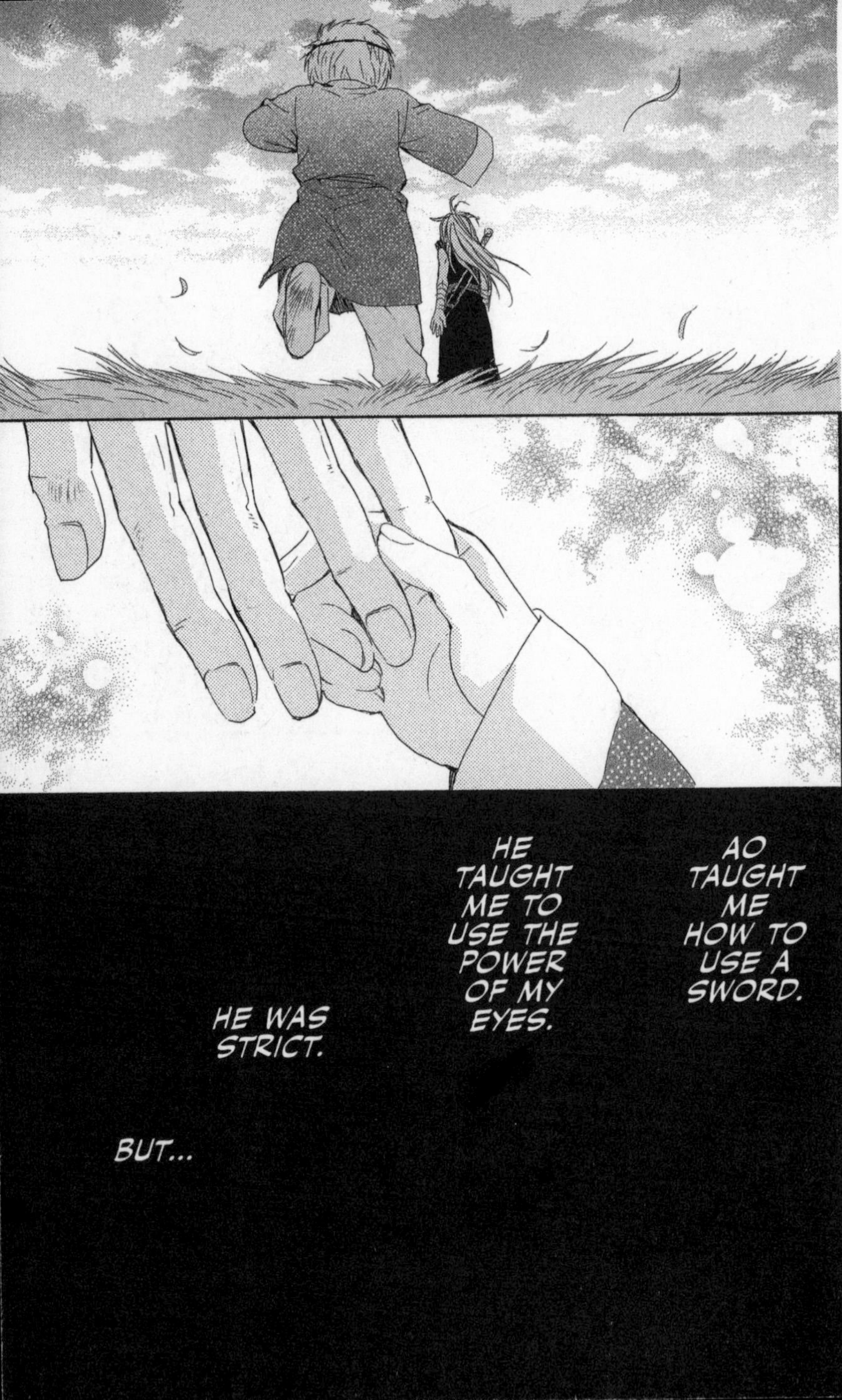
AO TAUGHT ME HOW TO USE A SWORD.
HE TAUGHT ME TO USE THE POWER OF MY EYES.
HE WAS STRICT.
BUT...

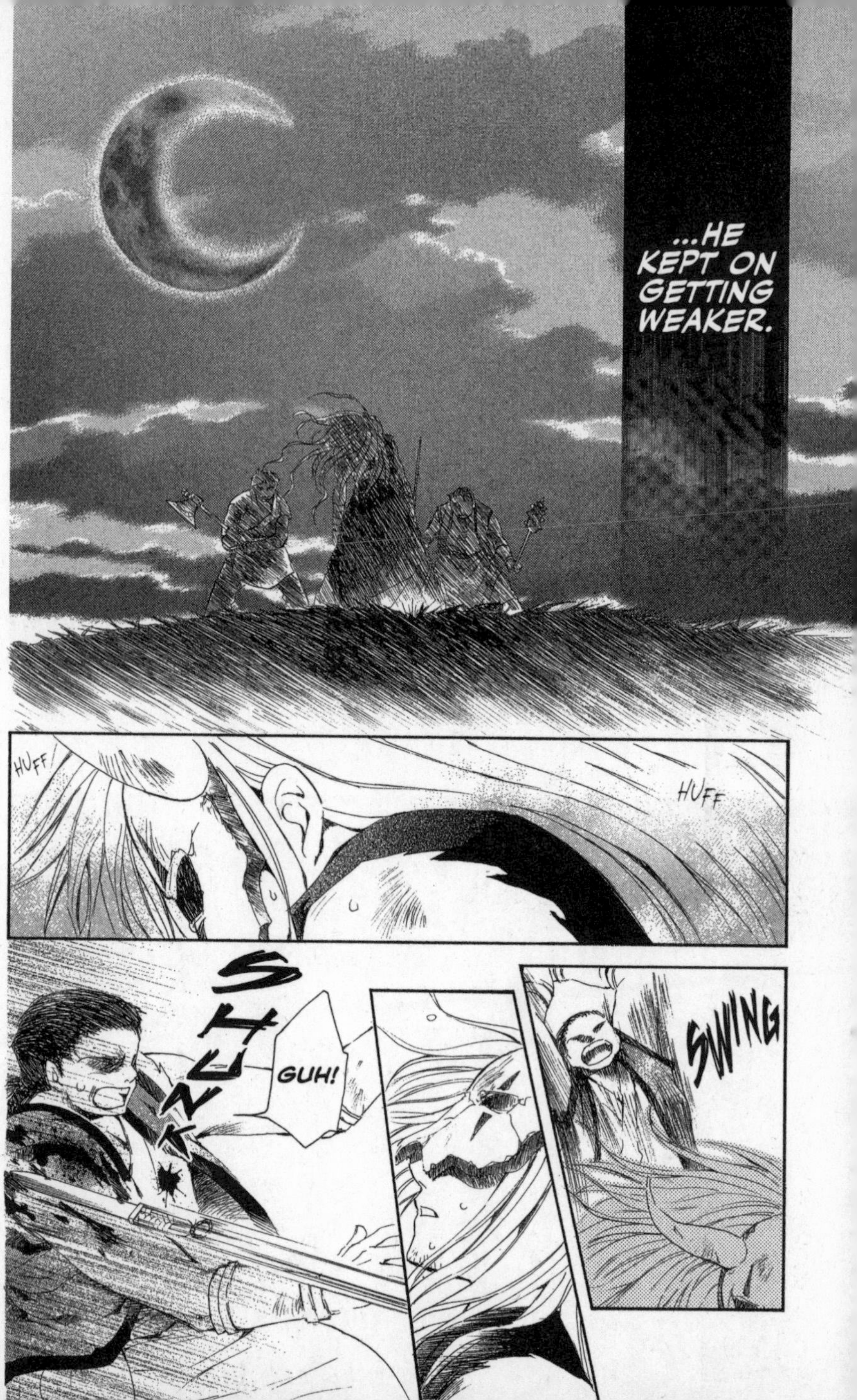
...HE KEPT ON GETTING WEAKER.
HUFF
HUFF!
SWING
SHUNK
GUH!

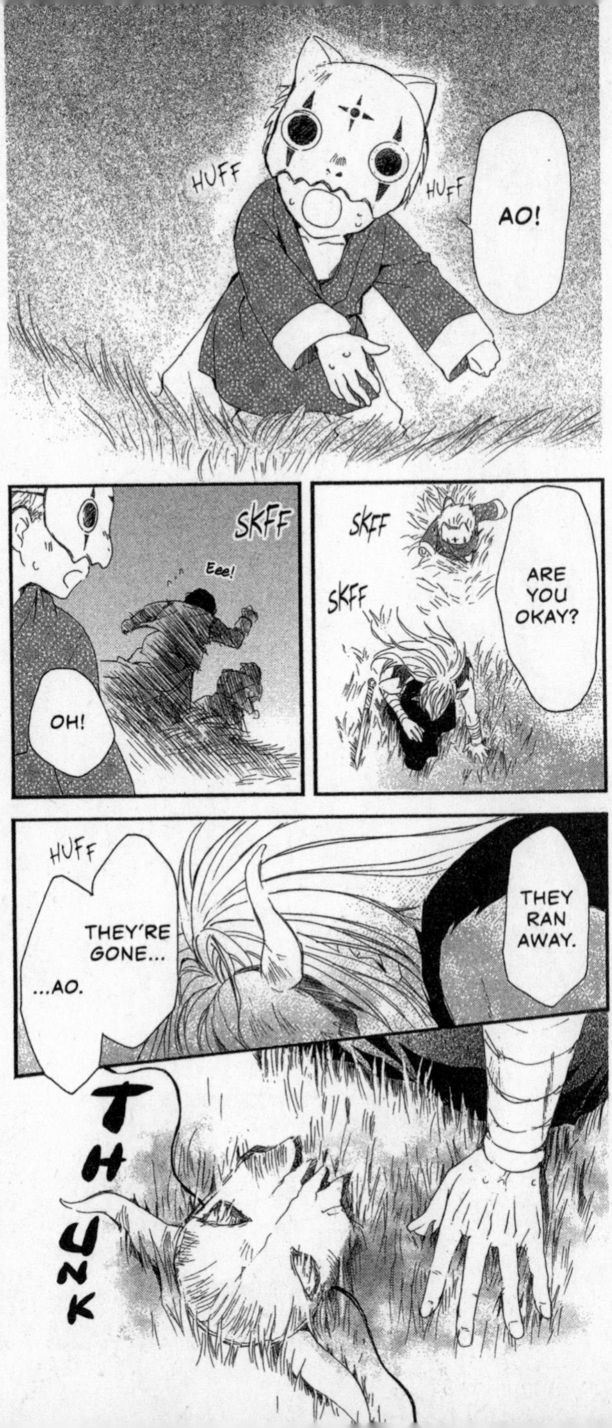

HUFF
HUFF
AO!
SKFF
SKFF
ARE YOU OKAY?
SKFF
Eee!
OH!
THEY RAN AWAY.
HUFF
THEY'RE GONE...
...AO.
THUNK

About the last panel of this page...

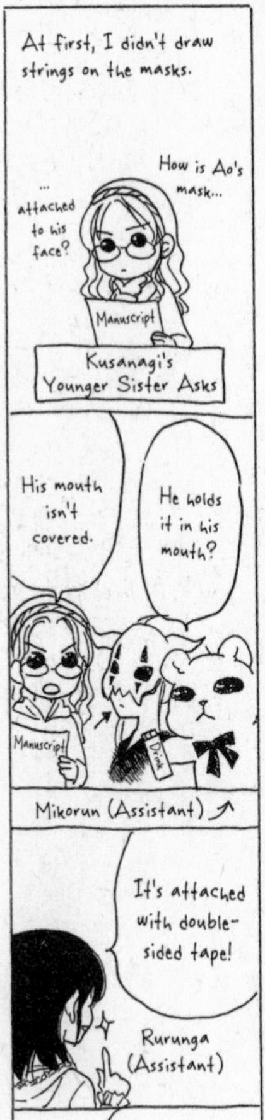

At first, I didn't draw strings on the masks.
How is Ao's mask...
...attached to his face?
Manuscript
Kusanagi's Younger Sister Asks
His mouth isn't covered.
He holds it in his mouth?
Manuscript
Drink
Mikorun (Assistant)
It's attached with double-sided tape!
Rurunga (Assistant)
I think it works like the NuBra!
Kyoko (Assistant)
Drink

If you ever visit the Village of the Blue Dragon, get me one of their famous masks made of NuBra material!

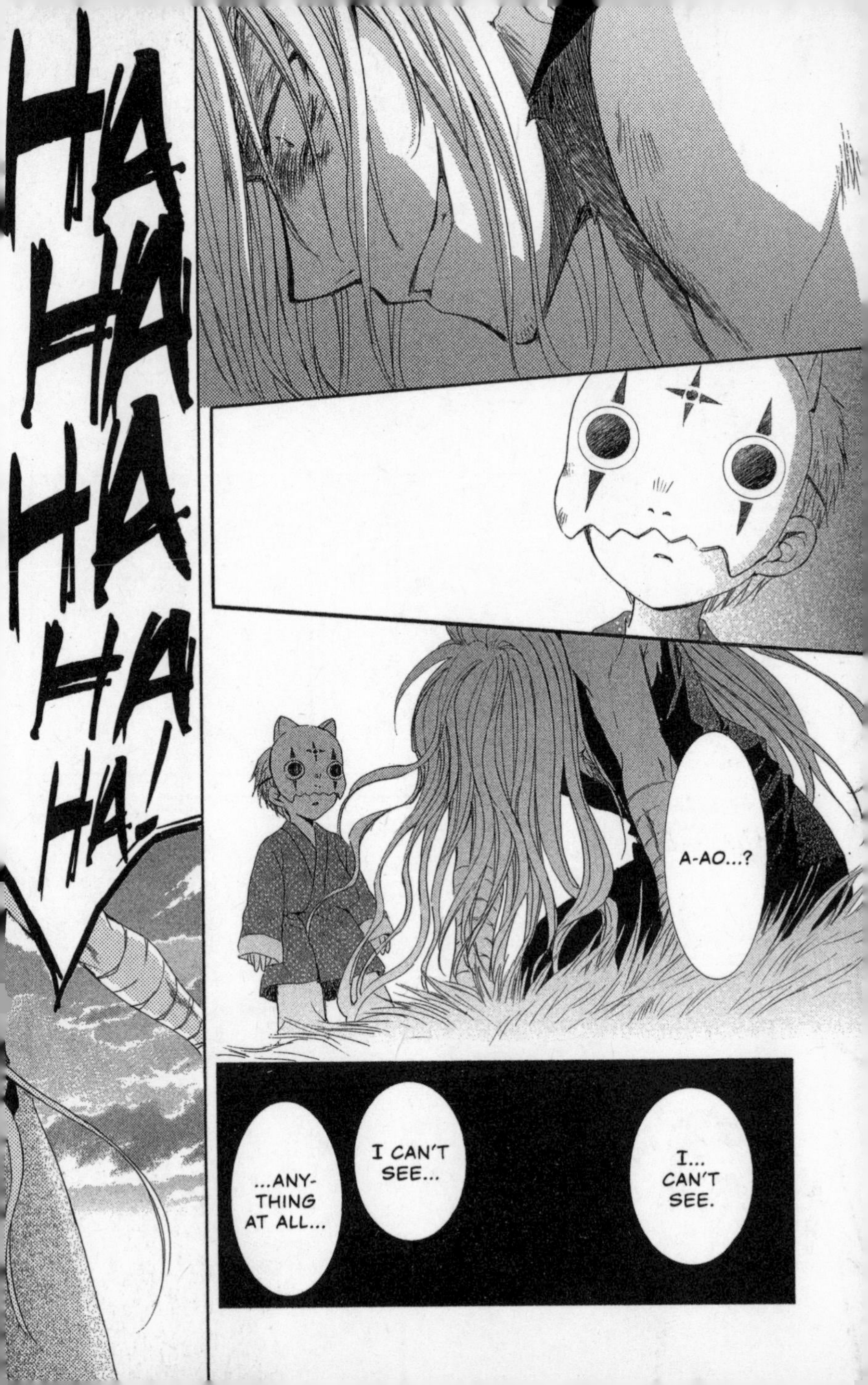
A-AO...?
I... CAN'T SEE.
I CAN'T SEE...
...ANY-THING AT ALL...
HA HA HA HA HA HA HA!

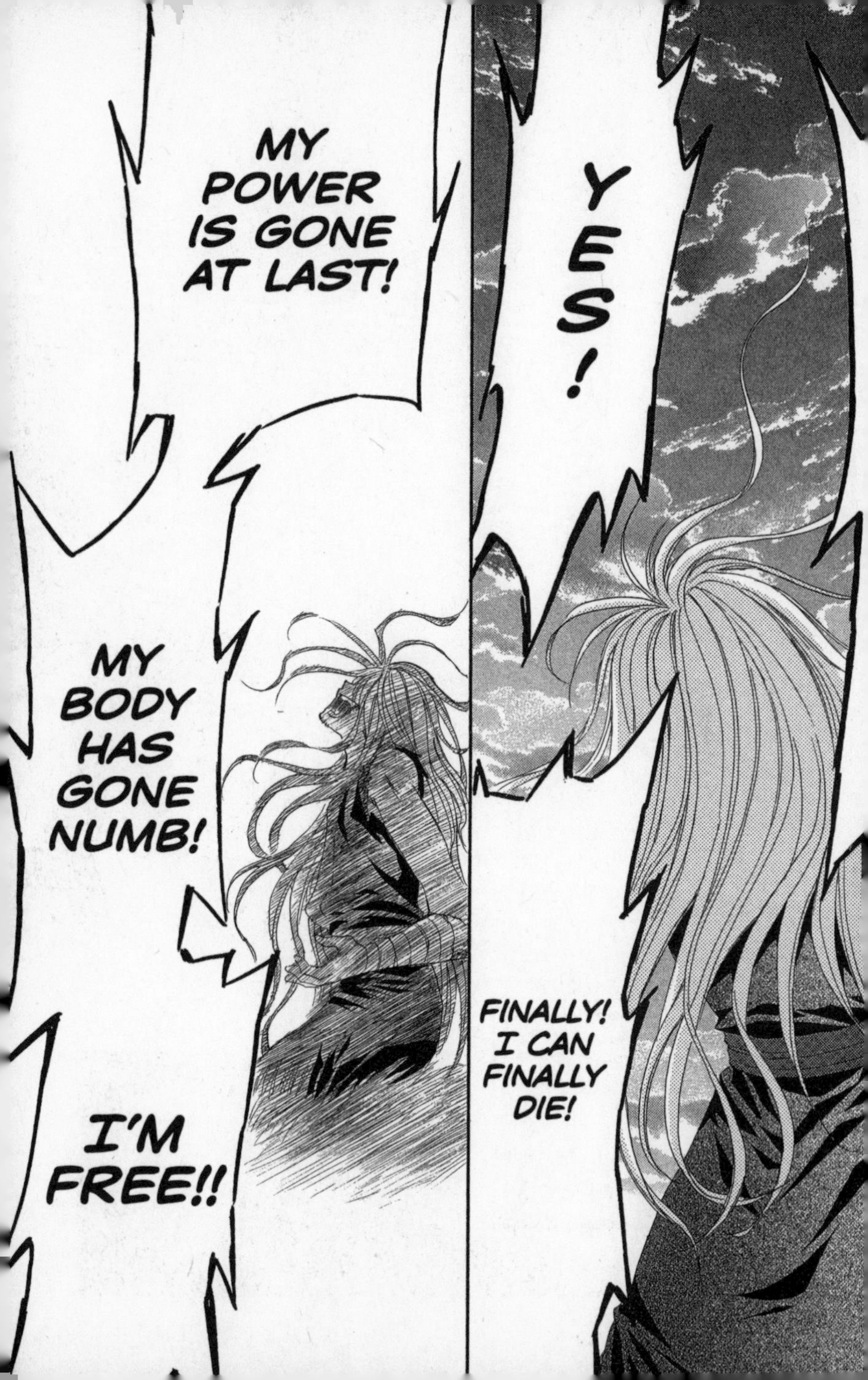
YES!
FINALLY! I CAN FINALLY DIE!
MY POWER IS GONE AT LAST!
MY BODY HAS GONE NUMB!
I'M FREE!!

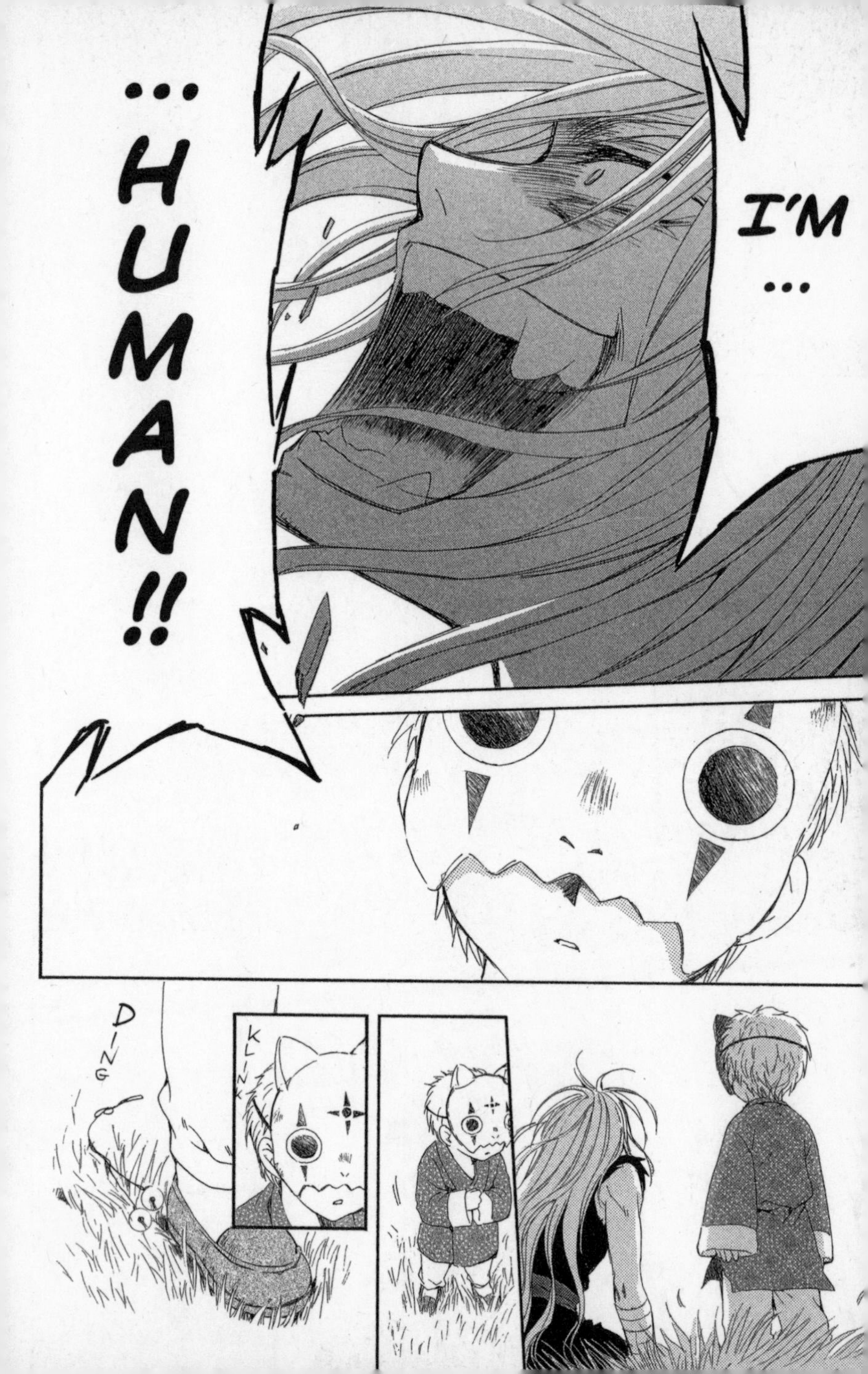
I'M ...
...HUMAN!!
KLINK
DING

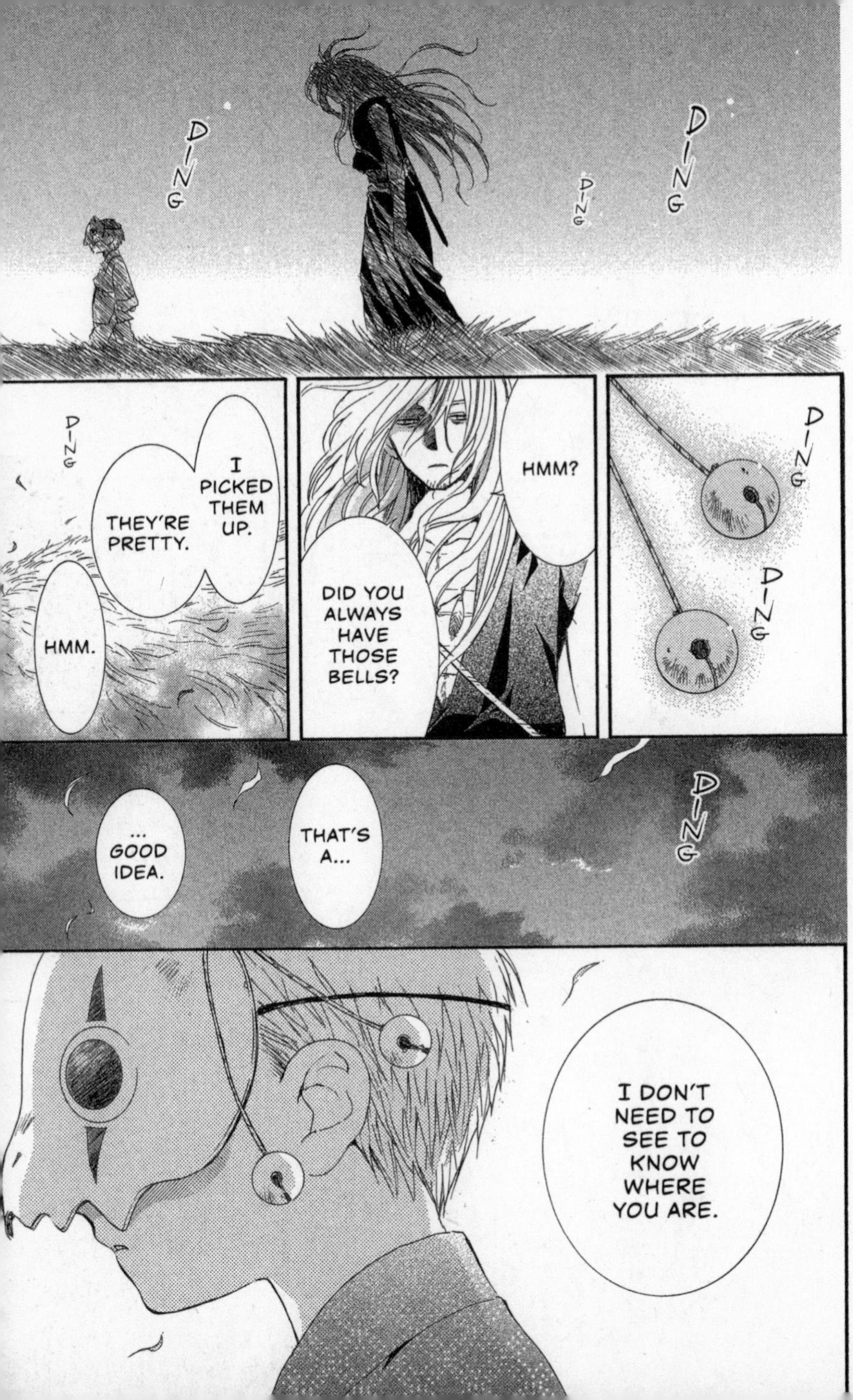
DING
DING
DING
DING
DING
HMM?
DID YOU ALWAYS HAVE THOSE BELLS?
I PICKED THEM UP.
THEY'RE PRETTY.
HMM.
DING
DING
THAT'S A...
...GOOD IDEA.
I DON'T NEED TO SEE TO KNOW WHERE YOU ARE.

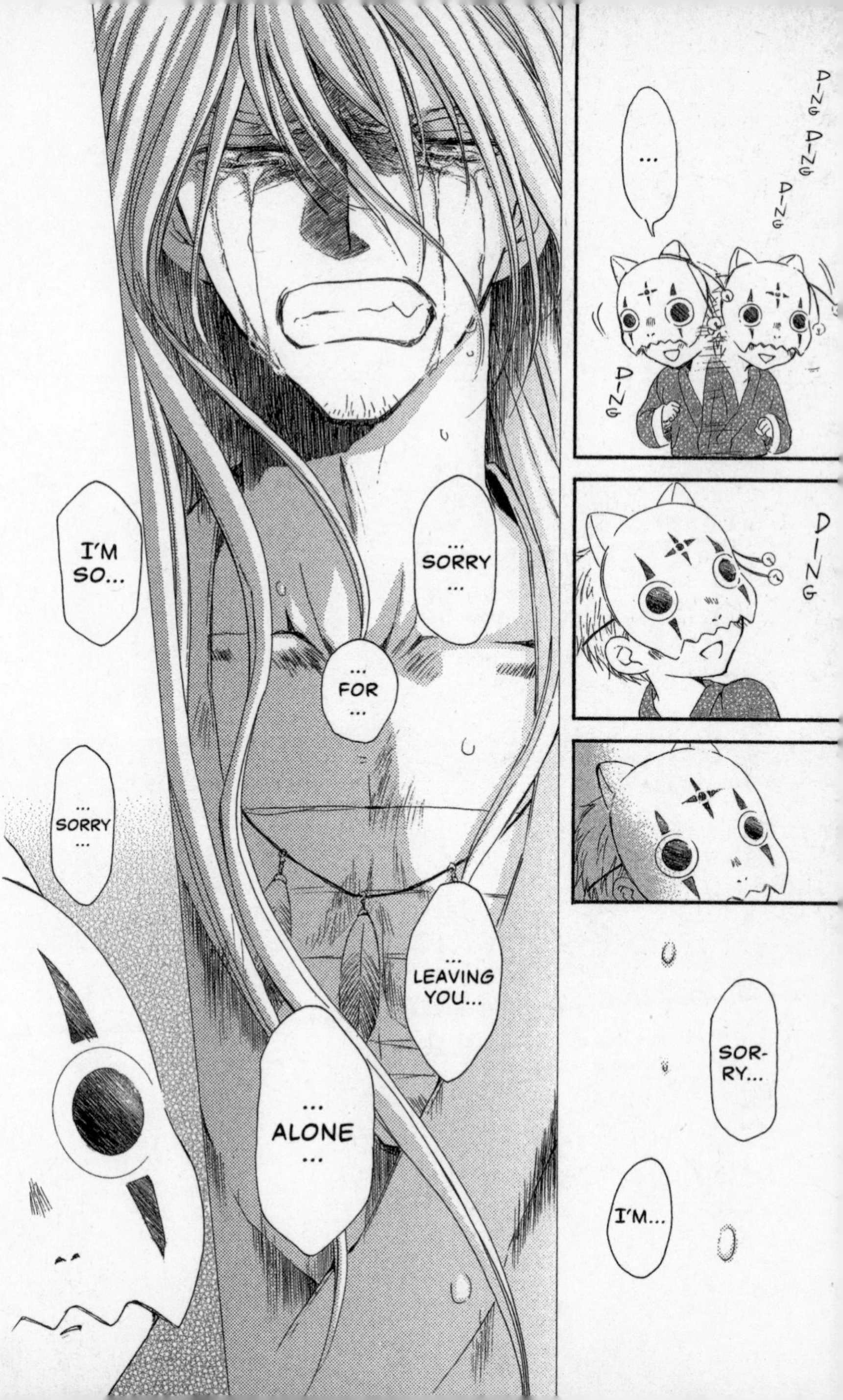

DING DING DING
...
DING
DING
SOR-RY...
I'M...
I'M SO...
... SORRY ...
... FOR ...
... SORRY ...
... LEAVING YOU...
... ALONE ...

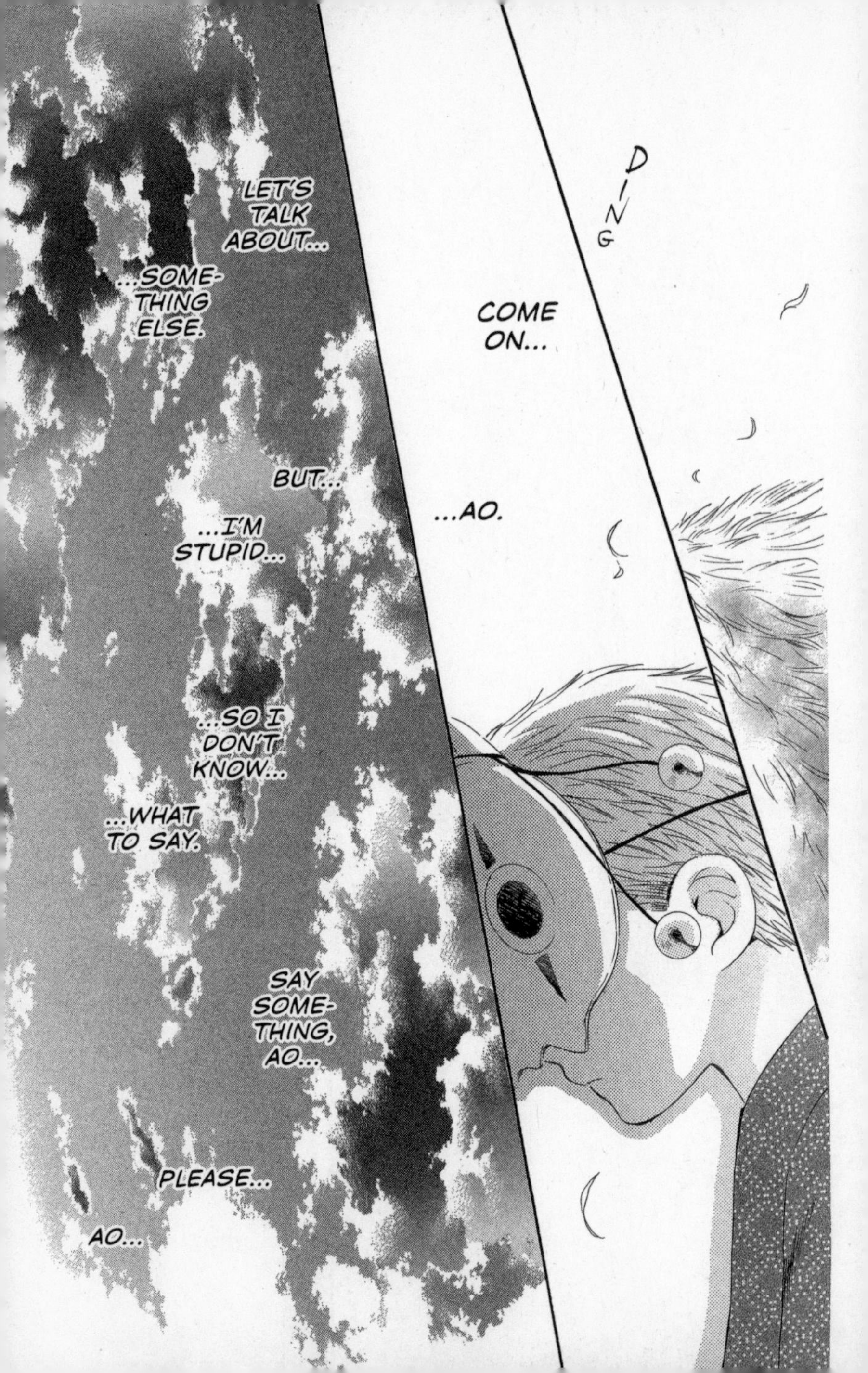
DING
COME ON...
...AO.
LET'S TALK ABOUT...
...SOME-THING ELSE.
BUT...
...I'M STUPID...
...SO I DON'T KNOW...
...WHAT TO SAY.
SAY SOME-THING, AO...
PLEASE...
AO...

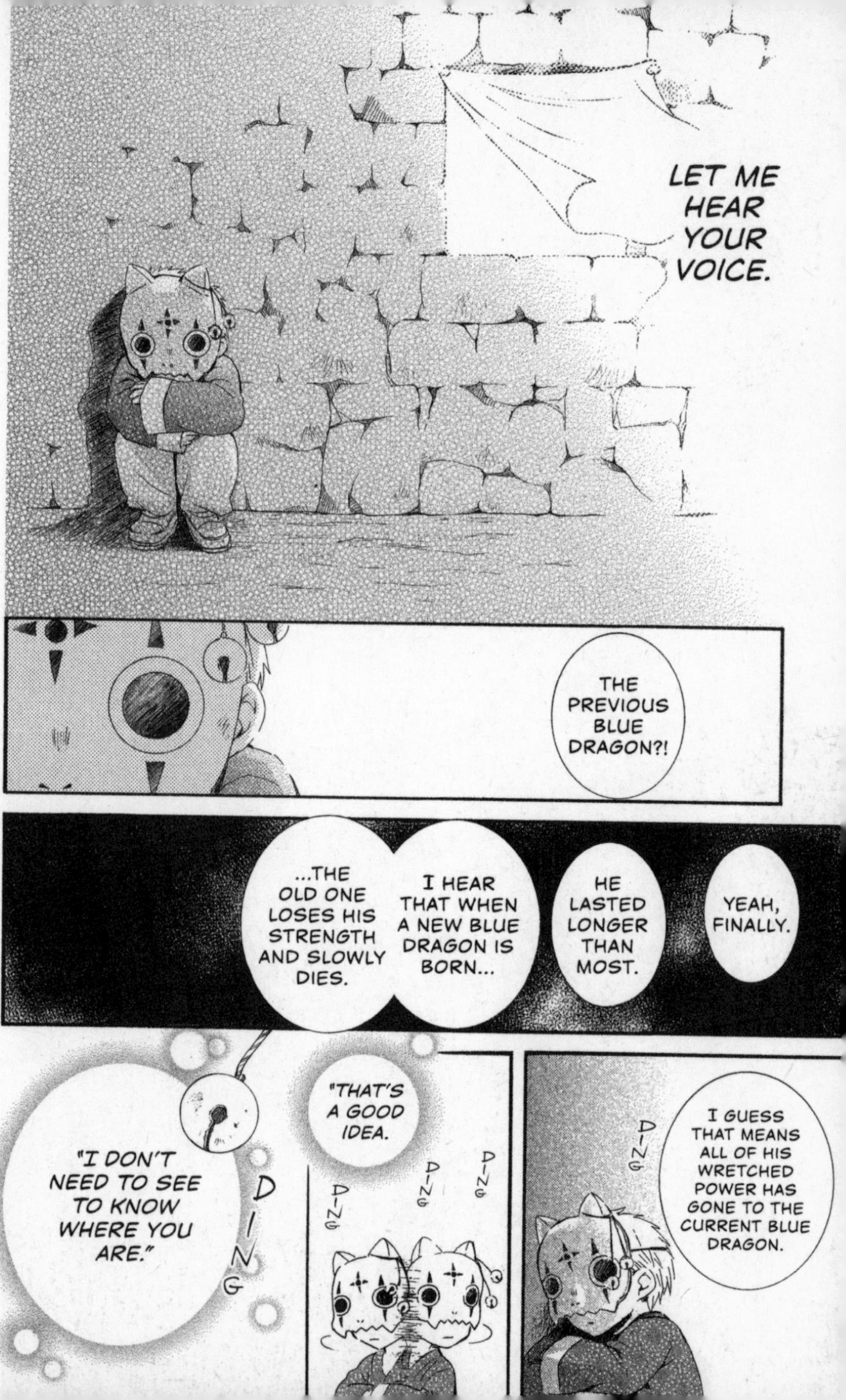
LET ME HEAR YOUR VOICE.
THE PREVIOUS BLUE DRAGON?!
YEAH, FINALLY.
HE LASTED LONGER THAN MOST.
I HEAR THAT WHEN A NEW BLUE DRAGON IS BORN...
...THE OLD ONE LOSES HIS STRENGTH AND SLOWLY DIES.
DING
I GUESS THAT MEANS ALL OF HIS WRETCHED POWER HAS GONE TO THE CURRENT BLUE DRAGON.
DING
DING
DING
"THAT'S A GOOD IDEA.
DING
"I DON'T NEED TO SEE TO KNOW WHERE YOU ARE."

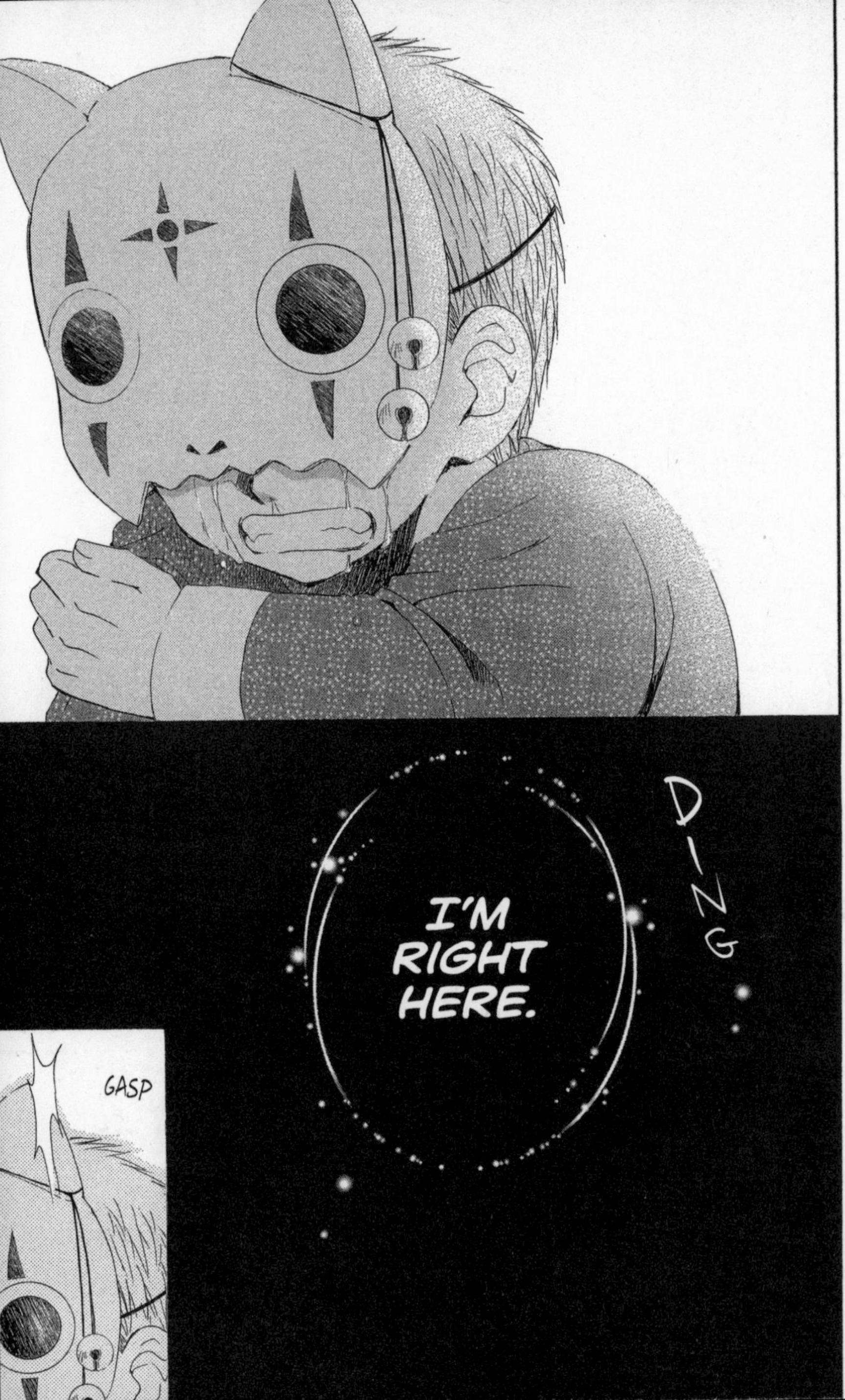
DING
I'M RIGHT HERE.
GASP

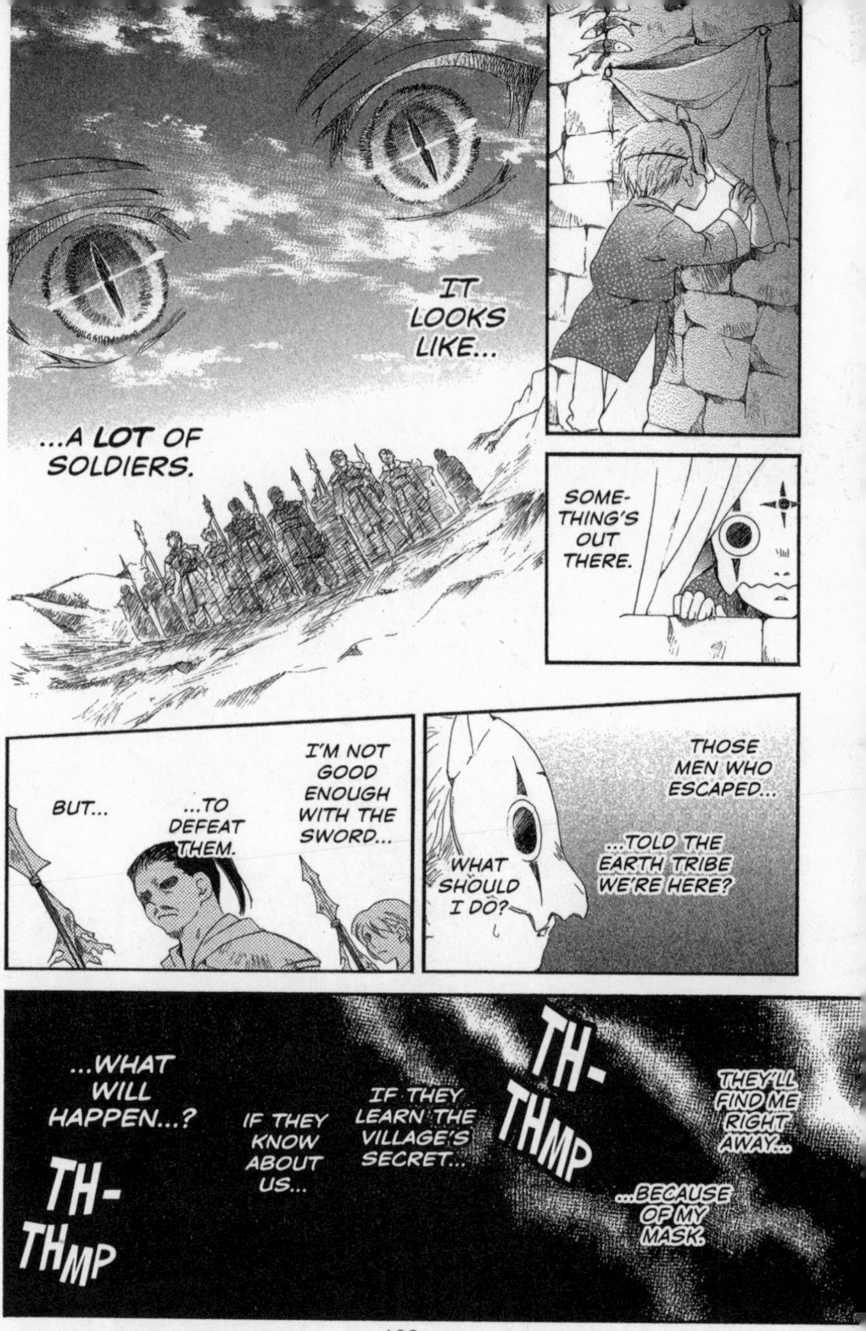
SOME-THING'S OUT THERE.
IT LOOKS LIKE...
...A LOT OF SOLDIERS.
THOSE MEN WHO ESCAPED...
...TOLD THE EARTH TRIBE WE'RE HERE?
WHAT SHOULD I DO?
I'M NOT GOOD ENOUGH WITH THE SWORD...
...TO DEFEAT THEM.
BUT...
THEY'LL FIND ME RIGHT AWAY...
...BECAUSE OF MY MASK.
TH-THMP
IF THEY LEARN THE VILLAGE'S SECRET...
IF THEY KNOW ABOUT US...
...WHAT WILL HAPPEN...?
TH-THMP

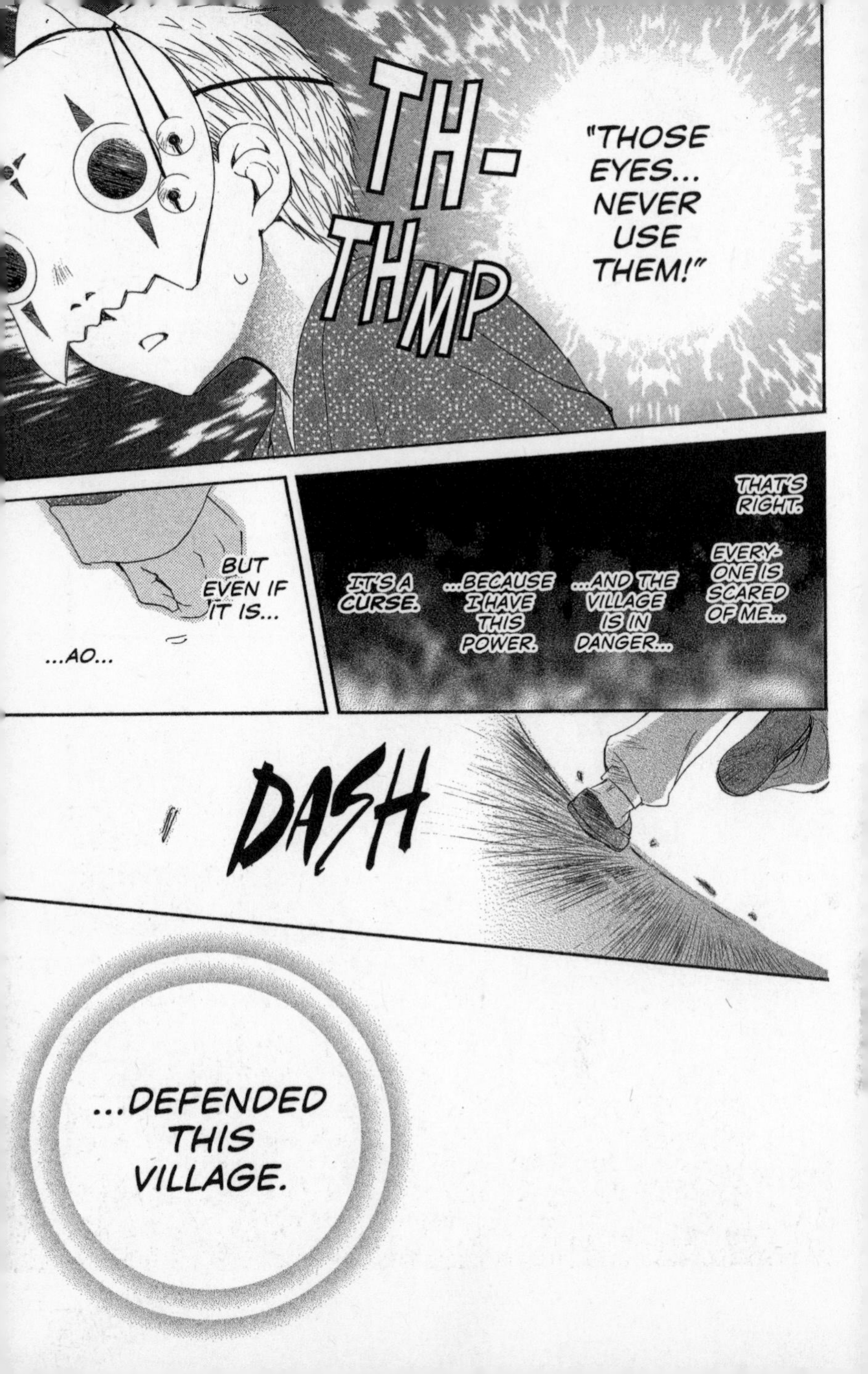
"THOSE EYES... NEVER USE THEM!"
TH-THMP
THAT'S RIGHT.
EVERY-ONE IS SCARED OF ME...
...AND THE VILLAGE IS IN DANGER...
...BECAUSE I HAVE THIS POWER.
IT'S A CURSE.
BUT EVEN IF IT IS...
...AO...
DASH
...DEFENDED THIS VILLAGE.

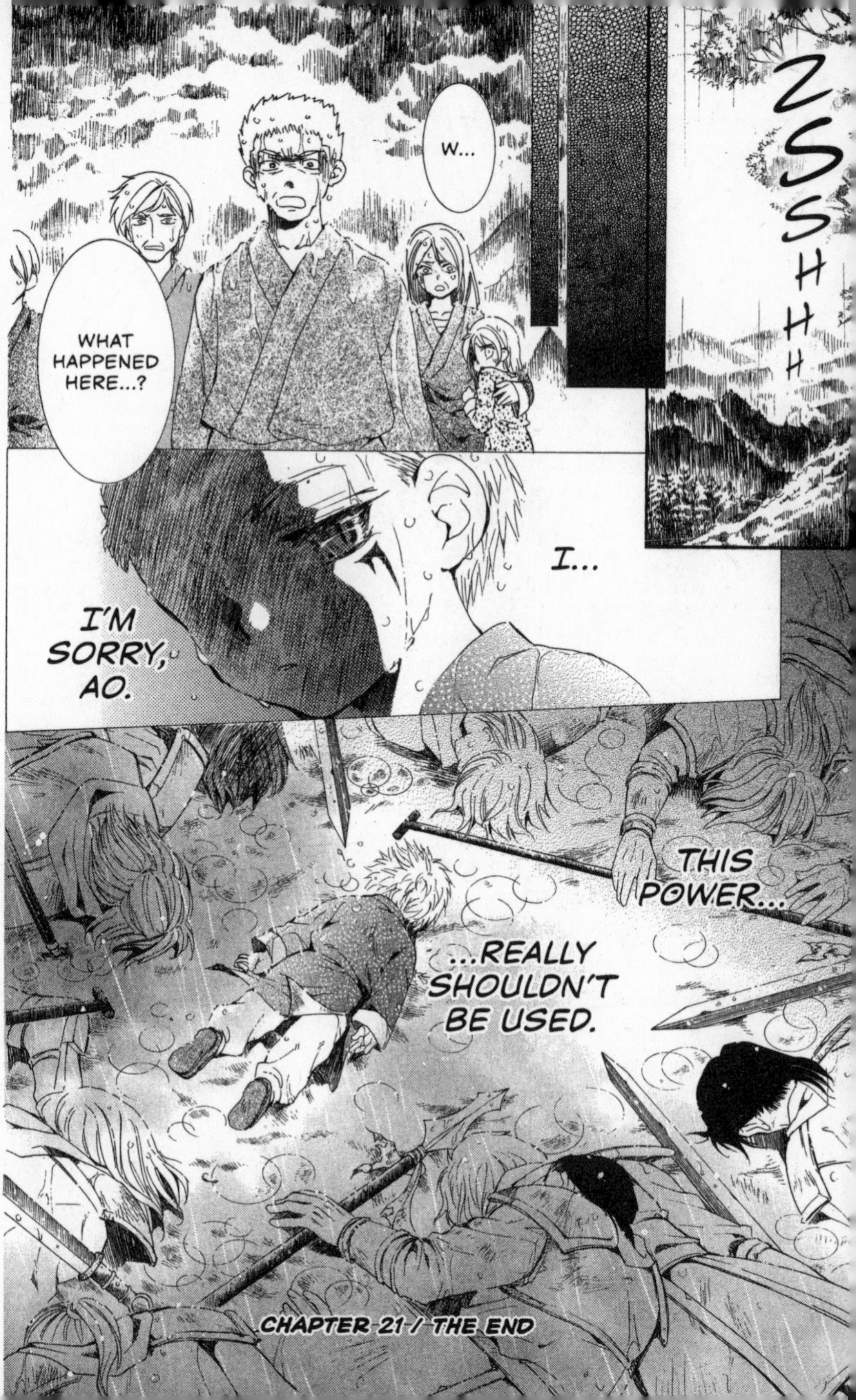
ZSSHHH
W...
WHAT HAPPENED HERE...?
I...
I'M SORRY, AO.
THIS POWER...
...REALLY SHOULDN'T BE USED.
CHAPTER 21 / THE END

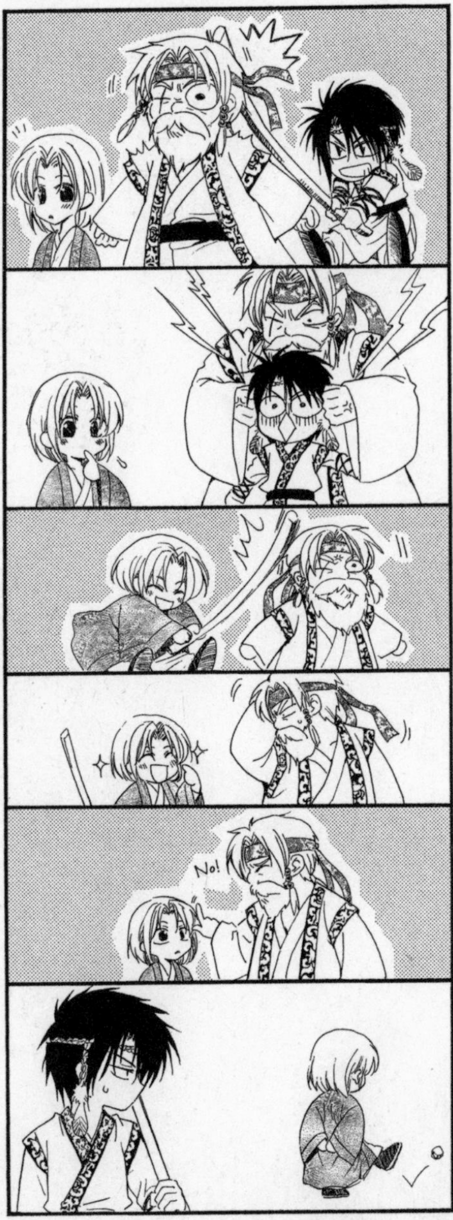
No!

Long time no see.

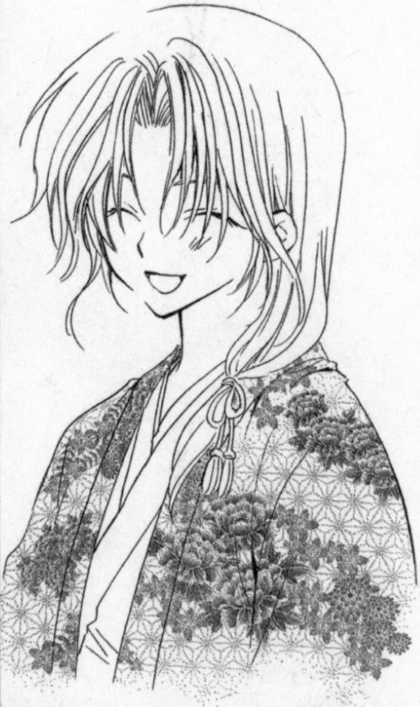

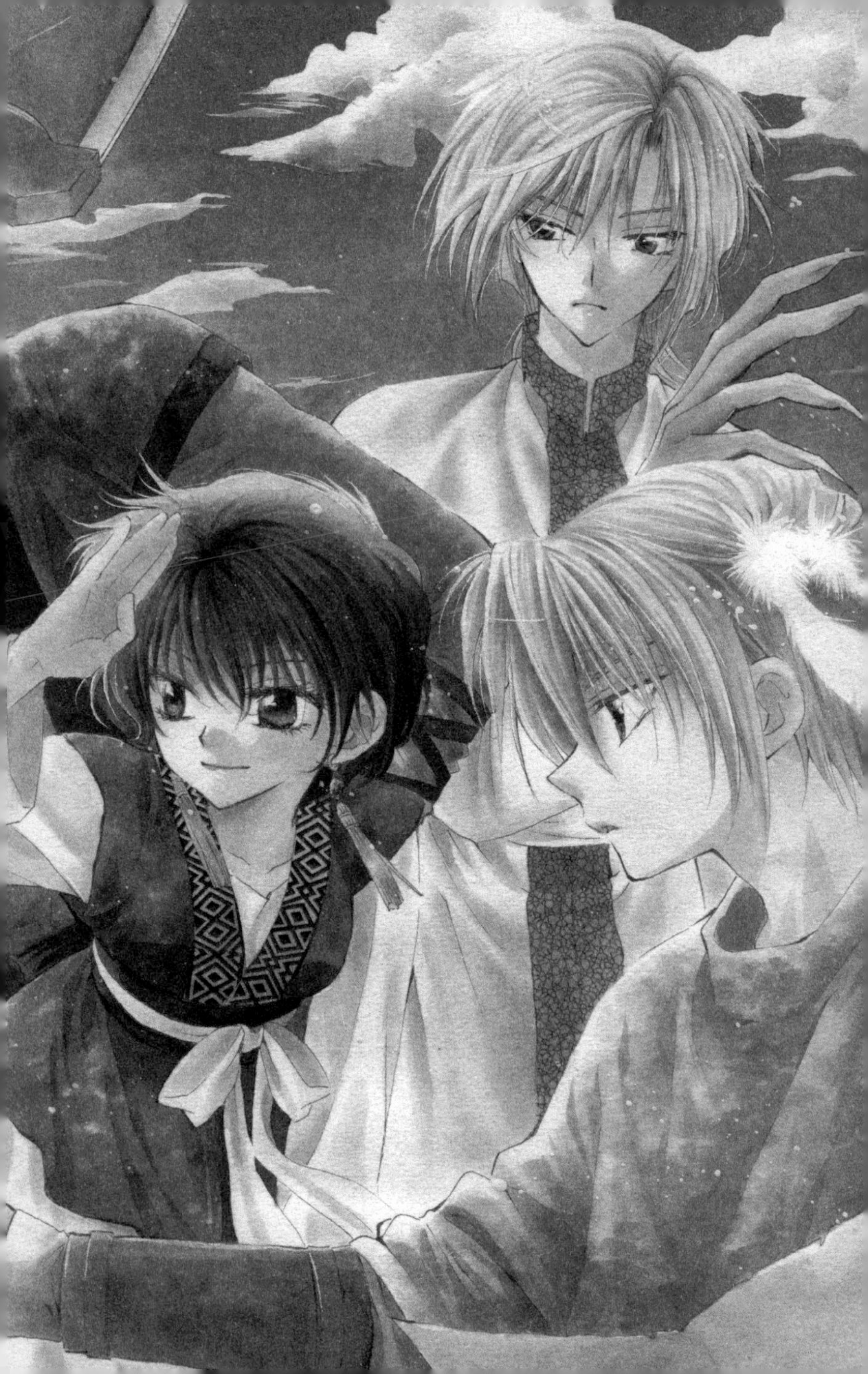

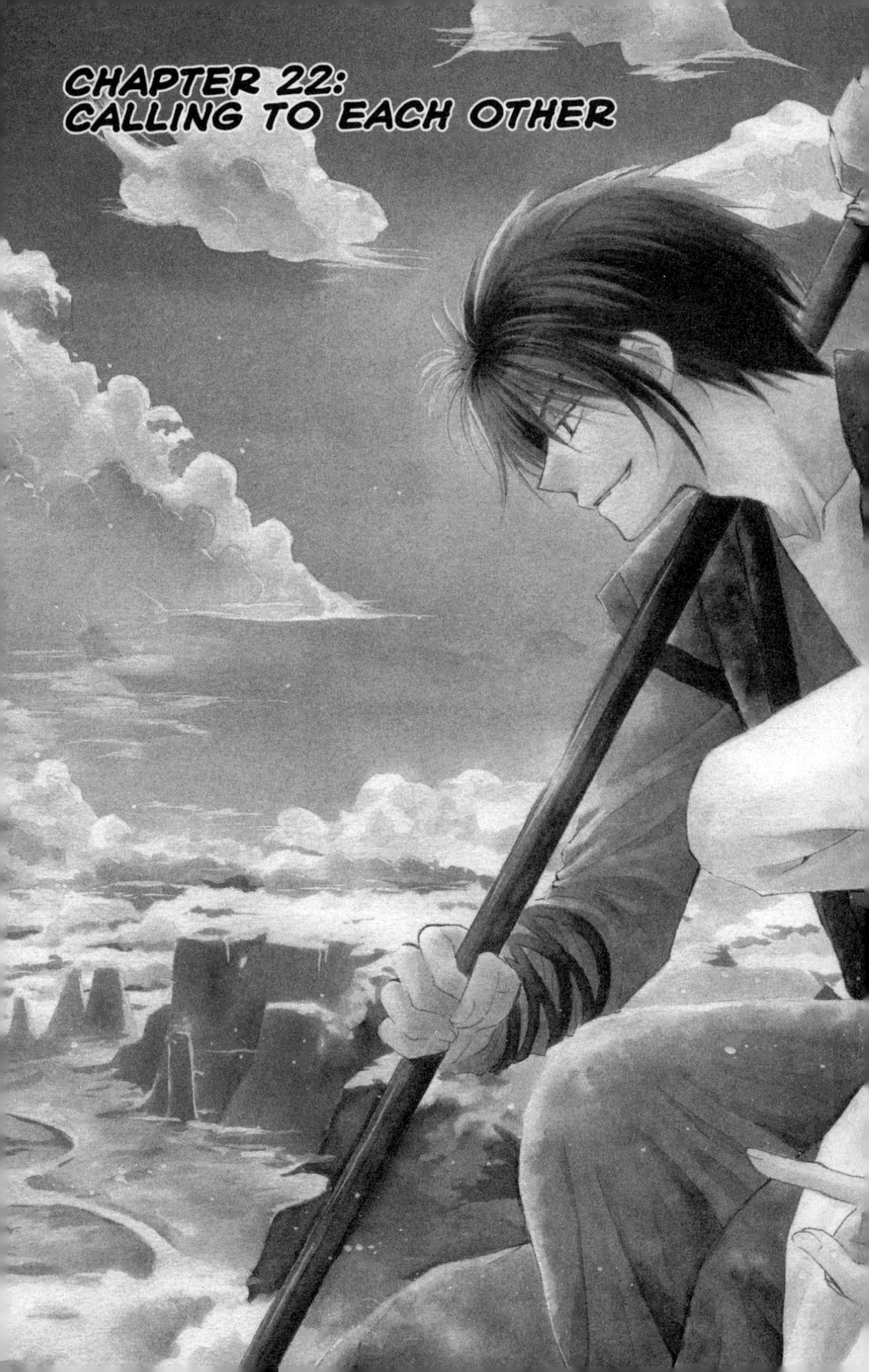
CHAPTER 22:
CALLING TO EACH OTHER

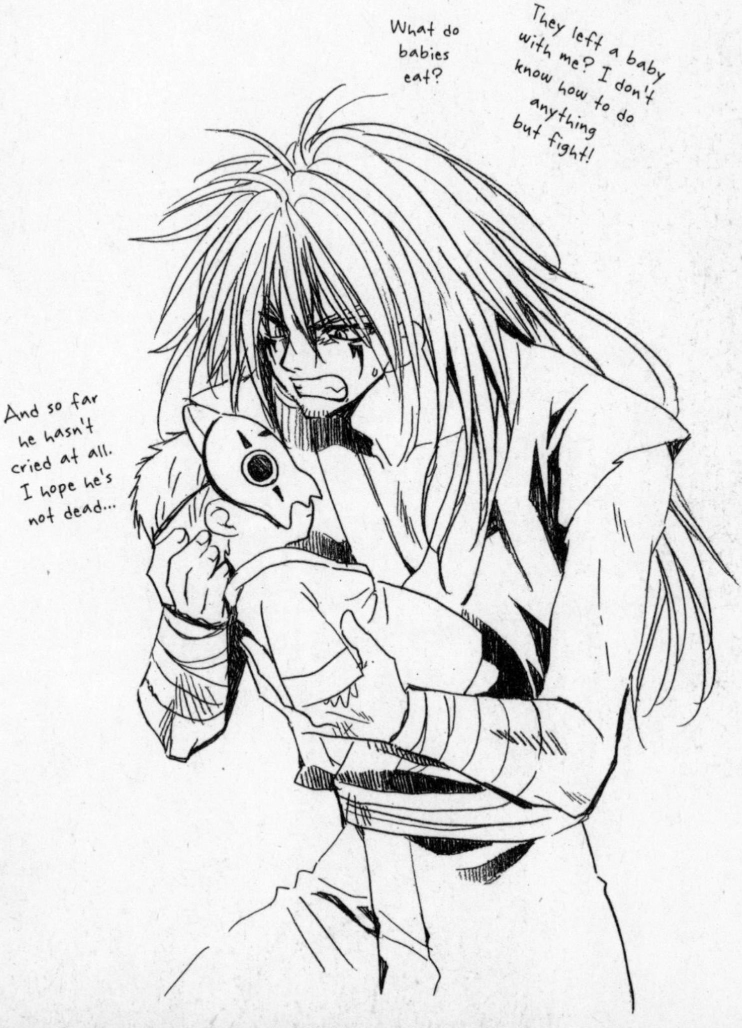
They left a baby with me? I don't know how to do anything but fight!
What do babies eat?
And so far he hasn't cried at all. I hope he's not dead...

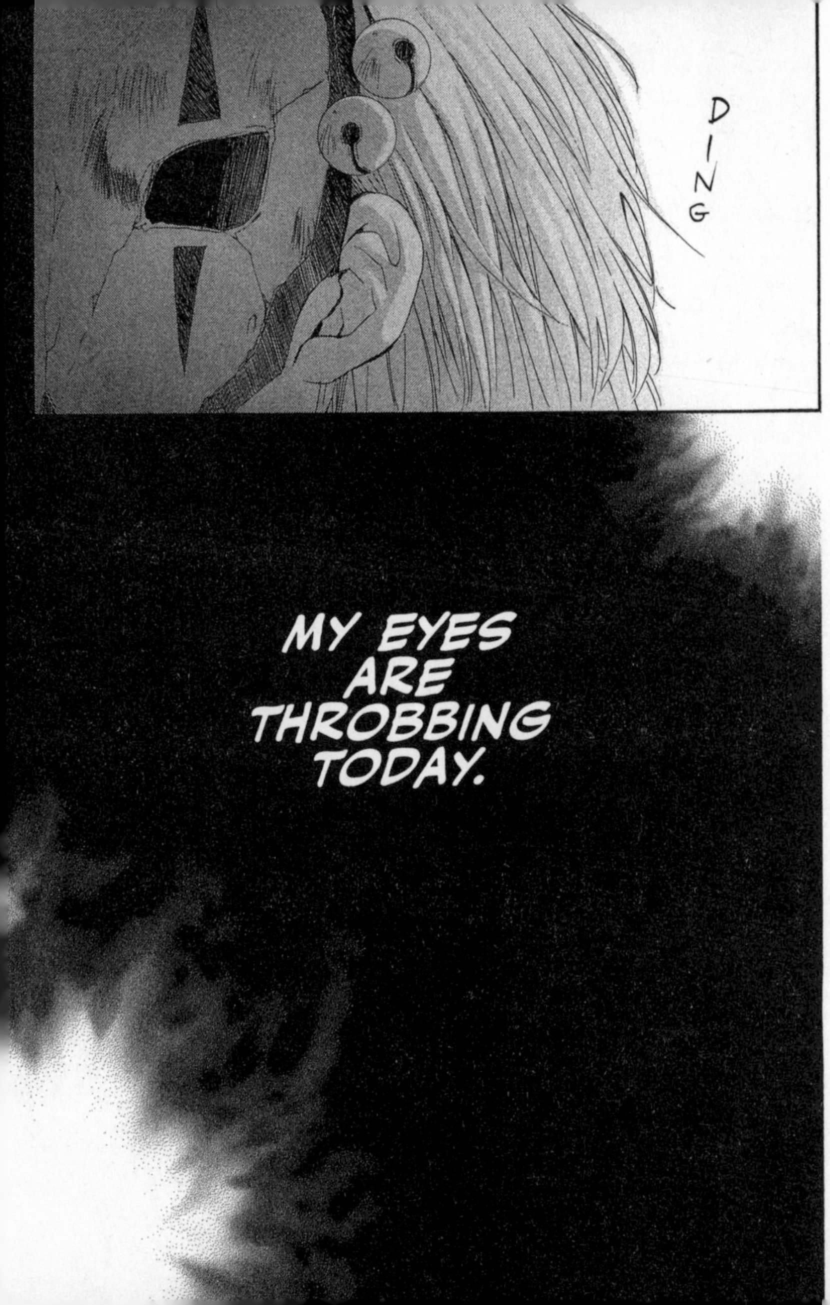
DING
MY EYES ARE THROBBING TODAY.

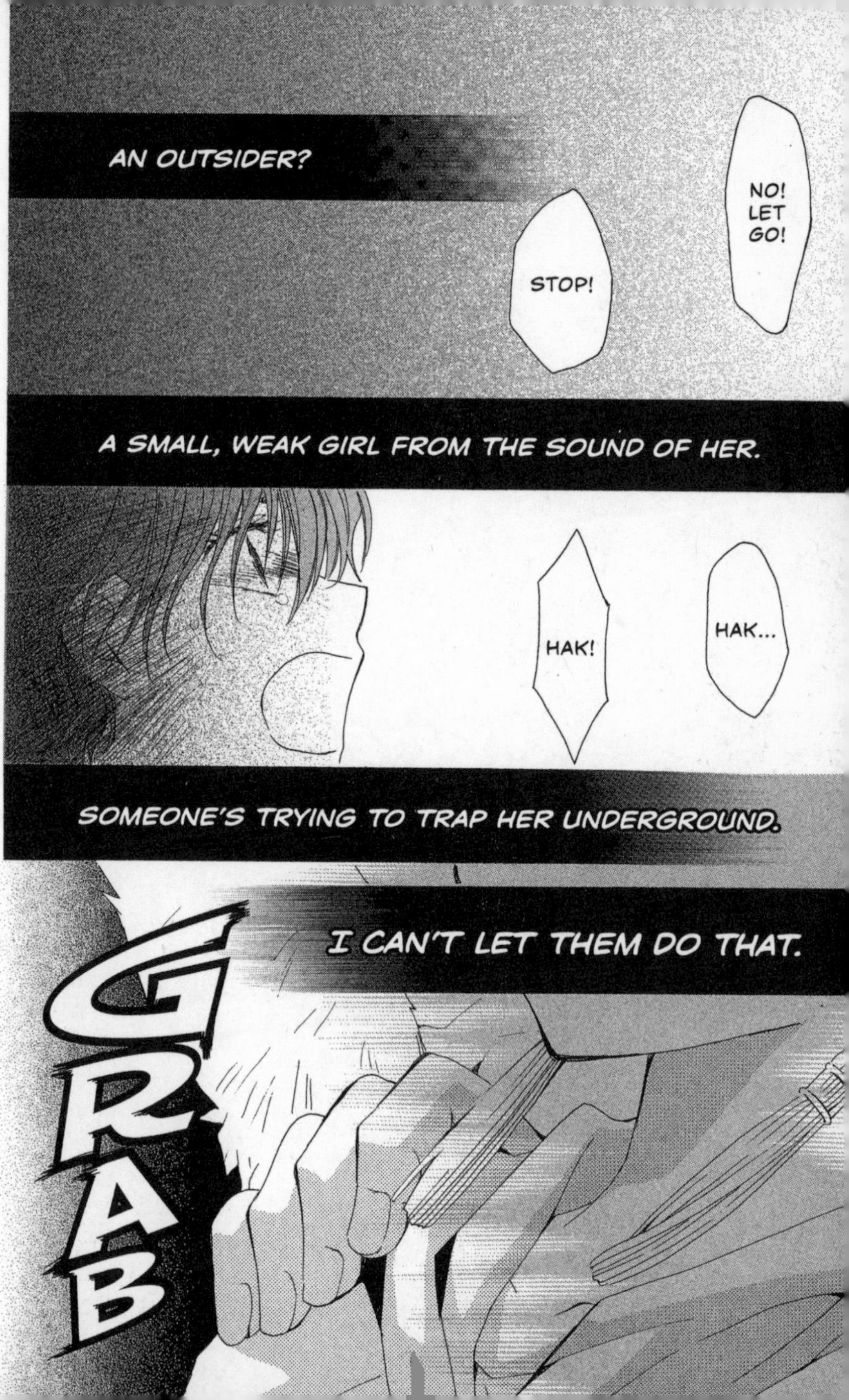
NO! LET GO!
STOP!
AN OUTSIDER?
A SMALL, WEAK GIRL FROM THE SOUND OF HER.
HAK...
HAK!
SOMEONE'S TRYING TO TRAP HER UNDERGROUND.
I CAN'T LET THEM DO THAT.
GRAB

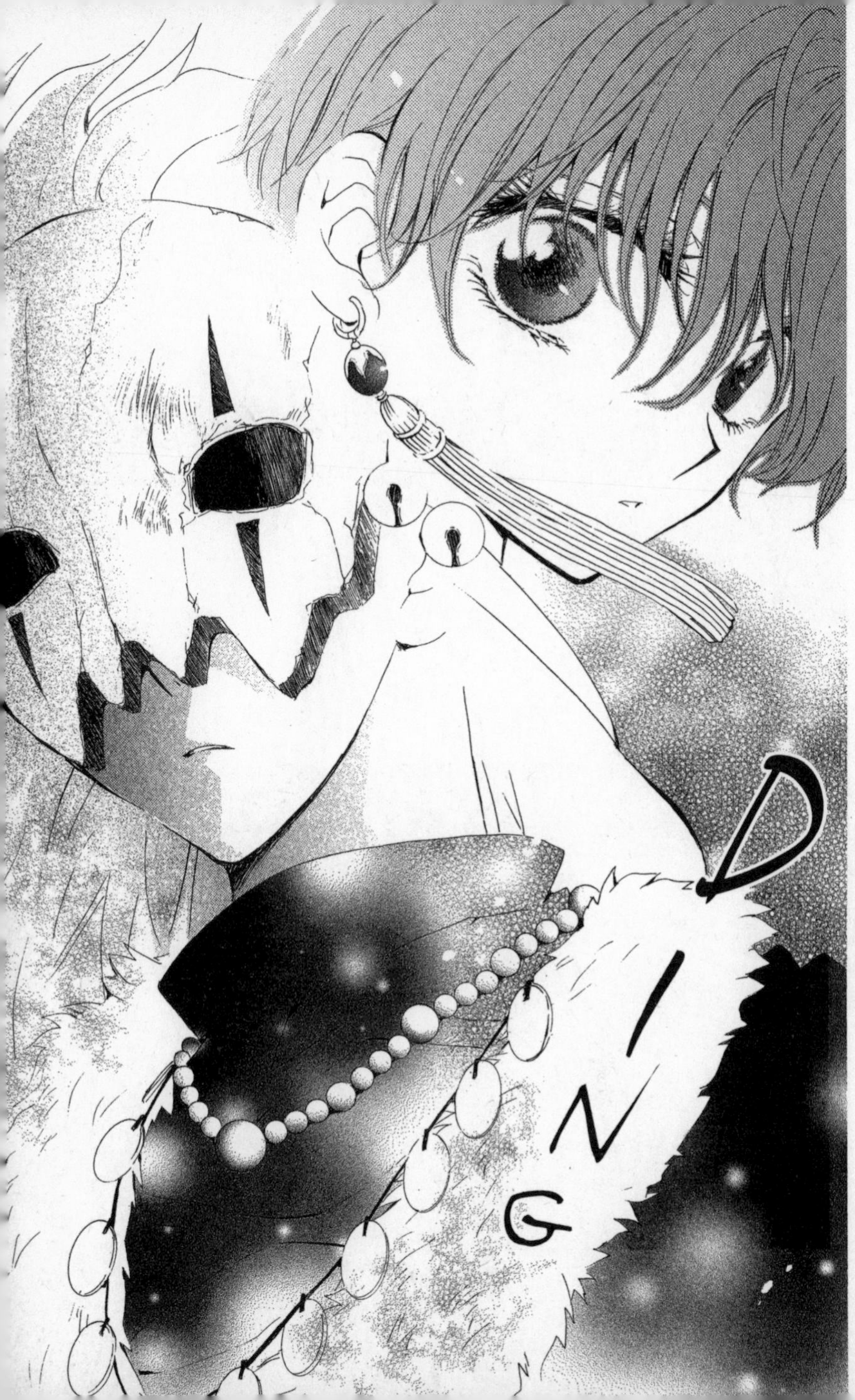
DING

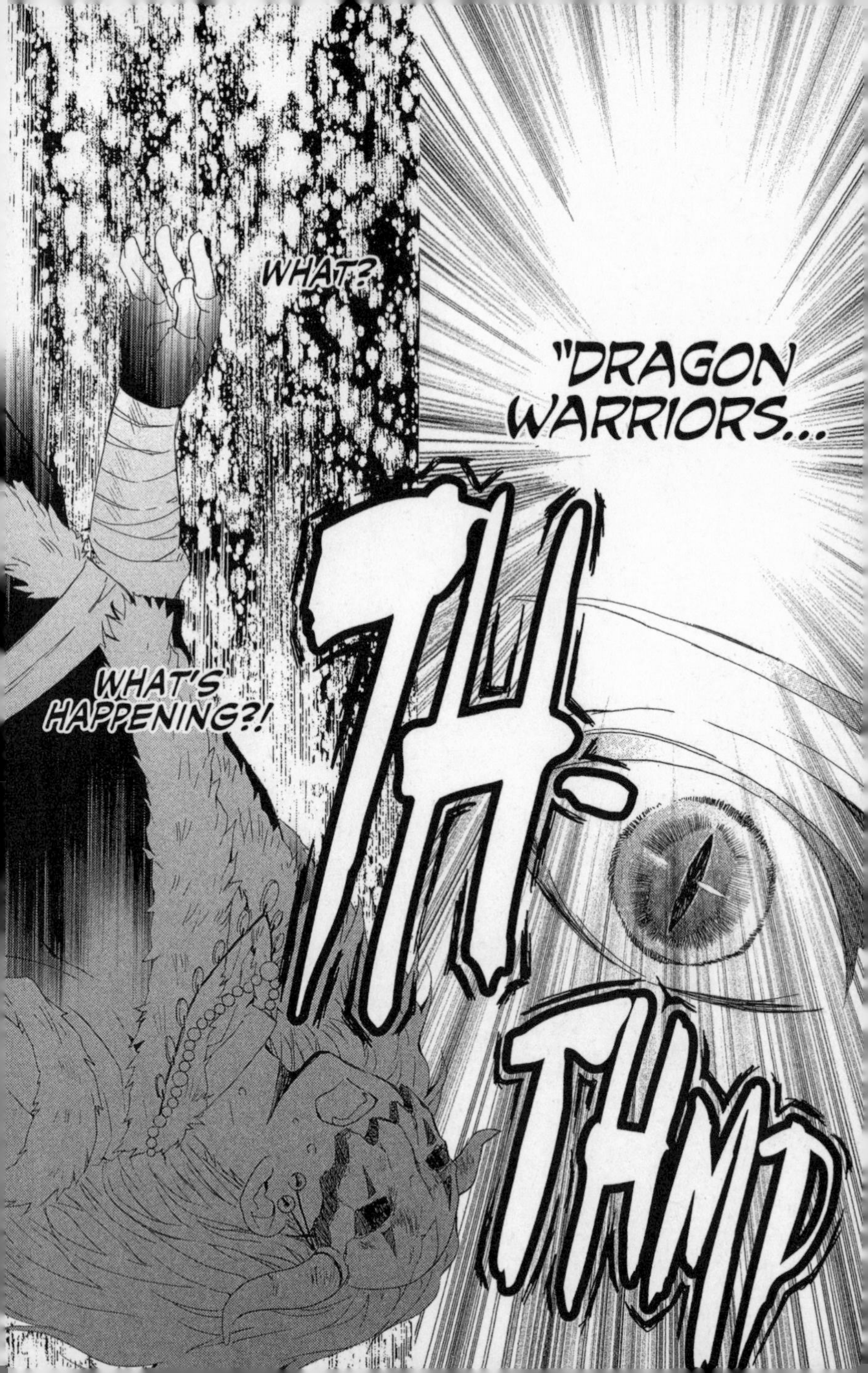
"DRAGON WARRIORS...
TH-THUMP
WHAT?
WHAT'S HAPPENING?!

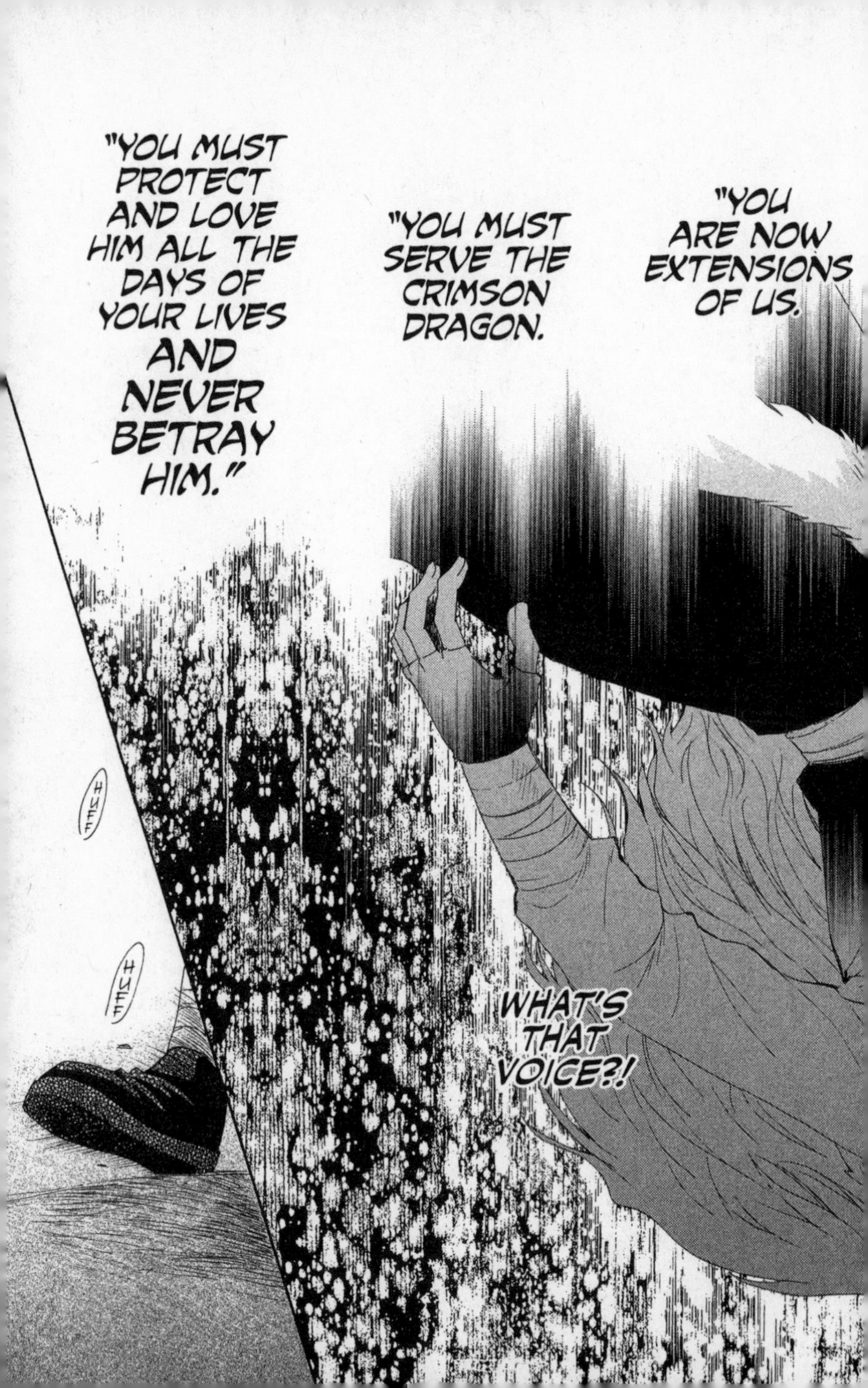
"YOU ARE NOW EXTENSIONS OF US.
"YOU MUST SERVE THE CRIMSON DRAGON.
"YOU MUST PROTECT AND LOVE HIM ALL THE DAYS OF YOUR LIVES AND NEVER BETRAY HIM."
WHAT'S THAT VOICE?!
HUFF
HUFF

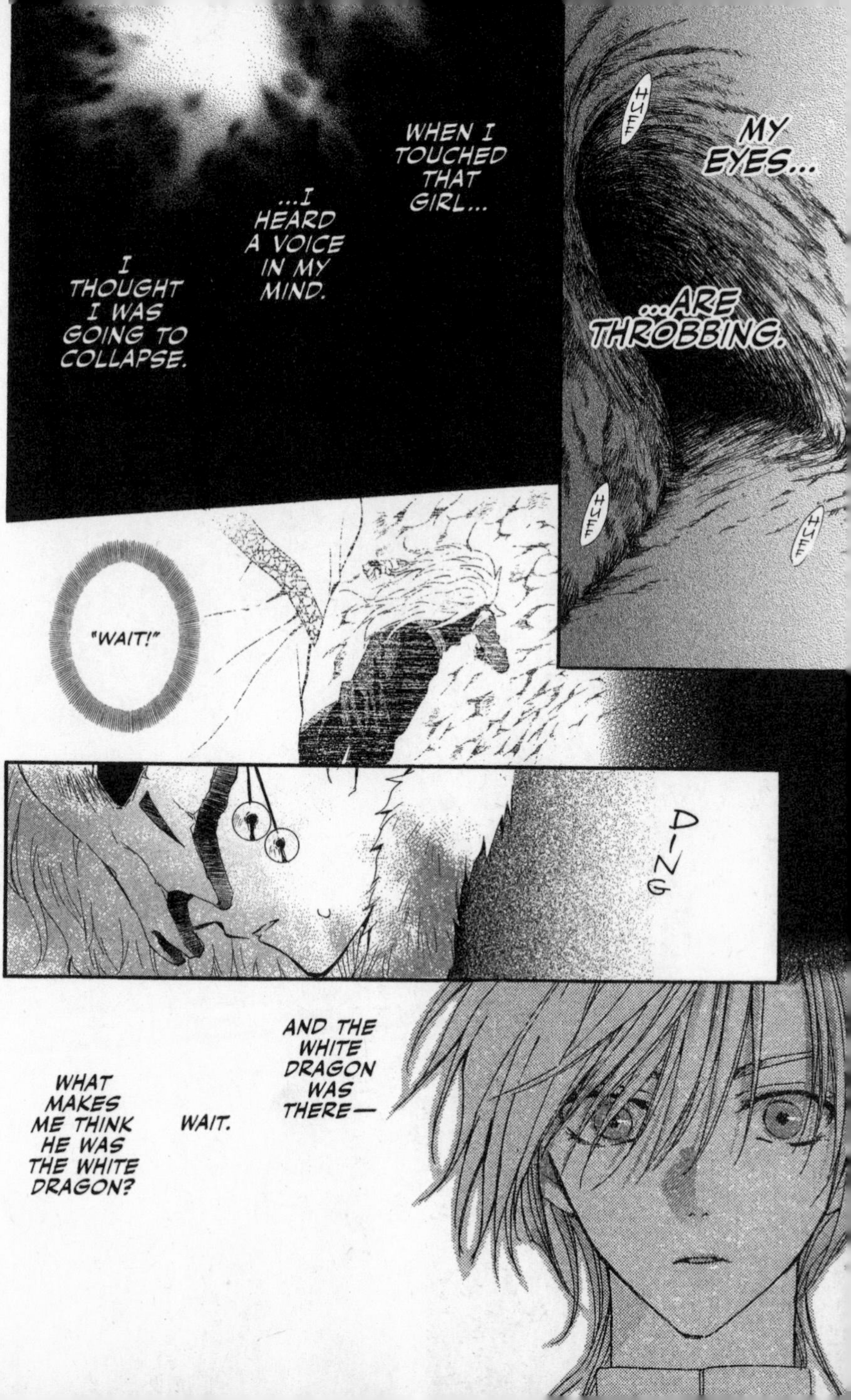
HUFF
MY EYES...
...ARE THROBBING.
HUFF
HUFF
WHEN I TOUCHED THAT GIRL...
...I HEARD A VOICE IN MY MIND.
I THOUGHT I WAS GOING TO COLLAPSE.
"WAIT!"
DING
AND THE WHITE DRAGON WAS THERE—
WAIT.
WHAT MAKES ME THINK HE WAS THE WHITE DRAGON?

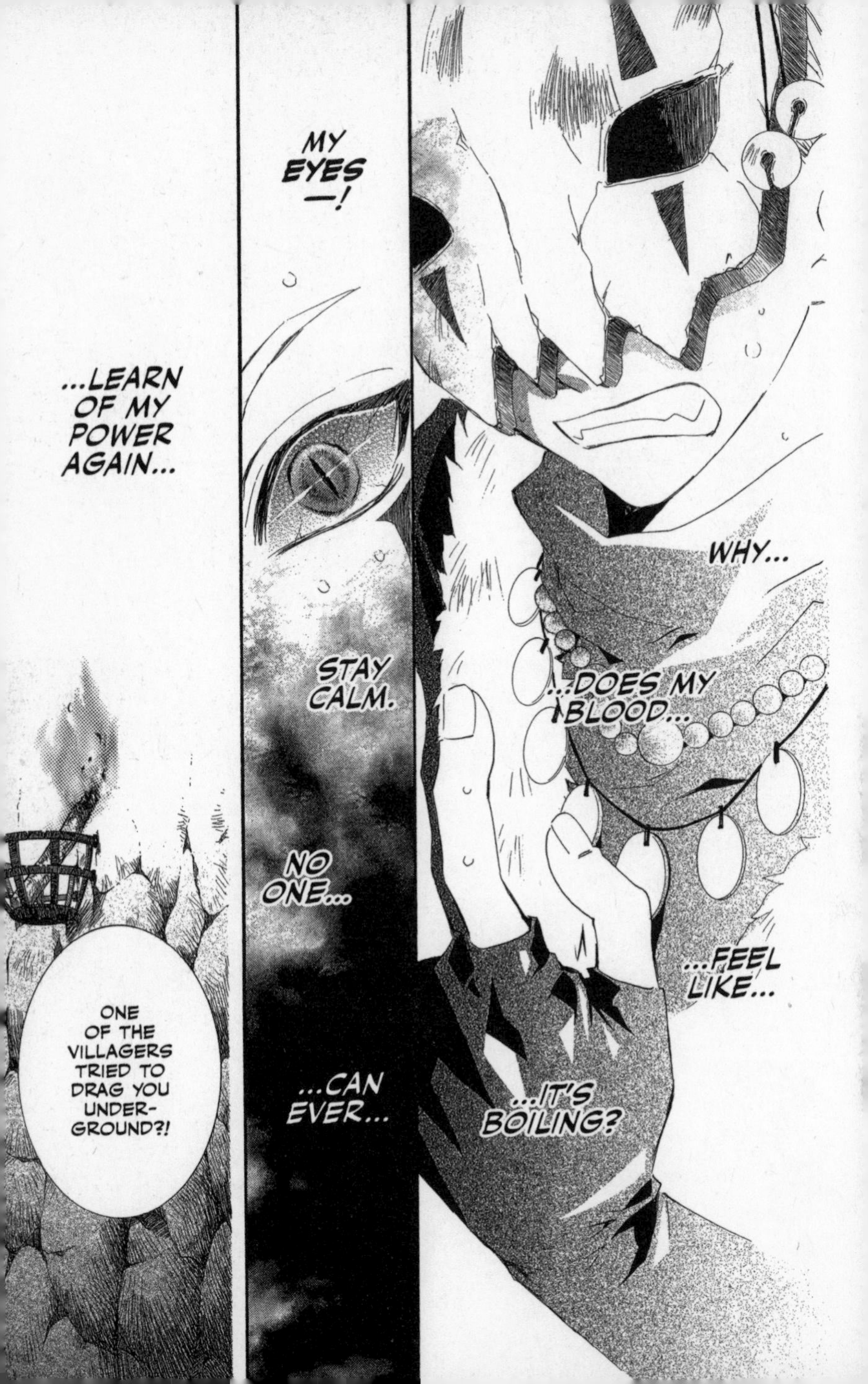
WHY...
...DOES MY BLOOD...
...FEEL LIKE...
...IT'S BOILING?
MY EYES—!
STAY CALM.
NO ONE...
...CAN EVER...
...LEARN OF MY POWER AGAIN...
ONE OF THE VILLAGERS TRIED TO DRAG YOU UNDER-GROUND?!

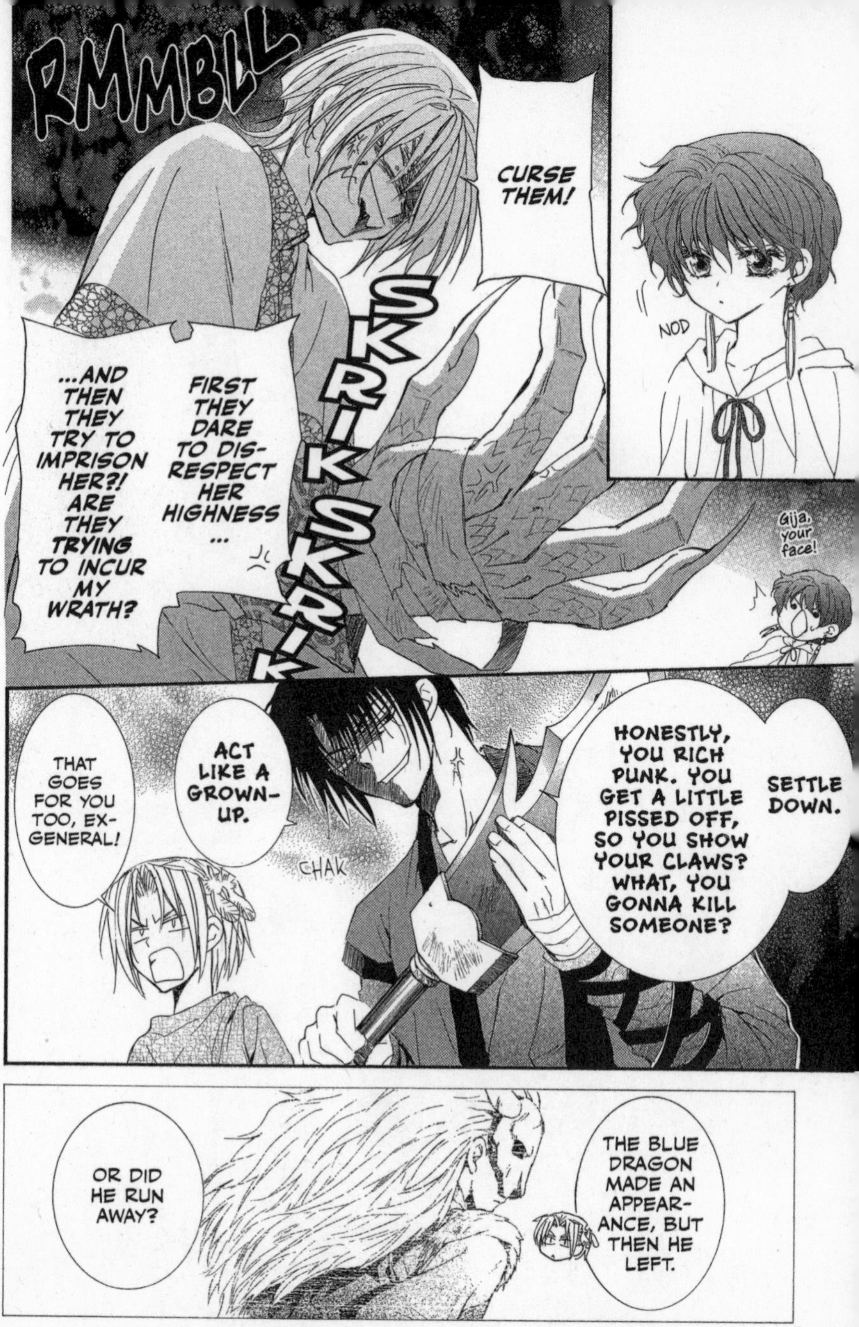
RMMBLL
CURSE THEM!
NOD
FIRST THEY DARE TO DIS-RESPECT HER HIGHNESS...
...AND THEN THEY TRY TO IMPRISON HER?! ARE THEY TRYING TO INCUR MY WRATH?
SKRIK SKRIK
Gija, your face!
SETTLE DOWN.
HONESTLY, YOU RICH PUNK. YOU GET A LITTLE PISSED OFF, SO YOU SHOW YOUR CLAWS? WHAT, YOU GONNA KILL SOMEONE?
CHAK
ACT LIKE A GROWN-UP.
THAT GOES FOR YOU TOO, EX-GENERAL!
THE BLUE DRAGON MADE AN APPEAR-ANCE, BUT THEN HE LEFT.
OR DID HE RUN AWAY?

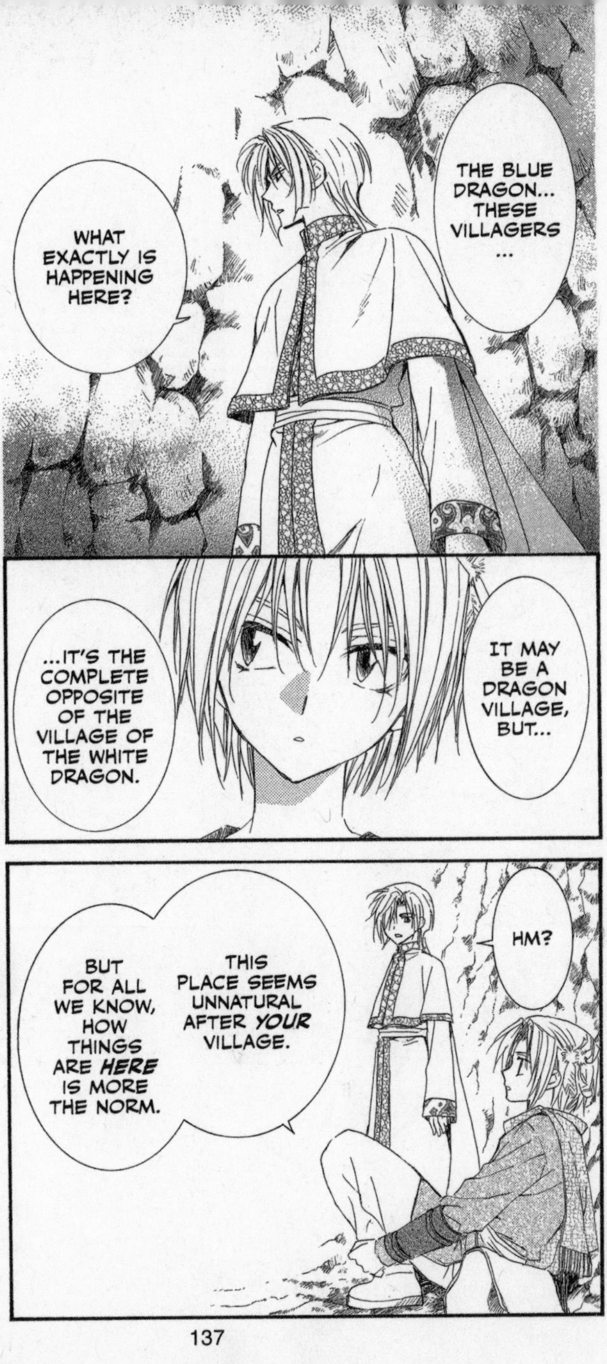
THE BLUE DRAGON... THESE VILLAGERS ...
WHAT EXACTLY IS HAPPENING HERE?
IT MAY BE A DRAGON VILLAGE, BUT...
...IT'S THE COMPLETE OPPOSITE OF THE VILLAGE OF THE WHITE DRAGON.
HM?
THIS PLACE SEEMS UNNATURAL AFTER *YOUR* VILLAGE.
BUT FOR ALL WE KNOW, HOW THINGS ARE *HERE* IS MORE THE NORM.

Ao is featured in the story about the Blue Dragon's past. Of all the characters in any of my series, he's probably the kind of guy I like most. (Laugh)

But "favorite character" and "favorite character type" are slightly different things. I just really like bestial people with long, scraggly hair and scruffy faces.

I wanted to keep drawing Ao, but alas, he's a one-off character. I'm glad I got to draw him though.

He may be my favorite type, but that doesn't mean I put more effort into him than the other characters! I focus on the heroine and her companions the most, because I want the heroes to do their very best.

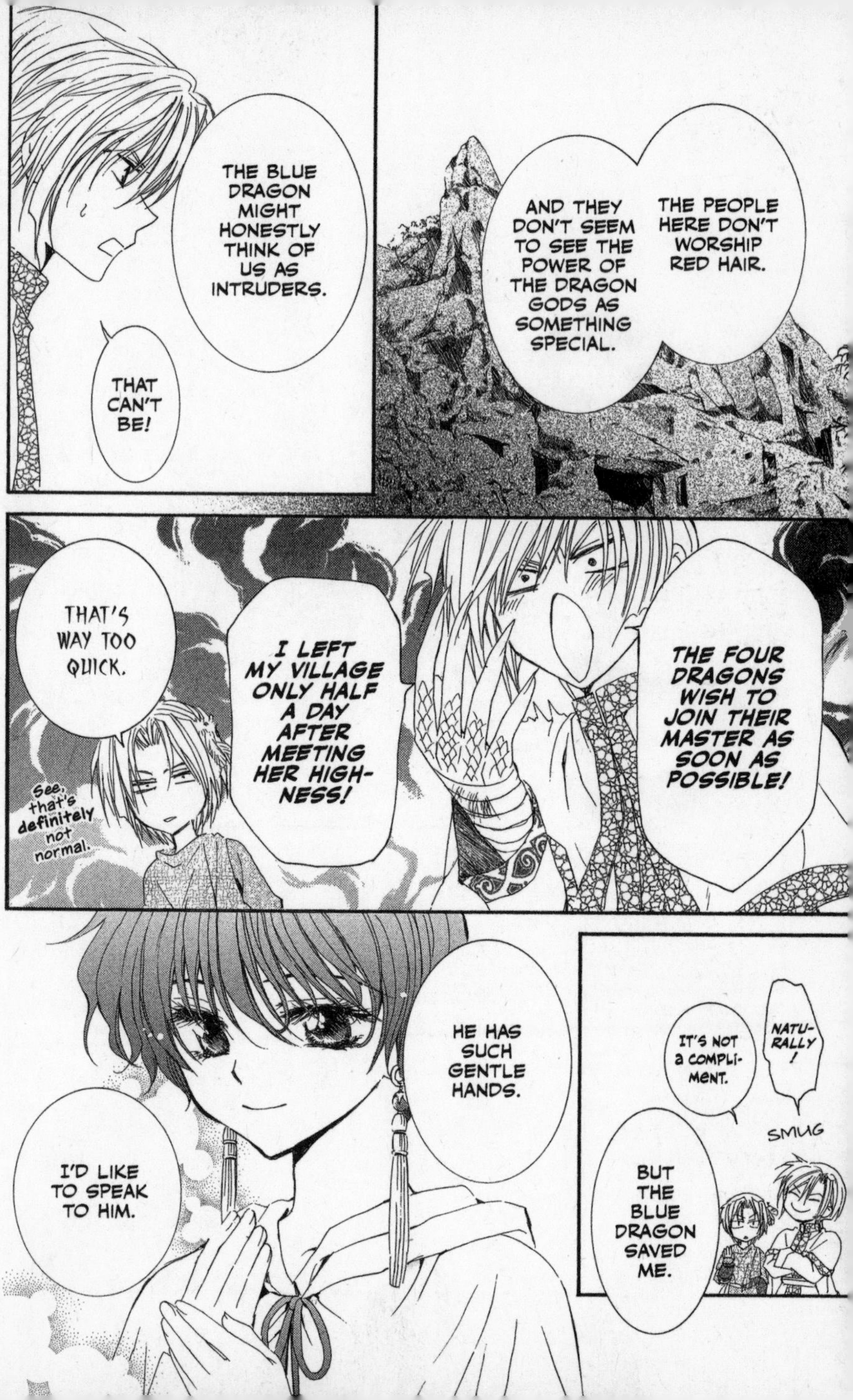
THE PEOPLE HERE DON'T WORSHIP RED HAIR.
AND THEY DON'T SEEM TO SEE THE POWER OF THE DRAGON GODS AS SOMETHING SPECIAL.
THE BLUE DRAGON MIGHT HONESTLY THINK OF US AS INTRUDERS.
THAT CAN'T BE!
THE FOUR DRAGONS WISH TO JOIN THEIR MASTER AS SOON AS POSSIBLE!
I LEFT MY VILLAGE ONLY HALF A DAY AFTER MEETING HER HIGHNESS!
THAT'S WAY TOO QUICK.
See, that's definitely not normal.
NATURALLY!
IT'S NOT A COMPLIMENT.
SMUG
BUT THE BLUE DRAGON SAVED ME.
HE HAS SUCH GENTLE HANDS.
I'D LIKE TO SPEAK TO HIM.

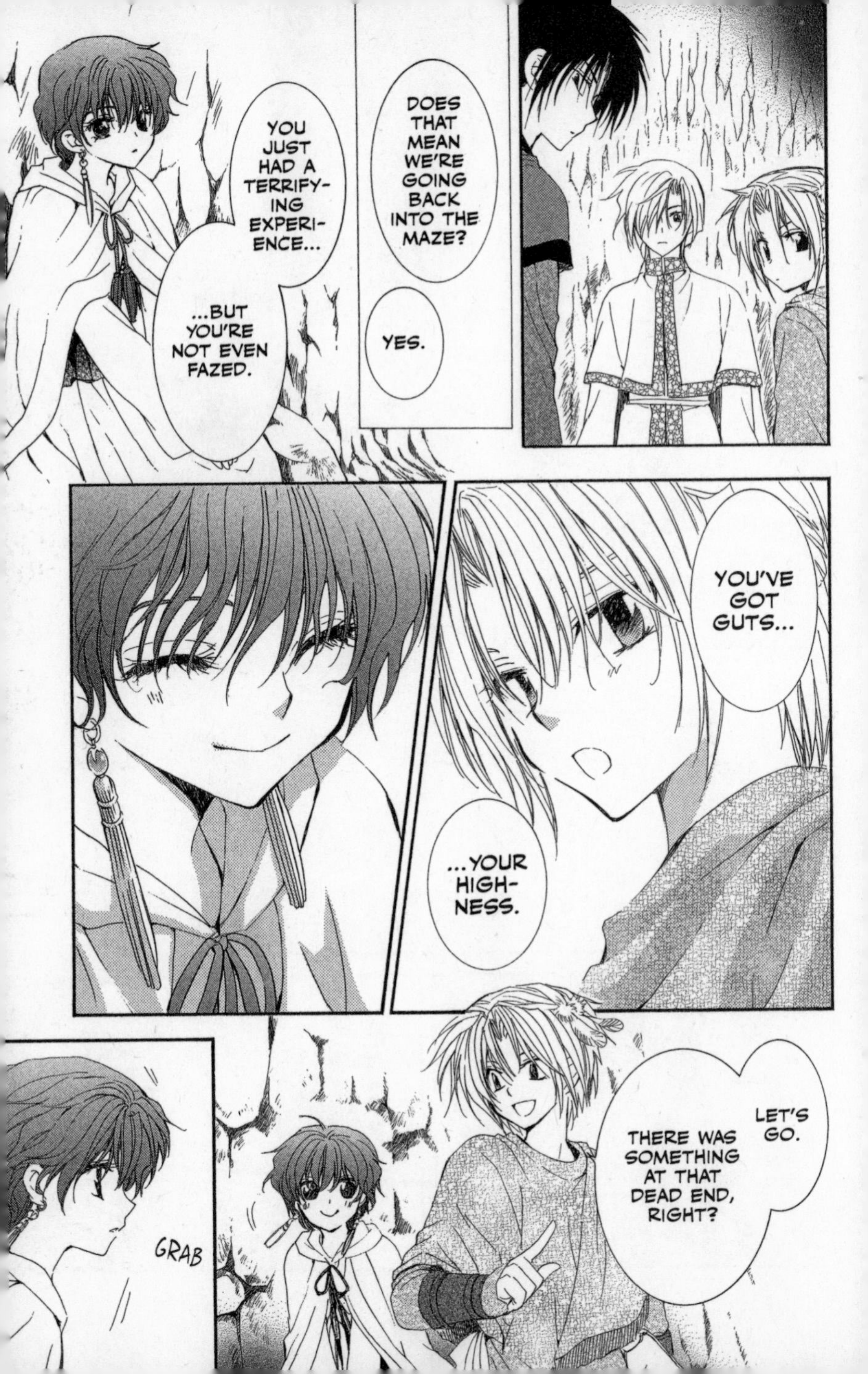
DOES THAT MEAN WE'RE GOING BACK INTO THE MAZE?
YES.
YOU JUST HAD A TERRIFYING EXPERIENCE...
...BUT YOU'RE NOT EVEN FAZED.
YOU'VE GOT GUTS...
...YOUR HIGHNESS.
LET'S GO.
THERE WAS SOMETHING AT THAT DEAD END, RIGHT?
GRAB

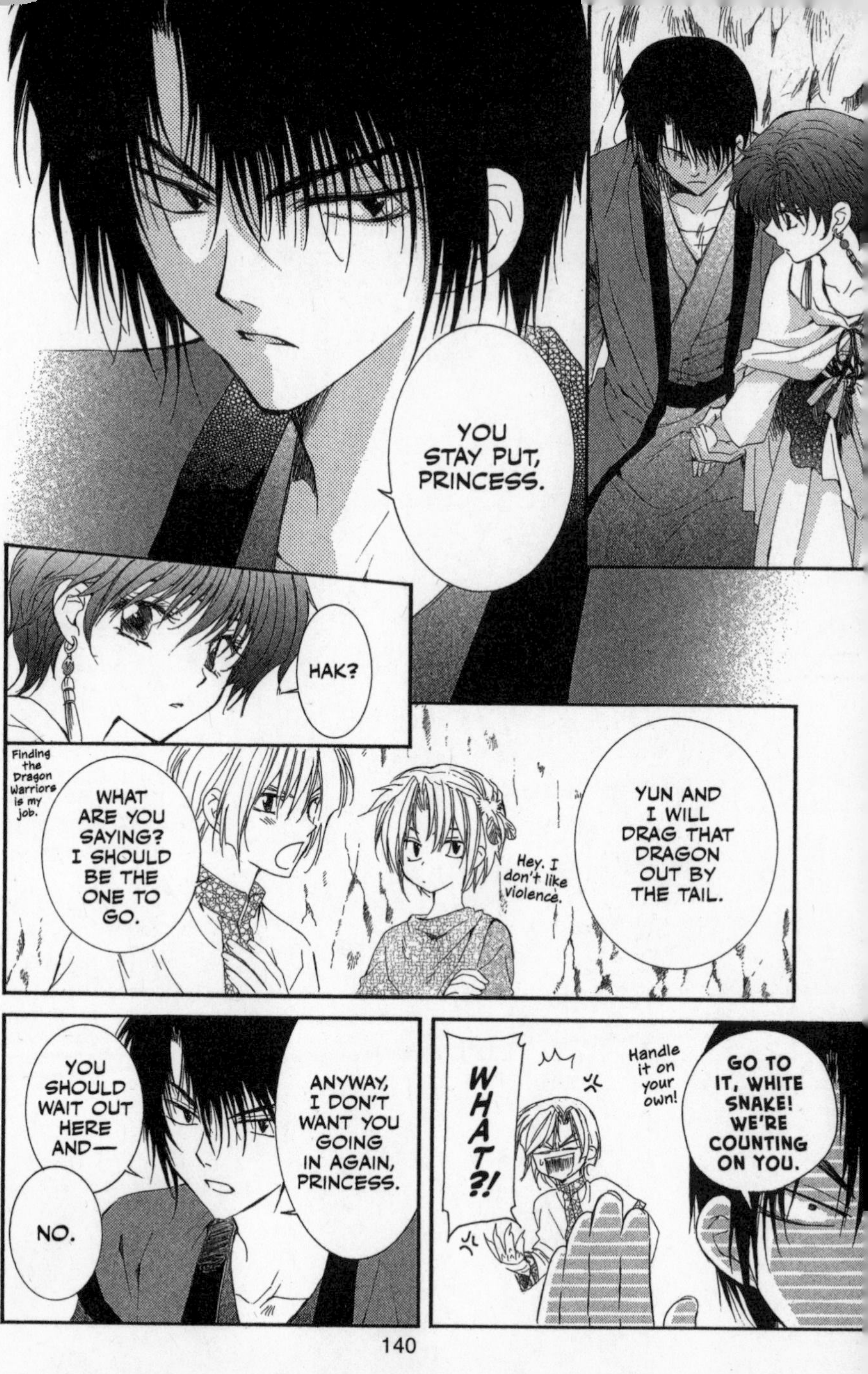
YOU STAY PUT, PRINCESS.
HAK?
YUN AND I WILL DRAG THAT DRAGON OUT BY THE TAIL.
Hey. I don't like violence.
WHAT ARE YOU SAYING? I SHOULD BE THE ONE TO GO.
Finding the Dragon Warriors is my job.
GO TO IT, WHITE SNAKE! WE'RE COUNTING ON YOU.
Handle it on your own!
WHAT?!
ANYWAY, I DON'T WANT YOU GOING IN AGAIN, PRINCESS.
YOU SHOULD WAIT OUT HERE AND—
NO.

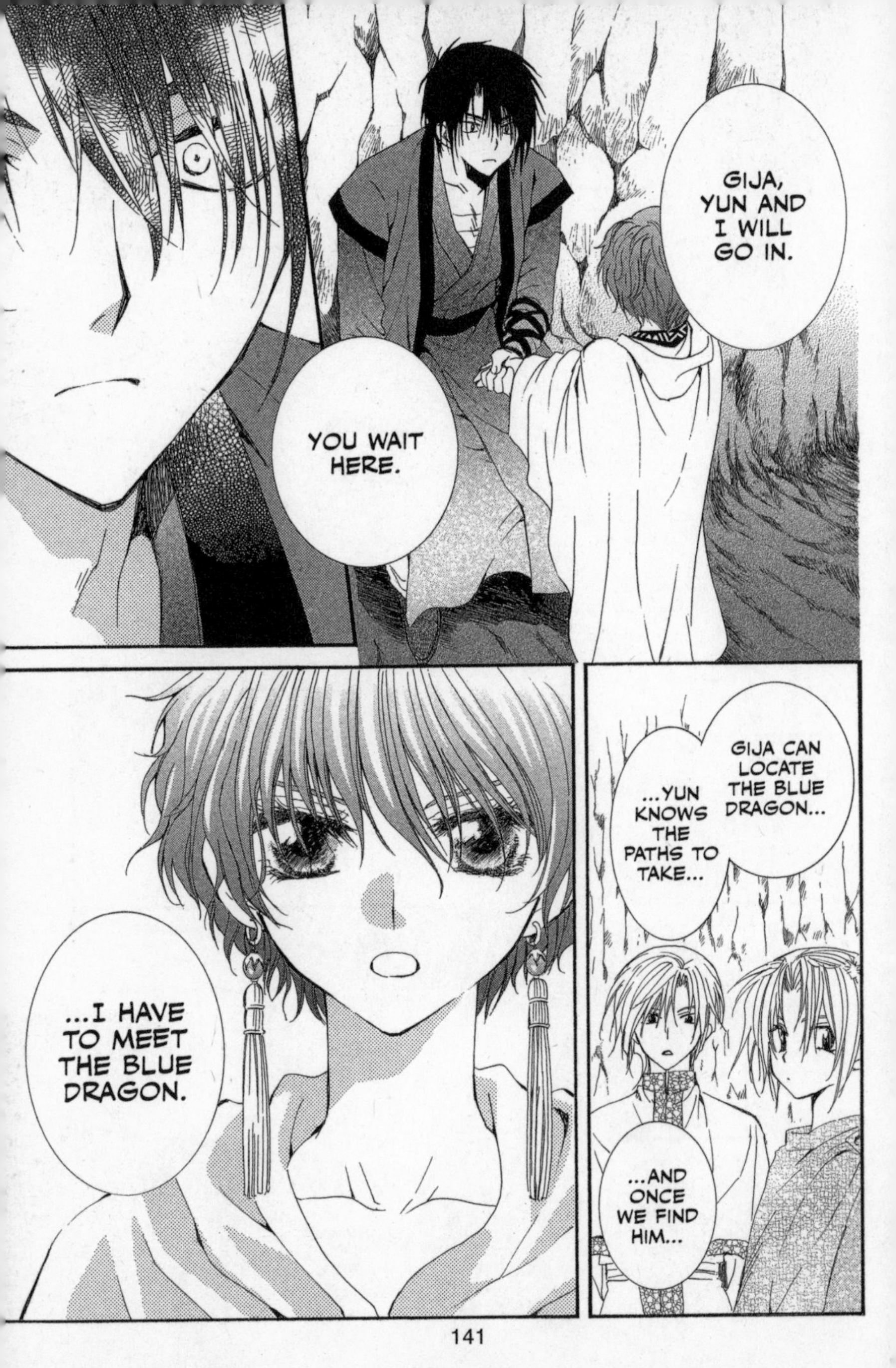
GIJA, YUN AND I WILL GO IN.
YOU WAIT HERE.
GIJA CAN LOCATE THE BLUE DRAGON...
...YUN KNOWS THE PATHS TO TAKE...
...AND ONCE WE FIND HIM...
...I HAVE TO MEET THE BLUE DRAGON.

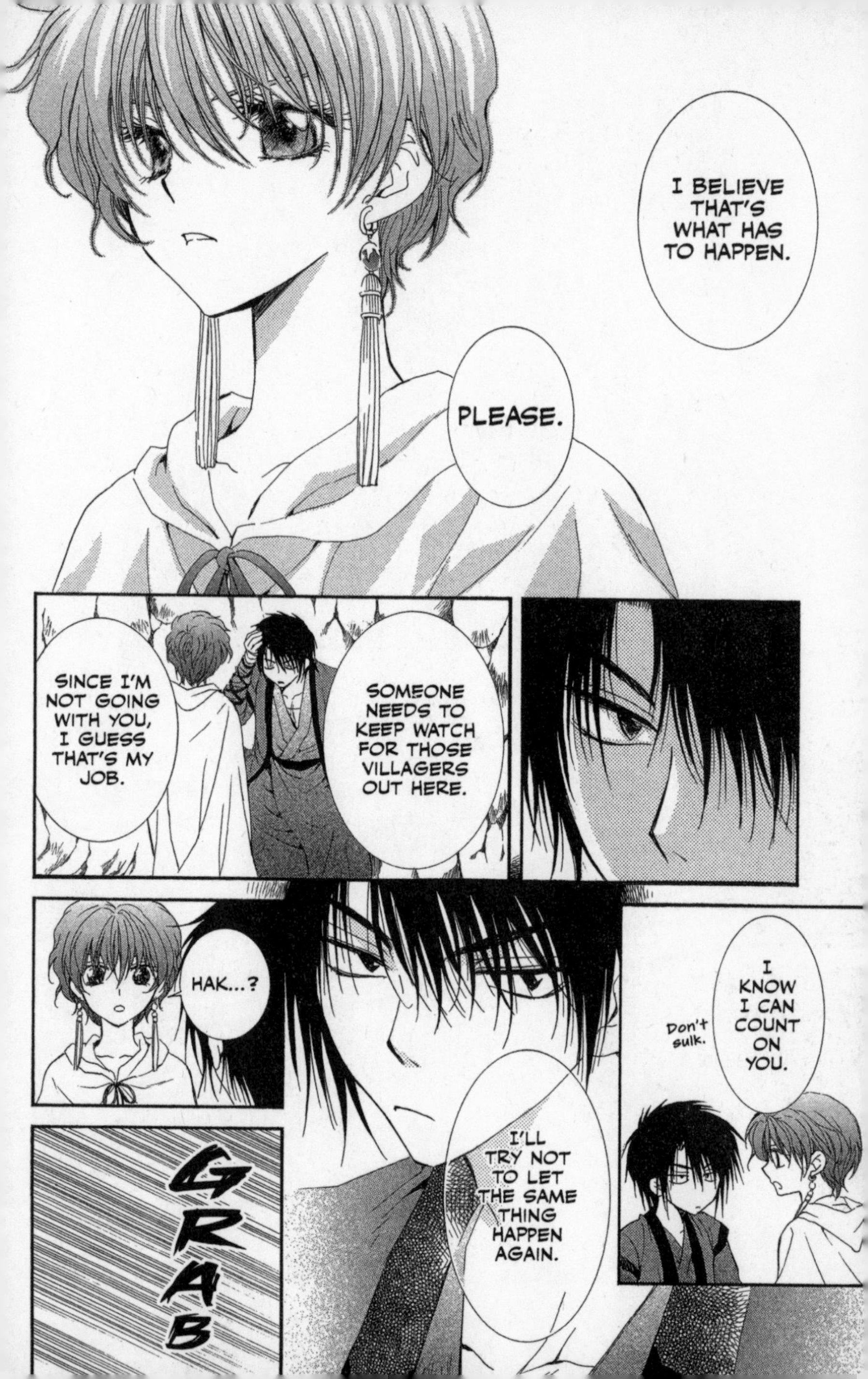
I BELIEVE THAT'S WHAT HAS TO HAPPEN.
PLEASE.
SOMEONE NEEDS TO KEEP WATCH FOR THOSE VILLAGERS OUT HERE.
SINCE I'M NOT GOING WITH YOU, I GUESS THAT'S MY JOB.
I KNOW I CAN COUNT ON YOU.
Don't sulk.
I'LL TRY NOT TO LET THE SAME THING HAPPEN AGAIN.
HAK...?
GRAB

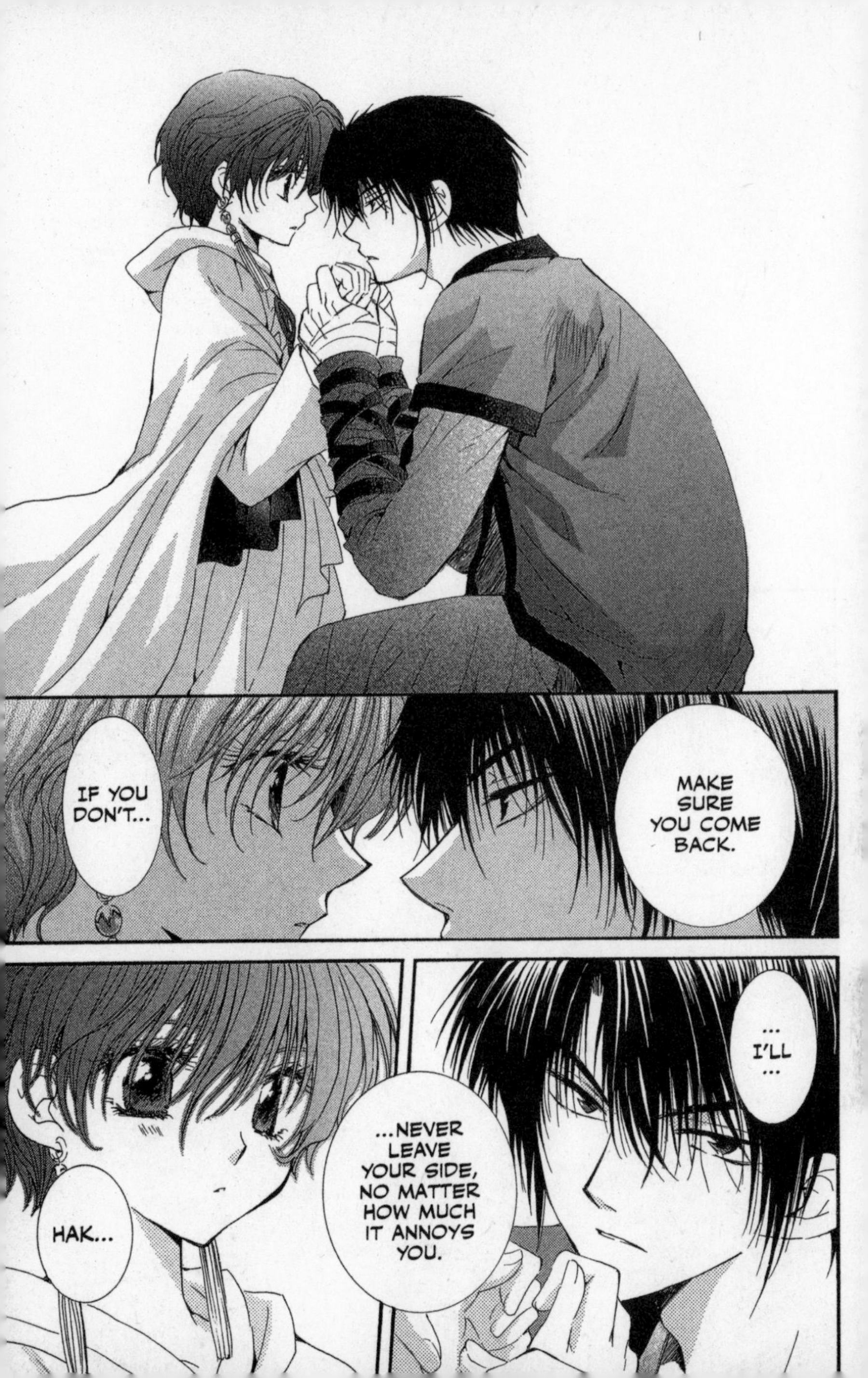
MAKE SURE YOU COME BACK.
IF YOU DON'T...
... I'LL ...
...NEVER LEAVE YOUR SIDE, NO MATTER HOW MUCH IT ANNOYS YOU.
HAK...

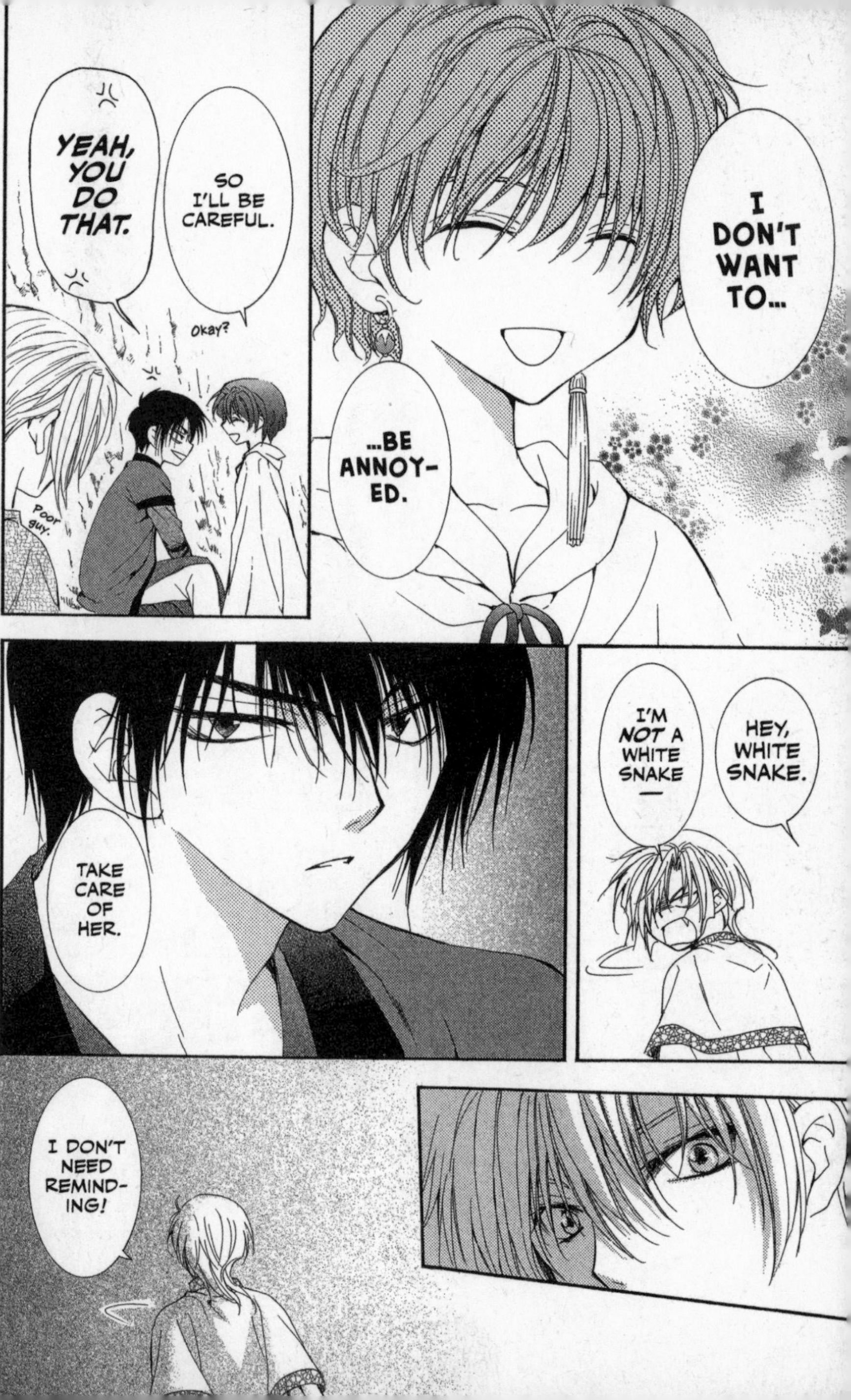
I DON'T WANT TO...
...BE ANNOY-ED.
SO I'LL BE CAREFUL.
Okay?
YEAH, YOU DO THAT.
Poor guy.
HEY, WHITE SNAKE.
I'M NOT A WHITE SNAKE—
TAKE CARE OF HER.
I DON'T NEED REMIND-ING!

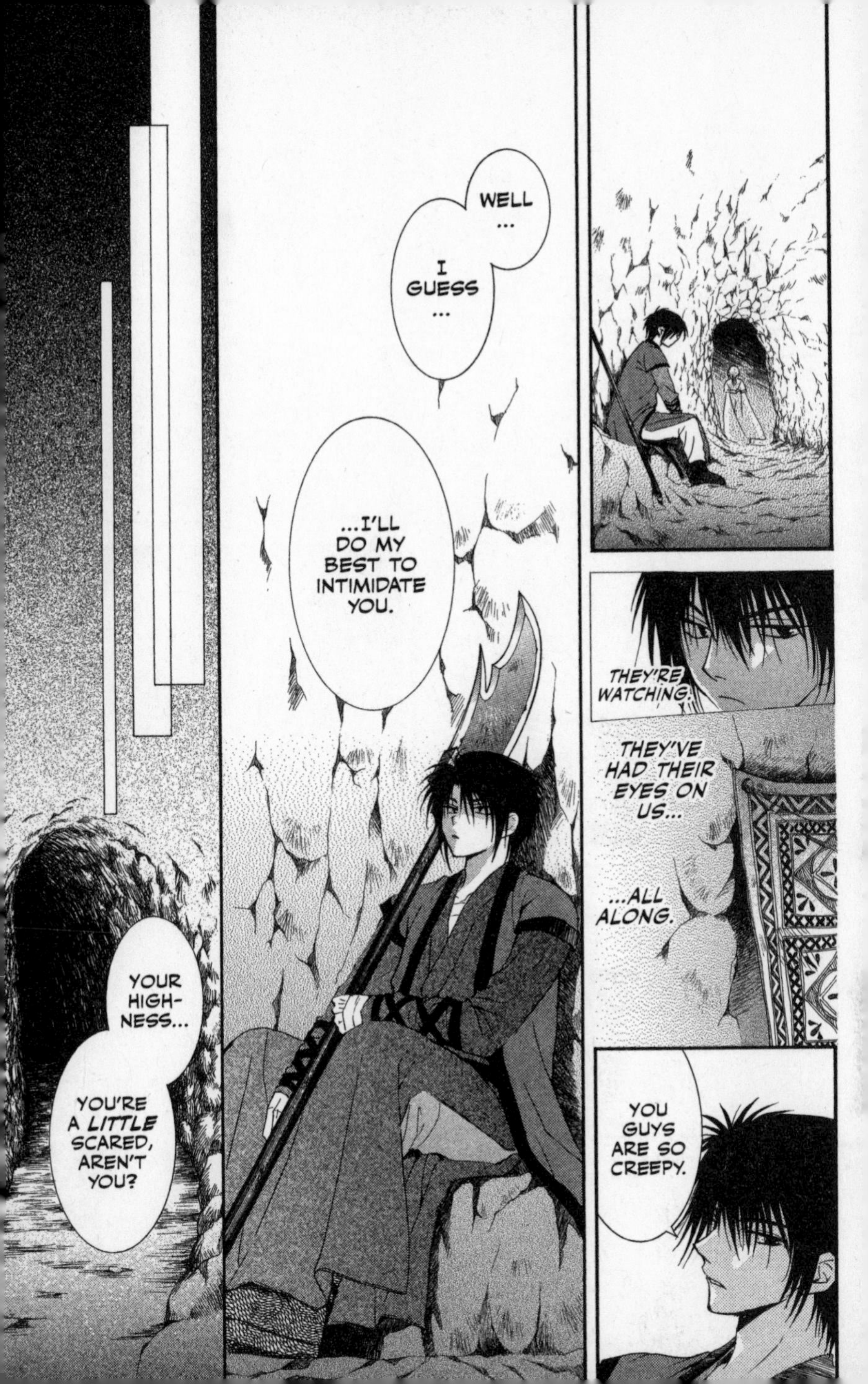
THEY'RE WATCHING.
THEY'VE HAD THEIR EYES ON US...
...ALL ALONG.
YOU GUYS ARE SO CREEPY.
WELL... I GUESS...
...I'LL DO MY BEST TO INTIMIDATE YOU.
YOUR HIGHNESS...
YOU'RE A *LITTLE* SCARED, AREN'T YOU?

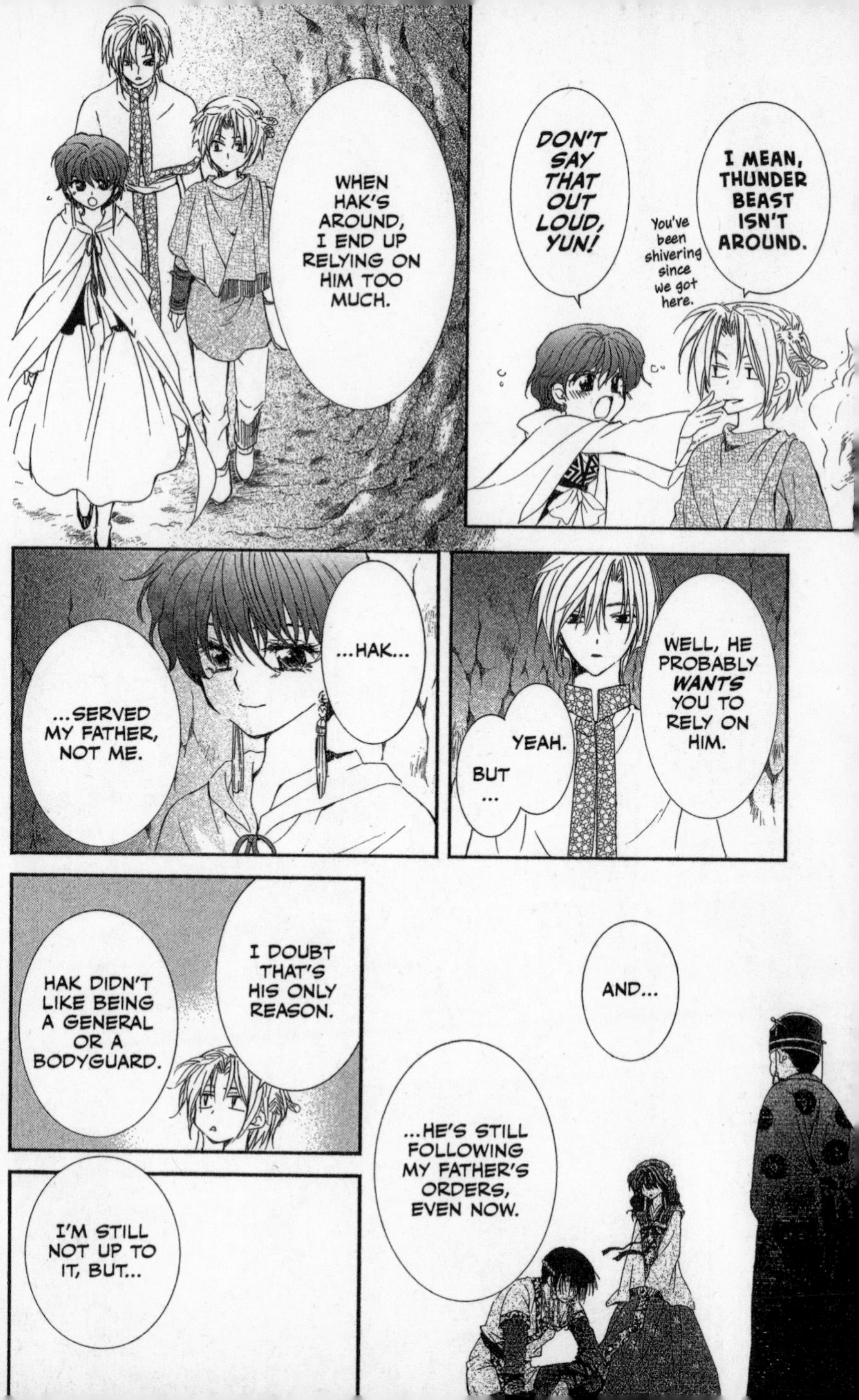

I MEAN, THUNDER BEAST ISN'T AROUND.
You've been shivering since we got here.
DON'T SAY THAT OUT LOUD, YUN!
WHEN HAK'S AROUND, I END UP RELYING ON HIM TOO MUCH.
WELL, HE PROBABLY WANTS YOU TO RELY ON HIM.
YEAH.
BUT ...
...HAK...
...SERVED MY FATHER, NOT ME.
AND...
...HE'S STILL FOLLOWING MY FATHER'S ORDERS, EVEN NOW.
I DOUBT THAT'S HIS ONLY REASON.
HAK DIDN'T LIKE BEING A GENERAL OR A BODYGUARD.
I'M STILL NOT UP TO IT, BUT...

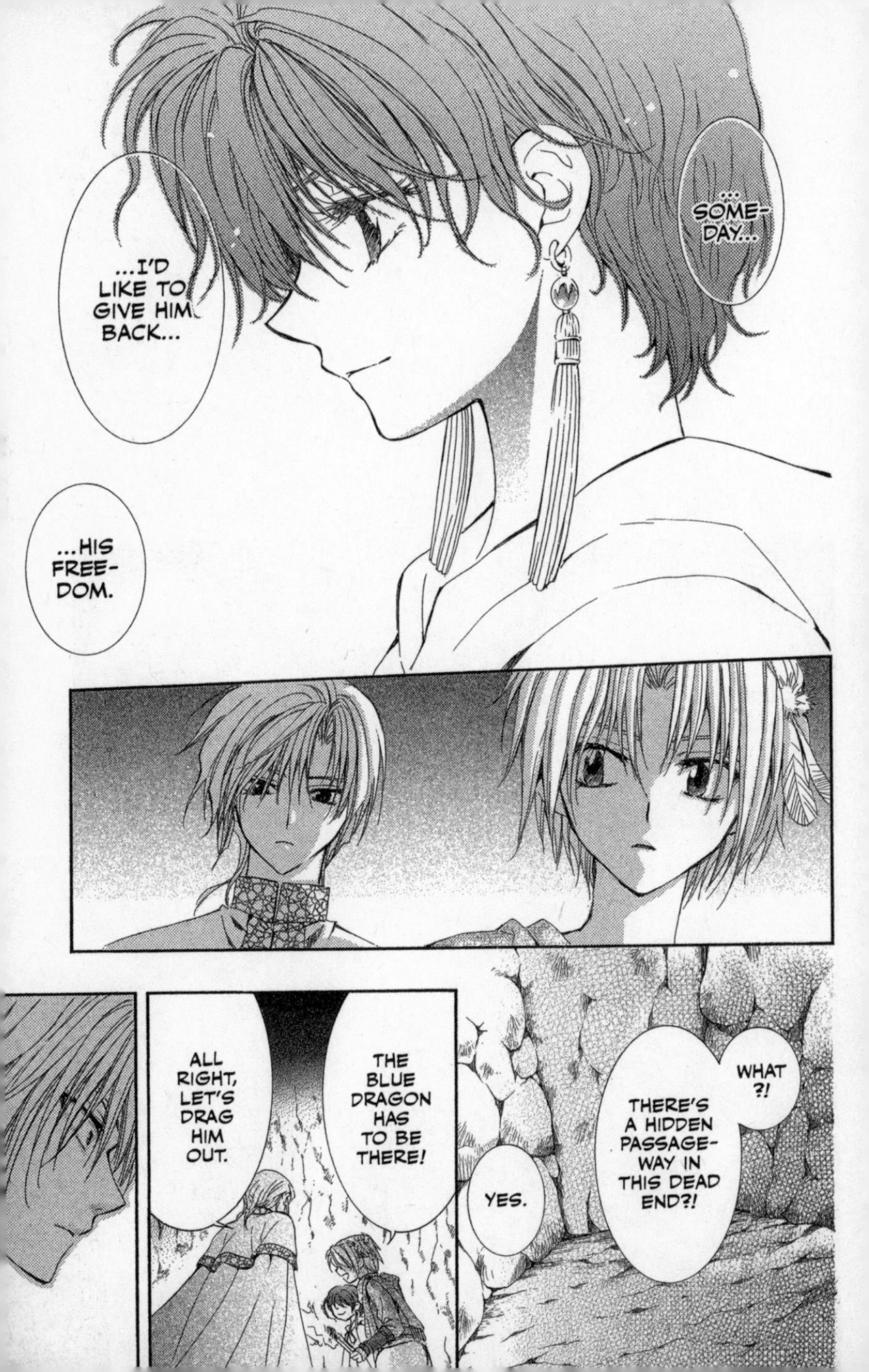
...SOME-DAY...
...I'D LIKE TO GIVE HIM BACK...
...HIS FREE-DOM.
WHAT?!
THERE'S A HIDDEN PASSAGE-WAY IN THIS DEAD END?!
YES.
THE BLUE DRAGON HAS TO BE THERE!
ALL RIGHT, LET'S DRAG HIM OUT.

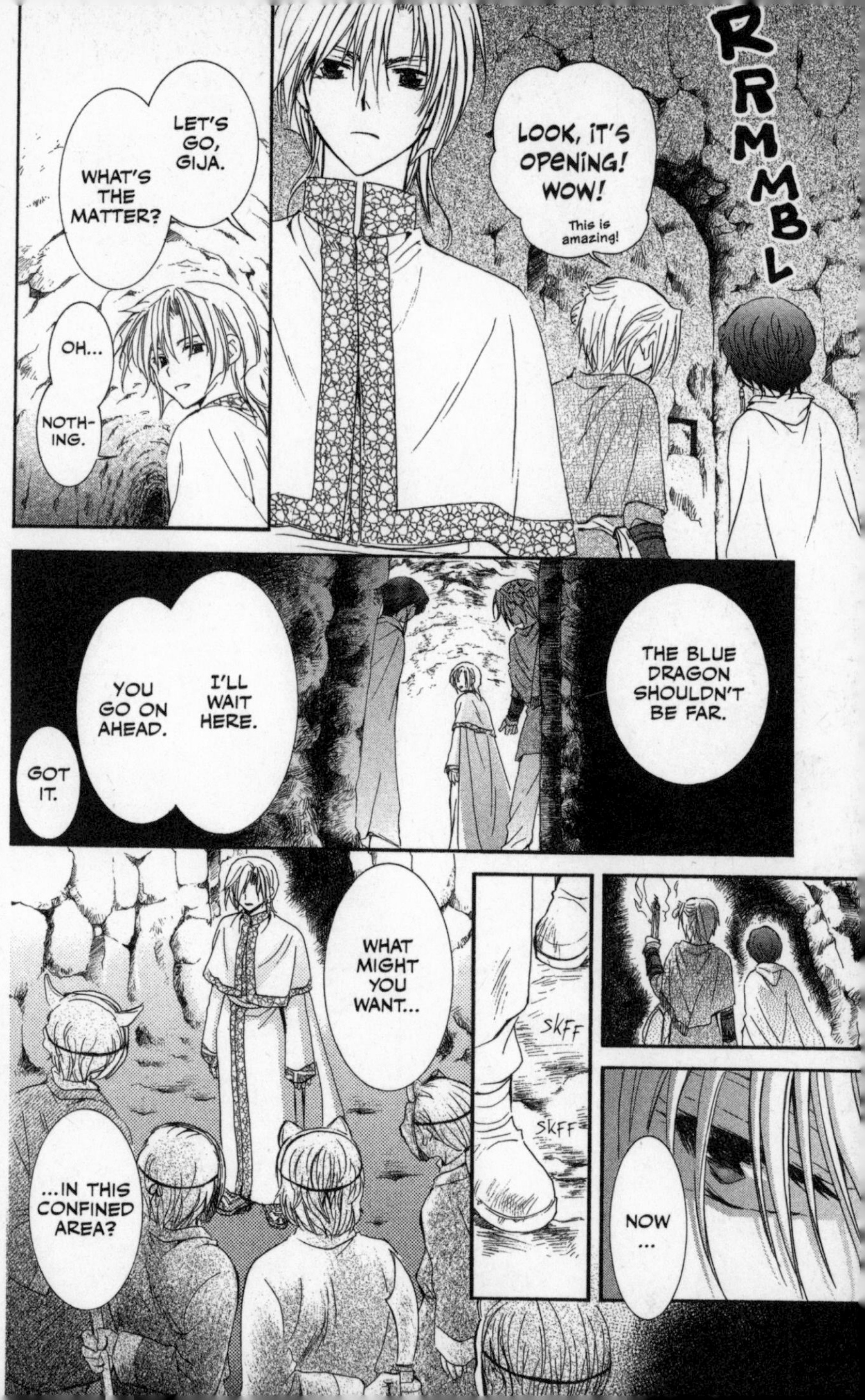
RRMMBL
LOOK, IT'S OPENING! WOW!
This is amazing!
LET'S GO, GIJA.
WHAT'S THE MATTER?
OH...
NOTHING.
THE BLUE DRAGON SHOULDN'T BE FAR.
I'LL WAIT HERE.
YOU GO ON AHEAD.
GOT IT.
NOW ...
SKFF
SKFF
WHAT MIGHT YOU WANT...
...IN THIS CONFINED AREA?

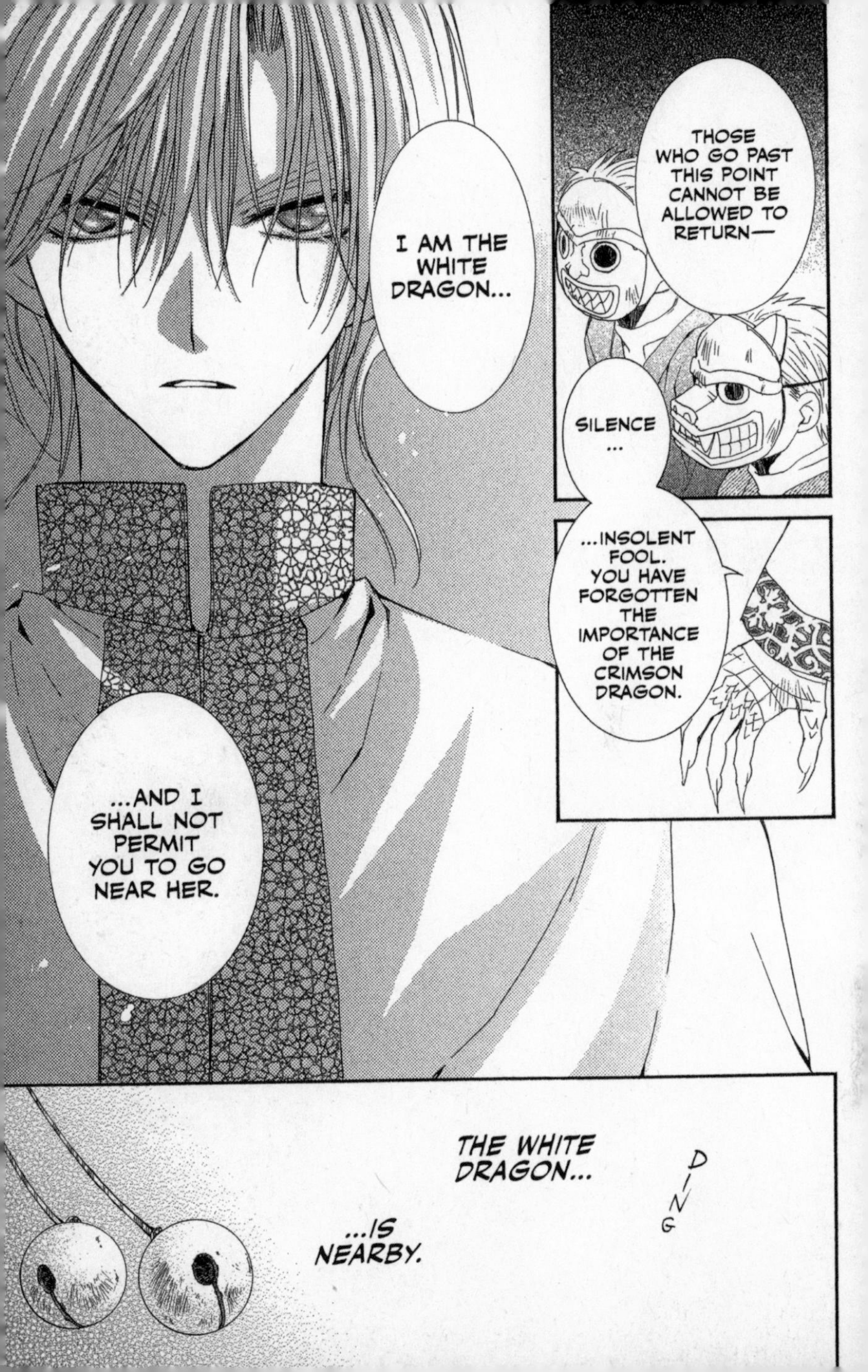
THOSE WHO GO PAST THIS POINT CANNOT BE ALLOWED TO RETURN—
SILENCE...
...INSOLENT FOOL. YOU HAVE FORGOTTEN THE IMPORTANCE OF THE CRIMSON DRAGON.
I AM THE WHITE DRAGON...
...AND I SHALL NOT PERMIT YOU TO GO NEAR HER.
DING
THE WHITE DRAGON...
...IS NEARBY.

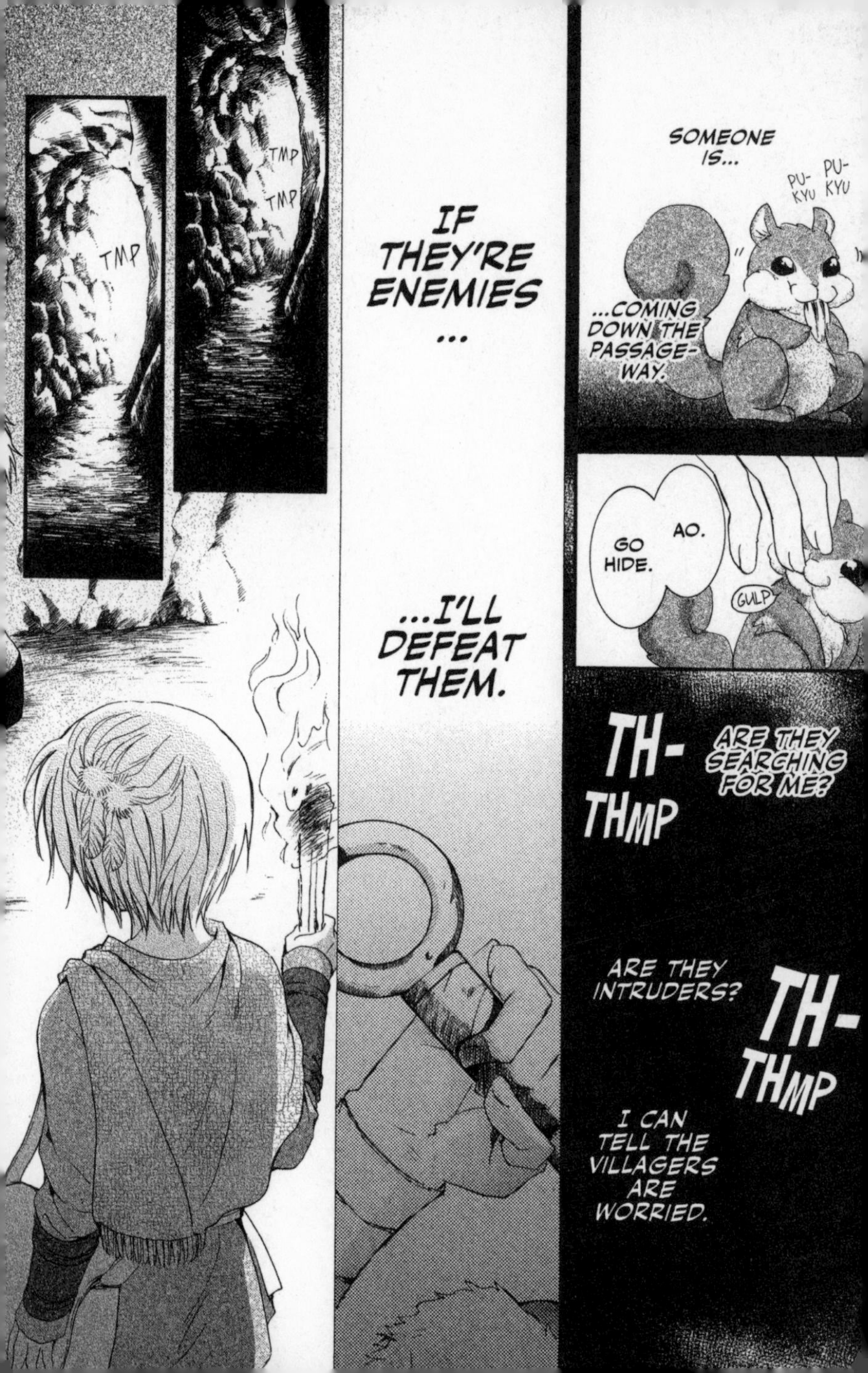
SOMEONE IS...
PU- KYU
PU- KYU
...COMING DOWN THE PASSAGE-WAY.
AO.
GO HIDE.
GULP
TH-THMP
ARE THEY SEARCHING FOR ME?
TH-THMP
ARE THEY INTRUDERS?
I CAN TELL THE VILLAGERS ARE WORRIED.
IF THEY'RE ENEMIES ...
...I'LL DEFEAT THEM.
TMP
TMP
TMP

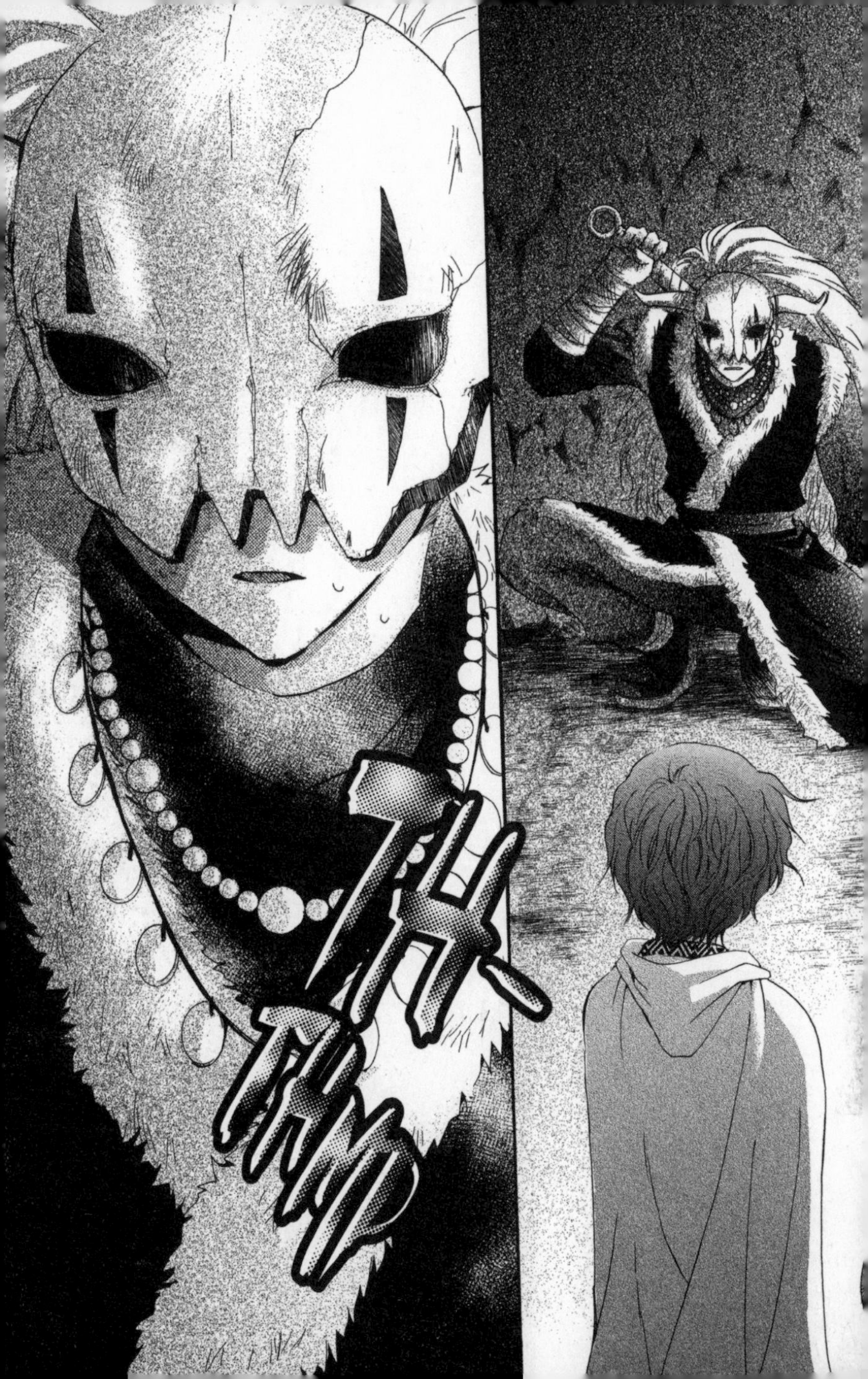
TH THMP

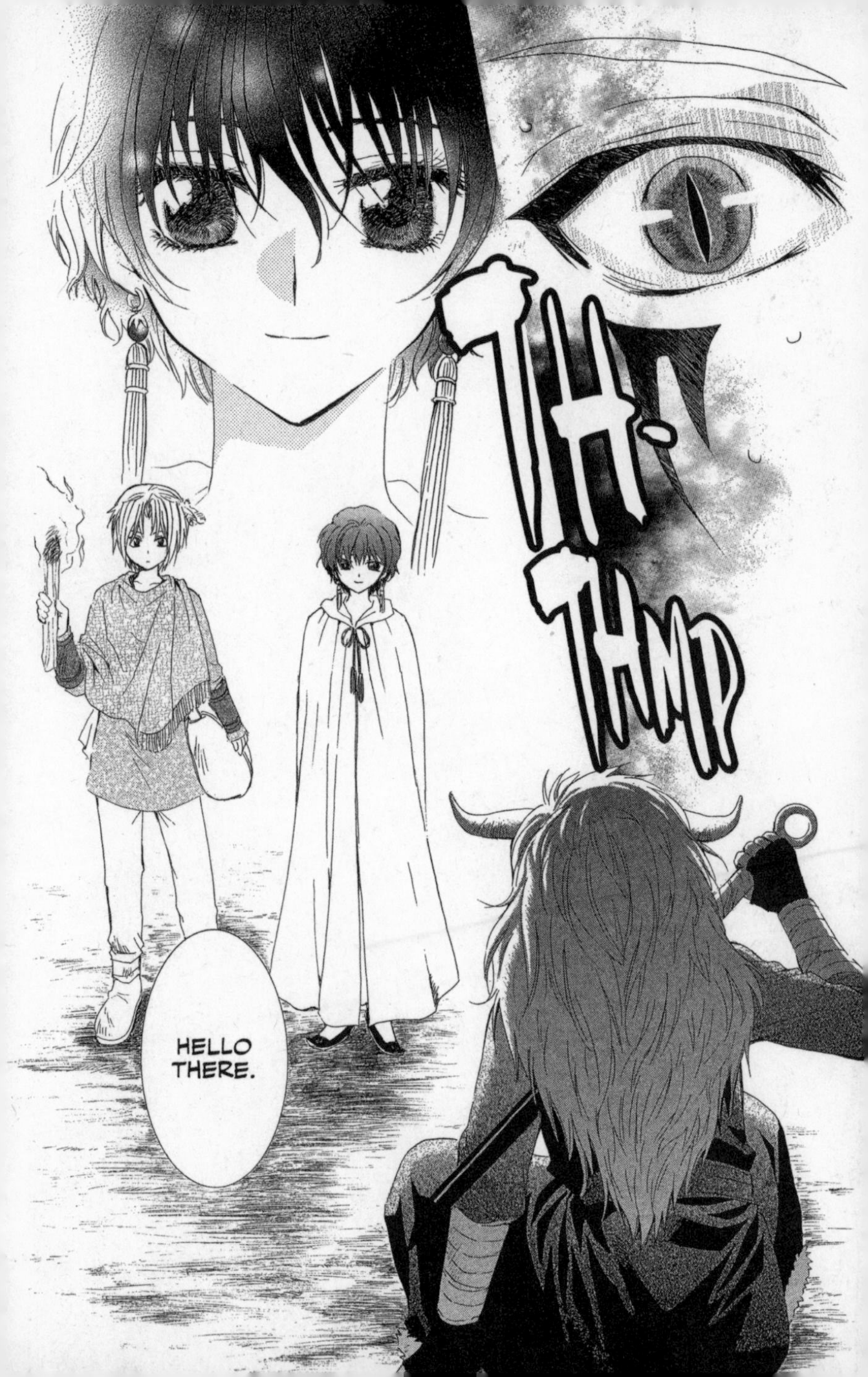
TH-THMP
HELLO THERE.

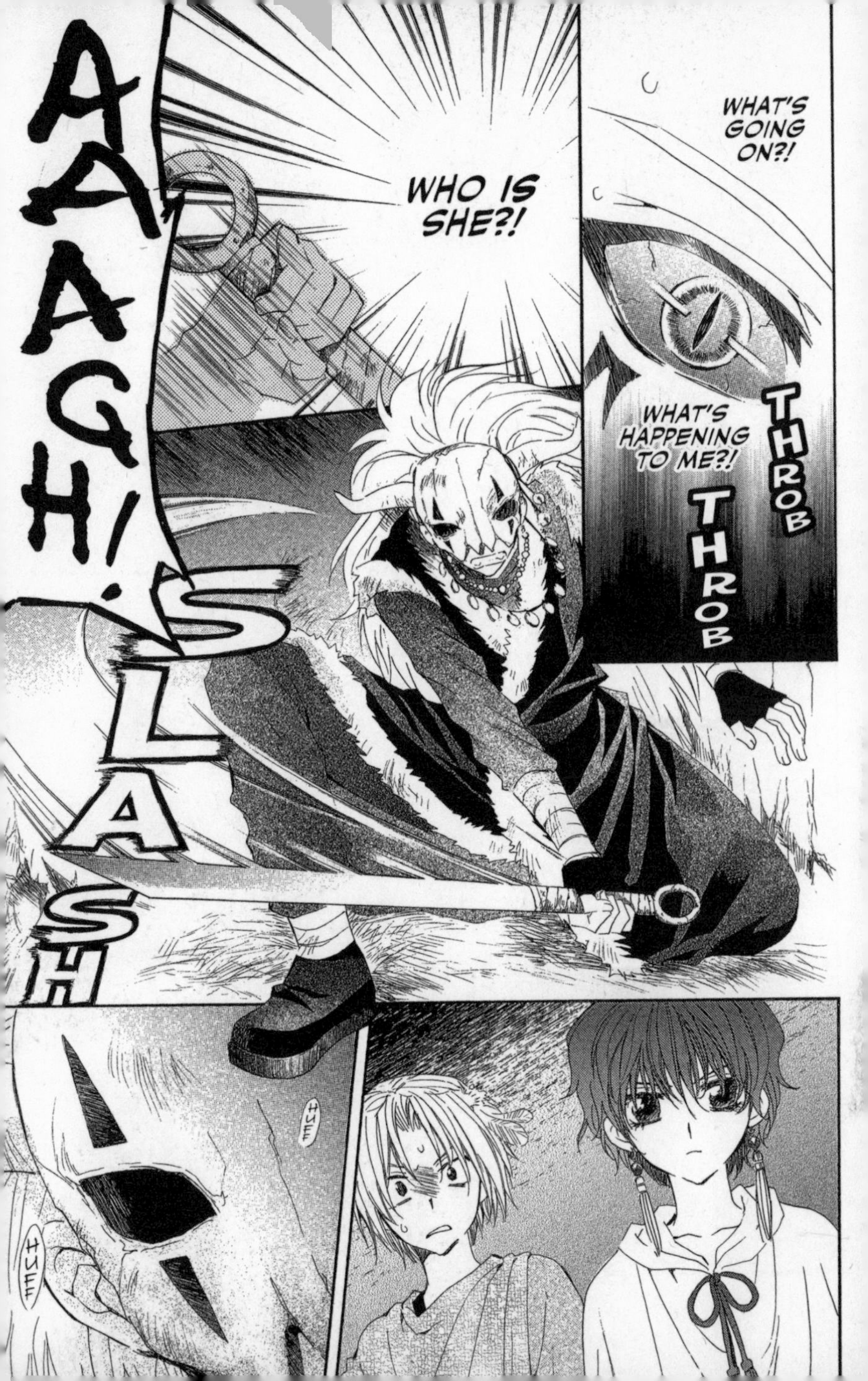
WHAT'S GOING ON?!
WHAT'S HAPPENING TO ME?!
THROB
THROB
WHO IS SHE?!
AAGH!
SLASH
HUFF
HUFF

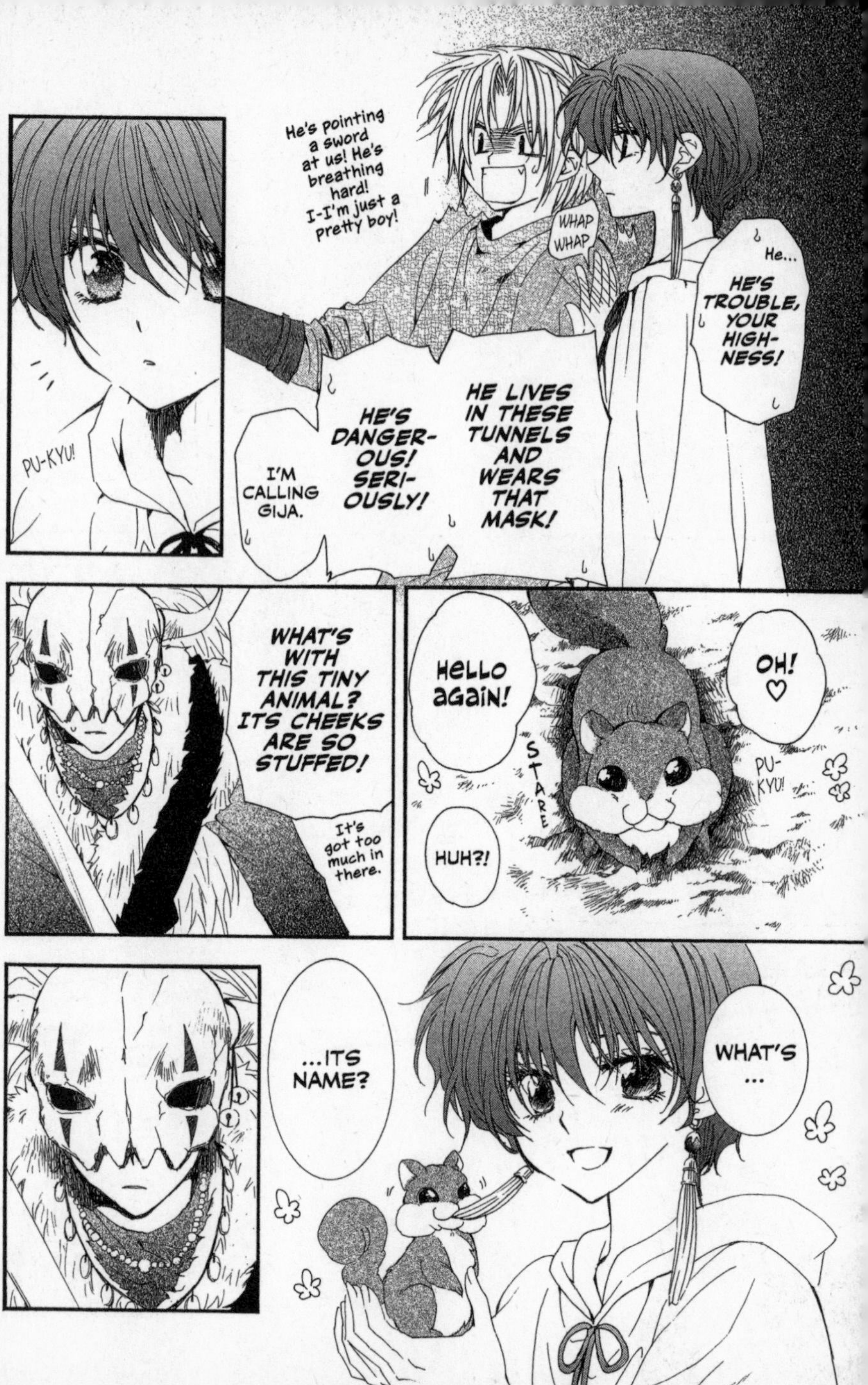
He...
HE'S TROUBLE, YOUR HIGHNESS!
HE LIVES IN THESE TUNNELS AND WEARS THAT MASK!
HE'S DANGEROUS! SERIOUSLY!
I'M CALLING GIJA.
WHAP WHAP
He's pointing a sword at us! He's breathing hard! I-I'm just a pretty boy!
PU-KYU!
OH! ♥
PU-KYU!
Hello again!
STARE
HUH?!
WHAT'S WITH THIS TINY ANIMAL? ITS CHEEKS ARE SO STUFFED!
It's got too much in there.
WHAT'S...
...ITS NAME?

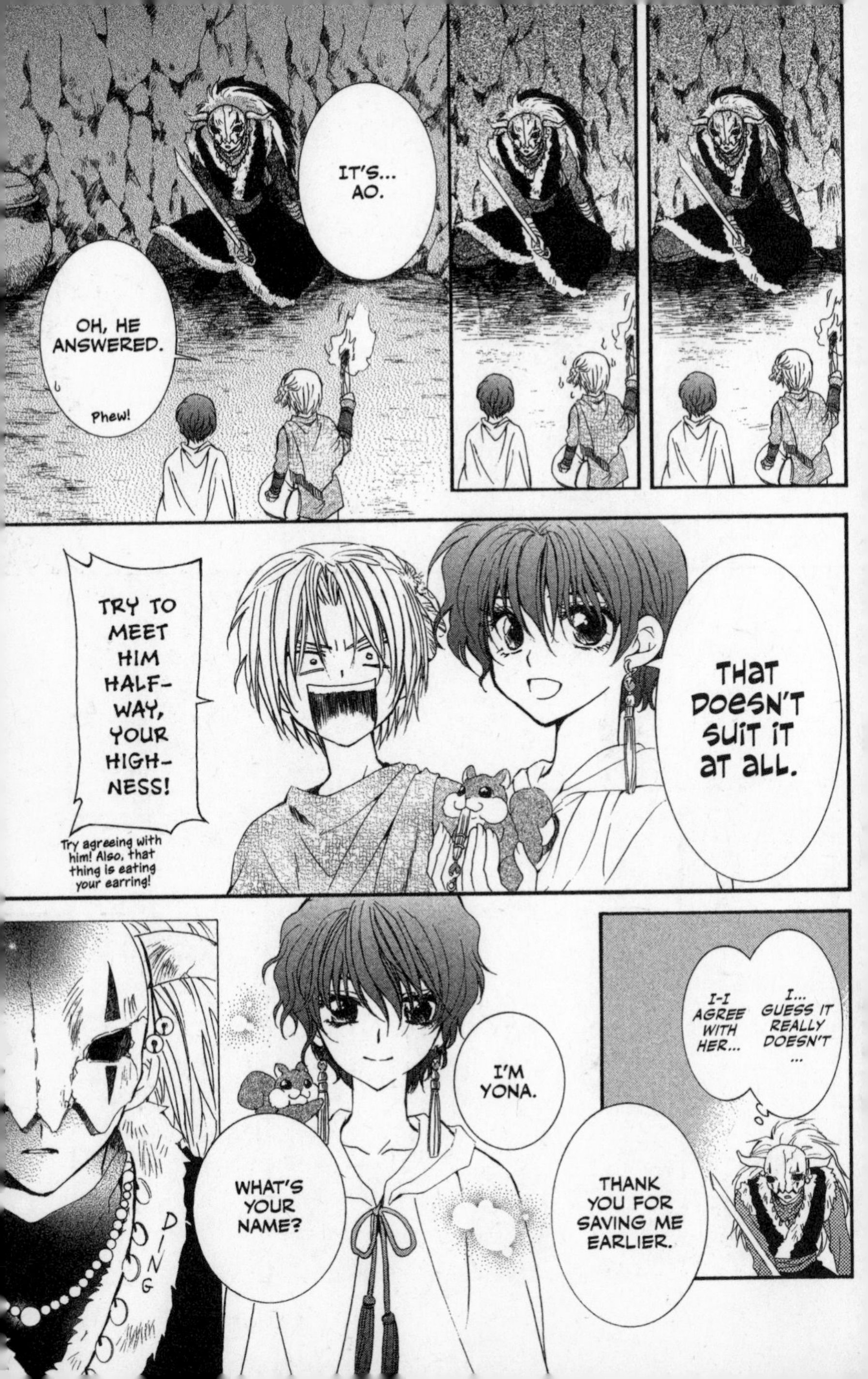
IT'S... AO.
OH, HE ANSWERED.
Phew!
THAT DOESN'T SUIT IT AT ALL.
TRY TO MEET HIM HALF-WAY, YOUR HIGH-NESS!
Try agreeing with him! Also, that thing is eating your earring!
I... GUESS IT REALLY DOESN'T ...
I-I AGREE WITH HER...
I'M YONA.
THANK YOU FOR SAVING ME EARLIER.
WHAT'S YOUR NAME?
DING

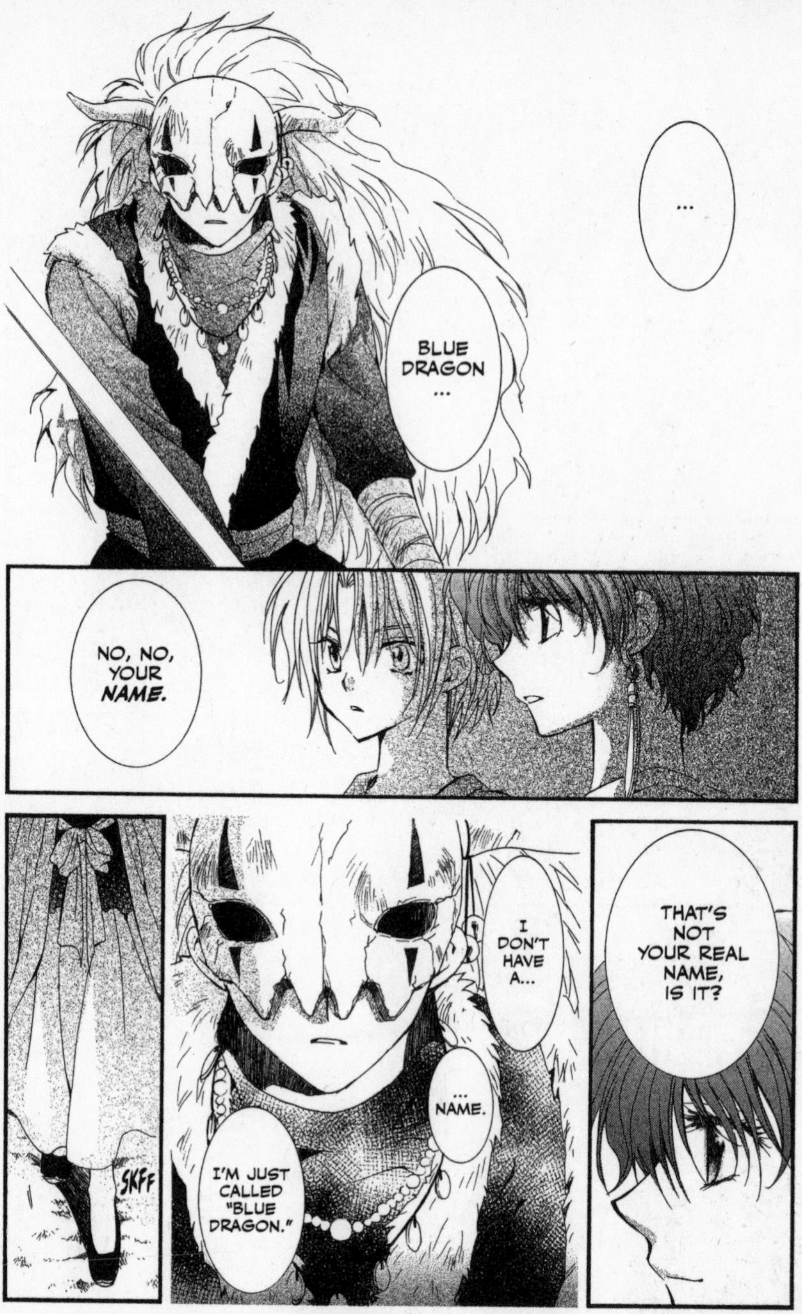
...
BLUE DRAGON ...
NO, NO, YOUR NAME.
THAT'S NOT YOUR REAL NAME, IS IT?
I DON'T HAVE A...
... NAME.
I'M JUST CALLED "BLUE DRAGON."
SKFF

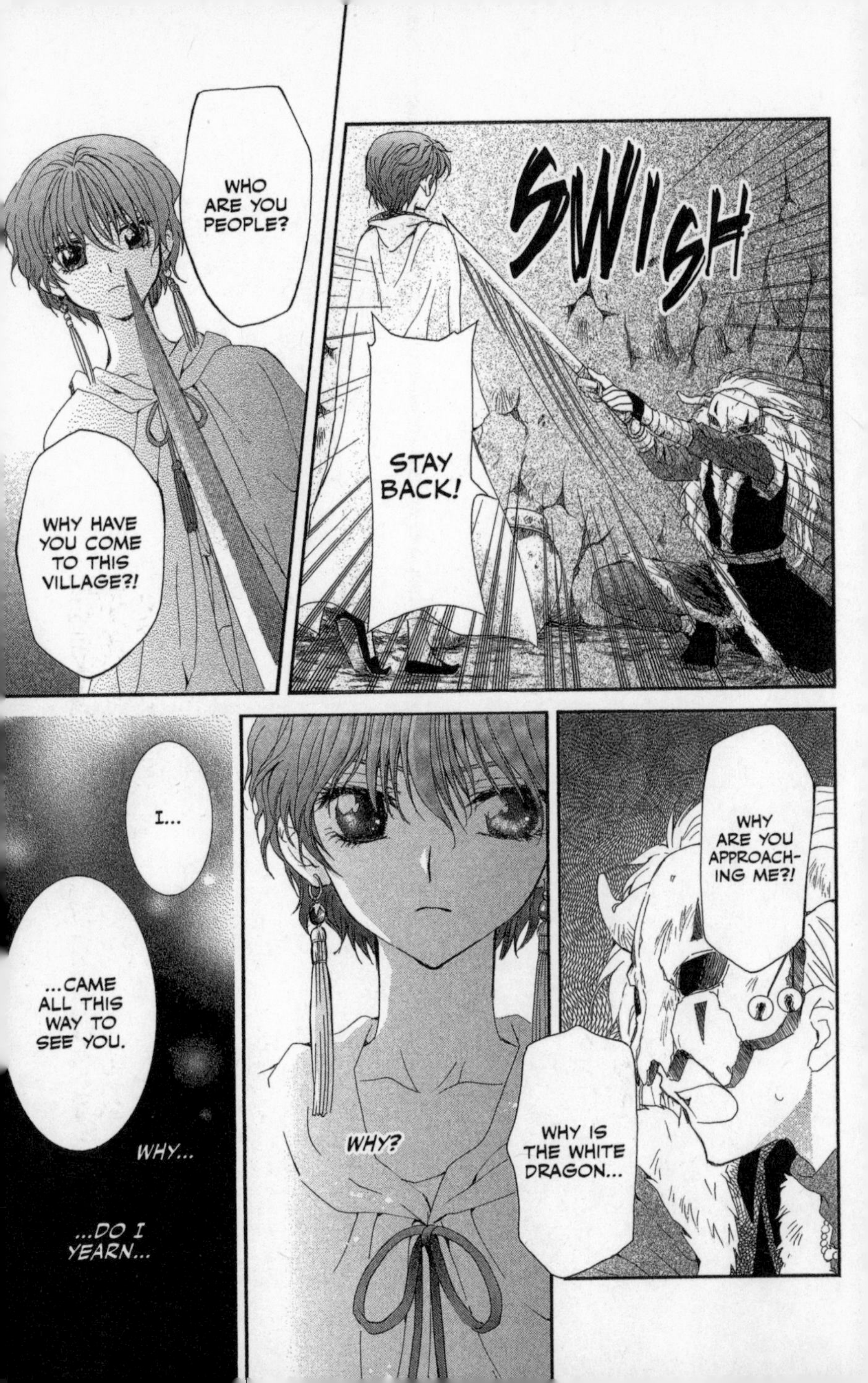
SWISH
STAY BACK!
WHO ARE YOU PEOPLE?
WHY HAVE YOU COME TO THIS VILLAGE?!
WHY ARE YOU APPROACHING ME?!
WHY IS THE WHITE DRAGON...
WHY?
I...
...CAME ALL THIS WAY TO SEE YOU.
WHY...
...DO I YEARN...

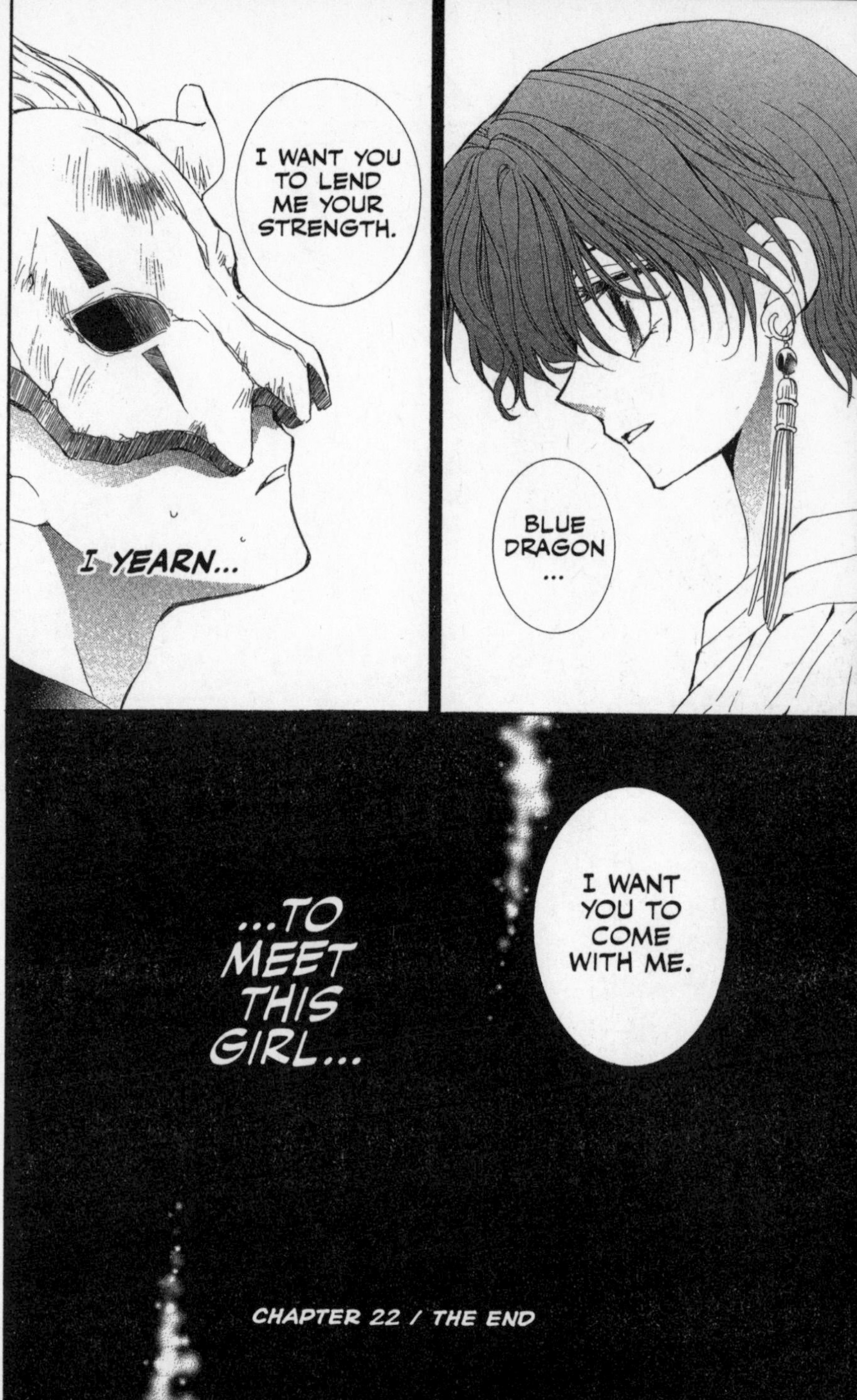
BLUE DRAGON ...
I WANT YOU TO LEND ME YOUR STRENGTH.
I YEARN...
I WANT YOU TO COME WITH ME.
...TO MEET THIS GIRL...
CHAPTER 22 / THE END

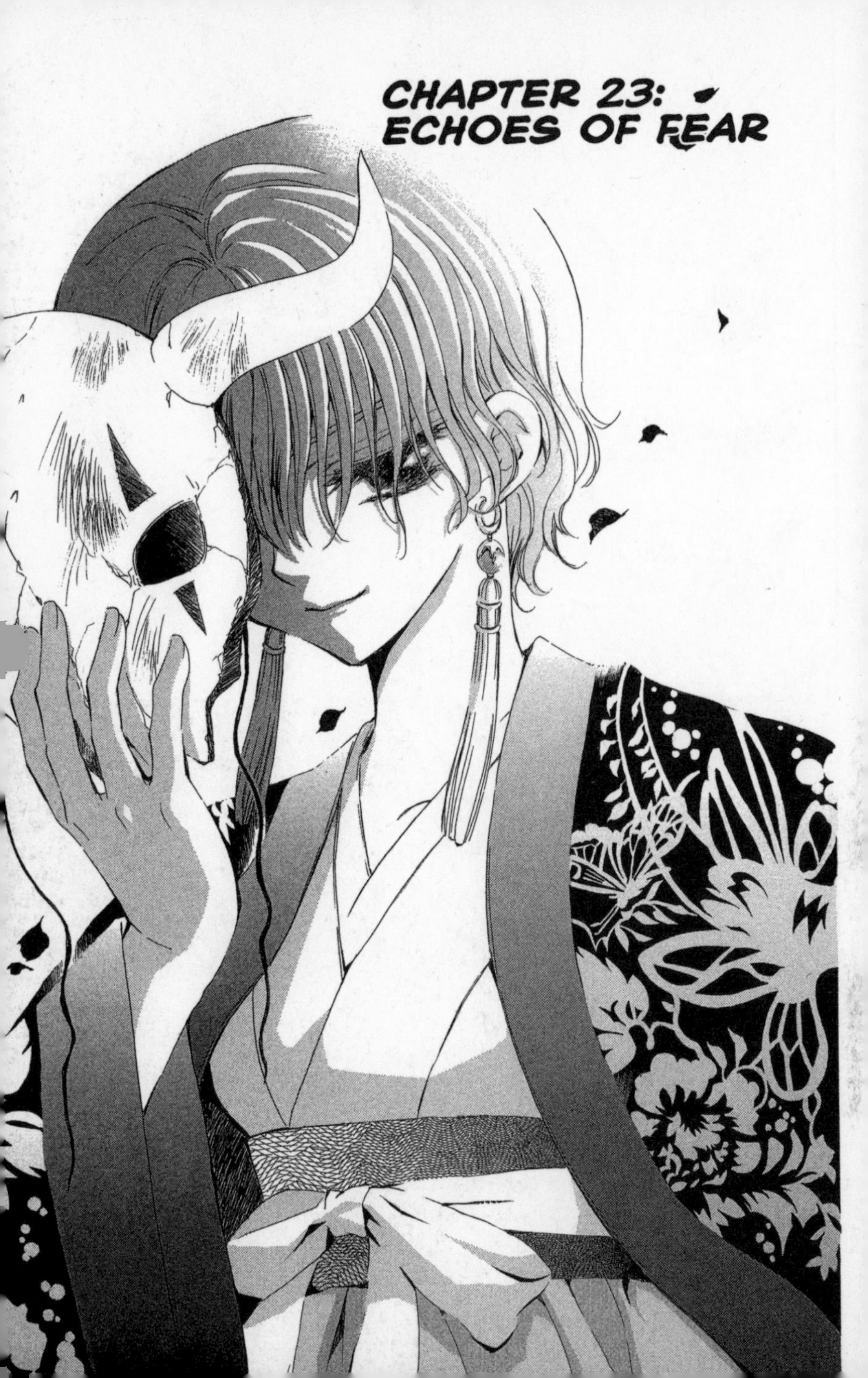
CHAPTER 23:
ECHOES OF FEAR

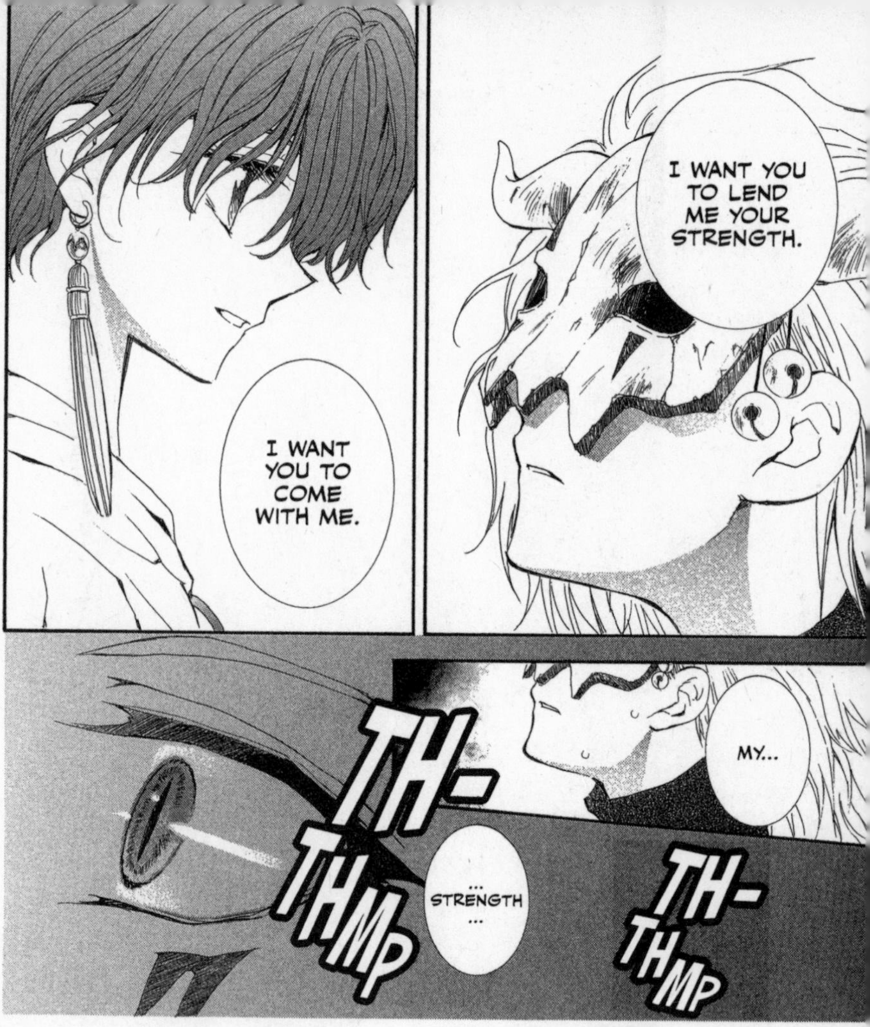
I WANT YOU TO LEND ME YOUR STRENGTH.
I WANT YOU TO COME WITH ME.
MY...
TH-THMP
...STRENGTH...
TH-THMP

A special thanks! ♥
My assistants → Mikorun, Kyoko, Rurunga, Ryo Sakura and my little sister...
My editor Yamashita, the *Hana to Yume* editorial office and Naato...
Everyone who helped me create and sell this manga...
Family and friends who supported me, and my readers! ♥
Thank you for always helping me out. And thank you for making me want to continue drawing this manga!

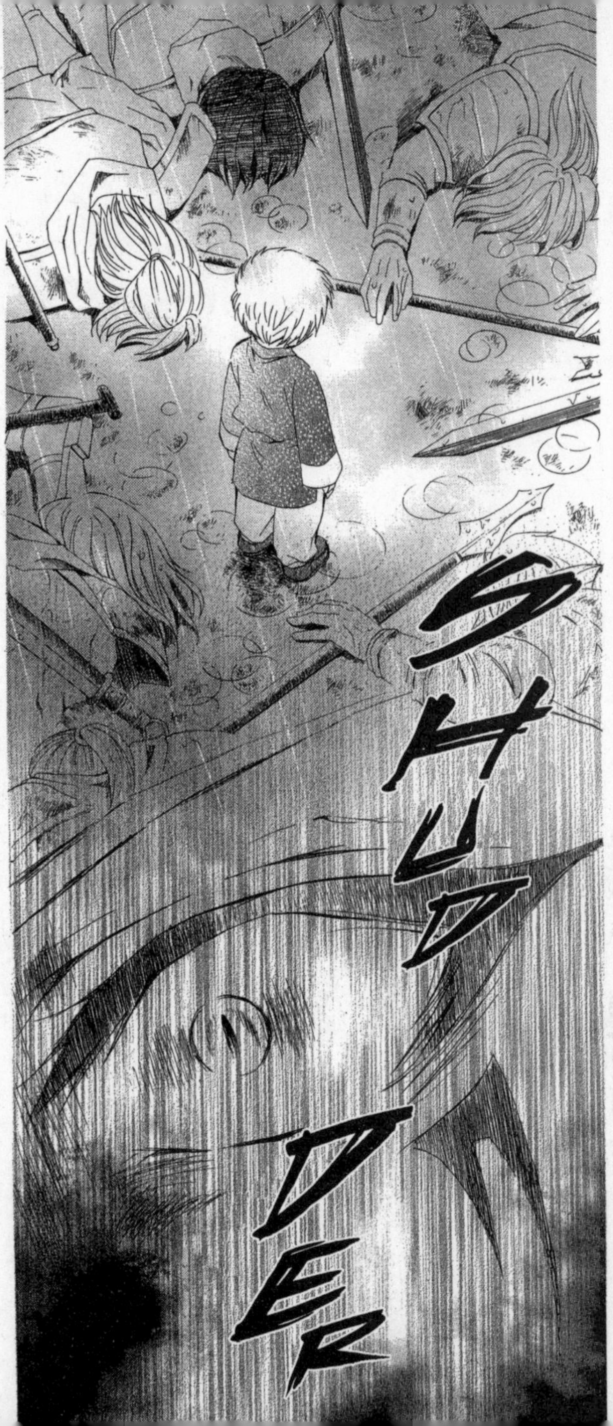
SHUDDER

The Blue Dragon has a squirrel named Ao, but the name doesn't really suit it, so at our workplace, we call it "Pu-kyu."✧ It gets confusing since the previous Blue Dragon had the same name. If any of you get confused, please call it Pu-kyu too! There's always something stuffed in its cheeks.✧

Su-won hasn't made an appearance lately. I felt bad for any Su-won fans, so I drew a mini comic with tiny Su-won (and the ever-popular Mun-deok). I eventually have plans for Su-won, but it looks like the search for the Dragon Warriors will continue for a while longer. Coming up next is volume 5. I hope you'll read it! Thank you very much!

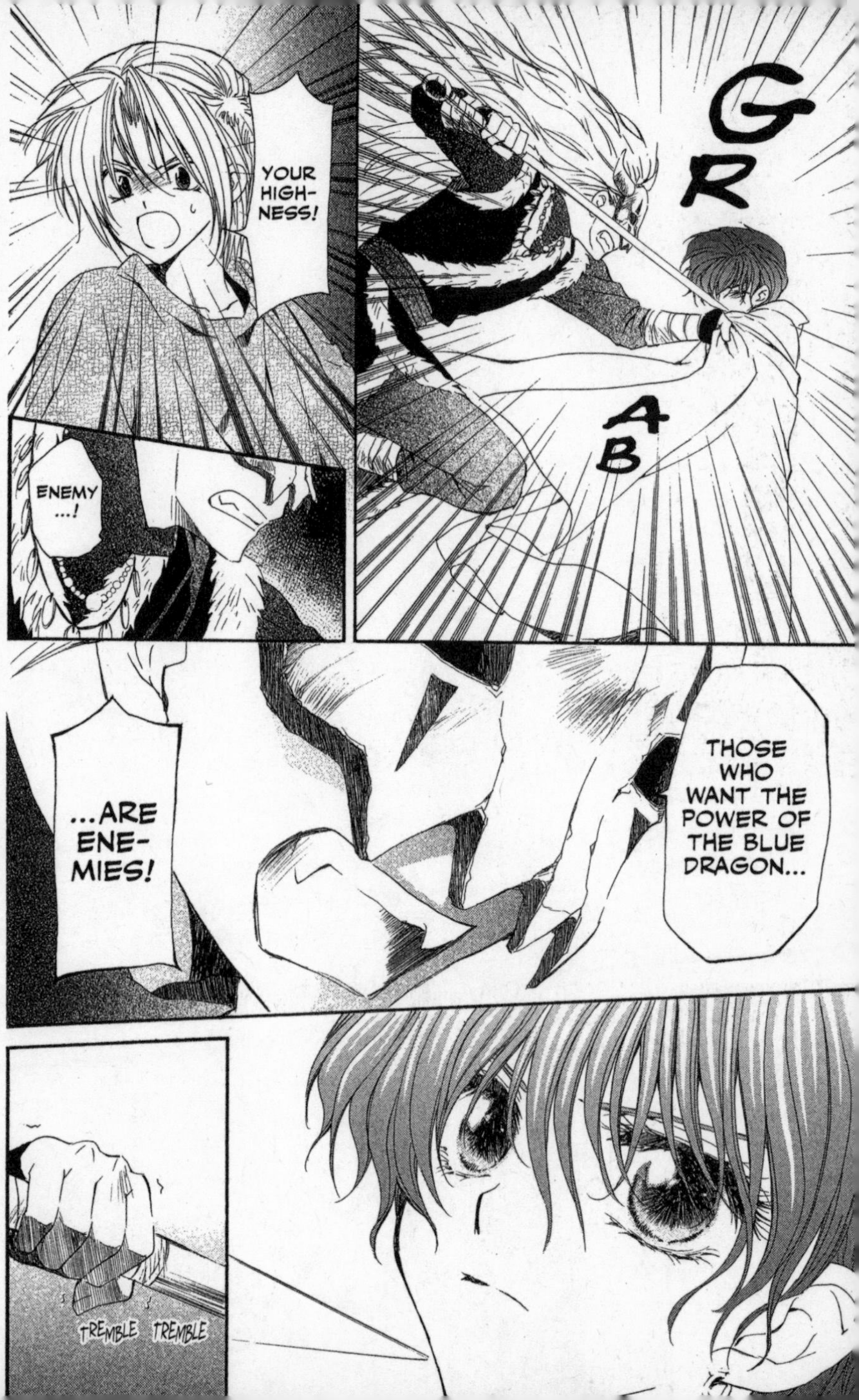
GRAB
YOUR HIGHNESS!
ENEMY ...!
THOSE WHO WANT THE POWER OF THE BLUE DRAGON...
...ARE ENEMIES!
TREMBLE TREMBLE

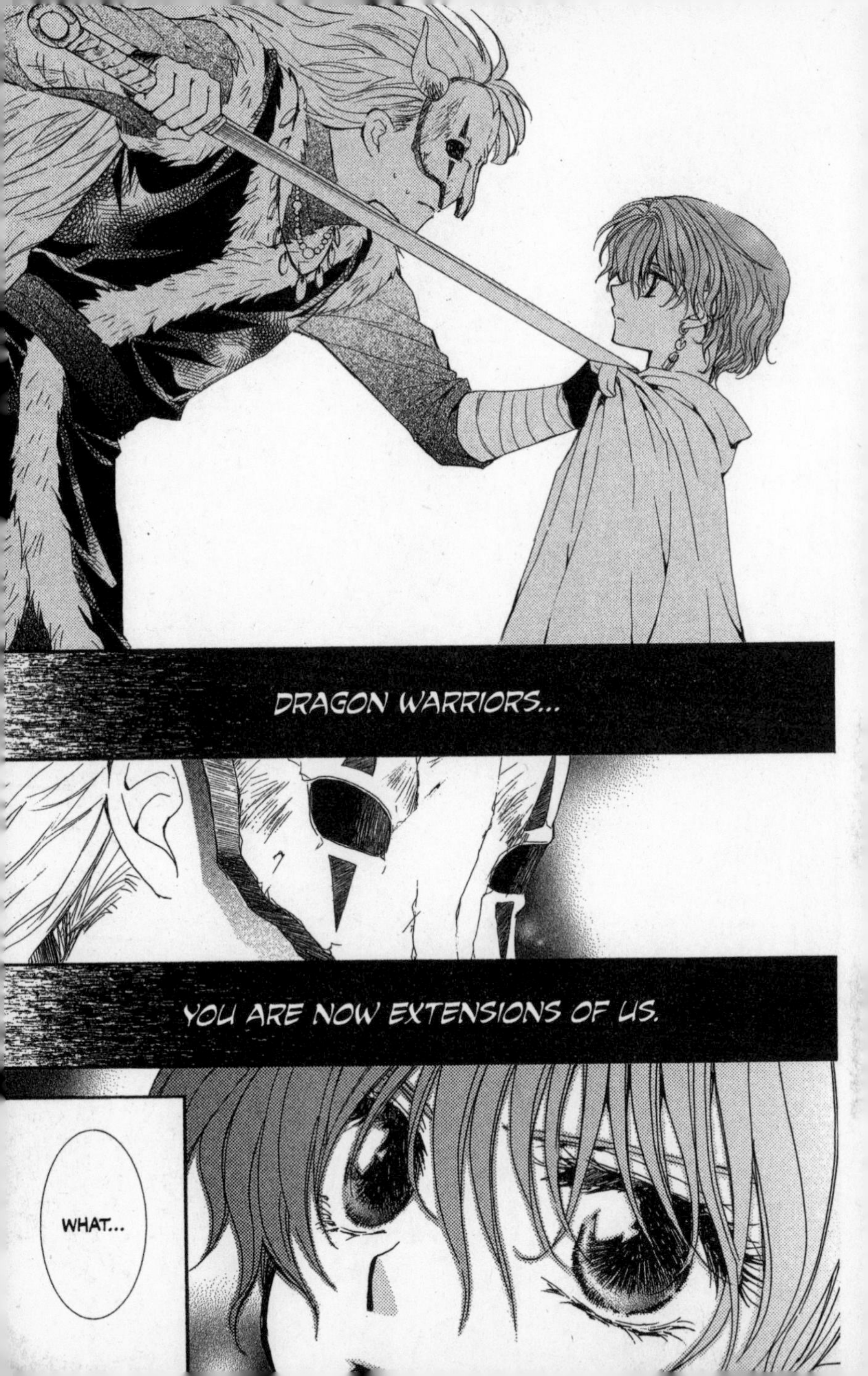
DRAGON WARRIORS...
YOU ARE NOW EXTENSIONS OF US.
WHAT...

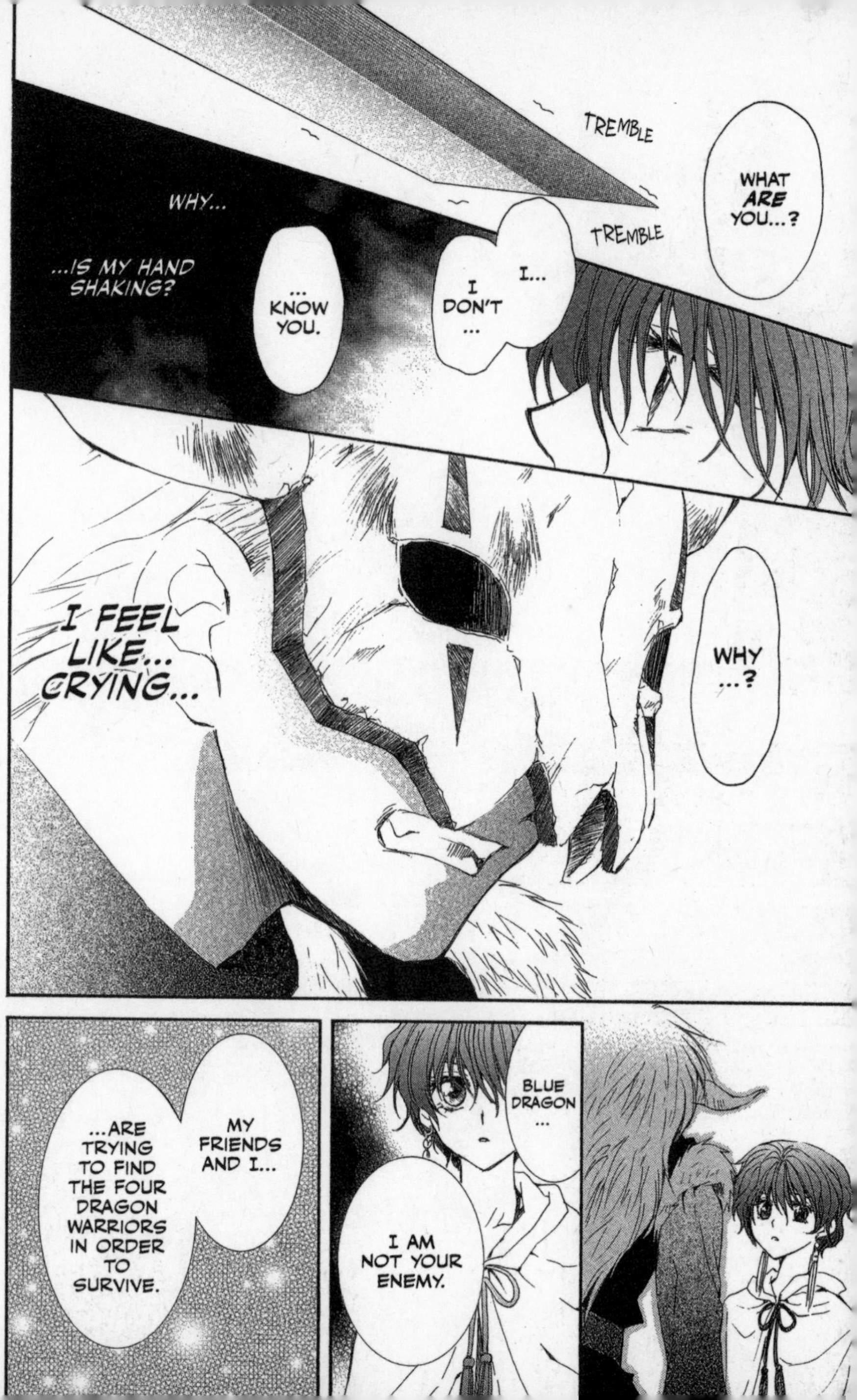
WHAT ARE YOU...?
TREMBLE
TREMBLE
I... I DON'T ...
... KNOW YOU.
WHY...
...IS MY HAND SHAKING?
WHY ...?
I FEEL LIKE... CRYING...
BLUE DRAGON ...
I AM NOT YOUR ENEMY.
MY FRIENDS AND I...
...ARE TRYING TO FIND THE FOUR DRAGON WARRIORS IN ORDER TO SURVIVE.

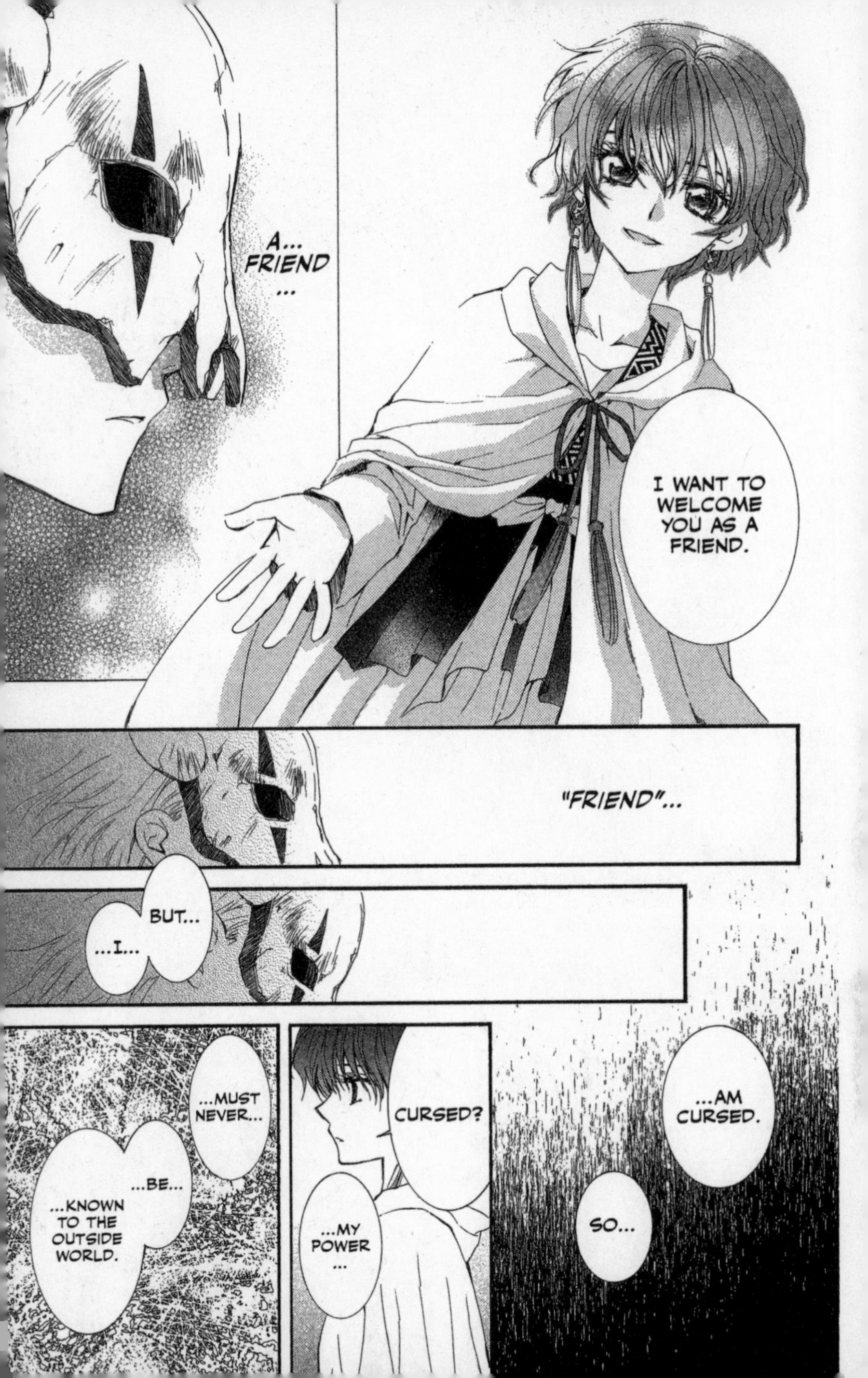
I WANT TO WELCOME YOU AS A FRIEND.
A... FRIEND ...
"FRIEND"...
BUT...
...I...
...AM CURSED.
SO...
CURSED?
...MY POWER ...
...MUST NEVER...
...BE...
...KNOWN TO THE OUTSIDE WORLD.

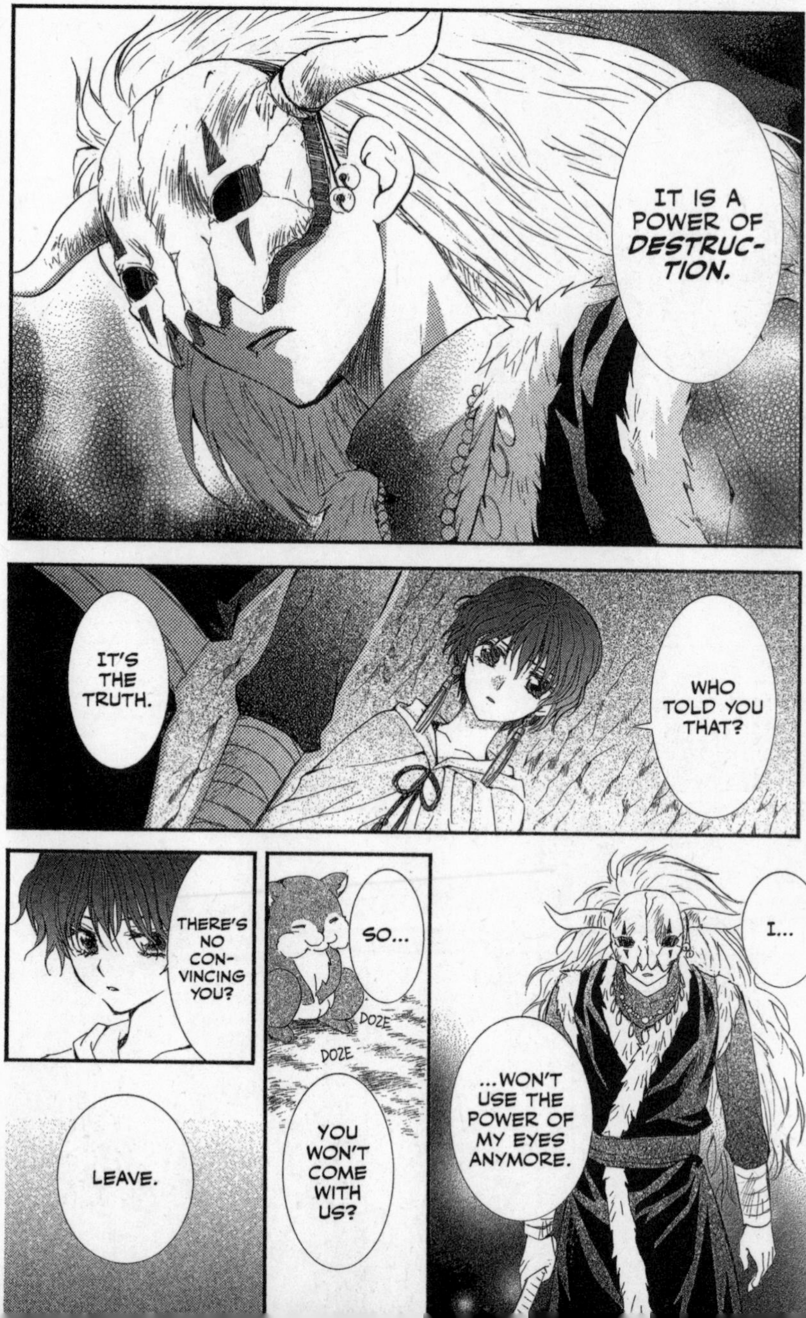
IT IS A POWER OF DESTRUCTION.
WHO TOLD YOU THAT?
IT'S THE TRUTH.
I...
...WON'T USE THE POWER OF MY EYES ANYMORE.
SO...
DOZE
DOZE
YOU WON'T COME WITH US?
THERE'S NO CON-VINCING YOU?
LEAVE.

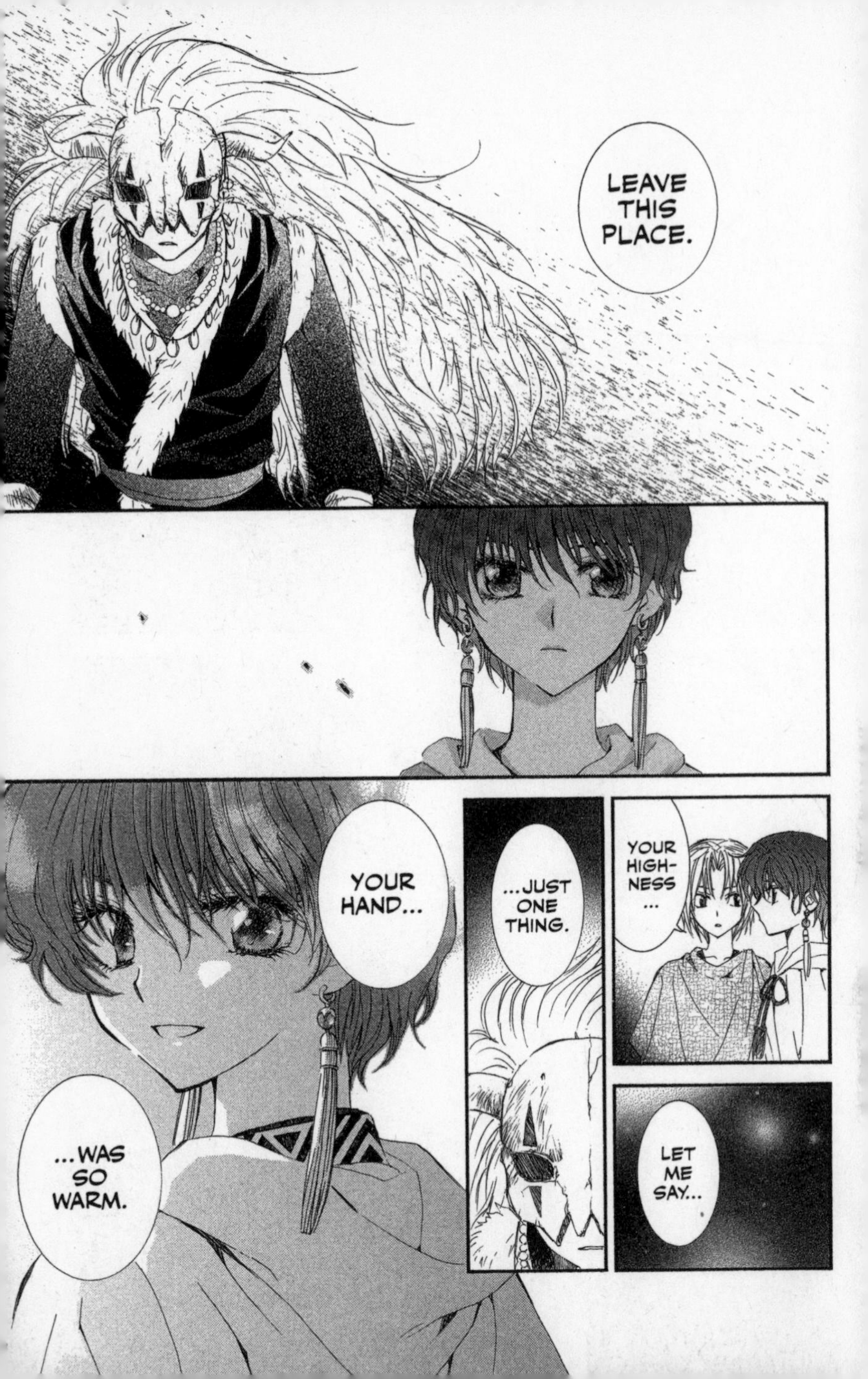
LEAVE THIS PLACE.
YOUR HIGH-NESS ...
LET ME SAY...
...JUST ONE THING.
YOUR HAND...
...WAS SO WARM.

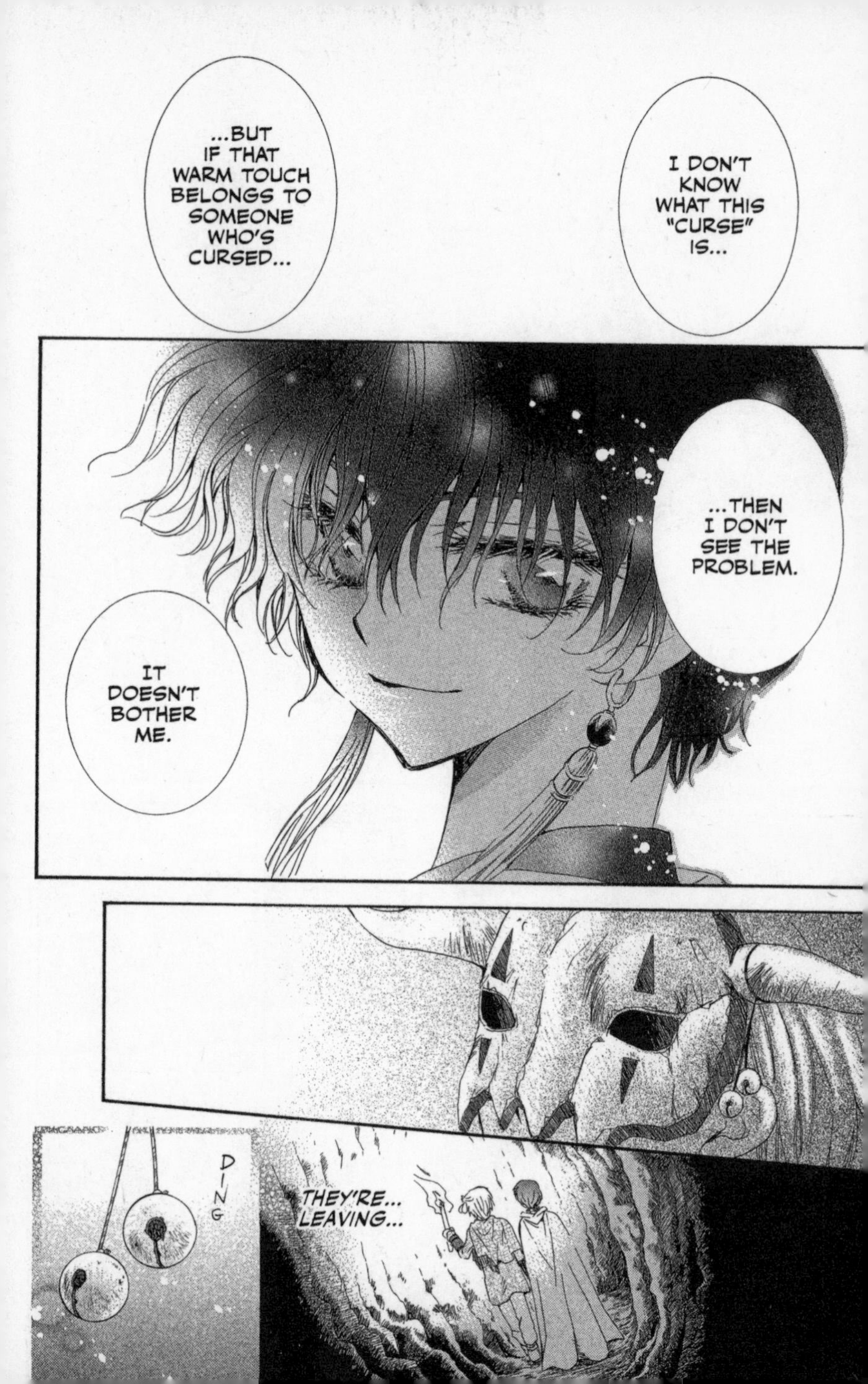
I DON'T KNOW WHAT THIS "CURSE" IS...
...BUT IF THAT WARM TOUCH BELONGS TO SOMEONE WHO'S CURSED...
...THEN I DON'T SEE THE PROBLEM.
IT DOESN'T BOTHER ME.
THEY'RE... LEAVING...
DING

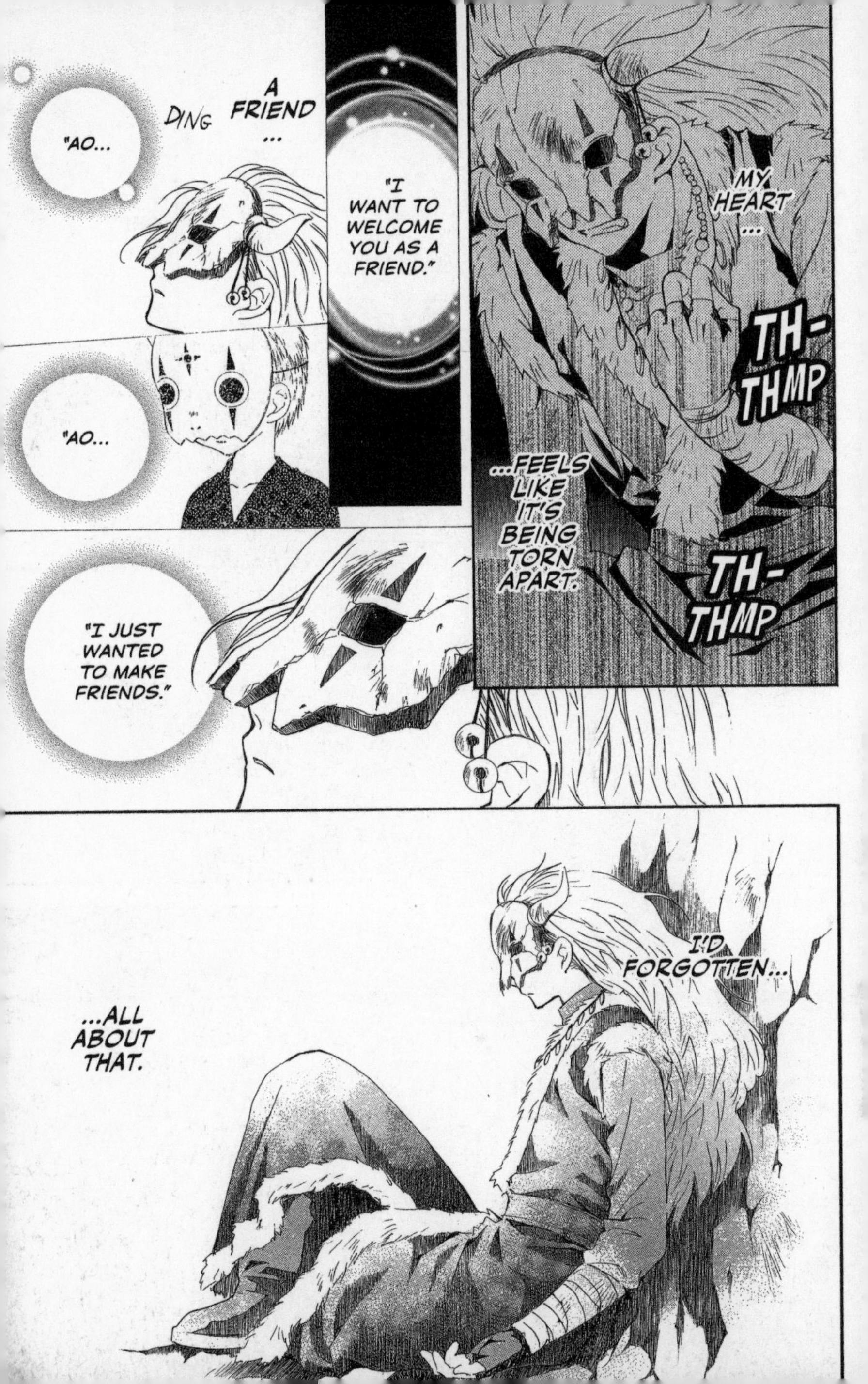
MY HEART...
TH-THMP
...FEELS LIKE IT'S BEING TORN APART.
TH-THMP
"I WANT TO WELCOME YOU AS A FRIEND."
A FRIEND...
DING
"AO...
"AO...
"I JUST WANTED TO MAKE FRIENDS."
I'D FORGOTTEN...
...ALL ABOUT THAT.

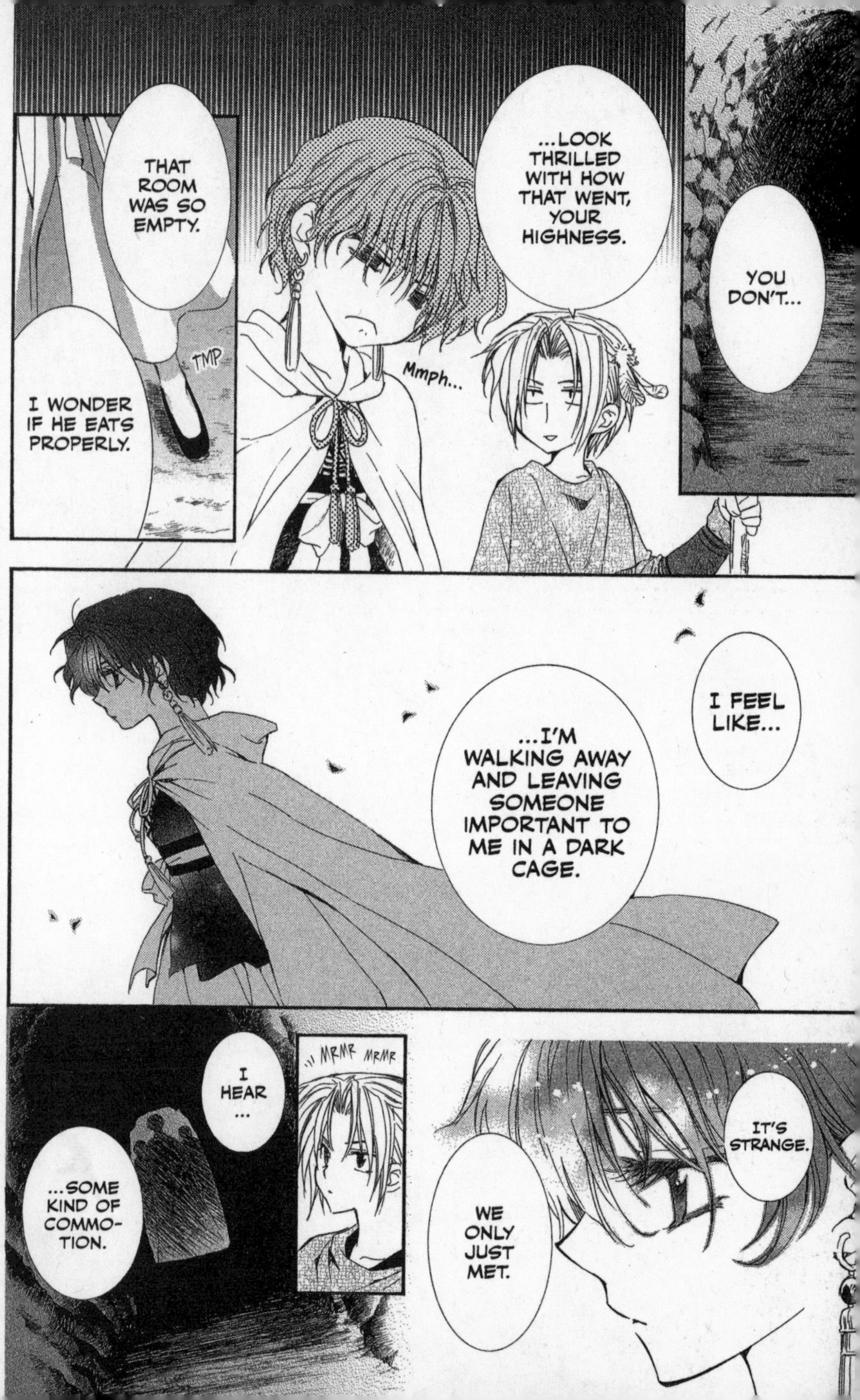
YOU DON'T...
...LOOK THRILLED WITH HOW THAT WENT, YOUR HIGHNESS.
Mmph...
THAT ROOM WAS SO EMPTY.
TMP
I WONDER IF HE EATS PROPERLY.
I FEEL LIKE...
...I'M WALKING AWAY AND LEAVING SOMEONE IMPORTANT TO ME IN A DARK CAGE.
IT'S STRANGE.
WE ONLY JUST MET.
MRMR MRMR
I HEAR...
...SOME KIND OF COMMO-TION.

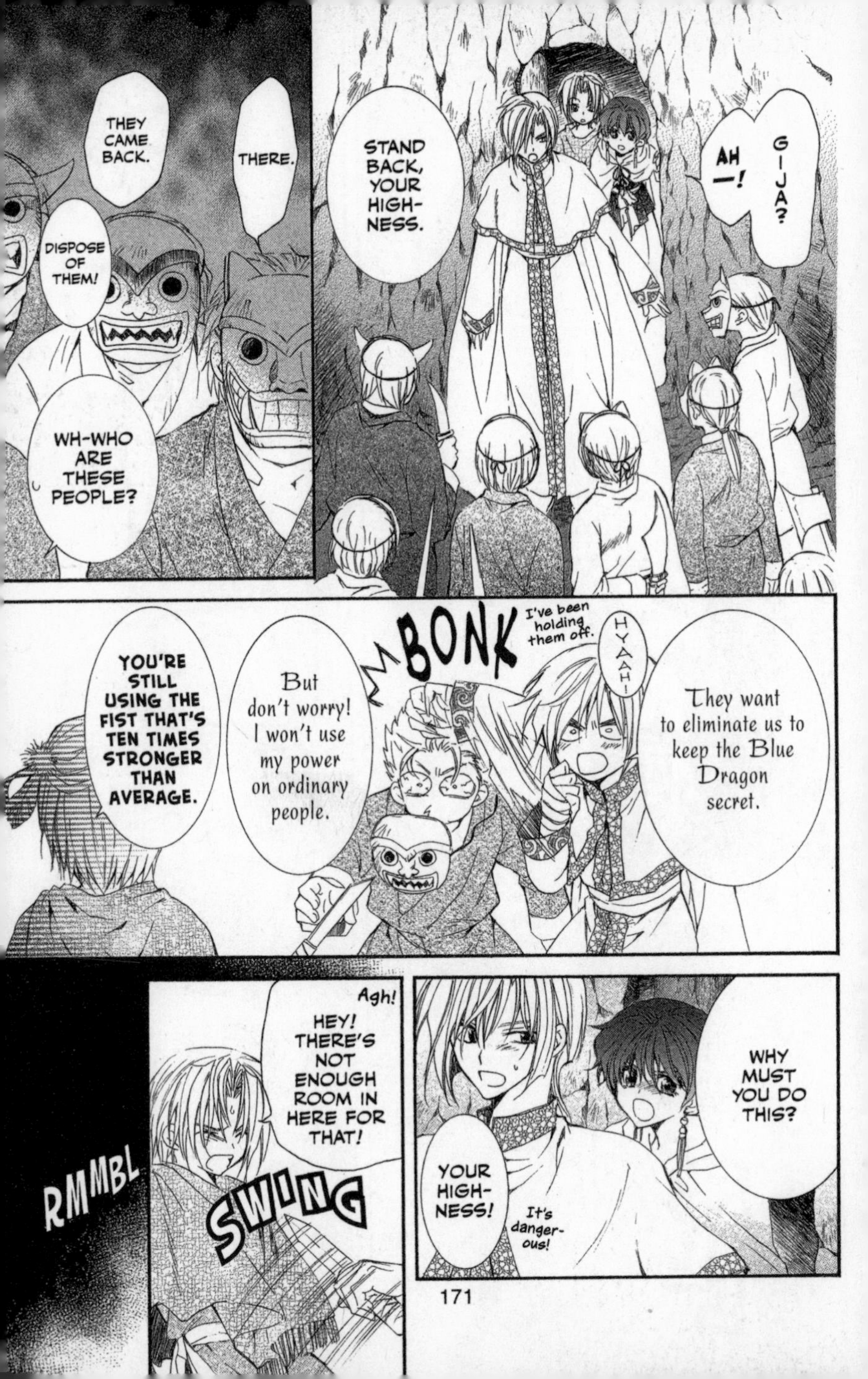
GIJA?
AH—!
STAND BACK, YOUR HIGHNESS.
THERE.
THEY CAME BACK.
DISPOSE OF THEM!
WH-WHO ARE THESE PEOPLE?
They want to eliminate us to keep the Blue Dragon secret.
HYAAH!
I've been holding them off.
BONK
But don't worry! I won't use my power on ordinary people.
YOU'RE STILL USING THE FIST THAT'S TEN TIMES STRONGER THAN AVERAGE.
WHY MUST YOU DO THIS?
YOUR HIGHNESS!
It's danger-ous!
Agh!
HEY! THERE'S NOT ENOUGH ROOM IN HERE FOR THAT!
SWING
RMMBL

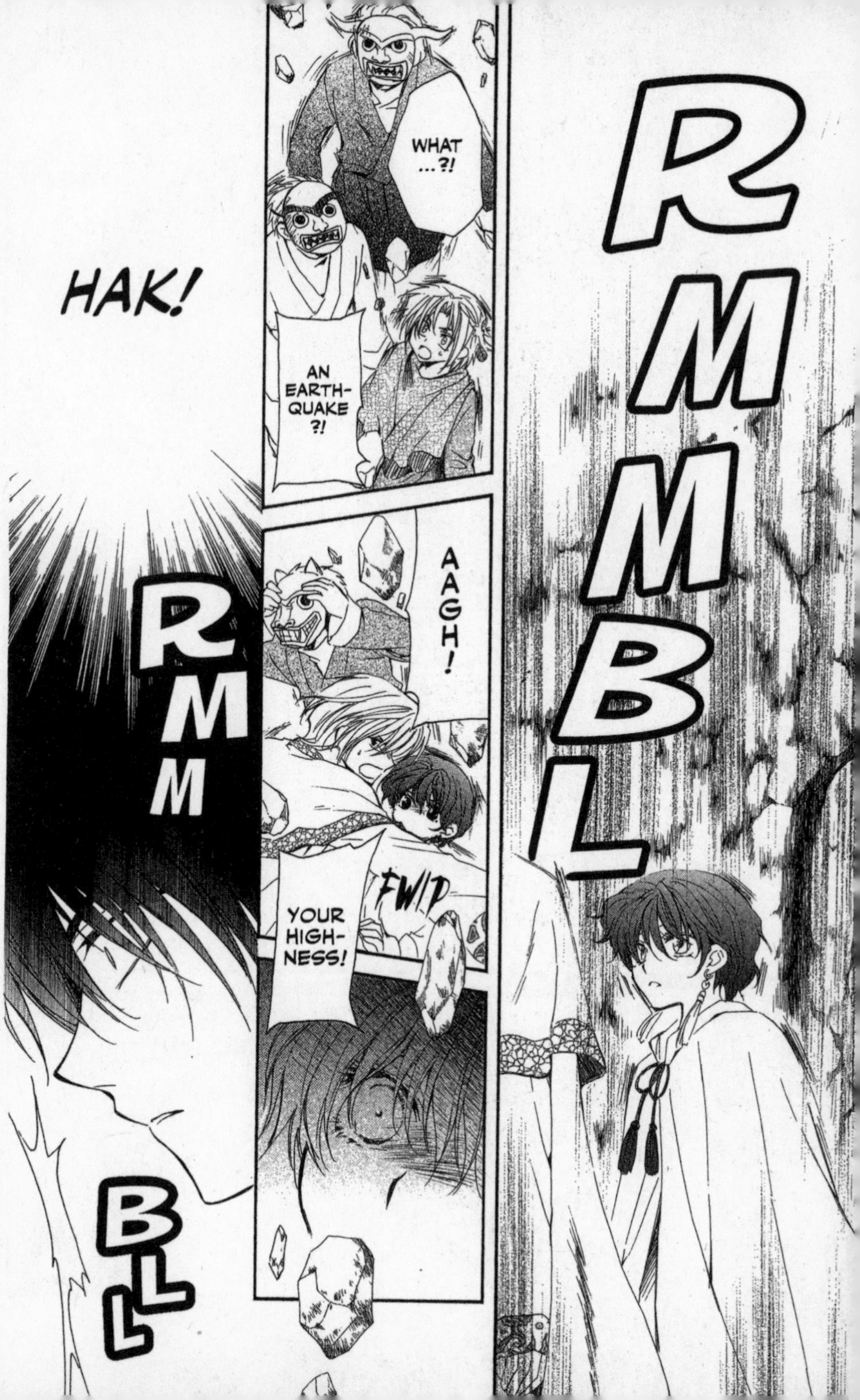
RMMBL
WHAT ...?!
AN EARTHQUAKE ?!
AAGH!
FWIP
YOUR HIGHNESS!
HAK!
RMMBLL

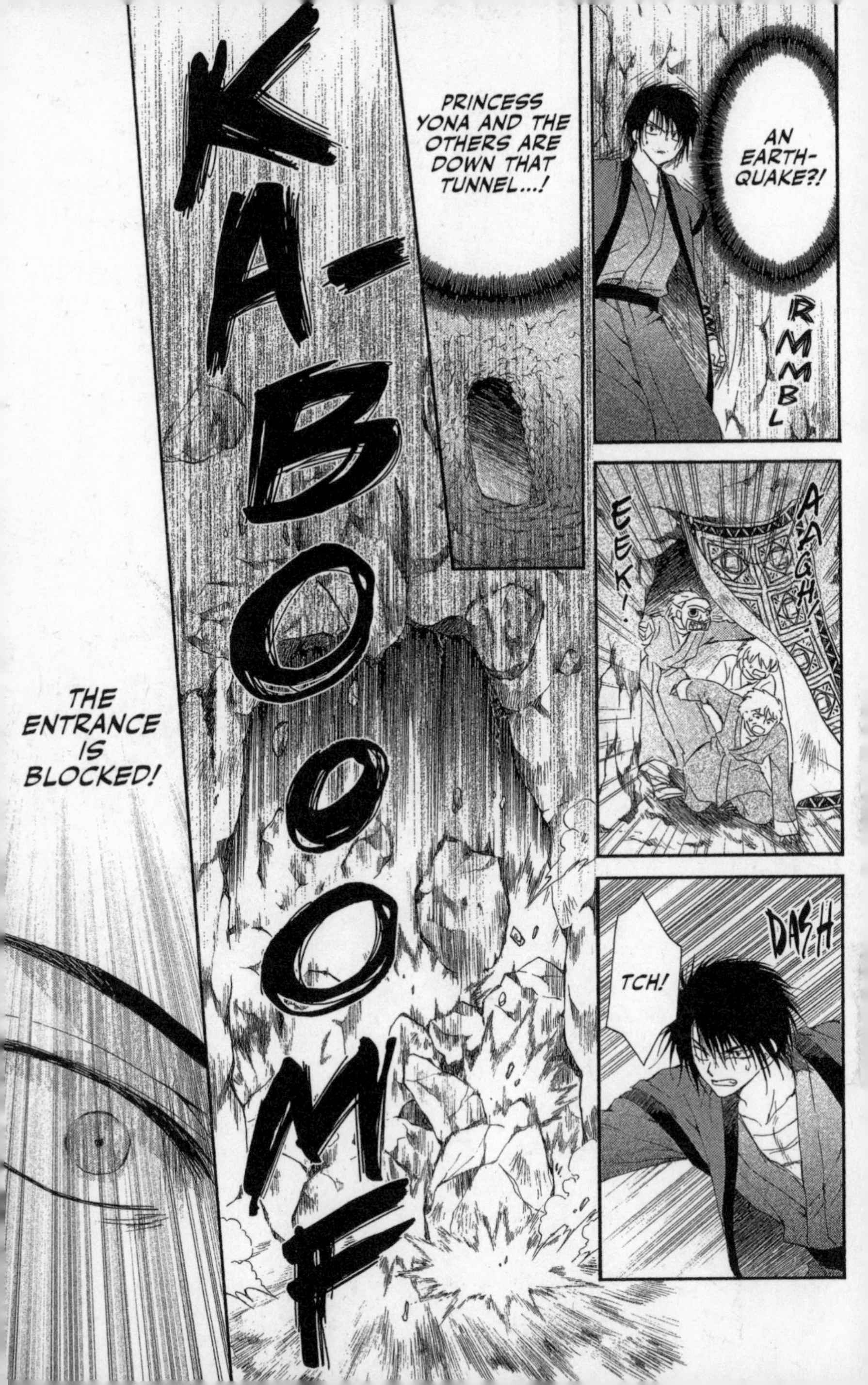

AN EARTH-QUAKE?!
RMMBL
PRINCESS YONA AND THE OTHERS ARE DOWN THAT TUNNEL...!
AAGH!
EEK!
DASH
TCH!
KA-BOOOOMF
THE ENTRANCE IS BLOCKED!

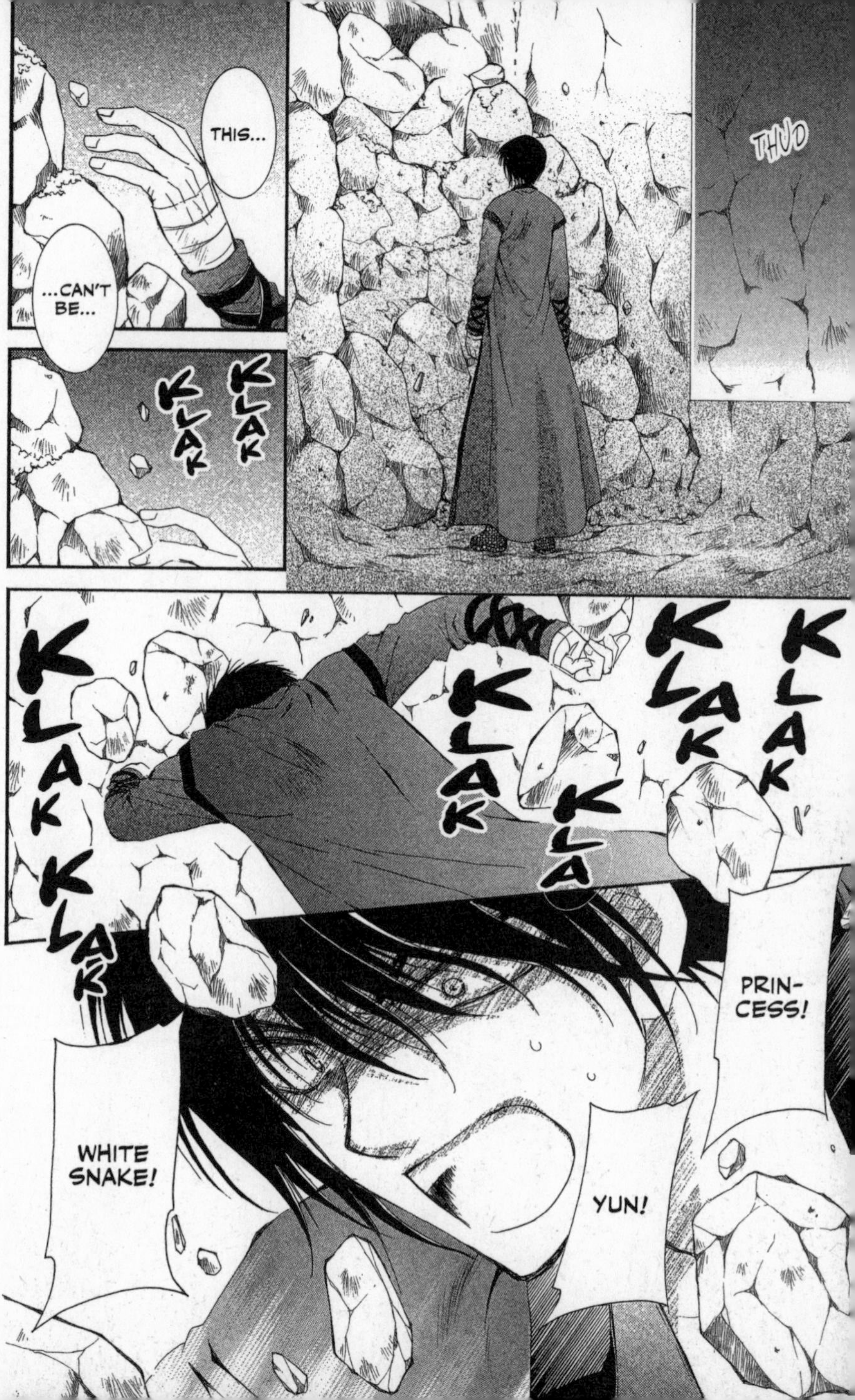
THUD
THIS...
...CAN'T BE...
KLAK KLAK
KLAK KLAK
KLAK KLA
KLAK
KLAK KLAK
PRIN-CESS!
YUN!
WHITE SNAKE!

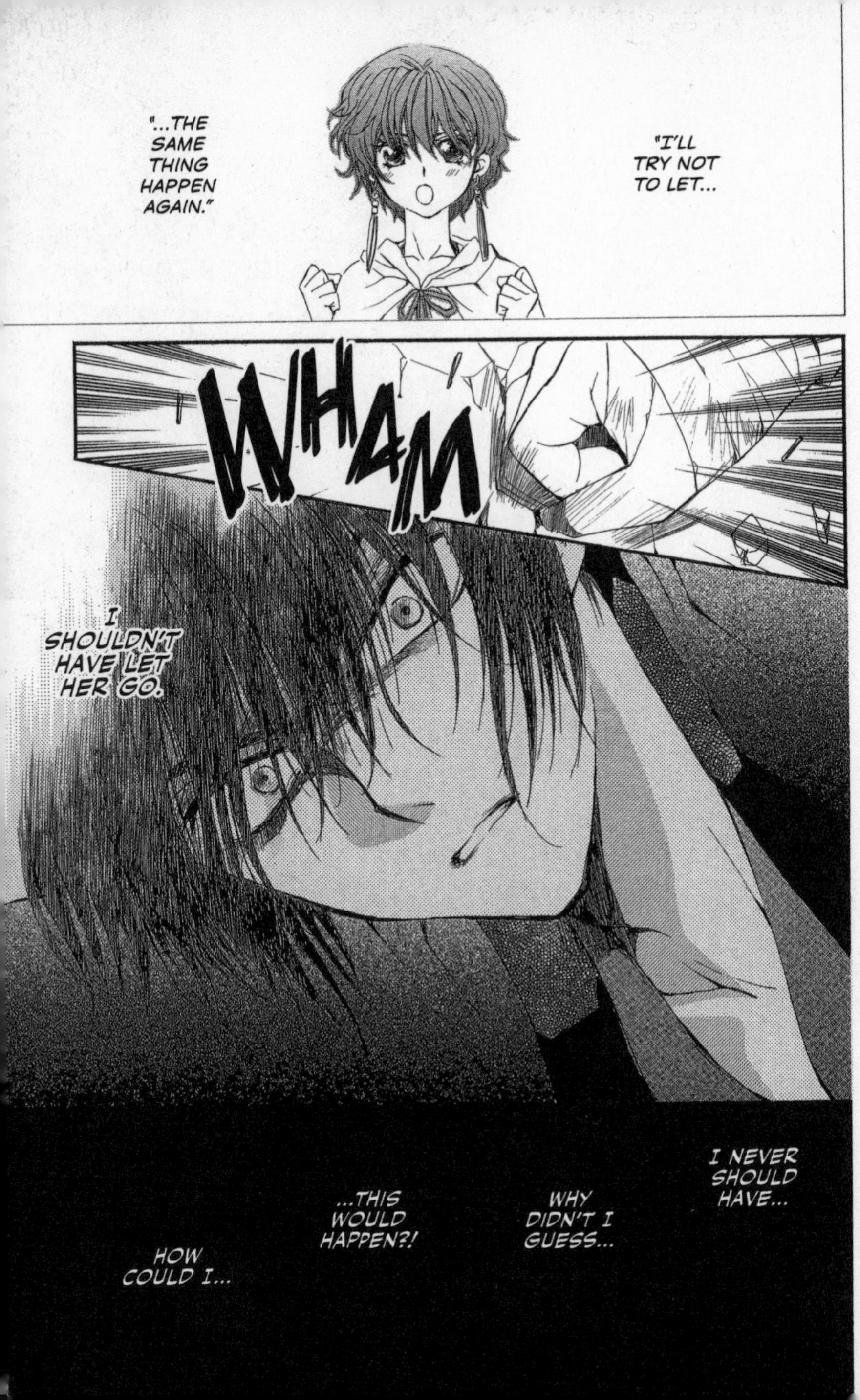
"I'LL TRY NOT TO LET...
"...THE SAME THING HAPPEN AGAIN."
WHAM
I SHOULDN'T HAVE LET HER GO.
I NEVER SHOULD HAVE...
WHY DIDN'T I GUESS...
...THIS WOULD HAPPEN?!
HOW COULD I...

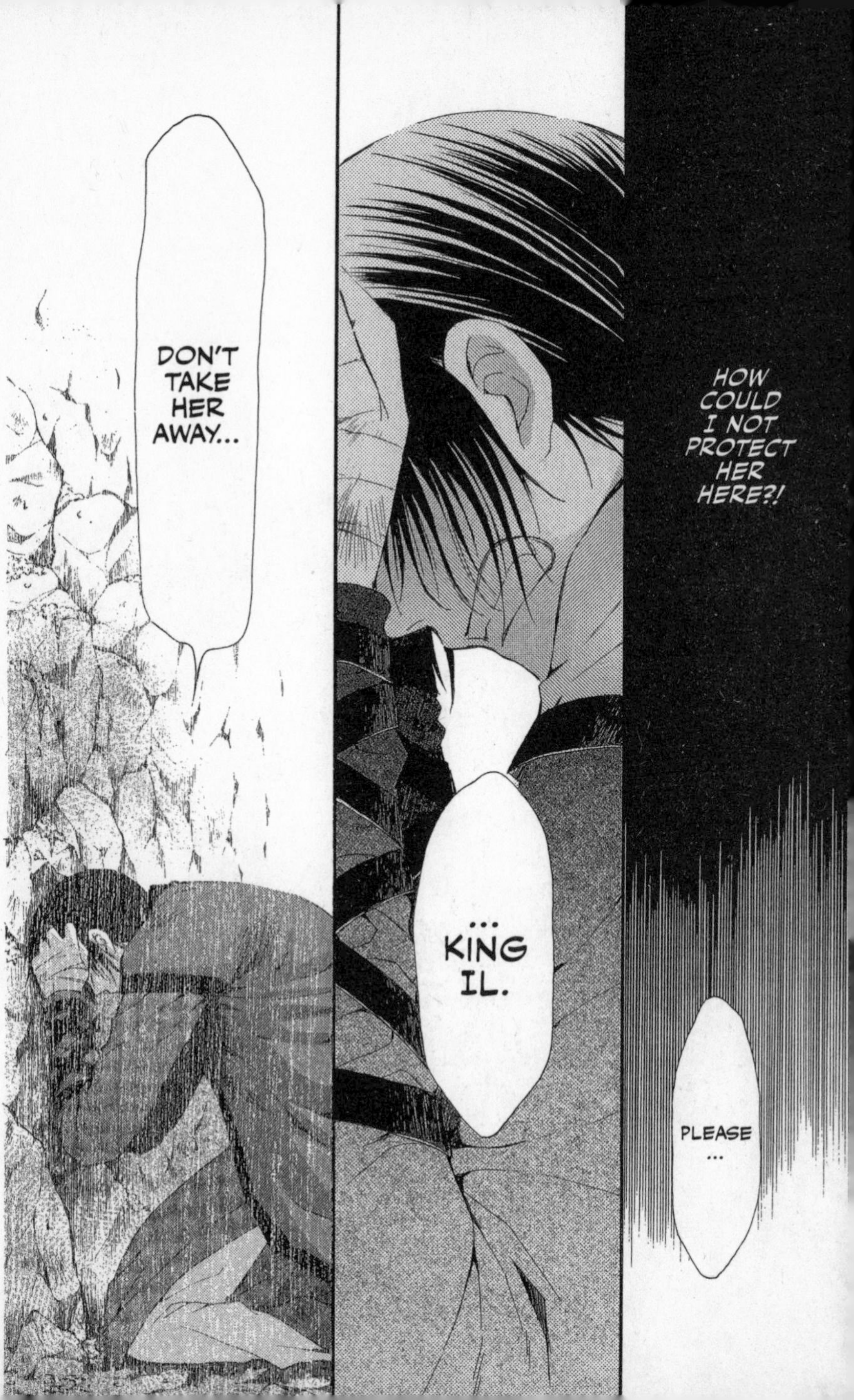
HOW COULD I NOT PROTECT HER HERE?!
PLEASE ...
... KING IL.
DON'T TAKE HER AWAY...

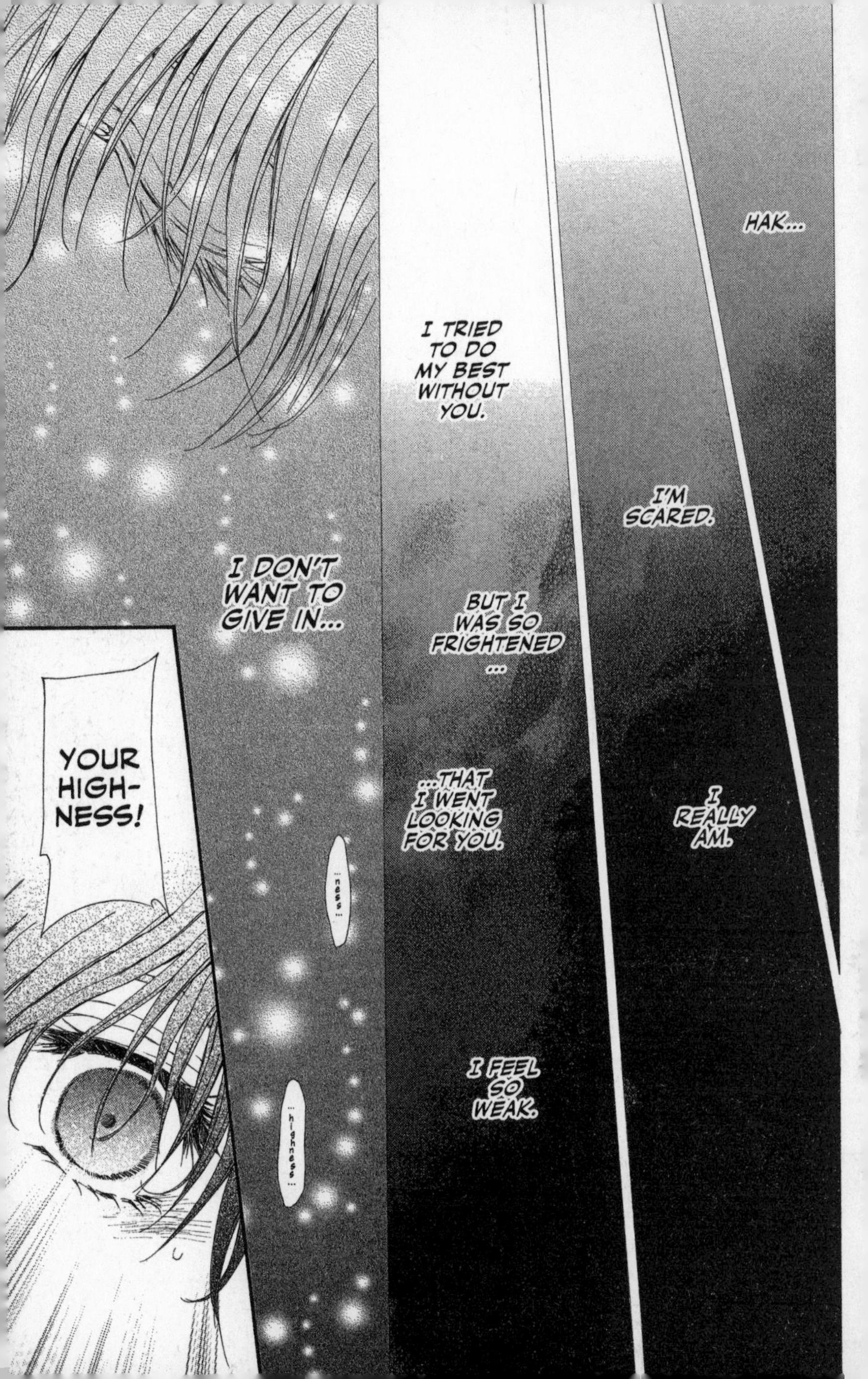
HAK...
I'M SCARED.
I REALLY AM.
I TRIED TO DO MY BEST WITHOUT YOU.
BUT I WAS SO FRIGHTENED...
...THAT I WENT LOOKING FOR YOU.
I FEEL SO WEAK.
I DON'T WANT TO GIVE IN...
...ness...
...highness...
YOUR HIGHNESS!

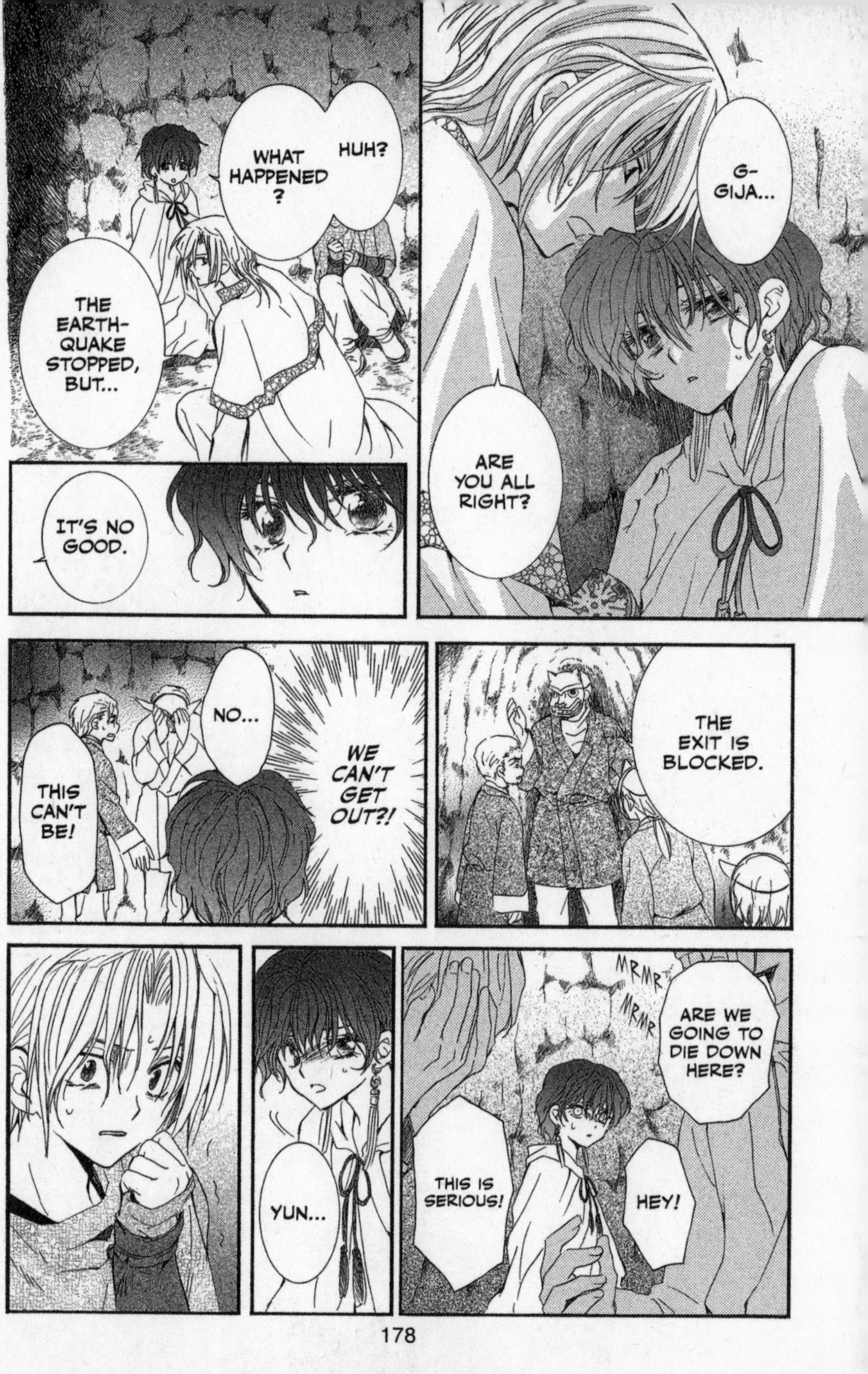
G-GIJA...
ARE YOU ALL RIGHT?
HUH?
WHAT HAPPENED?
THE EARTHQUAKE STOPPED, BUT...
IT'S NO GOOD.
THE EXIT IS BLOCKED.
NO...
WE CAN'T GET OUT?!
THIS CAN'T BE!
MRMR
MRMR
ARE WE GOING TO DIE DOWN HERE?
HEY!
THIS IS SERIOUS!
YUN...

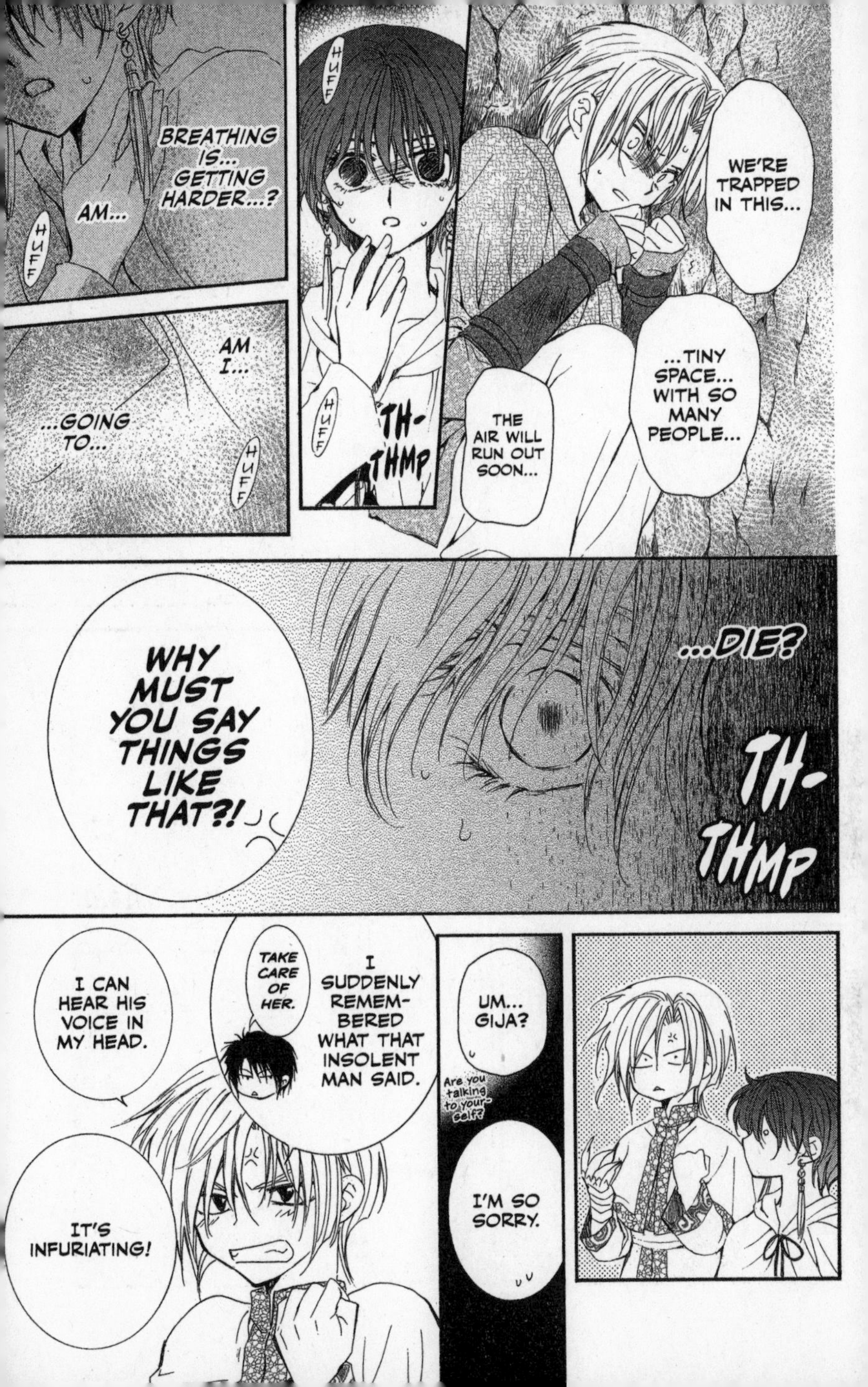
WE'RE TRAPPED IN THIS...
...TINY SPACE... WITH SO MANY PEOPLE...
THE AIR WILL RUN OUT SOON...
HUFF
HUFF
TH-THMP
BREATHING IS... GETTING HARDER...?
AM...
HUFF
AM I...
...GOING TO...
HUFF
...DIE?
TH-THMP
WHY MUST YOU SAY THINGS LIKE THAT?!
UM... GIJA?
Are you talking to yourself?
I'M SO SORRY.
I SUDDENLY REMEM-BERED WHAT THAT INSOLENT MAN SAID.
TAKE CARE OF HER.
I CAN HEAR HIS VOICE IN MY HEAD.
IT'S INFURIATING!

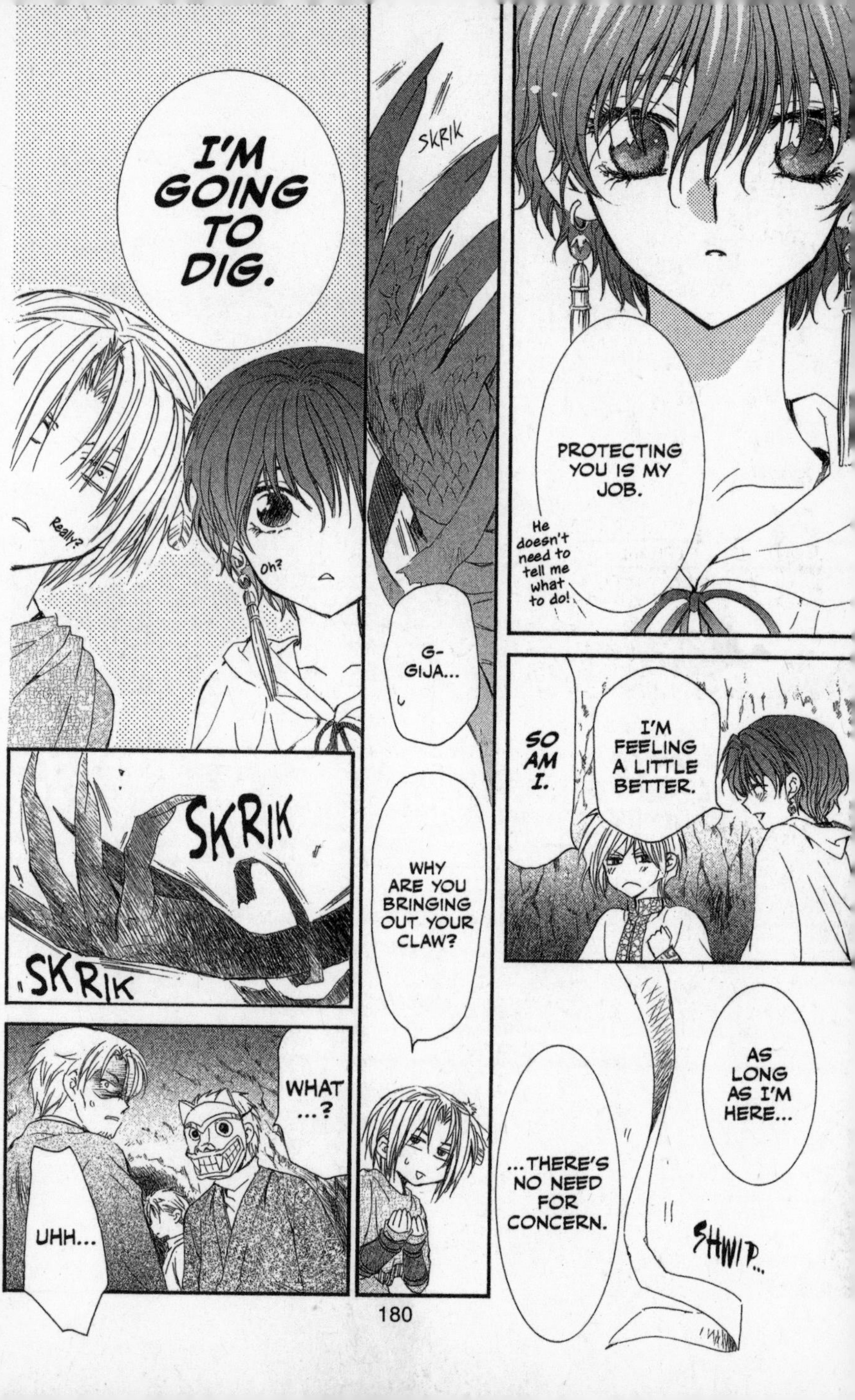
PROTECTING YOU IS MY JOB.
He doesn't need to tell me what to do!
I'M FEELING A LITTLE BETTER.
SO AM I.
AS LONG AS I'M HERE...
...THERE'S NO NEED FOR CONCERN.
SHWIP...
SKRIK
G-GIJA...
WHY ARE YOU BRINGING OUT YOUR CLAW?
I'M GOING TO DIG.
Oh?
Really?
SKRIK
SKRIK
WHAT...?
UHH...

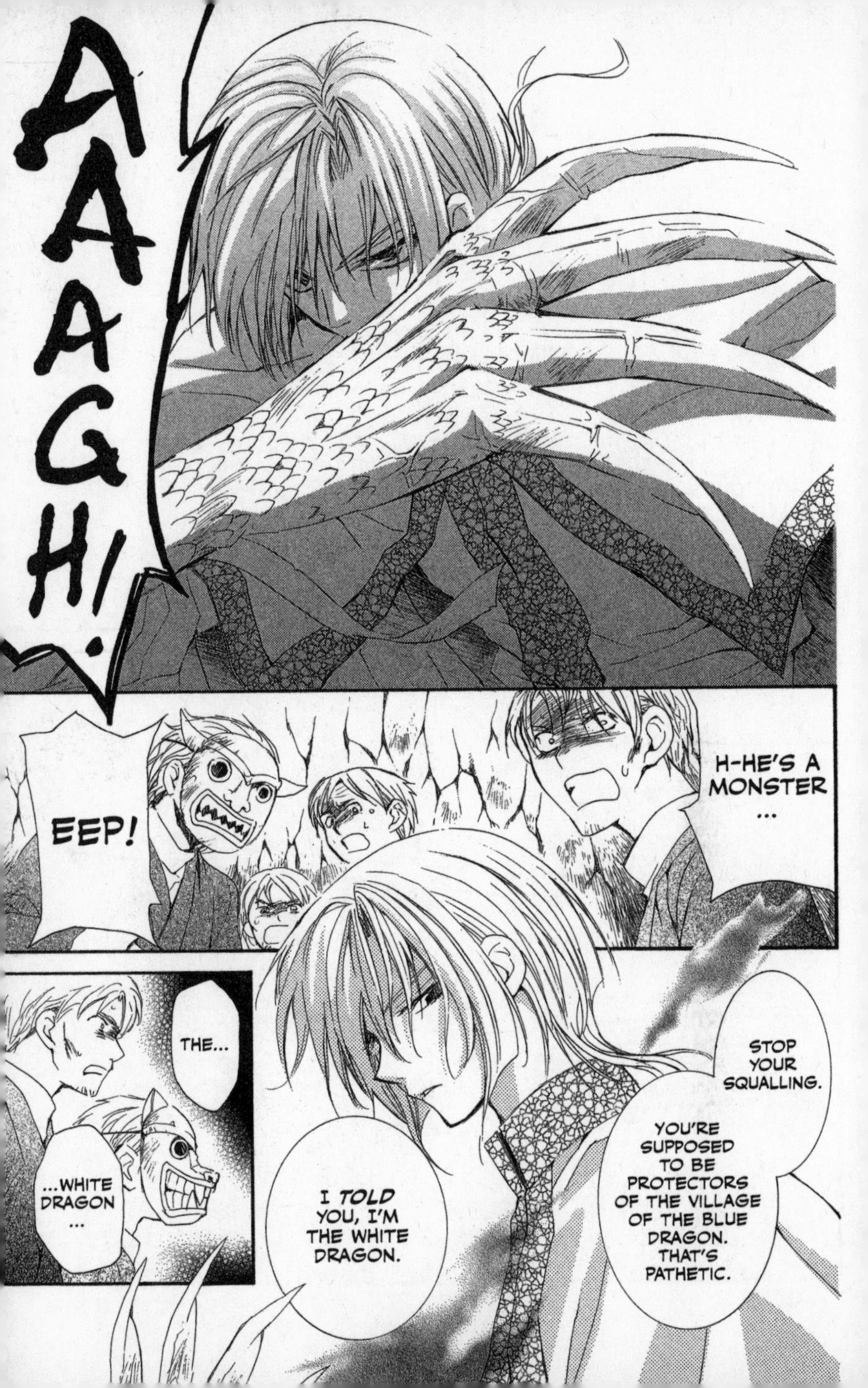
AAGH!
H-HE'S A MONSTER ...
EEP!
STOP YOUR SQUALLING.
YOU'RE SUPPOSED TO BE PROTECTORS OF THE VILLAGE OF THE BLUE DRAGON. THAT'S PATHETIC.
I *TOLD* YOU, I'M THE WHITE DRAGON.
THE...
...WHITE DRAGON ...

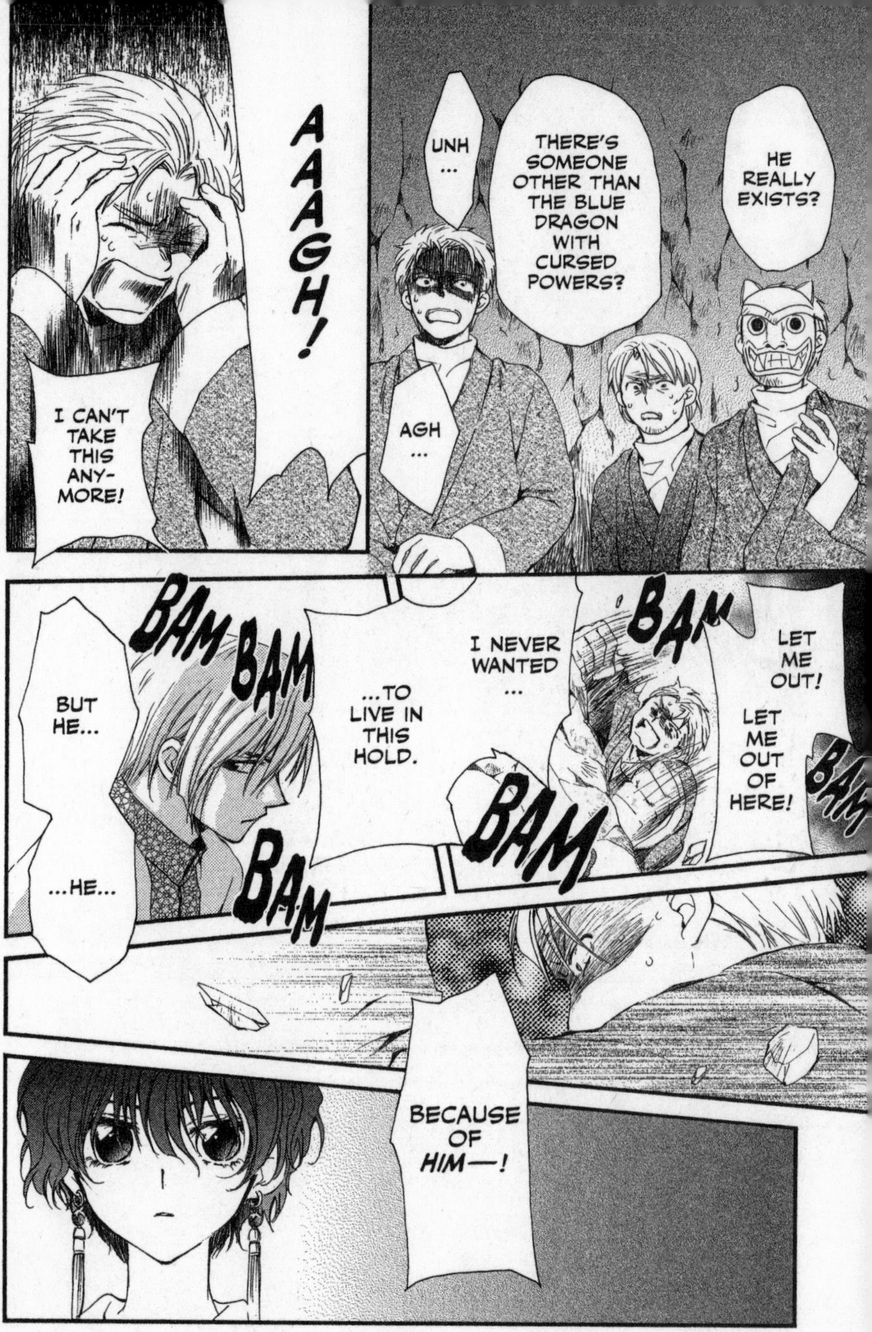
HE REALLY EXISTS?
THERE'S SOMEONE OTHER THAN THE BLUE DRAGON WITH CURSED POWERS?
UNH ...
AGH ...
AAAAGH!
I CAN'T TAKE THIS ANY-MORE!
BAM
LET ME OUT!
LET ME OUT OF HERE!
BAM
I NEVER WANTED ...
BAM
...TO LIVE IN THIS HOLD.
BAM BAM
BUT HE...
BAM
...HE...
BECAUSE OF *HIM*—!

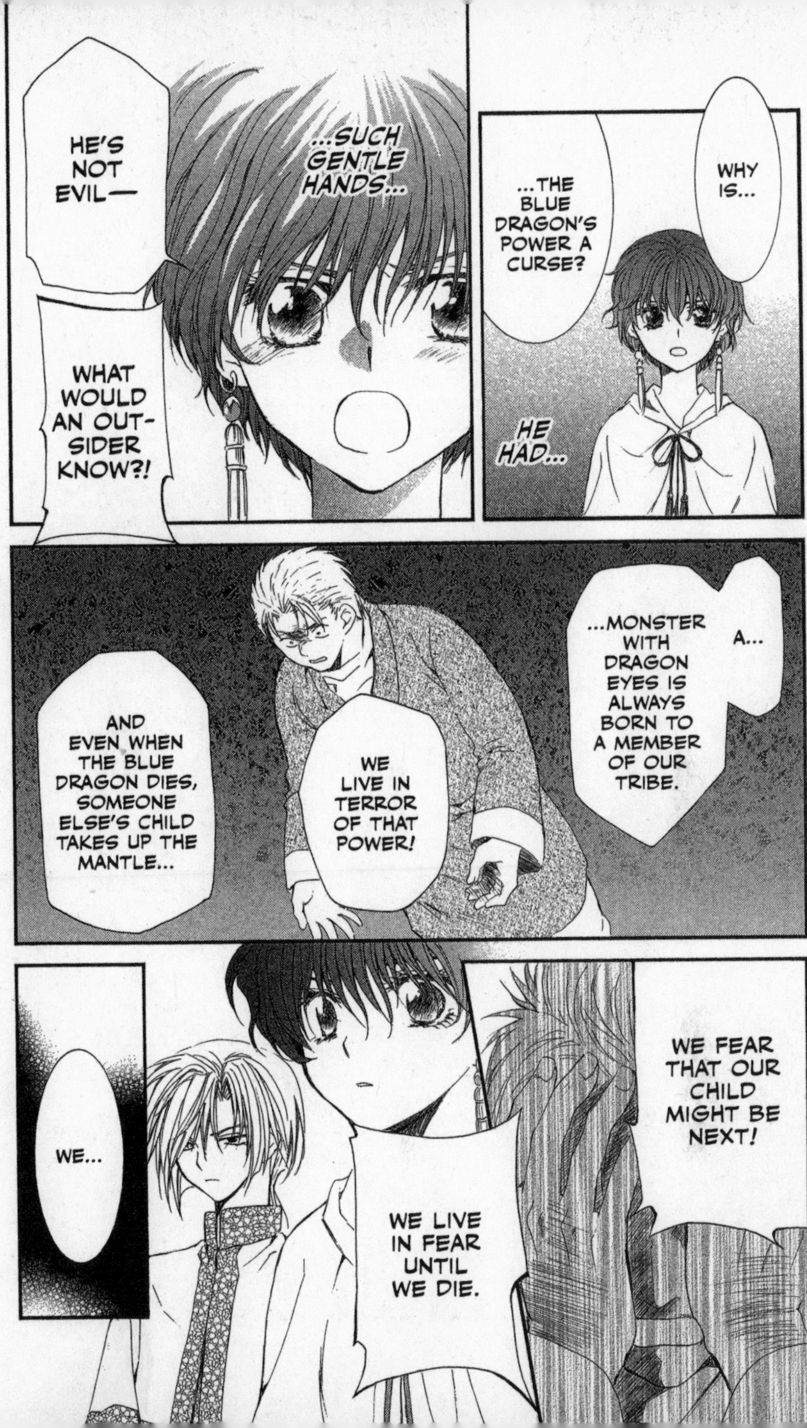

WHY IS...
...THE BLUE DRAGON'S POWER A CURSE?
HE HAD...
...SUCH GENTLE HANDS...
HE'S NOT EVIL—
WHAT WOULD AN OUT-SIDER KNOW?!
A...
...MONSTER WITH DRAGON EYES IS ALWAYS BORN TO A MEMBER OF OUR TRIBE.
WE LIVE IN TERROR OF THAT POWER!
AND EVEN WHEN THE BLUE DRAGON DIES, SOMEONE ELSE'S CHILD TAKES UP THE MANTLE...
WE FEAR THAT OUR CHILD MIGHT BE NEXT!
WE LIVE IN FEAR UNTIL WE DIE.
WE...

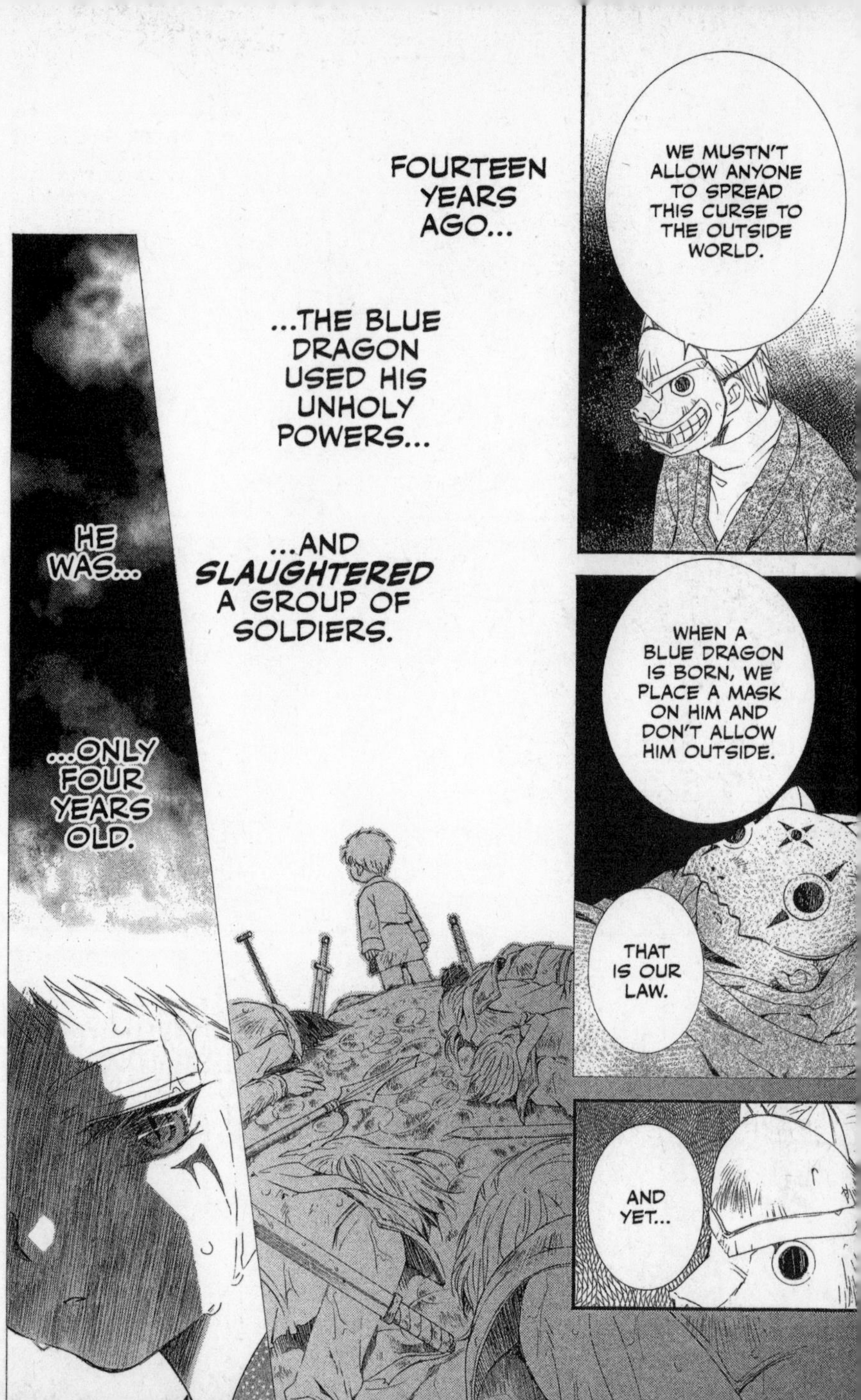
WE MUSTN'T ALLOW ANYONE TO SPREAD THIS CURSE TO THE OUTSIDE WORLD.
WHEN A BLUE DRAGON IS BORN, WE PLACE A MASK ON HIM AND DON'T ALLOW HIM OUTSIDE.
THAT IS OUR LAW.
AND YET...
FOURTEEN YEARS AGO...
...THE BLUE DRAGON USED HIS UNHOLY POWERS...
...AND *SLAUGHTERED* A GROUP OF SOLDIERS.
HE WAS...
...ONLY FOUR YEARS OLD.

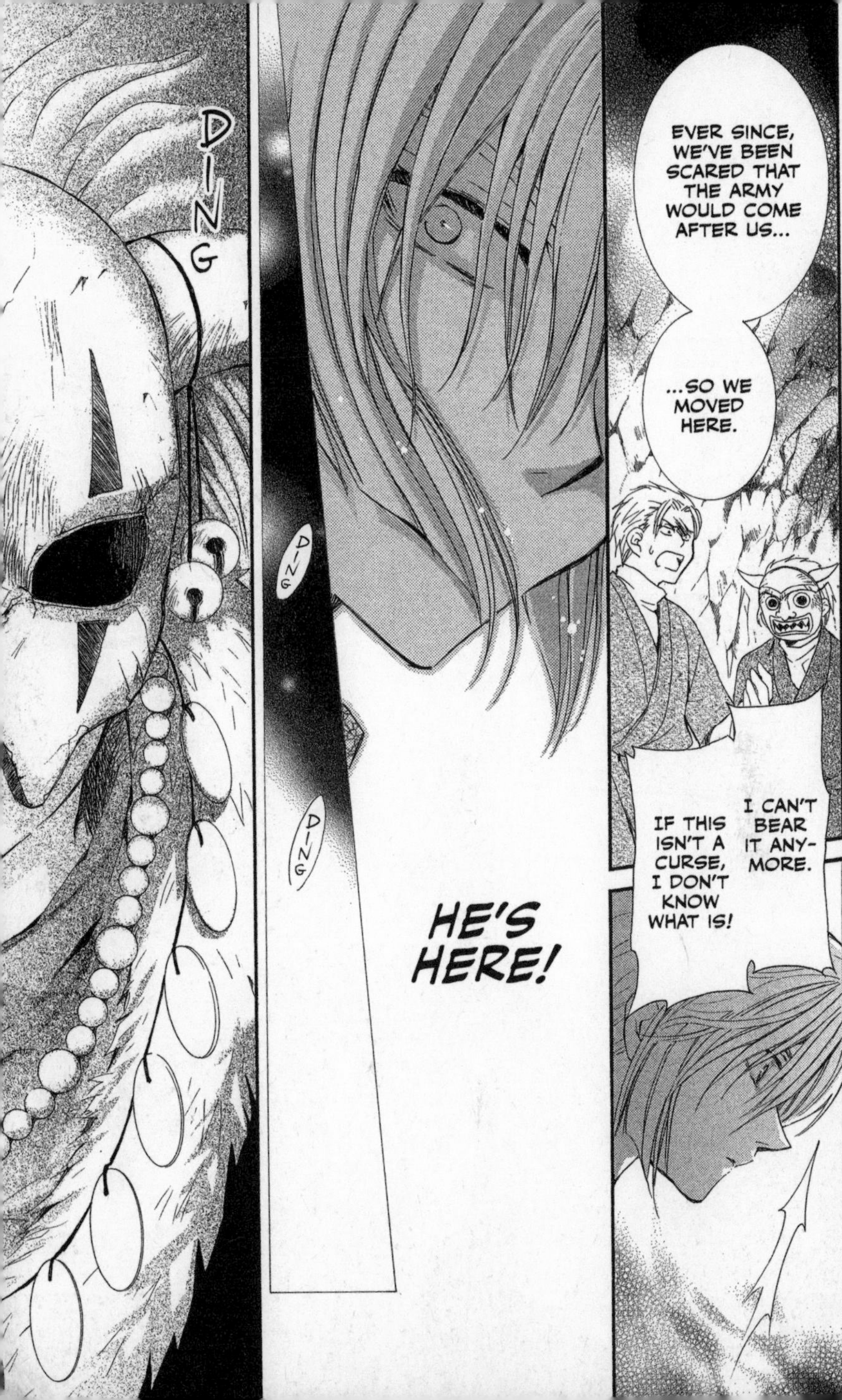
EVER SINCE, WE'VE BEEN SCARED THAT THE ARMY WOULD COME AFTER US...
...SO WE MOVED HERE.
I CAN'T BEAR IT ANY-MORE.
IF THIS ISN'T A CURSE, I DON'T KNOW WHAT IS!
DING
DING
HE'S HERE!
DING

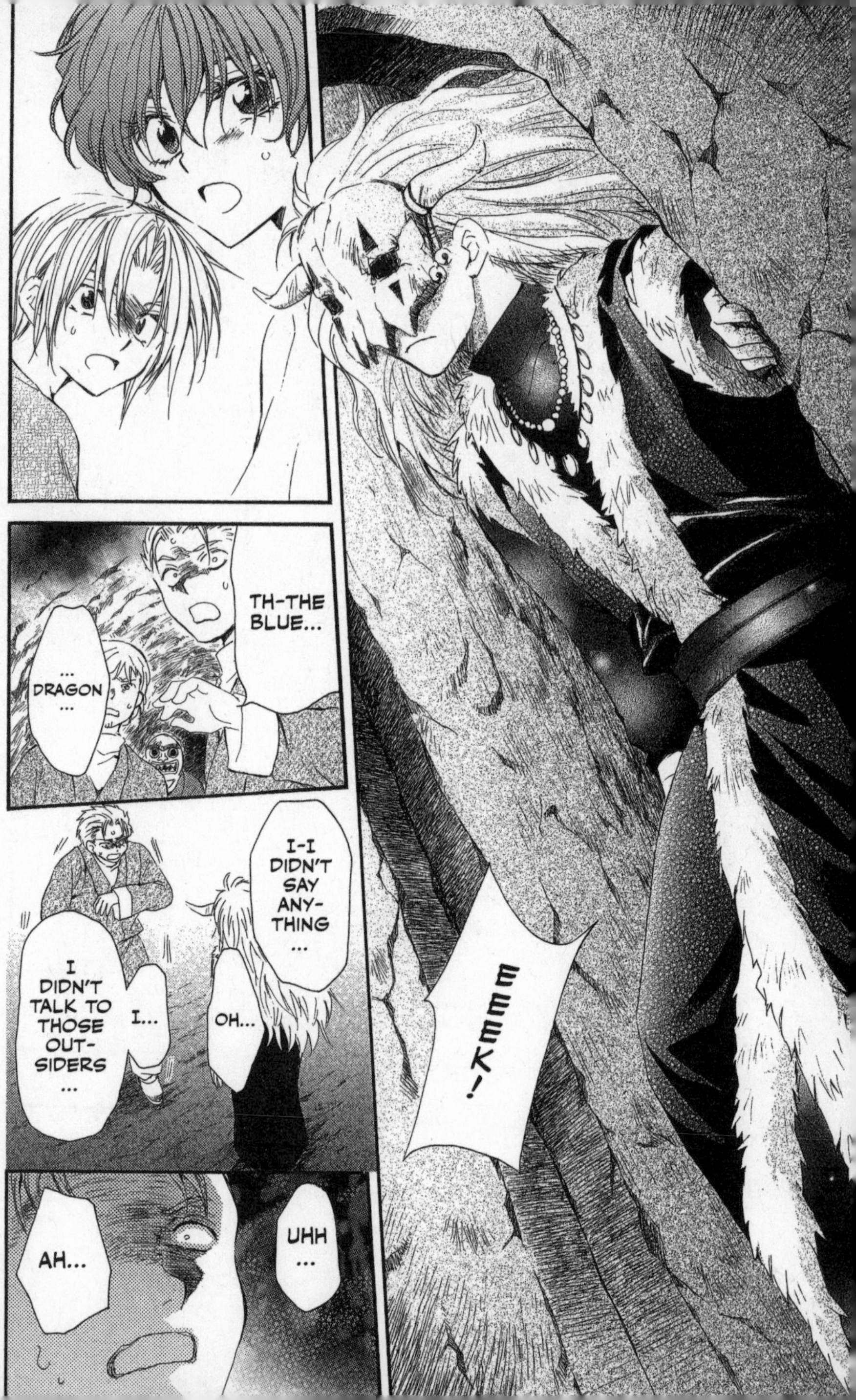
EEEEK!
TH-THE BLUE...
...DRAGON...
I-I DIDN'T SAY ANYTHING...
OH...
I...
I DIDN'T TALK TO THOSE OUTSIDERS...
UHH...
AH...

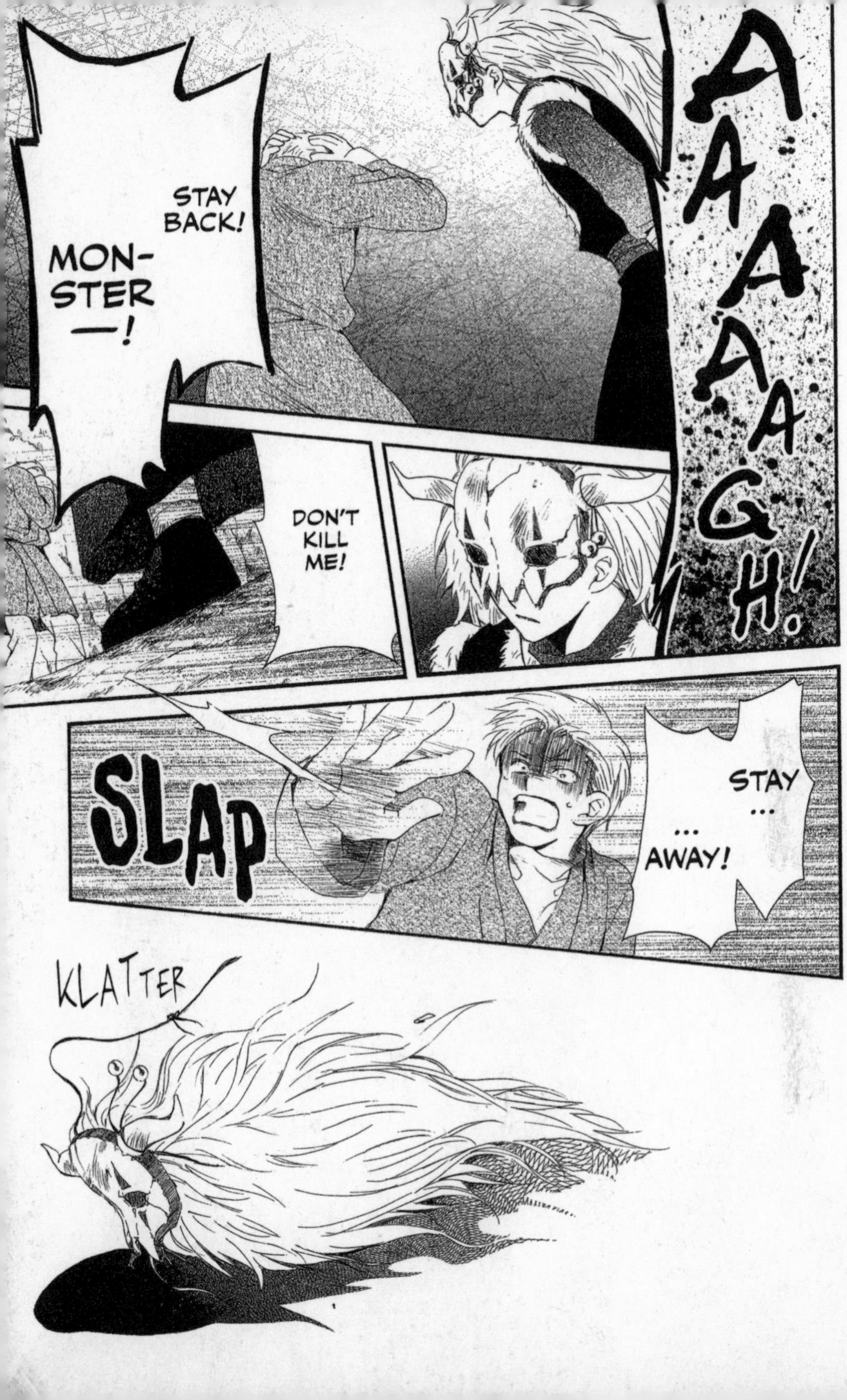

AAAAAGH!
STAY BACK!
MON-
STER
—!
DON'T KILL ME!
STAY ...
... AWAY!
SLAP
KLATTER

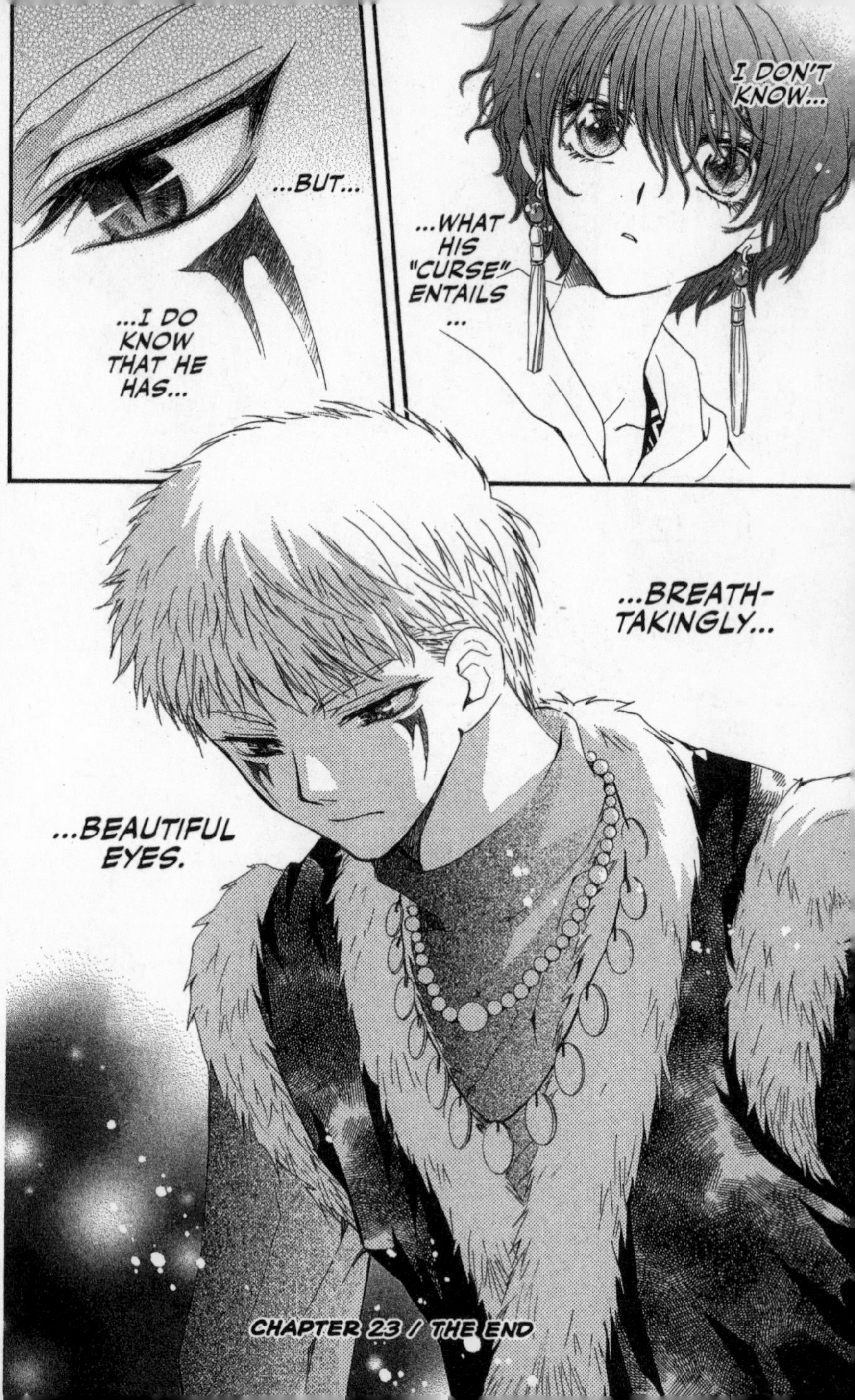
I DON'T KNOW...
...WHAT HIS "CURSE" ENTAILS...
...BUT...
...I DO KNOW THAT HE HAS...
...BREATH-TAKINGLY...
...BEAUTIFUL EYES.
CHAPTER 23 / THE END